SUBCONTRACTING PEACE

Subcontracting Peace
The Challenges of the NGO Peacebuilding

Edited by
OLIVER P. RICHMOND
University of St Andrews, UK

HENRY F. CAREY
Georgia State University, USA

Routledge
Taylor & Francis Group

LONDON AND NEW YORK

First published 2005 by Ashgate Publishing

Reissued 2018 by Routledge
2 Park Square, Milton Park, Abingdon, Oxon OX14 4RN
711 Third Avenue, New York, NY 10017, USA

Routledge is an imprint of the Taylor & Francis Group, an informa business

First issued in paperback 2018

A Library of Congress record exists under LC control number: 2005927753

Notice:
Product or corporate names may be trademarks or registered trademarks, and are used only for identification and explanation without intent to infringe.

Publisher's Note
The publisher has gone to great lengths to ensure the quality of this reprint but points out that some imperfections in the original copies may be apparent.

Disclaimer
The publisher has made every effort to trace copyright holders and welcomes correspondence from those they have been unable to contact.

ISBN 13: 978-0-815-39725-0 (hbk)
ISBN 13: 978-1-138-62071-1 (pbk)
ISBN 13: 978-1-351-14840-5 (ebk)

Contents

List of Contributors   *ix*
Foreword   *xv*
List of Abbreviations   *xxi*

Part One: Conceutalising NGO Roles in Peacebuilding

1   Expanding Involvement of NGOs in Emerging Global Governance   3
    Chadwick F. Alger

2   The Dilemmas of Subcontracting the Liberal Peace   19
    Oliver P. Richmond

3   Up to No Good? Recent Critics and Critiques of NGOs   37
    Kim D. Reimann

4   Politics Beyond the State: Globalisation, Migration and the
    Challenge of Non-State Actors   55
    Fiona Adamson

Part Two: NGOs in Peacemaking

5   Building Peace Norwegian Style: Studies in Track I½ Diplomacy   69
    Ann Kelleher and James Larry Taulbee

6   Voices from the Parallel Table: The Role of Civil Sectors in the
    Guatemalan Peace Process   85
    Susan Burgerman

7   Practicing Peace: The Role of NGOs in Assisting
    'Zones of Peace' in Colombia   93
    Catalina Rojas

8   The NGOs' Dilemmas in the Post-War Iraq: From Stabilisation
    to Nation-Building   101
    Mahmood Monshipouri

9   A Necessary Collaboration: NGOs, Peacekeepers and Credible
    Military Force – The Case of Sierra Leone and East Timor   109
    Michael Gordon Jackson

Part Three: NGOs in Peacebuilding

10   When Civil Society Promotion Fails State-Building:
The Inevitable Fault-Lines in Post-Conflict Reconstruction   119
Julie Mertus and Tazreena Sajjad

11   Private Military Companies in Peacebuilding   131
Marek Pavka

12   Promoting NGOs as Agents of Social Stabilisation: Trauma
Management and Crime Prevention Initiatives in the
Southern African Region   143
Wole Olaleye and David Backer

13   A Rights-Based Approach to Natural Resources Management:
Roles and Responsibilities of IGOs, States and NGOs   155
Clark Efaw and Avtar Kaul

14   The Challenges of an NGO in Post-Communist Europe:
The Soros Health Education Program   161
Susan Shapiro

15   Community Peacebuilding in Somalia – Comparative
Advantages in NGO Peacebuilding – The Example of the Life
and Peace Institute's Approach in Somalia (1990–2003)   173
Thania Paffenholz

16   The Role of NGOs in Institution-Building in Rwanda   183
Joanna Fisher

17   Orangi Pilot Project: An NGO Helping to Build Community   191
Steven Barmazel

Part Four: NGOs and Norm Development and Monitoring

18   Transnational Activism Against the Use of Child Soldiers   201
Heather Heckel

19   NGOs and Depleted Uranium: Establishing a Credible and
Legitimate Counter Narrative   209
Chenaz B. Seelarbokus

20   Postconflict Election Observers   221
Henry F. Carey

21   NGOs and the Rule of Law in El Salvador and Guatemala   229
      JoAnn Fagot Aviel

22   Conclusion   237
      Henry F. Carey

Index   *251*

List of Contributors

Fiona Adamson is an Assistant Professor of International Relations and Director of the Program in International Public Policy at University College London. She holds a PhD in Political Science from Columbia University, and a BA in International Relations from Stanford University. She has also held research fellowships with the Center for International Security and Cooperation (CISAC) at Stanford University, the Belfer Center for Science and International Affairs (BCSIA) at Harvard University, the John M. Olin Institute for Strategic Studies at Harvard University and the Social Science Research Council (SSRC). Adamson's research interests are in theories of international relations, international security, transnational and non-state actors, migration and diaspora politics, and globalization and democratization.

Chadwick F. Alger is Mershon Professor of Political Science and Public Policy Emeritus, The Ohio State University. His research and teaching is focused on three themes: (1) the UN system of some thirty organizations, with special interest in the roles of NGOs, (2) the world relations of people in local communities and (3) the development of long term strategies for peacebuilding. He is editor of *The Future of the UN System: Potential for the Twenty-First Century,* UN University Press, 1998. He has served as President of the International Studies Association (1978–79) and Secretary General of the International Peace Research Association (1983–87).

JoAnn Fagot Aviel is Professor and Chair of International Relations at San Francisco State University. She has published numerous articles in comparative foreign policy and international relations, including 'Placing Human Rights and Environmental Issues on ASEAN's Agenda: The Role of Non-Governmental Organizations' (*Asian Journal of Political Science*) and co-editing *Multilateral Diplomacy and the United Nations Today* (Westview Press, 1999).

David Backer is an Assistant Professor of Government at the College of William and Mary. During the 2005–06 academic year, he is on leave as a Post-Doctoral Scholar at the Stanford University Center for Democracy, Development and the Rule of Law. He previously taught in the Department of Political Science at the University of Michigan, from which he received his PhD in 2004. His research focuses on victims' attitudes in relation to South Africa's Truth and Reconciliation Commission. He has also published articles on the role of non-state actors in transitional justice processes, the dilemmas of constructive engagement by NGOs in Liberia and the dynamics of episodes of ethnic violence in Rwanda and Burundi. During 2000–01, he worked in the Transition and Reconciliation Programme at the Centre for the Study of Violence and Reconciliation, a South African NGO with which he remains affiliated as a Research Associate.

Steven Barmazel is a freelance journalist based in Santa Rosa, California. He worked as the Karachi correspondent for *AsiaWeek* in the early 1990s, where he visited Orangi and Orangi Pilot Project many times. After returning to the United States, he was associated for several years with an NGO that worked to improve landmine-clearing techniques and equipment.

Susan Burgerman is a Washington, DC-based consultant on international political development. Previously, she was Associate Director of the Institute of Latin American Studies at Columbia University. Her publications include *Moral Victories: How Activists Provoke Multilateral Action* (Cornell University Press, 2001); 'Building the Peace by Mandating Reform: United Nations-Mediated Human Rights Agreements in El Salvador and Guatemala', *Latin American Perspectives* (May 2000); and a contributing author to *Implementing US Human Rights Policy* (Debra Liang-Fenton, editor, US Institute of Peace Press, 2004).

Henry F. Carey is Associate Professor of Political Science at Georgia State University. He is author or editor of five books, including: *Romania since 1989: Politics, Economics and Society* (Lexington Books 2004). *Mitigating Conflict: the Role of NGOs*, special issue of *International Peacekeeping* (co-editor with Oliver P. Richmond, Frank Cass, 2003), *National Reconciliation in Eastern Europe* (Columbia University Press, 2003), and *Dilemmas of NGO Peacebuilding Among Former Enemies* (London: Palgrave, 2006), forthcoming. He is chair of the international law section of the International Studies Association.

Clark Efaw is Program Officer for CARE. Formerly leading an effort in the Department of Agriculture and Natural Resources on a rights-based approach to development, he is now part of CARE's Impact Measurement and Learning Team (IMLT).

Joanna Fisher has worked in the NGO sector in Rwanda during the past decade.

Felice D. Gaer directs the Jacob Blaustein Institute of Human Rights and was previous Executive Director of the International League for Human Rights. She is author of numerous academic articles and manuscripts on human rights, NGOs and the UN. She is also the US-nominated, independent expert in Geneva on the Torture Committee, which reviews states parties' reports under the International Torture Convention.

Michael Gordon Jackson received his PhD in Politics from Brandeis University in 1991. Since 1992, he has been working and teaching at Brown University. His research interests include the study of national security issues and international peacekeeping.

Heather D. Heckel is Assistant Professor of Political Science at Bridgewater College in Virginia. Before becoming a professor, she worked with youth from low income communities through a non-profit organization and as a public school teacher. Her previously published work includes a study of NGOs and the campaign against corruption. She received her PhD from Georgia State University in 2005, with a dissertation on transnational advocacy movements and child rights.

Julie Mertus is an Associate Professor and Co-Director of the MA program in Ethics, Peace and Global Affairs at American University. A graduate of Yale Law School, her books include: *Bait and Switch: Human Rights and American Foreign Policy* (Routledge, 2004) and *Human Rights and Conflict* (United States Institute of Peace, 2004) (co-editor); *Kosovo: How Myths and Truths Started a War* (U. Cal. Press 1999), *War's Offensive Against Women: The Humanitarian Challenge in Bosnia, Kosovo, and Afghanistan* (Kumarian, 2000); *The Suitcase: Refugees' Voices from Bosnia and Croatia* (U. Cal. Press, 1999); and *Local Action/Global Change* (UNIFEM 1999) (with Mallika Dutt and Nancy Flowers).

Avtar Kaul, late, retired from CARE on July 1, 2004 and passed away on December 1, 2004.

Ann Kelleher currently holds an appointment as Professor of Political Science at Pacific Lutheran University. Her teaching specializations include international conflict reduction/resolution, development, and international relations. Kelleher has published in the fields of international development and international education and has initiated programs in Norway and, in cooperation with Norwegian educators, in Namibia.

Julie Mertus is an Associate Professor and Co-Director of the MA program in Ethics, Peace and Global Affairs at American University in Washington, DC. A graduate of Yale Law School, her work focuses on ethno-national conflict, human rights, refugee and humanitarian law and policy, gender and conflict and post-war transitions. Her books include: *Bait and Switch: Human Rights and American Foreign Policy* (Routledge, 2004) and *Human Rights and Conflict* (United States Institute of Peace, 2004)(editor, with Jeffrey Helsing); *Kosovo: How Myths and Truths Started a War* (U. Cal. Press 1999), *War's Offensive Against Women: The Humanitarian Challenge in Bosnia, Kosovo, and Afghanistan* (Kumarian, 2000); *The Suitcase: Refugees' Voices from Bosnia and Croatia* (U. Cal. Press, 1999); *Local Action/Global Change* (UNIFEM 1999) (with Mallika Dutt and Nancy Flowers).

Mahmood Monshipouri is Chair of the Political Science Department. at Quinnipiac University, Connecticut. He is author of *Democratization, Liberalization and Human Rights in the Third World* (Lynne Rienner, 1995) and *Islamism, Secularism, and Human Rights in the Middle East* (Lynee Reinner, 1998). He is also co-editor of *Constructing Universalisms: Human Rights in an Age of Globalization* (M.E. Sharpe, 2003).

Wole Olaleye is currently the Regional Policy Coordinator of ActionAid International's Southern African Programme, as well as a PhD candidate in Political Studies at the University of Cape Town. From 2000–2002, he was a Researcher at the Centre for the Study of Violence and Reconciliation, where he served as the Project Coordinator for the SADC Crime and Violence Prevention Project. He received an M.Phil. in Social Science Research Methodology from the University of Stellenbosch and a BA (Hons.) from the University of the Western Cape.

Thania Paffenholz lectures peace and development studies at the Institute of Political Science at the University in Berne, Switzerland. She received her PhD in international relations focusing on the theory and practice of mediation and peacebuilding in civil wars from the University of Frankfurt/Main, Germany. She was also Member of the Board of the UN Lessons Learned Unit, Department of Peacekeeping Operations (1996–2002) as well as Council member of the International Peace Research Association (1996–2000). She co-edited 'Peacebuilding: A field Guide' (Lynne Rienner Publishers, 2000) and has a wide range of other publication in peacebuilding.

Marek Pavka, a native of Hodonin, Czechoslovakia, has lecturing since 1998 at the Military Academy and since 2000 at Masaryk University, both in Brno. From 2001–2002, he was scholar in residence on University of Central Florida and received his PhD from Masaryk University in 2003.

Kim D. Reimann is an Assistant Professor in the Department of Political Science at Georgia State University in Atlanta. Her research interests include the role of NGOs and nonstate actors in international relations, transnational social movements, environmental politics, East Asian politics and the political economy of Japan. She has published work in academic journals and edited book volumes on both NGOs in Japan and NGOs in international politics more generally. She is currently finishing a book project on the emergence and growth of NGOs in Japan entitled 'Activism from Above'.

Oliver P. Richmond is a Reader at the School of International Relations at St. Andrews University. His forthcoming publications include a monograph called *The Transformation of Peace* (Palgrave), as well as co-edited volumes on *Spoilers in Peace Processes,* and *NGOs and Peacebuilding*. He edits a Palgrave Book Series called *Rethinking Conflict Studies.* His past books include: *Mitigating Conflict: NGOs in Peace Processes*, Special Issue of *International Peacekeeping* and book (co-edited with Henry F. Carey, Frank Cass 2003). M*aintaining Order, Making Peace* (Palgrave 2002); *The United Nations and Human Security: Beyond Peacekeeping.* (Co-edited with Edward Newman (Palgrave 2001); *The Work of the UN in Cyprus: Promoting Peace and Development.* (Co-edited with James KerLindsay, Palgrave 2001); and *Mediating in Cyprus: The Cypriot Communities and the United Nations* (Frank Cass Series on Peacekeeping, 1998.)

Catalina Rojas is a Colombian political scientist and doctoral candidate at the Institute for Conflict Analysis and Resolution at George Mason University. Her areas of research include intrastate conflict, refugees and internally displaced persons, civil society and women's peace initiatives, and post-conflict reconstruction and development. Ms. Rojas has taught and conducted research in various Colombian universities, and she has over 10 years experience working with peace organizations. She holds a masters degree in peace and development. Ms. Rojas work has been published several countries including Colombia, Venezuela, Spain and the United States. She currently resides in Alexandria, VA.

Tazreena Sajjad, a citizen of Bangladesh, is a candidate for a Masters degree in International Peace and Conflict Resolution at American University in Washington DC. Her research interests include gender, human rights, international law and post-conflict reconstruction. Her other publications include, 'Addressing the Gray Areas of International Law and Women Guerillas: Marching Toward True Freedom?'

Chenaz B. Seelarbokus is a PhD candidate, Department of Political Science, Georgia State University. She holds a BS in Chemistry and Environmental Studies from the University of Mauritius (1990); MS in Environmental Management from the Louisiana State University, Baton Rouge (1998); MA in Political Science from GSU (2002); and MPA (2002) from the Andrew Young School of Policy Studies, GSU, with specialization in nonprofit administration. Chenaz has participated in the 1994 UNEP/UNESCO International Postgraduate Diploma Course in Environmental Management for Developing Countries, Dresden, Germany. Chenaz has also served in the Ministry for the Environment, Government of Mauritius, from 1990–1994.

Susan Shapiro helped to conceive and develop the Soros Health Education Program as its project director, She is co-author of *The Curtain Rises: Oral Histories of the Fall of Communism in Eastern Europe* with Ronald Shapiro (McFarland Publishers, Jefferson, North Carolina, 2004). She is also co-author, among many studies, of the Russia Health Education Project Strategic Plan, 1998–2001.

James Larry Taulbee is Associate Professor of Political Science at Emory University. His written work has addressed questions relating to the legal control of terrorism, the use of mercenaries and private military companies, the effectiveness of human rights initiatives, the International Criminal Court and the utility of non-conventional defense strategies.

Foreword

Felice D. Gaer

Non-governmental organizations and other local actors have conducted some of their most valuable and effective work over the years in the area of peacebuilding, as detailed vividly in the chapters of this book. This was not always the case: it became possible because of the space created for their activities as a result of the vision and leadership of top UN officials. Two United Nations leaders – separated in time and career by some 40 years – stand out for having created the new space within which NGOs were able to function more fully and to assist the world body to become more than a debating society. This foreword recalls and honors their legacies.

Both Dag Hammarskjold and Sergio Viera de Mello understood that the UN would only be able to build a lasting peace if it could do more than negotiate agreements with broad verbal promises to end conflict. Both understood that after signing peace agreements, many countries would lapse back into violence unless there were extra efforts for economic development, security, and reconciliation measures on the ground. Engaging local populations that were once at war to focus on pragmatic concerns – from going about their daily lives to building new institutions to sustain peace – might help prevent a return to armed conflict.

Hammarskjold made it possible for UN forces to be positioned between combatant armies in countries in which peace agreements were being negotiated or had been concluded. De Mello understood that for complex peacekeeping and peacebuilding situations, it was necessary to engage the talents of more than peacekeepers who were military personnel – and that an array of civilian actors and organizations – based within the country as well as those based abroad who brought special skills to bear – were allies of the United Nations in responding to the challenges within failed states and post-conflict situations. He recruited NGO leaders to work on-site, and he consulted broadly with diverse and local NGOs. In addition, both UN leaders understood that it was impossible to separate the security factor in peacebuilding from the human rights factor, and that UN programs had to be more proactive in linking these dimensions if they were to keep armed conflict from reoccurring.

Hammarskjold served as UN Secretary General in the 1950s, the second person to hold that position. Viera de Mello was the third UN High Commissioner for Human Rights, serving from 2002–2003; immediately following his term as executive head of the UN's Peace Operation in East Timor, one of its most complex on-the-ground projects. While separated by decades in their UN careers, both Hammarskjold and Viera de Mello shared a common fate, each having died tragically in office, while traveling or stationed in countries far from UN headquarters, serving the UN in the field in efforts to bring peace to trouble spots. Dag Hammarskjold died in an air crash in Congo in 1962; the year 2005 marks the centennial of his birth. His death was a huge setback for the United Nations at the height of the cold war. Sergio Viera de Mello was the victim of a terrorist attack on UN headquarters in Iraq, where he was serving on an interim basis, as head of the UN's mission, in 2003, while on leave as High Commissioner for Human Rights. Many viewed him as a future Secretary General; his death demoralized the UN and its supporters globally. Both men understood the importance of peacebuilding, and both saw NGOs as crucial contributors to the UN's work in this regard.

Dag Hammarskjold is commonly associated with the UN's work to advance peace and security. He operated in an era when the UN's human rights efforts were at their infancy, muzzled by the cold war, and highly controversial within the organization. Hammarskjold is widely credited with transforming the world body into an independent, impartial international organization with a professional secretariat, and, perhaps most significantly, launching peacekeeping operations as a new conflict prevention tool of the UN, one unforeseen by the Charter. Hammarskjold engaged actively in preventive diplomacy. Soviet leader Nikita Khrushchev demanded his resignation, but Hammarskjold refused to step down.

In 1956, Dag Hammarskjold addressed the subject of human rights before the American Jewish Committee (AJC) in New York. He declared that human rights was fundamental to all he was engaged in as Secretary-General, explaining that 'we know the question of peace and the question of human rights are closely related. Without recognition of human rights, we shall never have peace, and it is only within the framework of peace that human rights can be fully developed.'

Hammarskjold argued in those pre-human rights treaty years that there was still room for the world body to act: Even in the rarefied political atmosphere of that period, the UN could promote human rights, just as it could promote peace. Hammarskjold's efforts were often behind the scenes, and he encouraged NGO actors, among them the AJC, to press for codification of human rights instruments and for factual reports, and to keep the rights issue before the world body even as he worked to advance peacekeeping and peacebuilding programs in trouble spots overseas.

In a prominent 1963 Dag Hammarskjold Memorial Lecture at Columbia University, inspired by example the Swedish UN head set in expanding UN executive authority during his term in office, former AJC president Jacob Blaustein called for establishment of a post of High Commissioner for Human Rights. Reflecting on what Hammarskjold was able to accomplish creatively as Secretary General, Blaustein argued that it was now also time 'to strengthen the executive powers of the United Nations in the field of human rights'. This speech launched the High Commissioner concept, which was debated again and again over the next thirty years until the post was finally established in 1993. In the interim, it was the NGO community that kept the idea before the community of nations.

Human rights activities in the United Nations have come a long way since those days. Conference room diplomacy in human rights, exemplified by the UN Commission on Human Rights, was not enough: it would be essential to move human rights programs into the field, as a component of peacekeeping and development and other UN programs.

Dag Hammarskjold was an international civil servant who looked for new ways to use the international organization to build peace on the ground; so did Sergio Viera de Mello, as a head of peacekeeping missions and High Commissioner for Human Rights (the only one of the four officeholders to date to have had hands-on experience with United Nations peace operations at the country level). De Mello had served in Cambodia and Bosnia, as the head of the Office for Coordination of Humanitarian Affairs (OCHA), and in 2002 was Special Representative of the Secretary General in East Timor. There, he learned even more clearly how much security, development, and human rights interact in the real world, and how valuable NGOs are in such settings.

NGOs around the globe articulated their regrets on the death of de Mello in Iraq in 2003 – perhaps none more strongly or movingly than those from East Timor. Yet some human rights NGOs, such as Human Rights Watch, initially expressed doubts about De Mello's qualifications for the post of UN High Commissioner, acknowledging his diplomatic experience in the field, but questioning that De Mello 'lacks hands-on human rights experience'.[1] The NY-based organization asked whether the new appointee would 'stand up to governments', implying that in his previous political assignments he had made too many compromises and, as one of De Mello's former aides put it, 'shaken too many dirty hands'.[2] In one of his earliest press conferences, De Mello characteristically brushed the issue aside, challenging journalists to 'judge me on the basis of results …'[3] De Mello was convinced that peacebuilding in the real world required both a variety of skills and an awareness of when to use them. He understood the complexity of what is needed to bring a genuine end to conflict.

Though de Mello had interacted with NGOs in his varied UN positions, it was only in East Timor that he came to recognize them as essential. The Herald Tribune recalled that de Mello was 'most widely and justly praised' for his UN work overseeing the transition in East Timor. However, de Mello 'began his work there with too heavy an authoritarian hand, but he soon … increased the role of the Timorese in the transition. From that work, he learned a key lesson, which he brought to Iraq: 'do everything possible to give the local population control of its own destiny.'[4] The challenge was how to be both principled and pragmatic.

While serving as High Commissioner, de Mello suggested a new approach emphasizing not only the universal human rights instruments, but the rule of law more generally. Whether in peace operations or other activities UN field operations in human rights, this would be the centerpiece of the UN's concern. At his first press conference, de Mello emphasized that his 'overarching theme' would be 'fostering the rule of law, without which it is not possible to have respect for

---

[1] Human Rights Watch Press release, July 22, 2002.
[2] Interview, 19 May 2004, notes with author.
[3] Transcript of Press Conference by Sergio Vieira de Mello, the New High Commissioner of Human Rights, Geneva, 20 September 2002, p. 6.
[4] 'A Nation-Builder Slain', Herald Tribune, 21 August 2003.

human rights, democracy and good governance'. He called it 'the lynchpin of human rights protection – it is not just about morals. It is not just about politics ... it is both ...'[5]

Institutional development remained central: 'I intend to focus on rule of law as an overarching theme. The rule of law requires that the entire range of institutional arrangements that function under the national constitutional and legal order play an active role to ensure that human rights ... are advanced, enjoyed, and defended ... We need to make this dynamic concept operational and accessible to everyone around the globe.'[6] De Mello repeated this in his first appearance as High Commissioner for Human Rights before the Third Committee of the General Assembly, remarking that 'conflict often emerged where the rule of law collapsed'.[7]

Rule of law was an 'overarching principle' that De Mello planned to stress together with equality, dignity, and security.[8] Citing the key role of non-governmental organizations in peacebuilding and reconciliation efforts, de Mello clarified that the triad of 'rule of law, popular participation, and responsibility – as well as accountable governance' was 'crucial for our cooperation with governments and civil society'.[9] He noted that he had established a capacity for rule of law and democracy promotion at the OHCHR. Further, the rule of law is not only universal but is extraordinarily portable, and can be built throughout the world.

When de Mello reported to the UN General Assembly's Third Committee, a representative of the European Union asked de Mello whether his office would strengthen its work with NGOs. De Mello responded that cooperation would continue and that instead of just establishing a 'focal point' for non-governmental organizations, he would establish a unit that 'would not only liaise but also be the entry point for coordination of cooperation with NGOs in all fields of human rights'.[10]

De Mello's formal report to the Commission on Human Rights[11] a few months later provided the usual acknowledgment of 'the importance of working with civil society and to strengthening our partnership with NGOs active in the field of human rights'. And he cited awareness of 'the vital contribution of these organizations which provide information, insights, ideas and courage in the defense of human rights information, insights, ideas and courage in the defense of human rights'.

But de Mello also envisaged that NGOs would play a broader role in building respect for rule of law and enforcing it at country level. Whereas some saw human rights groups primarily as information gatherers and transmitters, de Mello understood that field-based human rights NGOs could be engaged not merely in monitoring, but in other locally-focused programs, from training to

---

[5] Ibid., pp. 1, 2.
[6] Opening address by Sergio Vieira de Mello, 76th session of the Human Rights Committee, UN HCHR, Geneva, 14 October 2002, p. 1.
[7] UN Press release, 4 November 2002, AM.
[8] Sergio Vieira de Mello, Address to the Permanent Council of OSCE, 21 November 2002.
[9] Ibid., p. 3.
[10] UN press release, 4 November 2002, Third Committee, AM.
[11] UN document E.CN.4/2003/14, paragraph 45.

mediation to relief and to dealing with 'the past'. At an NGO conference organized in New York on February 18, 2003, de Mello was more candid: it is important for NGOs to address power, he explained. Asked whether human rights assistance should replace human rights protection activities, he agreed it should not – but technical assistance is in itself useful. People in the field don't need more human rights workshops and conferences, he remarked there and elsewhere. They need to find ways to renew a commitment to protecting and promoting human rights in their own societies which have broken down. While some activists argued that the human rights movement with its emphasis on norms and monitoring was worn out, Sergio De Mello saw it otherwise: thinking of the field, he said the movement has just begun.

Sergio De Mello understood the need to gain support for sustainable peace from all components of a post-conflict society. If his emphasis on rule of law was successful, it would do more than ensure the formal guarantee of human rights norms – it would also provide practical avenues through which to advance peace: ensuring access to and participation in political decision making, encouraging economic growth on a more fair basis, and advancing social accord among diverse groups.[12] De Mello sought to overcome the stereotyped divide: 'peace or justice?' With rule of law, he hoped to advance both.

In his opening address to the Commission on Human Rights on March 17, Sergio Vieira de Mello also cited the key role of NGOs in the protection of civilians in war, which he called a paramount principle of international law. In this way he linked the human rights and security elements that Hammarskjold and Annan had emphasized and pointed unmistakably to the new functions of NGOs in the field of peacebuilding in the twenty-first century: 'The role of NGOs and or civil society more broadly in protection cannot be overestimated. NGOs are critically important in the work that lies ahead ...'[13]

This was De Mello's last major reference to the NGO role on the ground before his departure to Iraq, and he was very probably thinking of Iraq at the time. In Iraq, De Mello engaged with political leaders, consulted with NGOs and tried to find a role for the United Nations in a situation in which the world body was clearly a side actor. In July, he brought human rights organizations from abroad to meet with and discuss with Iraqi civil society leaders and NGOs on a range of transitional justice topics, including future trials of gross human rights abusers. At issue was how to move the society forward by dealing with its past. Sadly, before he would have the chance to test his approach, on August 19, 2003, UN headquarters in Baghdad, barely protected and outside the US-British security zone, was attacked by a truck-bomb. The talented visionary High Commissioner was one of its casualties. De Mello's loss catalyzed attention to the issue of what unarmed UN forces can achieve – on the ground – in building peace locally that is not a

---

[12] See Carnegie Corporation Report on Preventing Deadly Conflict, December 1997, pp. 89-90.
[13] Statement to the Opening of the 59th Session of the Commission on Human Rights by Sergio Vieira de Mello, 17 March 2003.

matter of merely collecting information. They also refocused attention on core concepts of security in UN field operations.

UN Secretary General Kofi Annan has seized on the lessons learned about the value of field-based peacebuilding, He wrote in his 2005 plan for UN reform that there can be no security without development; no development without security, and *neither* without human rights – an expansion of the earlier Hammarskjold formula.

Kofi Annan has also called for a new Human Rights Council as a standing body to restore the credibility of the United Nations in the field of human rights, and he envisions the Council would function alongside a new Peacebuilding Council, which would aim to enable the UN to concentrate on aiding countries in transition from war to peace. There is a certain irony in the absence of any role or mention of NGOs in connection with the proposed Peacebuilding Council. However, it is possible that this is being held for a second stage, once the new organ is created.

Annan has also asked for human rights components in many of the UN peacekeeping presences around the world. Perhaps De Mello's emphasis on field experience and his conviction that all components of society must ne engaged in this complex task, has encouraged Annan to press for a stronger relationship between NGOs and the UN's human rights activities in the UN's work.

The Secretary General has also taken up his deceased friend's emphasis on the rule of law. In his proposed reform plan, 'In Larger Freedom', Annan notes that 'Through hard experience, we have become more conscious of the need to build human rights and rule-of-law provisions into peace agreements and ensure that they are implemented'[14] and 'The rule of law as a mere concept is not enough. New laws must be put into place, old ones must be put into practice and our institutions must be better equipped to strengthen the rule of law …'[15]

While final agreement has not yet been reached, the UN's Peacebuilding Council will likely be aimed at bringing 'together all relevant actors to marshal resources and advise on and propose comprehensive strategies for peacebuilding and post-conflict recovery …' The Council will not focus on early warning, but on action to advance the transition from war to post-conflict recovery.

If the Peacebuilding Council is created with this mandate, it will serve as a living memorial to the visions of Dag Hammarskjold and Sergio Vieira de Mello. All it will need is a mandate and means to engage the talents and skills of NGOs throughout the world. It would be a fitting tribute to the leadership of both men and their commitment to peace and the institutions that entrench it.

---

[14] Paragraph 129.
[15] Paragraph 133.

List of Abbreviations

ACBAR	Agency Coordinating Body for Afghan Releif
AHSAO	Afghan Health and Social Assistance Organization
AIA	Afghan Interim Authority
AMA	Afghan Medical Aid
AWC	Afghan Women's Council
AWN	Afghan Women's Network
BINGOs	Big International, Nongovernmental Organizations
CCW	Convention on Conventional Weapons
CIDA	Canadian International Development Agency
CDO	Centar za Dramski Odgoj [Centre for Drama in Education]
CMOCs	Civil-Military Co-operation Centres
CP	Conflict Prevention
CPAU	Cooperation for Peace and Unity
DPRK	Democratic Republic of Korea
DRC	Democratic Republic of the Congo
DONGOs	Donor Created Nongovernmental Organizations
ECHO	European Community Humanitarian Office
EPLF	Eritrean People's Liberation Front
GDI	Global Development Initiative
HCIC	Humanitarian Coordination Information Centre
HINGOs	Humanitarian International Nongovernmental Organizations
ICC	International Criminal Court
ICRC	International Committee of the Red Cross
ICTR	International Criminal Tribunal for Rwanda
ICTY	International Criminal Tribunal for Yugoslavia
IGOs	Inter-Governmental Organizations
INGOs	International Nongovernmental Organizations
LNGOs	Local Nongovernmental Organizations
MAPA	UN Mine Action Program for Afghanistan
MICIVIH	UN/OAS Civilian Verification Mission in Haiti
MSF	Médicins Sans Frontières
NEGAR	Defence of Afghanistan Women's Rights
NGOs	Nongovernmental Organizations
NPFL	National Patriotic Front of Liberia
ODA	Official Development Assistance
OHR	Office of the High Representative
OLS	United Nations Operation Lifeline Sudan
OAS	Organization of American States
OSCE	Office of Security and Cooperation in Europe
PEACE	Poverty Eradication and Community Empowerment

PHR	Physicians for Human Rights
PrepComs	Preparatory Commissions
QUANGOs	Quasi Nongovernmental Organizations
RAWA	Revolutionary Association of the Women of Afghanistan
RPF	Rwanda Patriotic Front
SAD	Society of Afghan Doctors
SPLA	Sudan People's Liberation Army
SPLM	Sudan People's Liberation Movement
SRRA	Sudan Relief and Rehabilitation Association
SSIA	South Sudan Independence Army
TPLF	Tigray People's Liberation Front
UEO	Unexploded Ordnance
UN	United Nations
UNDP	United Nations Development Programme
UNFPA	United Nations Fund for Population Activities
UNHCR	United Nations High Commissioner for Refugees
USAID	United States Agency for International Development
VDCs	Village Development Committees

Part One:
Conceutalising NGO Roles in Peacebuilding

Chapter 1

Expanding Involvement of NGOs in Emerging Global Governance

Chadwick F. Alger

The rapidly growing involvement of nongovernmental organisations (NGOs) in world relations has created escalating challenges to both NGO participants and analysts. The growing literature on NGOs offers ever more comprehensive insights into their emergence, broad involvement in national and international politics, diverse activities, and challenges to achieve their goals. The four sections of this volume clearly reveal the broad scope of NGO peacebuilding with former enemies, especially: (1) *Coordination* among different NGOs and between NGOs and other actors; (2) *Negotiations* attempting to resolve or mitigate conflicts; (3) *Development* of post-conflict institutions; and (4) *Monitoring* the performance of new institutions. This chapter places these contributions in the scholarly context of understanding how and why NGOs are involved in emerging global governance.

Minear and Weiss succinctly summarize the challenge to assess the role of NGOs in the response of the international community to violence against humanity: 'The sheer diversity of external NGOs – a universe in its own right – is mind-boggling'.[1] Katarina West provides a useful metaphor of the NGO landscape as 'like a pyramid that has a few big multinational NGOs at the top, thousands of small local NGOs at the bottom, and a number of medium-sized NGOs in the middle'.[2]

Although there is no doubt that the number of NGOs involved in world relations has greatly increased in recent years, historically, NGOs are not a new phenomenon. Secretary General Kofi Annan reminded his audience at a 1998 commemoration of the 50th anniversary of the Universal Declaration of Human Rights:

> Before the founding of the United Nations, NGOs led the charge in the adoption of some of the Declaration's forerunners. The Geneva conventions of 1864; multilateral labour conventions adopted in 1906; and the International Slavery Convention of 1926; all stemmed from the world of NGOs who infused the international community with a spirit of reform.[3]

Keck and Sikkink also remind us of the emergence of the 1833–65 campaign to end slavery in the United States, efforts of the international suffrage movement to secure the vote for women between 1888 and 1928, the campaign from 1874 to 1911 by Western missionaries and Chinese reformers to eradicate footbinding in

China, and efforts by Western missionaries and British colonial authorities to end the practice of female circumcision among the Kikuyu of Kenya in 1920–23.[4]

Before going further, it is also important to recognize that the use of the term 'NGO' by some or even the majority of those focusing on their roles in world relations are concerned with only a small percentage of the total NGO population. Two volumes applying terminology from sociology make this tendency clear. Smith et. al., in *Transnational Social Movements and Global Politics*, define this category of NGOs as 'clusters of relatively marginalized actors [that] promote some form of social or political change' and identify them as 'social movements'.[5] Their volume focuses on transnational social movements (TSMOs), i.e. those active across state borders. Keck and Sikkink, in *Activists Beyond Borders*, prefer the term 'transnational network':

> By importing the network concept from sociology and applying it transnationally, we bridge the increasingly artificial divide between international and national realms ... The networks we describe in this book participate in domestic and international politics simultaneously, drawing on a variety of resources, as if they were part of an international society.[6]

The complexity of the political processes in which NGOs that are the focus of this volume are involved is not only a result of the 'sheer diversity' of those NGOs working for social and political change, but also NGOs providing humanitarian relief, as well as from the array of other state and intergovernmental actors with which they must interact. Minnear and Weiss list eight kinds of actors involved in humanitarian actions, five outside the borders of the state in which the activity is being undertaken, and three inside: *Outside*: (1) The UN System and regional inter-state organisations, (2) bilateral state agencies, (3) International Committee of the Red Cross, (4) military forces and (5) NGOs. *Inside*: (1) host government, (2) armed opposition and (3) local NGOs.[7] Because each of these actors has its strengths and weaknesses, they assert that 'identifying who does what best in particular circumstances can help improve the humanitarian system of the future'.[8] For their part, Keck and Sikkink offer a complimentary list of major actors in 'transnational advocacy networks': (1) international and domestic nongovernmental research and advocacy organisations, (2) local social movements, (3) foundations, (4) the media, (5) churches, trade unions, consumer organisations, and intellectuals, (6) parts of regional and international intergovernmental organisations and (7) parts of the executive and/or parliamentary branches of governments.[9]

An issue that is frequently raised in research on NGOs/transnational social movements/transnational networks is the degree to which they make world politics more or less democratic. On the one hand, many point out that leaders of these organisations tend not to be democratically elected, and the same can be said for leaders in many of the organisations on which they depend for funding. On the other hand, Sikkink advises that the standard against which to measure NGOs is against 'the existing degree of democracy in international institutions and in international governance'. This leads her to conclude that 'most efforts by NGOs and networks bring a greater diversity of viewpoints and information into international institutions than would be otherwise available'. [10] Nevertheless, whether and in what way NGOs make an activity more or less democratic must be evaluated in each specific case.

The goal of this chapter is to make a modest effort to illuminate the global political framework in which the NGO peacebuilding activities presented in this volume take place. When reading about specific coordination, negotiation, monitoring and other NGO peacebuilding in this volume, it becomes clear that simultaneously these same NGOs are involved in a diversity of other activities around the world. These other activities affect what NGOs attempt and are able to achieve in particular cases.

In order to illuminate this framework with relative brevity, while at the same time offering very concrete insights on NGO activity, I have drawn primarily on three approaches to NGO activity. [11] Based on these works, I shall present a fourfold framework of NGO efforts necessary for greater peacebuilding. First, it is necessary for NGOs involved in peacebuilding to create and mobilize global networks. Second, in organising these networks and acquiring support for their operations, NGOs must enhance public participation. Third, such peacebuilding NGOs must become involved with, and endeavor to influence, the activities of International Governmental Organisations (IGOs). Fourth and finally, NGOs must become deepen their involvement in a diverse array of Field Activities.

I. Create and Mobilize Global Networks

We need to study the supporting organisations and activities enhance NGO peacebuilding. [12] Sociologists studying transnational social movements offer insights on the importance of taking into account the resource mobilisation structures and activities of NGOs. [13] These NGOs tend to emerge out of more informal networks composed of local individuals and organisations that are linked through common concerns. These can develop into a transnational organisation with headquarters, periodic meetings of representatives from a number of countries for making policy on one or more global issues, and secretariats to promote and implement these policies. These networks gather information on local conditions in places like East Timor, Sierra Leone and Guatemala through contacts around the world. At times, these efforts may involve systematic monitoring of local conditions. When appropriate, this information is then used to alert networks of supporters about conditions requiring attention. Then, if evidence merits action, they must create an emergency response network around the world. When conditions limit, or make very costly, challenges within states, they may mobilize pressure from the outside, as in the case when pressure from the outside against the Argentine government was exercised through awarding the Nobel Peace Prize to Perez Esquivel.

II. Enhance Public Participation

To create and sustain their efforts, NGOs must become directly and publicly involved in those issues which are their *raison d'etre*.[14] Of course, these efforts tend to be directed toward activating people in support of the goals and policies of specific NGOs, not in broadening public participation itself as a worthy goal. Obviously, NGOs must overcome the general tendency for the public to be less knowledgeable and involved in foreign policy issues than in domestic issues and to feel even more distant from policy-making in IGOs. Thus NGOs are severely challenged in their efforts to enhance public understanding. At times NGOs can enhance public participation in transnational efforts by linking to local partners and facilitating the latter's transnational reach.

Many of the issues on NGO agendas are not in the headlines. NGOs act out in organisations familiar to few, in conferences rarely reported by journalists who mostly have no knowledge, slight awareness and little interest in these issues. Thus, NGOs are challenged to devise ways to inform government officials and others involved that people are concerned about these issues and taking action. In other words, they must remind government officials that they are being watched. This presents them with the difficult challenge of increasing the transparency of international negotiations and institutions.

III. Participate in IGOs

Most significant peacebuilding issues, including all cases in this volume, are placed on the agendas of organisations in the UN System and other IGOs. As a result, NGOs are increasingly involved in IGOs. They not only mobilize NGOs and build NGO coalitions around issues in IGOS, but they also attempt to place new issues on IGO agendas. Successful completion of these tasks requires NGOs to make efforts to improve their skills in what many refer to as 'conference diplomacy'. In light of their growing involvement in IGOs, some NGOs have become involved in supporting the development of IGOs by member states and their citizens.

The remainder of this third section will provide very brief overviews of NGO (1) participation in UN decision-making bodies, (2) facilitation of inter-state cooperation in IGOs, and (3) relationships with UN secretariats.

1. Participation in UN Decision-Making Bodies[15]

Article 71 of the UN Charter provides that 'the Economic and Social Council may make suitable arrangements for consultation with non-governmental organisations'. Through practice over the years, the involvement of NGOs has extended beyond consultation with ECOSOC to include more active involvement in ECOSOC, in the General Assembly, the Security Council, and in other UN agencies:

a.   *Public meetings* NGOs not only observe public meetings but also have addressed public UN sessions, such as the Special Political and Decolonisation Committees of the General Assembly and the Commission on Human Rights. They have been asked to make panel presentations to committees of the General Assembly. NGOs with ECOSOC consultative status regularly submit documents to a variety of UN bodies.

b.   *Private meetings* Public meetings of UN bodies are frequently preceded by a variety of private meetings in order to facilitate decision-making. NGOs are now involved in some of these meetings. Sometimes they are only observers, but on other occasions they participate in discussions. An NGO Working Group on the Security Council that was convened in 1995 by several NGOS: the Global Policy Forum, Amnesty International, Earth Action, Lawyers' Committee on Nuclear Policy, World Council of Churches and the World Federalist Movement. In 1997, a special Consultation Group of this Working Group began to meet informally with Presidents of the Security Council. NGOs, even those without ECOSOC status, also regularly consult the independent, expert members of the six, treaty-based, human rights committees, such as the Committee Against Torture, the Committee on the Elimination of Discrimination Against Women, and the Human Rights Committee itself.

2. Facilitate Inter-State Cooperation in IGOs[16]

In addition to participation in decision-making bodies of IGOs, NGOs attempt to facilitate cooperation among member states in a number of ways. Toward this end, NGOs sometimes provide reliable background information, which reveals the extent of a problem and reasons why multilateral agreements are necessary. This is sometimes achieved through preparing background papers and reports. Education of delegates may become more activist and include luncheon meetings or weekend seminars, as well as lobbying in meetings and receptions. A special kind of education takes place in efforts to educate representatives to narrow the technical gap between delegates. This is illustrated by the Neptune Group's enhancing technical competence of some African, Asian and Latin American delegates with respect to certain highly technical, Law of the Sea issues.

Often, movement toward inter-state agreement may not be inhibited by the lack of information, but rather by a flood of contending viewpoints, all of whom claim expertise. In such cases, some trusted NGOs can serve as third party sources of information. Agreement may also be impossible when groups of states hold tenaciously to opposing policy options. In such occasions, NGOs can facilitate agreement by expanding policy options one of which may be acceptable to opposing groups of states. NGO facilitation or mediation may be practiced in very informal ways, in corridors, receptions, luncheons, etc. that are a normal part of multilateral diplomacy.

Another contribution of 'NGOs' is the creation and strengthening of international human rights norms. Ann Marie Clark has drawn up a list of requirements for 'a third-party model of norm generation', which is usefully complementary to the NGO activities in cases in this volume. She concludes that such an NGO will be effective when: (1) it appears to be independent from one state or group's point of view; (2) it has information and expertise that states would not gather, or be able to gather, on their own; (3) it can convey a sense that its independence is a result of representativeness, either of principle or broad public opinion, or both; and (4) it invokes existing principles in a way that refers to concrete behavior and extends the reference to real or potential new cases of violations.[17]

3. Relations with Secretariats[18]

Members of IGO secretariats are, of course, deeply involved in parliamentary diplomacy. They are present at all public meetings, often sitting on either side of the Chair. In this context, NGOs can establish contact with those who organize public meetings and those who are expected to carry out their decisions. This can build contact and collaboration with relevant UN secretariats.

In recent years, Secretary Generals have paid increasing attention to NGOs. Secretary-General Boutros Boutros Ghali, addressing NGO representatives at the UN in September 1994, made this very clear: 'I want you to consider this your home'. According to Rice and Ritchie:

> Until recently, these words might have caused astonishment. The United Nations was considered to be a forum for sovereign states alone. Within the space of a few short years, this attitude has changed. Non-governmental organisations are now considered full participants in international life.[19]

In 1995 this Secretary General named his Special Political Adviser as the focal point in his executive office on NGOs. She was made chair of an inter-departmental working group on NGO relations and asked to propose innovative ways through which relations with NGOs could be enhanced.[20]

Some UN offices have regularly scheduled meetings with NGOs. The UN High Commissioner for Refugees in 1999 'consulted with leaders of about 30 major human rights and relief NGOs – a meeting that resulted in a follow-up dialogue process'. The Office of Coordination of Humanitarian Affairs has monthly meetings with NGOs, co-chaired by the Office and an NGO representative, Inter-Action. In addition, The Office of Coordination of Humanitarian Affairs has an Inter-Agency Standing Committee with NGO representation. The International Fund for Agricultural Development has an Annual Consultation with NGOs. The World Trade Organisation has symposia on specific issues of interest to civil society.[21] Finally, the World Bank has established national steering committees for examining the impacts of Bank policies on social groups. Composed of representatives of local NGOs, governments and World Bank members, these committees hold national public fora and participatory field investigations.[22] Some NGOs and UN agencies jointly research, implement and monitor programs. Finally, some UN agencies provide training and financial support for NGO establishment and development.

In conclusion, an array of opportunities exist for public and private NGO participation in UN decision-making bodies and secretariats. Particularly fascinating is that on some occasions, secretariats support and even finance NGOs, and on others the support flows in the opposite direction. Thus, our inventory leads to challenging research questions about this emerging global governance and the future potential of the diverse styles for NGO participation.

IV. Field Activities

1. Typology of Field Activities

NGOs are involved in a remarkable diversity of kinds of humanitarian field activities. It is useful to first place them in the context of the six-fold typology provided by Katarina West in the introduction to her volume on humanitarian NGOs in Rwanda and Afghanistan: (1) general humanitarian, (2) preventive, (3) protective, (4) relief, (5) forcible, and (6) restorative.[23] Her first two categories usefully link NGO field activities with their external roots, discussed extensively above.

West defines *general humanitarian* action as 'activities whose primary aim is not to deal with a particular humanitarian crisis, but, instead, to raise awareness about humanitarian issues in donor countries and develop general principles of humanitarian action'.[24]

Prevention is anticipating and avoiding humanitarian crises before they occur by monitoring, fact-finding, early warning, lobbying and information-sharing. Toward this end, NGOs raise awareness about 'alarming humanitarian developments, and pressure governments and IGOs to take action'.[25] Thus, NGO preventive activities link their field activities to participation in IGOs, as discussed above.

Protective activities seek to maintain basic order and to shield civilians from fighting. West cites prison visits, landmine-clearance, minimum refugee camp standards, and protective accompaniment of people in danger.

Relief action involves traditional humanitarian action, i.e. providing clothing, shelter, medicine, and other things necessary for survival. Thus, relief can expand into more sustained efforts that include sanitation, health care, construction of temporary and more long-term shelters, etc.

Forcible humanitarian actions are efforts to help enforce penalties for severe violations of international humanitarian law. For example, the UN Security Council created international tribunals for such violations in 1993 for the former Yugoslavia and 1994 for Rwanda. By investigating and adducing evidence, NGOs have assisted prosecutions at both ad hoc tribunals.

Restorative humanitarian action is both conflict resolution and peacebuilding, a central focus of the case studies in this volume. Conflict resolution NGOs attempt to find agreement between belligerents in order to terminate fighting. West defines peacebuilding as efforts to 'improve general security, establish a legitimate government and rehabilitate the local economy and civil society'.[26]

2. Preparing for the field

Peacebuilding: A Field Guide, by Reychler and Paffenholz,[27] is a 543-page handbook for members of NGOs active in peacebuilding in the field. A quick overview of the 55 contributions to this volume, by 57 scholars and NGO participants, usefully illuminates the diversity of NGO challenges in field activities. Several authors comment on most of the 17 aspects of field activity presented in three sections: (1) Preparing for the field, (2) Working in the field, and (3) Surviving in the field. Thus the field guide does not provide those preparing for the field with a simple manual for overcoming the challenges that they will face. But it does challenge them to ponder in advance how to cope with these challenges. In the following, several brief comments will be presented from these 17 field activities, which epitomize NGO participation in global governance.

The first section on *preparing for the field* opens with a discussion of concepts and analytical tools for efforts to move from conflict to sustainable peacebuilding. This is essentially a very brief 17-page summary of how much recent research has contributed to knowledge for entering the field.[28]

Preparing for the field also involves *selecting people*, training people and creating awareness of multicultural environments and gender issues. Some may be surprised with this warning to potential recruits, 'Do not join to do someone a favor'. It is feared that 'feelings of paternalism or guilt that may motivate some volunteers hinder effective peacebuilding work'. It is felt that 'total personal commitment may lead to lack of overall perspective and objective judgment' (34). Emphasis is also placed on ability to cope with violent situations and the risk of physical injury.

Discussion of *training people* opens with a listing of peacebuilding activities in which NGOs are involved: mediation and confidence building, humanitarian assistance, reintegration, rehabilitation, reconstruction, stabilisation of economic structures, monitoring and improving human rights, interim administration, information and education. It concludes with concern that 'at best civilians are introduced to their mission tasks through short-term courses' (36). Instead it is advocated that 'there is a need for comprehensive training programs that fit the needs of field operations' (36).

Creating awareness places emphasis on preparing to cope with a multicultural environment and gender issues. Multicultural issues include concern that basic attitudes toward acceptance of third parties varies in different contexts and that Western assumptions about conflict resolution are not accepted in other cultures. Awareness of gender issues involves understanding of the linkages between gender-equality issues, conflict and peacebuilding. It is noted that different gender dimensions arise in preconflict situations, during conflict and during reconstruction and rehabilitation. In evaluating results of peacebuilding, participants are advised to ask how many peace negotiators were women, the voting rates of women, the male/female ratio of displaced people and the varying impact of projects on women and men.

3. Working in the field

The long section of the field guide on Working in the field (75-442) reveals the diversity of challenges confronted by NGO peacebuilders in the field and the broad range of competences they require to meet these challenges. They are divided into nine topics:

1. Selecting approaches to mediation
2. Identifying key actors in conflict situations
3. Designing the mediating process
4. Monitoring
5. Relief aid and development cooperation
6. Training local peacebuilders
7. Media
8. Dealing with the past and imaging the future
9. Security

All nine of these tasks are confronted by NGOs involved in peacebuilding activity that is analyzed in chapters in the book that you are now reading. This nine-part typology of work in the field can help the reader to place one activity, such as monitoring or negotiation in the context of the full array of actual, and potential, activities in which NGOs in the field are involved.

Selecting approaches to mediation (75-144) indicates the need to choose among approaches that range from low to more intrusive mediation, i.e. ranging from good offices (low intervention), to facilitation (talk to the parties separately), to consultation (advise the conflicting parties), to negotiation (both parties are present with the third party). Also presented are the need to choose from different types of mediation, with that involving states referred to as Track 1, and that involving other parties, including NGOs, referred to as Track 2. This offers the context for the chapter in this volume on NGOs and Track-one-and-a-half diplomacy.

Identifying key actors in mediation (145-198) asserts that NGOs in the field are challenged to identify three levels of leadership. Top Leadership includes military/political/religious leaders with high visibility. Middle Leadership includes respected ethnic/religious, academics/intellectual and humanitarian leaders. Grassroots Leadership includes leaders of indigenous NGOs, community developers, local health officials and refugee camp leaders. Lederach advises that different approaches are required at each of these levels. In dealing with top leadership, the goal is to achieve a negotiated settlement in which high level leaders are brought to the negotiating table. Lederach believes that a theory for approaching middle leadership has not yet been developed, but he recommends three approaches: problem-solving workshops (workshops in which members of both parties, in the presence of third parties, discuss the conflict) conflict resolution training, and the development of peace commissions.[29] The grassroots, or bottom-up approach, must cope with massive numbers of people. These can involve local peace commissions, grassroots training, prejudice reduction, and psychosocial work in postwar trauma.

Designing the mediation process   (173-198) is responsive to the fact that NGOs are involved in facilitating mediation at all three levels, not only the much publicized mediation between representatives of states. It opens with the warning that 'people and organisations are usually more sensitive about how a decision is reached than what the decision itself is' (173). NGOs involved in establishing mediation among parties are basically urged to proceed thoughtfully and avoid haste. They are advised to involve representatives of parties in each stage of the process, including information gathering, definition of the problem, and reporting back to people affected by the process. It is also suggested that in certain situations more than one problem-solving forum may be needed.

Monitoring   (199-237) offers guidance for NGOs involved in monitoring an array of peace-building activities: human rights, democratic transitions, elections and minority conflicts. Advice to those monitoring democratic transitions offers insight on the challenges faced by monitors and how far some NGOs have come in developing monitoring competence. Monitors are advised that they must be aware, and prepared to cope with, contending definitions of democracy. They are made aware of transition strategies for moving from undemocratic regimes to solid democratic institutions. And they are warned against anticipating quick and easy transitions to democracy.

Relief aid and development cooperation   (238-276) reflects growing awareness of relief NGOs that they must be aware of the impact of relief aid on conflicts within societies, on sustainable development and on peace-building. In response, NGOs involved in relief aid are instructed in the development of ways in which they can at the same time contribute to long-term conflict prevention, support peace processes and address localized violence. Local participation is seen as important in development work that leads to these broader goals. A high turnover rate of NGO personnel is believed to undermine local learning that makes these goals feasible.

Training local peace-builders   (277-300) is, of course, necessary in achieving local participation. Training trainers has recently become a higher priority for NGOs in the field. Those participating are challenged to study new developments in knowledge about peacebuilding and to acquire knowledge about the local peacebuilding context and appropriate norms and ethics for relations with local people being trained. Also important is the need for follow-up contact and counseling of those that have been trained.

Media   (301-321) can obviously play an important role in conflict resolution and peacebuilding. NGOs are increasingly aware of this fact and of the need for them to monitor media coverage of situations in which they are involved and to promote media coverage compatible with their aims. Toward this end these recommendations for NGOs have been developed: (1) Promote laws that monitor the media and ensure that media do not undermine peacebuilding values. (2) Encourage international sanctions against hate speech in the media. (3) Promote peace media that can counter the distortions of hate media. (4) Develop capacity to keep track of untruthful rumors. (5) Provide a forum through which moderate voices can be heard in the media. (6) Help train the media to cover local peace-building needs.

Dealing with the past and imagining the future (322-375) can have a fundamental impact on movement from extreme peacelessness to a process of peace-building. NGOs are contending with growing knowledge that a policy dominated by revenge and punishment may undermine peacebuilding. As a result they are attempting to apply knowledge attained by the South African Truth and Reconciliation Commission, other similar truth commissions, and reconciliation and restorative justice policies applied elsewhere. At the same time, some see the need for an image of a peaceful future as a necessary tool for peacebuilding. Toward this end NGOs are urged to develop workshops composed of local people who work together to develop images of a future with peace.

Security (376-442) is a term used to define NGO involvement in an array of issues that are concerned with diminishing and controlling the use of arms. These include peacekeeping, diminishing access to small arms, demobilising and reintegrating former combatants, rebuilding police forces into democratic policing, and removing mines. This array of issues reflects the fact that peacebuilding begins while efforts are still underway to bring weapons of violence under control. Some NGOs are involved in these activities, focused on diminishing past use of violence. At the same time, other NGOs are participating in peacebuilding guided by a vision of the future. Success requires the development of strategies that are aware of the linkages between them.

4. Surviving in the field (443-533)

It is essential for academic analysts to be aware of the survival challenges confronted by members of NGOs attempting to achieve their goals in strange, challenging, disruptive and often violent conditions. Four dimensions are emphasized in the Field Guide.

Managing stress differentiates among four types of stress and emphasizes the need for preventive measures to be taken before departure abroad and measures that should be taken during the mission. Basic stress is that encountered by anyone in a strange culture, far from home, and confronted with a challenging work environment. Dysfunctional stress can be generated by shortcomings of the organisation, such as lack of information and uncertainty about the mission. Cumulative stress can be caused by long-term exposure to daily challenges in the field. Traumatic stress is referred to as 'critical incident stress', defined as a totally unexpected event causing great fear while experiencing mortal danger against which one is totally helpless. In response to the challenge presented by stress, High Risk Job (HRJ) NGOs, such as International Red Cross and Doctors Without Borders, have developed a stress-prevention structure within their organisations.

Dialogue and listening   play an important role in ending violent conflict so NGOs now recognize the need for their field workers to be self-consciously aware of their listening and communications skills. In his practical guide to mediating disputes, Karl Slaikeu offers instructions for active listening, self-disclosing and questioning that will lead toward dialogue that provides the basis for mutual understanding.[30] Of course, NGOs in the field must place these instructions in the context of cross-cultural dialogue. Luc Reychler advocates training courses in order to shorten the learning curve of neophytes about the culture in general and the conflicts of cultures that are being encountered in the field.

Dealing with moral dilemmas   is a challenge to field workers. For example, an NGO that has a mission devoted to an array of basic principles, reaching across civil, political and economic rights will find specific situations that require maximising one at the cost of minimising another. Another challenge is whether an NGO is concerned only with doing good deeds in the present or broadens its concern to include the long term consequences of these deeds. An example provided by Hugo Slim is whether it is deemed good to heal some people's wounds if they then return to battle and kill children.[31] Slim believes that poor morale in relief agencies is often a result of moral confusion. He believes that 'improved ethical analysis can contribute to morale within agency staff and beyond to the people they are working with'.

V. Conclusion

Our goal has been to provide a brief framework placing specific activities of NGOs involved in peacebuilding in the context of other activities in which these NGOs are involved. We have focused on (1) creation and mobilisation of global networks, (2) enhancing public participation, (3) participation in IGOs and (4) field activities. This overview has revealed that effective involvement in most peacebuilding activities requires NGOs to be active in a diversity of arenas: (1) within their own networks, (2) within states, (3) in IGOs and (4) in inter-state relations that help to shape their negotiations in IGOs. This array of activities and responsibilities makes their direct involvement in specific peacebuilding issues possible. But efforts to coordinate activities in this array of arenas may be very challenging for organisations with limited personnel and resources.

    Perhaps the section of our analysis that most vividly portrays the emerging involvement of NGOs in global governance is our overview of NGO participation in IGOs, which we illustrated primarily with information on NGO involvement in the UN. Covered were the involvement of NGOs in public inter-state decision-making sessions, as well as participation in private sessions, efforts to facilitate inter-state cooperation outside these meetings and NGO relations with UN Secretariats.

Some are challenging us to ponder the difficulties that they see emerging from growing involvement of NGOs in global governance. For example, Katrina West has noticed competition for funds between big international NGOs and other NGOs. She perceives that 'it looks likely that it will be polarized even further [in the future] ... Because the top NGOs are shifting closer to the UN agencies, there will be a greater gap between international NGOs and other NGOs than between international NGOs and the UN agencies'.[32] She also draws attention to growing competition between 'international NGOs', 'other NGOs' and UN agencies for aid projects. She notes that NGOs 'make use of a considerable part of the total humanitarian funds'. For example, during the latter half of the 1990s NGOs had more resources in Afghanistan than UN agencies. '... Currently many donors seem to prefer "NGO-like qualities": that is, speed, flexibility, relative cheapness, high implementation capacity and the lack of bureaucracy ...'[33] 'If the UN continues to have financial problems, it will have to come down to the same level as NGOs to compete for funds.'[34]

Rieff, in *A Bed for the Night: Humanitarianism in Crisis*, perceives a different type of challenge resulting from growing involvement of NGOs in the United Nations. For example:

> Independent humanitarianism does many things well and some things badly, but the things it is now being called upon to do, such as helping to advance the cause of human rights, contributing to stopping wars, and furthering social justice, are beyond its competence, however much one might wish it otherwise.[35]

Also, '... Most humanitarian NGOs seem more than willing to abandon their independence for seats at the big table with officials of the great powers and the United Nations'.[36] Thus, as a result of his focus on NGO competence to cope with humanitarian crises, he observes that simultaneous concern with the long-term impact of humanitarian aid (human rights, stopping wars, furthering social justice) may tend to detract from achieving immediate humanitarian goals. At the same time, he fears that involvement in UN politics by NGOs may result in loss of their capacity to independently fulfill their humanitarian mission.

Nevertheless, at the same time that there is extension of the diversity and quantity of NGO-peace-building activities in the field, their global reach is broadening. One dimension is NGO Issue Networks that are attempting to strengthen NGO competence to cope with specific peacebuilding issues. Some examples are: World Organisation Against Torture (OMCT), International Federation for Human Rights (FIDH), Human Rights Links, Human Rights NGOs, International Campaign to Ban Landmines (ICBL), Coalition to Stop the Use of Child Soldiers, International Action Network on Small Arms, and Coalition for the International Criminal Court. There are also a number of NGO organisations with broad agendas for furthering NGO effectiveness. Their broad focus enables members of NGOs to understand the larger movement in which they are involved. A few examples are: NGO Links, The NGOs Network, Global Policy Forum, and the Global Communication Center for Development Organisations. All of these organisations have web sites that facilitate information sharing and opportunities for collaboration among NGOs.

Another aspect of the extending global reach of NGOs is their creation of their own global conferences. One development has been parallel conferences to UN world conferences on issues such as environment, women and population and development. This then led to NGOs having their own conferences, sometimes before and sometimes after NGO world conferences. These were followed by a People's Millennium Forum in December 2000 which met as a companion to the Millennium Assembly of the UN General Assembly. Participating were 1350 representatives of over 1000 NGOs from more than 100 countries. Planning is now underway for an international conference of 'civil society actors' at UN Headquarters in 2005 to develop a program on 'The Role of Civil Society in the Prevention of Armed Conflict'.[37] This plan is in response to a request from Secretary General Kofi Annan in June 2001: 'I urge NGOs with an interest in conflict prevention to organize an international conference of local, national and international NGOs on their role in conflict prevention and future interaction with the United Nations in this field'.[38] Some tend to see these more recent developments as leading towards fulfillment of proposals for a second UN General Assembly that began emerging several decades ago. More recent proposals include the International Network for a Second Assembly (1982), Childers and Urquhart's (1994) proposal for a UN Parliamentary Assembly and a proposal for an annual Forum of Civil Society.[39]

When the peace-building activities of NGOs analyzed in this volume are placed in the broader context of their roles in emerging global governance, challenging questions arise for readers attempting to understand and evaluate these activities. Seven questions follow. They are a challenge to compare the cases. Because of diversity in the kinds of NGOs involved, in the issues confronted and in the array of other actors involved, there will no doubt be different answers for a specific question when examining different cases:

1. In the light of insights offered by Reychler and Paffenholz's field guide, do NGOs involved in each of these cases seem to have been adequately prepared to perform their functions?
2. Do specific cases offer insights on how the mobilising and financing structures of NGOs have affected their performance of their specific peacebuilding activities?
3. How did decisions in IGOs affect NGO performance in specific cases?
4. Do individual cases reveal any NGO involvement in and tensions between UN organisations or other IGOs?
5. In what way has NGO involvement in specific cases affected the degree to which outcomes are more or less democratic?
6. Do any of the actors in specific cases reveal a future vision for NGO involvement in peacebuilding?

The chapters that follow will take the reader into laboratories where NGOs are facing challenging tasks as they try to develop effective roles for NGOs in peacebuilding. As you read them keep questions such as these in mind. They will offer insights on the dimensions of global governance that are emerging out of everyday experience around the world. They will challenge you to ponder which options would most adequately fulfill your vision of a peaceful world. What vision do you have of a preferred future role for NGOs in peacebuilding? What vision do you have of a preferred future for the role of NGOs in global governance?

Notes

1 Larry Minnear and Thomas G. Weiss, *Mercy Under Fire: War and the Global Humanitarian Community* (Boulder, CO: Westview, 1995), p. 157.
2 Katarina West, *Agents of Altruism: The Expansion of Humanitarian NGOs in Rwanda and Afghanistan* (Aldershot, UK: Ashgate.2001), p. 217.
3 UN Secretary General, 'Report of the UN Secretary-General on the Prevention of Armed Conflict', Recommendation 27 (New York: United Nations, 1998), p. 10.
4 Margaret E. Keck and Kathryn Sikkink, *Activists Beyond Borders: Advocacy Networks in International Politics* (Ithaca, NY: Cornell University Press, 1998), p. 39.
5 *Transnational Social Movements and Global Politics: Solidarity Beyond the States*, Jackie Smith, Charles Chatfield and Ron Pagnucco (eds) (Syracuse, NY: Syracuse University Press, 1997), p. 59.
6 Keck and Sikkink, p. 4.
7 Minnear and Weiss, pp. 141-198.
8 Minnear and Weiss, p. 141.
9 Keck and Sikkink, 1998, p. 9.
10 Kathryn Sikkink, 'Restructuring world Politics: The Limits and Asymmetries of Soft Power', in Sanjeev Khagram, James V. Riker, and Kathryn Sikkink (eds), *Restructuring World Politics: Transnational Social Movements, Networks and Norms* (Minneapolis, MN: University of Minnesota Press, 2002), p. 316.
11 Chadwick F. Alger, 'Evolving roles of NGOs in member state decision-making in the UN System', *Journal of Human Rights* Vol.2 (2003), pp. 407-424; Chadwick F. Alger, 'Strengthening Relations Between NGOs and the UN System: Toward a Research Agenda', *Global Society* 13 (1999): 393-409; Chadwick F. Alger, 'Transnational Social Movements, World Politics and Global Governance', in Jackie Smith (et. al.), pp. 260-275; West, *Agents of Altruism: The Expansion of Humanitarian NGOs in Rwanda and Afghanistan*; *Peacebuilding: A Field Guide*, Luc Reychler and Thania Paffenholz (eds) (Boulder, CO: Lynne Rienner, 2001).
12 Alger, pp. 261-263.
13 John D. McCarthy, 'The Globalization of Social Movement Theory', in Jackie Smith (et. al.), pp. 249-254.
14 Alger, pp. 266-268.
15 Ibid., pp. 411-414.
16 Ibid., pp. 264-265.
17 Clark, pp. 17-18.
18 Alger, pp. 414-416.

19 Andrew E. Rice and Cyril Ritchie, 'Relationship Between International Non-Governmental Organizations and the United Nations: A Research and Policy Paper', *Transnational Associations*, 47/5 (1995), pp. 256-257.

20 UN Non-Governmental Liaison Service, *Go-Between* (NGLS) (bi-monthly) (Geneva and New York, 1995), p. 5.

21 World Trade Organization, 'Relations with NGOs' (Geneva: WTO, 1998).

22 UN Non-Governmental Liaison Service, p. 7.

23 West, pp. 13-18.

24 Ibid., p. 17.

25 Ibid., p. 14.

26 Ibid., p. 17.

27 Reychler and Paffenholz, *Peacebuilding: A Field Guide*.

28 Hugo Slim, 'Dealing with Moral Dilemmas', in Luc Reychler and Thania Paffenholz (eds), *Peacebuilding: A Field Guide* (Boulder, CO: Lynne Rienner, 2001), p. 498.

29 John Paul Lederach, "From War to Peace." *MCS Conciliation Quarterly*, (Winter 1991), Vol.10, no.1. pp.12-15.

30 Karl Slaikeu, *When Push Comes to Shove: A Practical Guide to Mediating Disputes* (San Francisco, CA: Jossey-Bass, 1996).

31 Hugo Slim, p. 503.

32 West, p. 217.

33 Ibid., p. 213.

34 Ibid., p. 218.

35 David Rieff, *A Bed for the Night: Humanitarianism in Crisis* (New York: Simon and Schuster, 2002), p. 334.

36 Rieff, p. 335.

37 European Platform for Conflict Prevention and Transformation, 'The Global Partnership for the Prevention of Armed conflict: The Story So Far', *Conflict Prevention Newsletter*, 6/3 (2003): 13-28.

38 UN Secretary General, 'Report of the UN Secretary-General on the Prevention of Armed Conflict'.

39 Erskine Childers and Brian Urquhart, *Renewing the United Nations System* (Uppsala, Sweden: Dag Hammarskjold Foundation, 1994); Commission on Global Governance, *Our Global Neighborhood* (New York: Oxford University Press, 1995).

Chapter 2

The Dilemmas of Subcontracting
the Liberal Peace

Oliver P. Richmond

The essays in this volume provide a detailed analysis of the contributions, constraints and opportunities available for NGOs in peacebuilding. In this chapter, I will examine the tensions in construction of the 'liberal peace' in the specific context of the sort of grassroots peacebuilding undertaken by NGOs, necessitating their cooperation with local populations, officials, and institutions, as well as with intergovernmental organizations (IGOs), regional organisations, international financial institutions, major agencies and donors. This conditional relationship, inherent in the subcontracting of duties, rights, responsibilities as well as advocacy, has not yet been fully explored. The essays that follow this chapter outline the tensions inherent in these developments from a variety of empirical and theoretical perspectives, and as such, speak for themselves.

NGOs have become essential in building stable communities and effective institutions, especially in the past 15 years where it has become very apparent that there is space for such actors in peacebuilding, but also that they are actually vital to the project entailed in the construction of the liberal peace. Of course, many NGOs end up feeling their involvement in peacekeeping and peacebuilding is not sufficiently meaningful or effective, while some governments dislike the increasing pressure to make more room for civil society through NGO participation in peace deliberations, monitoring and services. Though hardly a panacea, NGOs have made an enormous difference to complex peace processes through both their independent interventions at the grass roots level, and via their cooperation with, or attempts to modify, state and multilateral interventions at the socio-political and developmental levels. Decisive judgment on NGO success or failure in these roles depends on where one stands and upon the timeframe envisaged (which is all too often limited by donor cycles and political interests, despite the often apparent need for generational change rather than merely short term projects).

In a previous study by the same editors,[1] it was concluded that for the most part analyses of NGOs roles, potentials, and problems, accept that the democratisation of intervention in conflict zones brought about by the development of the role of NGOs in conjunction with more traditional and local actors is generally positive. Despite this, there is concern about the many technical, normative, and political difficulties that have arisen as their role has expanded, either because NGOs themselves have sought more responsibility and more space in which to operate or because they have been delegated tasks by IGOs, states, and other organisations. These contradictions clearly need further investigation, as many of the essays in this volume illustrate. NGOs have a vital role in supporting societies emerging from conflicts. Assessments of best practices and lessons learned about the vast growth of NGO activity, both acting independently and in partnership with the UN, is needed. In particular, research is needed on the comparative advantages of utilising UN-NGO partnerships in postconflict situations. Analysis of ways to improve these approaches needs to evaluate how to improve both the political will and level of resources applied to these tasks. Since NGO efforts need to be owned by local civil societies to be effective, more study of how to empower local NGOs (which normally depend on external resources in most cases) needs to be undertaken.

NGOs and the Liberal Peace

NGOs and the networks that they tend to form are perceived as key providers of the resources necessary to institutionalise human security (HS) in conflict zones by liberal states and actors. They have inherited the role of building a 'civil peace' as a key component of the liberal peace, along with the parallel construction of the 'constitutional' peace (through democratisation) and the institutional peace (associated with the UN system), which are also components of the liberal peace.[2] This is an important stage in the institution-building process. Effectively, NGOs are crucial in building the institutions of the 'liberal peace' from the bottom-up,[3] including free market economies and development strategies, social reform, political democratisation, to human rights and humanitarian assistance. They are part of a 'peacebuilding consensus'[4] including donors, major states, IGOs, ROs, and IFIs, in which there is a broad concurrence on the liberal peace, though there may be disagreement on how this can be achieved in a technical sense. This essentially reflects what has been called the 'Wilsonian Triad', meaning peace, democracy and free markets.[5] This consensus effectively indicates that NGOs have become part of the external governance of post-conflict zones. The construction of the liberal peace now focuses on peace-as-governance, and NGOs are vital actors in this project within the broader context of the globalisation of the norms of the liberal peace, and of global civil society.

    In the context of a growing acceptance of the transnational nature of contemporary international relations, of globalisation and of grass roots contributions via a global civil society, a debate emerged in the early 1990s indicating that NGOs have a particular capacity to aid in peacemaking and peacebuilding, directly or through their humanitarian roles. The argument suggested that NGOs had very specific qualities and capacities that no other actor possessed and also that they were less oriented by self-interest. Since then there has been an intellectual backlash against some of the more idealistic assertions associated with NGOs, ever-increasing use in the field. However, globalisation, global civil society, human security, humanitarianism, and the nature, capacity and functions of NGOs are all contested concepts. This contestation mainly occurs between pragmatists in realist-positivist mode, who argue in a somewhat contradictory vein that NGOs have a role in state-rebuilding as long as they are monitored and controlled by intergovernmental institutions, and those who argue that a global civil society has now transcended state control and represent a cosmopolitan desire for human security. In the former view, NGOs are seen as inadequate compared to the assistance and direction of states in the context of the construction of the liberal peace. In the latter, NGOs are so essential that they may actually take complete responsibility for tasks associated with constructing a liberal peace in a conflict or crisis zone. In the post-September 11 world, some states have reasserted their sovereign prerogatives relating to basic strategic security, but since the Asian Tsunami of December 2004, an embryonic return to human security thinking appears to be emerging.

Non-state actors and NGOs have, of course, been instrumental in broadening our understanding of peace and security and their existence is also indicative of the liberal peace project. In 1914, there were 1083 non-governmental organisations (NGOs) and no firm conception of universal human rights affirmed by the international community, such that it was. Now the estimated number of NGOs stands at between 37,000 and 50,000.[6] Though contested, there are now firm conceptions of human rights as well as emerging humanitarian norms, and a discourse of human security, which provides a basis for non-state actor intervention. Many NGOs were formed in the 1990s as a response to the broad requirements of this synthesis of peacebuilding, humanitarianism, human rights monitoring and advocacy. Most NGOs operate on specific issues or bridge several aspects of these areas and contribute to, the construction and facilitation of global governance and globalisation in transnational networks to advocate liberal reform.[7] This assertion is, of course, rather problematic given the fact that all of these concepts are contested and there is little agreement in the relevant literatures even on the nature of NGOs.

Their antecedents began to emerge in the Nineteenth century in association with the creation of the International Committee of the Red Cross (ICRC), the ending of the slave trade, voting rights for women, international law and disarmament discourses, and many other activities organised by non-state actors aimed political, social, and economic reform. This formed an important strand of the evolving debate on the nature of peace and how it could be achieved in the context of the civil peace. Such actors soon began to proliferate: the International Rescue Committee (IRC) began its life rescuing Jews from Europe during WWII, and was later to be involved with retrieving Hungarian refugees after the failure of the 1956 rebellion and Cuban refugees after Fidel Castro came to power in Cuba in 1959.[8] Other such organisations followed, including the Catholic Relief Service, World Vision, and the Oxford Committee for Famine Relief (OXFAM). NGOs played an important role in highlighting the need for human rights to be included in the UN Charter at San Francisco in 1945, and have consistently worked to develop the UN Human Rights System. NGOs provided useful input into the drafting of the Universal Declaration of Human Rights. They have also been key actors in the creation of different UN treaties and conventions spanning issues from the elimination of discrimination against women (1979) to the rights of children (1989).

They have played important roles in many other human rights related UN working groups, as well in the creation of the position of the UN High Commission for Human Rights. In the UN system their roles have fallen into three main guises: setting standards, monitoring, and implementation.[9] NGOs have also been able to introduce human rights mechanisms into other international organisations such as the World Bank and its Inspection Panel, which was introduced in 1993 to examine the impact of the organisation's policies on human rights. International NGOs have been important in bringing to light abuses by states and advocating change in their practices, and local NGOs are often crucial in re-establishing human rights in conflict and crisis zones as 'norm entrepreneurs' in which NGOs are instrumental in bringing about the social, political and economic changes necessary to enhance peacebuilding.[10] This has raised the question of whether NGOs operate on a 'rights' or a 'needs' basis[11] distinguishing between victim and aggressor or simply providing assistance where it is required regardless of this distinction. Despite the controversy over this question, the role of NGOs has continually strengthened since the first Gulf War when UN Security Council resolution 688 of 5th April 1991 allowed NGO intervention to take precedence over state sovereignty (in this case, of Iraq) to deal with human rights issues, among others.

These developments, and their associated questions make it important to ask how the liberal peace is imagined and created in contemporary policy and academic approaches to the ending of conflict from the perspective of non-state actors and civil society. What is their role in constructing peace from inside the conflict environment, through what is often referred to as a bottom-up peacebuilding process? Such processes are often in close association with donor states, international organisations like the UN, agencies like UNDP or UNHCR, or the World Bank. The World Bank, the Asian Development Bank, and the World Trade Organisation, among many others, encourages relationships with civil society.[12] What are the implications for the nature of the civil peace that non-state actors attempt to construct from the group upwards? The discourses and practices associated with such human security oriented approaches involve both a normative commitment to a *just* and a *sustainable* settlement to conflict, the reframing of security debates, and the involvement of external non-state actors with access to conflict zones, or indigenous non-state actors. This is connected with the role and status that civil society now has in constructing the liberal peace. Non-state actors, agencies, and civil society focused intervention, are very important in the wider legitimisation of the liberal peace through the constitution of the civil peace, and also by contributing to the construction of a constitutional peace in a broader institutional context. At the same time, states and international institutions and organisations are provided with legitimate access to the norms, regimes, and institutions of civil society non-state actors and the human security discourses they deploy. Partly because of this the liberal peace has become an end that appears to legitimate the means used, giving rise to some significant contradictions in contemporary non-state practices designed to construct a liberal peace from below. Such processes can be directly linked to the civil society discourse of peace, of course, but they also contribute to the constitutional and institutional discourses of peace in that their role is conditional upon their contribution to democratisation, to free market reform, to legal reforms, and to the anchoring of the new liberal peace within an international institutional context of global governance. This conditionality also suggests a link with the victor's peace, historically also an aspect of the liberal peace, in that dominant actors (states and their associated agencies or institutions) in the state system define the agendas of bottom-up peacebuilding approaches inherent in the liberal peace. In terms of bottom-up peacebuilding different actors contribute to the liberal peace model by installing forms of peace-as-governance associated with the regulation, control, and protection of individuals and civil society.

The question of intervention on the part of non-state actors, and whether or not they intervene on a rights or needs basis, is important to identify the type of peace they construct. The fact that they bypass state sovereignty reinforces a civil notion of peace. The fact that they do this in an intimate conditional relationship with sponsors and recipients indicates that they are involved in a broader programme of social, political, economic, humanitarian, and developmental engineering. This indicates that the civil peace is contested to a large degree by state actors and organisations that gain access to civil society through NGOs, who aid in the normalisation of civil societies which have deviated from the expected norm. The debate over whether they intervene on a rights basis revolves around a set of norms and rights from within the liberal peace. In this sense, the question over intervention on a needs basis would see victims and aggressors being equally weighted, rather than evaluated according to their respective positions relative to the installation of the liberal peace. This represents the differing positions taken by humanitarian pragmatists and humanitarian idealists in which regulation of such activity to preserve an overarching normative framework is contrasted with the liberalisation of NGOs to provide assistance to those that need it regardless of their position as victim of aggressor, or their location within the overall normative framework of the international system. Furthermore, what is often overlooked in both views is that making a decision on the basis of pragmatic or idealistic humanitarian is itself a hegemonic act made by third parties about 'others'. This opposition can be observed in the position of the ICRC and *Médecins sans Frontièrs* (MSF).[13] Such actors are far from non-political actors (or even apolitical actors). They have increasingly adopted a liberal discourse of peace in order to justify the strategic choices they make in the field as to which actors they work with and for. The debate on needs-based involvement versus rights-based intervention means is that these actors have to make strategic choices in two directions: as to who they help and why; and whether, in order to court favour and amass resources, they accept the dominant, and perhaps even hegemonic liberal peace discourse engendered in the peacebuilding consensus and in their role as part of a governance framework intended to institutionalise a sustainable liberal peace from the outside.

Humanitarian NGOs are themselves divided about their role, its limits, and whether they should accept constraints, and in particular, those associated with more traditional forms of sovereignty. MSF defies many of these restrictions, and focuses upon the need to assist against human rights violations, respecting neither sovereignty nor political neutrality. The ICRC opposed this in the context of the

Biafran crisis, which effectively spurred the creation of MSF and these principles in 1971. The differentiation between rights and needs-based humanitarian assistance has become a key issue dividing NGOs in the field: MSF works on the basis that all victims have a *right* to humanitarian assistance. Of course, this still requires the identification of victims. For example during the Rwandan genocide the blurring of victim and aggressor did not solely depend upon identifying Hutu and Tutsi in the refugee camps, but also understanding the politics behind the Hutu power exploitation of Hutus fleeing from the Rwandan Patriotic Front and their exploitation of these camps for their own political purpose. Thus, the differentiation between the political and the humanitarian is not always easy. Similarly, for those that argue that peace lies in the exhaustion the means of war NGOs may provide resources which delays that exhaustion.[14]

Yet, NGOs have become important in the canon of the liberal peace, and owing to their unique access, legitimacy, and flexibility, have become a vital tool for states and international organisations and institutions in the construction of that peace. They can respond quickly, are not bureaucratically crippled, cannot coerce and therefore are widely respected. Most importantly, the combination of these assets means that they can fulfil roles and tasks which states and their liberal organisations simply cannot achieve. However, they also have certain limits that are only now beginning to be identified and reflected upon. They also require security. They cannot control what happens to the resources they bring into the conflict zone, and they may confer a level of legitimacy on to actors who are not adverse to the use of violence. There is a level of conditionality that is also introduced into the relationship between NGOs and their benefactors, especially when it comes to the economic, social, and political dimensions of the peace that they are helping construct in conflict zones. Obviously there is a significant tension between attempts to introduce conditionality into relationships between internationals, agencies, or NGOs and disputants, especially as this may undermine or impede attempts to act in a humanitarian manner.[15] Furthermore, there is also a problem with the sheer numbers of NGOs operating in conflict zones in terms of the division of labour and overlap of roles and responsibilities. Perhaps most controversially there is the issue of accountability: should NGOs be held accountable and what kind of frameworks can be constructed to ensure this? Would this undermine their independence and flexibility in identifying problems and responding to them? For this later problem there have been initiatives (such as SPHERE) that are intended to improve their effectiveness and accountability.[16] Despite such problems, it is important to recognise that NGOs are now a recognised part of the UN system and hold consultative status within ECOSOC, and therefore the peacebuilding consensus and contribution to the liberal peace that they represent are an integral part of the humanitarian discourse. NGOs have gained enormous influence on UN Charter-based, human rights institutions on issues relating to refugees, the environment, and development,[17] but also in the six treaty-based, expert human rights committees.[18] This is particularly important in the context of debates about human security and the emergence of a contested 'global civil society'.[19]

Normative Issues

Advocacy movements, epistemic communities, non-states actors, NGOs, and agencies are what Wallace and Josselin have described as 'norm entrepreneurs' which privilege democracy, human rights, and forms of development in their micro level interventions as well as in their discourse in the realm of international relations.[20] Disillusionment with the role of states in constructing peace in conflict zones has led to an increased role for non-state actors, organisations, and agencies. This evolution has been based upon the need for expertise in the field working on the different aspects of human oriented security, enabled by the development of transnationalism and the recognition of non-state actors as key agents in this area. Gradually, they have become important not just in providing technological expertise, but also in a normative sense, in fulfilling a role in the construction of the liberal peace. The relationship between positive and negative aspects of such forms of intervention is intricate: not producing harm through humanitarian assistance might mean not providing assistance where it may impinge upon human rights or create further incentives for conflict.[21] Despite such troubling choices to be made on the part of those intervening in the name of humanitarianism (and there are many who fervently oppose such decisions),[22] understanding the role of NGOs opens up the possibility of a private, civil society account of peacebuilding, and of its fraught relationship with agencies, international organisations, institutions and state-backed work. Such an understanding also sheds light upon what disputants and societies in conflict want from both their wars, and the coming peace they are assumed to be committed to.

In view of this it is important to examine how NGOs can operate to transport and emphasise norms of human security in failing regions and locales, or in areas where violence has already flared. It is possible to see a pattern of some similarities between global and civil norms, or between the universal and the local, reflected in the construction of institutions on the ground along the lines of those which exist already in stable democratic states. Effectively NGOs are in a position to carry out this process, but also to negotiate with local actors about how these institutions and norms should reflect both international norms and conditionality and the local situation. In support of this argument, both cosmopolitan and communitarian approaches to International Relations agree that a single framework of legitimate politics can emerge; contention lies in whether this will be a single world community or an association of communities.[23] This means that the sequence of kin, tribe, city, state, does not have to be extended to 'globe' and produce a universal normative structure; this structure can be produced through a 'practical association' between political communities.[24] This association is based on a dialogue about common social justice, and to relieve suffering. As Brown has pointed out, community therefore makes sense locally (at the level at which many NGOs operate, in particular) rather than globally.[25] Brown argues that '[t]he goal would be an association of socially just communities which was, itself, constructed on socially just lines'.[26] Thus a '... plurality of morally autonomous, just communities relating to each other in a framework of peace and law ...'[27] provides an important perspective of the construction of the liberal peace. NGOs have, both through their access to international networks, and capacity for relatively intimate local access, the capacity to build institutions that reflect both. As agents of change, they have an acute awareness of, legitimacy in, and access to local conflict environments; however, care must be taken that this is not seen as a mandate to impose outside norms and conditions that may only exacerbate conflict.

This, of course, raises the issue of intervention on the basis of universal norms. NGOs may help bypass this problem because of their unofficial nature, which is not necessarily beholden to sovereignty, and the linkage they provide between the local and the global. This means that NGOs are actually extremely useful in the overall project of constructing the liberal peace, because in their relationship with states and sponsors, NGOs and the networks they create have far greater access than international organisations or institutions alone specifically into civil societies in conflict zones. This begs the question of NGO agency in the face of what could be interpreted as state control (albeit indirect and through funding practices). How far are NGOs agents of emancipation against domestic, transnational, and international hegemonies, be they liberal or authoritarian, nationalist, or militaristic?

One possible avenue of investigation lies in the linkages NGOs provide as mediators between particularistic norms and global governance/globalisation. This linkage seems to imply that their intervention can occur in the context of local normative and cultural frameworks, derived from local and global notions of human security. It is here that the contribution of NGOs is potentially crucial as they fit themselves in between each level of analysis in the sequence of kin, city, state, regional organisation and international organisation, facilitating and monitoring activities all these levels of analysis. This is crucial to peacebuilding as NGOs have the ability to operate in this manner in these positions providing access, and independent monitoring and facilitation. In this way they mediate between the different levels of international society regardless of the issue area in which they operate; they promote a practical and normative exchange between them.

Non-state actors are conceptualised as contributing to peace in different ways. They are generally seen to be contributing to an inside, grass roots peace, based upon local community consent and legitimacy in the context of a global civil society. This conceptulisation lies at the more idealist and utopian end of the peace spectrum and is reflected in the work of OXFAM, Amnesty International, Greenpeace, and other groups concerned with issues like development and human rights, through which NGOs enable the diffusion of ethical norms associated with the liberal peace. At the other end of this spectrum, non-state actors are seen as thinly veiled fronts for powerful state interest in that they act as front for the insertion of realist state interests in a disguised form.[28] This is particularly so where they have very close relationships with donor states, agencies and IFIs, who generally subcontract work to NGOs precisely because of their access and legitimacy in civil society, and also because humanitarian, social, educational, conflict resolution, and developmental tasks play a significant role on the reconstruction of the state. What both approaches agree upon is that such actors provide a way of bypassing sovereignty and gaining internal access into societies, economies, and polities, with a high degree of legitimacy and flexibility. Both approaches also agree that this occurs in the context of the proselytisation of the liberal peace. Where they disagree is whether this peace is universal and this can be legitimately installed thought this process in the local environment, or whether local particularism needs to be built into any peace process. Furthermore, it is also possible that non-state actors might merely replicate the insensitivities of the actors who fund or run them.

Despite such difficulties, various key donors have moved to institutionalise the dominant NGO discourse about peace through the concept of human security.[29] This has been notable mainly because of its acceptance in key policy circles (such as within the UN organisation, and by donor states such as Japan or Canada), and in what has been identified as 'global civil society' – that interconnected space which links civil society, NGOs, international agencies and international organisations, donors, and international financial institutions.[30] This debate calls for the subjects of security to be redefined from the 'state' to the 'individual' – in other words from managing inter-state relations to building peace by introducing social, political and economic reforms. 'Freedom from want, freedom from fear' is its most common expression in policy circles mainly related to the UN, agencies and NGOs. These developments can be observed in the context of UN Agenda's for the reform of international approaches to peace published throughout the 1990s (including the Agendas for Peace, Democratisation and Development) and beyond, in which it is clear that the notion of peace envisaged depends to a large part of non-governmental actors because they tend to have unparalleled access to conflict zones, far beyond those actors which form part of the official political, economic and developmental discourse.[31] Yet, the concept of human security broadens the agents and structures identified as being causes of insecurity and responsible for its eradication so far that it becomes very difficult to prioritise crucial areas that may be most effective in ameliorating insecurity. Yet, at the same time HS recognises the complexity of security issues, and the breadth of issues and actors who are affected by them. Since their emergence HS oriented approaches and actors offer a vision of the liberal peace in which social welfare and justice can be incorporated into parallel constitutional and institutional projects for peace.

While it is likely that actors and strategies at this level effectively replicate state practice, this criticism also tends to overlook the agency of such actors that has also emerged at this level that enables them to act relatively independently in some instances of institutional and state control. Yet, there is also a broad concurrence between human security-oriented agents and their actions, and that of states and their organisations within the liberal peace context. While this concept and these types of actors seem to provide a challenge to the traditional conceptions of the international system, most humanitarian actors, NGOs and associated non-state actors, must, for their very existence, work within the confines of the dominant institutions and regimes of the states-system. This tempers the challenge that they create somewhat and reduces their role in the negotiation and re-negotiation of the peacebuilding consensus as subservient to that of states. However, most commentators agree that non-state actors and agencies are a vital and key part of peacebuilding, and indeed that global governance is not possible without their cooperation.[32] They have become integral to the overall project of the liberal peace because the many different actors involved in, and many approaches to, peacebuilding have been used to provide avenues of legitimate intervention for the broader state-led liberal peace project. These ever-deeper forms of intervention involve structural intervention whereby social, political, economic, and cultural, frameworks are altered or introduced to contribute to the creation of the liberal peace. From these strands have developed a powerful body of non-state actors, and a development of a language of rights and norms that has undermined the absolutism of Westphalian sovereignty and reinforced the agency of the individual. This has been an extremely important addition to the peacebuilding consensus, and so to the liberal peace project.

Key Issues for the Subcontraction of the Liberal Peace

One of the side effects of the deployment of this concept in practical terms, particularly in the context of UN organs and the humanitarian community has been that the provision of basic needs of populations in conflict zones has been privatised – to a degree. By the end of the 1990s most countries dispersed 25 per cent of their overseas aid through NGOs: the EU Commission Humanitarian Aid Office was using NGOs to disperse at least 60 per cent of its budget.[33] This dispersal has effectively created a market situation where NGOs have to compete for funds, and therefore must respect the conditionalities imposed upon them by donors intent on constructing the liberal peace. These processes have been characterised by their complex and multi-level, multidimensional nature, and represent a securitisation of development, economy, human rights, as well as politics.[34] This development, guided by the human security framework, has had a major impact on the practice and efficacy of intervention. In this, the UN and its relationship with NGOs has become crucial, because of its recognition of the multiple political, social, economic and humanitarian dynamics of 'peace' via the concept of human security. *Agenda for Peace* enabled the UN to become engaged in social justice and political issues, which was as close as this documentation came to a broad conceptualisation of peace. The *Agendas* for 'Democratisation' and for 'Development' moved the debate further into the terrain of the liberal peace.[35]

Various other documentation also support this hypothesis, including Oxfam's *Poverty Report* and the Report of the International Commission on Intervention and State Sovereignty on *The Responsibility to Protect*, which projected a similar concern with broad security issues and with the development of methods to address the broader roots of conflict through multiple forms of intervention.[36] The former grappled with the inverse relationship between peace and poverty while the latter examined the responsibility that the 'international community' has to intervene in conflicts and crises regardless of the norms of sovereignty. Both documents see international intervention in civil society as a vital response to human security problems, in coordination with international institutions and organisations. Such documentation also indicates a tension in the humanitarian discourse in which two opposing arguments are made as if they were unproblematic: firstly that outsiders should and can do more to intervene in conflict, development, and human rights problems within civil society; but secondly that recipients should do more to help themselves.[37] The implication of this is that both interveners and insiders effectively need to agree on what constitutes the peace to be installed, and how this is to be carried out. Human security effectively provides a response to these questions: the peace to be created protects the individual, and a mixture of international, local, official and unofficial actors can take part in its provision.[38]

Another characteristic of these developments was the emergence of democratisation as a key objective through which civil society could be stabilized, and human security could be guaranteed.[39] Kofi Annan saw this as an attempt to construct democratic governance at the local level, particularly in conflict zones, and to '... explore democratic principles at the global level'.[40] What this indicated was that any form of intervention in a conflict, whether state, IO, agency or NGO, has become implicitly contingent upon their contribution to democratisation processes. Similarly, this is also associated with arguments about the need for development, which is itself linked to the entry of the conflict zone into the globalised international economy. As can be seen from El Salvador to Angola, Mozambique and Cambodia, democratisation provides an umbrella for liberal constructions that are seen as integral to the creation of long term sustainable conditions of peace. From Bosnia, to Kosovo and East Timor, transitional administrations have taken a firm grip of this democratisation and neo-liberal development process,[41] and aid and its provision, normally through NGOs and agencies has now become linked to governance.[42] Non-state actors have become intricately entwined with official actors and transitional administrations through conditionalities relating to the construction of the liberal peace by donors vis-à-vis NGOs and their target populations. Indeed, Duffield argues (in the context of the Dinka in the transition zone in Sudan) that this relationship has acted as a form of cultural suppression, as it has attempted to reorder the communities into western socio-economic groups.[43]

The role of non-state actors in a human security framework is susceptible to this accusation.[44] Human security as a concept works as a form of 'biopower', which domesticates and normalises mainly non-western societies and communities caught up in humanitarian crises, bringing their political structures and socio-economic interactions into a liberal peace and governance framework. It is in this bottom-up guise that peace may become a form of biopower, which involves interveners in conflict taking on the role of 'administering life'. This requires the importation of expert knowledge into conflict zones, both for the many tasks associated with humanitarianism and security, and to establish 'governmentality' in which control is taken over most political, social, economic, and identity functions of groups involved in conflict and in the construction of peace at the level of civil society. This governmentality actually depends upon the maintenance of a space between the local and the state/international, in order to maintain its authority, even though this may undermine local consent. Both the community and the self are governed in a manner in which external actors expect will create peace.[45] These practices and discourses have rapidly become a normalised part of our understanding of the liberal peace.[46] Essentially, from this bottom-up level of analysis, the liberal peace can be said to be a hegemonic peace, broadly consensual from the perspective of the coalition of external actors involved in it. But, its consensuality also depends on the incentivisation of, or conditionality of, such forms of intervention.

What this indicates is that the privatisation of peace and the increasing subcontracting of peace activities to private actors also masks a tendency for bottom-up peacebuilding to represent international rather than local consensus, and to swamp the voices of local actors involved in such civil society strands of the construction of the liberal peace. In its defence, it must be said that the version of the liberal peace propagated at this level is more concerned with social welfare and justice than the more conservative version propagated directly by states. Non-state actors and agencies working effectively serve as a filter for the liberal peace, renegotiating its priorities, between its propagators and its recipients.

The expectation has been that where IOs, IFIs, ROs, agencies and NGOs have cooperated for humanitarian reasons, human security concerns have tended to transcend the interests of actors engaged in the conflict, making the creation of the liberal peace more plausible at the civil level. Such a coalition of actors would therefore be able to engage in the construction of a liberal, multidimensional, and multi-level peace, spanning the civil to constitutional, to institutional levels. Yet it may also be the case that the ideology of human security, and the relationship of dependency between disputants and interveners in constructing the liberal peace mean that these are also part of the relationship of dependency being formed around humanitarianism and the peacebuilding consensus. The question is whether they are dependent upon the liberal states and their institutions in creating this conditional relationship vis-à-vis disputants and the liberal peace, or whether they are agents themselves in this relationship? Given the nature of the conditionality surrounding the construction of the liberal peace, and non-state actor dependency upon donors, this is far from clear. What is very clear however, is that non-state actor legitimacy vis-à-vis their access within civil societies is very useful in the construction of the liberal peace, which depends on social engineering, as much as international stability or state institutions. It might be argued that the civil peace strand of the liberal peace conceptualisation both legitimises deep intervention at the civil level, and requires interventionary practices in order to expand the liberal peace. Non-state actors, NGOs, and international agencies and institutions have played an important role in this evolution. For example, human security motivated approaches to peacebuilding have become embedded into a governance approach to ending conflict in Kosovo since 1999, through the UN Interim Administration (UNMIK) and its four pillars, the presence of UNDP and NGOs. These actors cooperated over the establishment of the necessary liberal institutions of a democratic state, involving broad institution building to reconstruct the political, social, and economic infrastructure of the state. This is succinctly stated in the mandate and role of UNMIK.[47]

There is a contradiction between the discourse and practices of human security in such a governance context. Humanitarian assistance is not apolitical of course, but it provides states with a tool with which to become deeply engaged in conflicts, and also to avoid foreign policy engagement[48] through the work of the many agencies and NGOs involved in conflict zones. In this sense the main agents of the liberal peace have both options open to them, and therefore can use more traditional interest-based criteria to evaluate why they may want to become more directly involved. This is perhaps why it is more accurate to argue that the work of these actors has become part of foreign policy in the general sense of constructing a liberal peace. Despite the fact that the civil peace and the relevant actors' roles therein are often represented as a highly legitimate aim for the humanitarian community, this is also heavily contested. The liberal order is understood to be peaceful internally and progressive in its external impact on other states, as well as characterised by democracy, free trade, and human rights, and public consent for human security activity by NGOs, agencies, states and IFIs, and IOs is broadly present in most states. This differentiates the peacebuilding consensus from past imperial orders,[49] but even at the level of civil society, the liberal peace often rests on coercion and conditionality in order to install liberal norms and regimes in regions where they are being resisted.[50] Implicit in this understanding of the liberal peace, as Laffey illustrates, is the return of the 'language of empire' divided between accounts of US imperialism and accounts of a more general liberal empire.[51] This has important implications both in terms of the universalism that is often claimed for humanitarianism and the many agents of human security, and for the role of the many non-state actors that claim legitimacy for their interventions on this basis.

These developments have highlighted a tension between transnationalism and inter-governmentalism. The UN system has been forced to assign more of the increasingly complex duties associated with constructing the liberal peace to outside and non-state actors, because it and its member states cannot fulfil such duties alone. This contracting out of such services to NGOs and specialised agencies means that transnational agendas are replacing intergovernmental agendas.[52] In other words, the civil peace is gradually being reconstructed and is shifting away from an emphasis on the security of the state as an umbrella for that of the person, to an independent discourse of security for the person in which specific states acting as donors within the liberal transnational framework are influential. But this discourse is based upon an agreement on how such security can be provided in a manner that legitimates and empowers liberal states and their organisations to intervene under what they claim to be a peacebuilding consensus to construct the liberal peace in conflict zones. Given that the liberal peace encompasses a civil peace, non-state actors are vital to this process given the access and legitimacy they have in conflict zones as agents of humanitarian goods. They are effectively the only actors in a good position to negotiate the importation of new norms and institutions in conflict zones with civil societies, whilst also remaining loyal to the conditionality of the liberal peace in both its regulative and restrictive forms.

Conclusion

Clearly, the discourse of humanitarianism and human security has become an important indicator of the agency of international organisation, agencies, and non-state actors in their contribution to the civil peace. This contribution also is very important with regard to the development of the constitutional and institutional aspects of the liberal peace project. Furthermore, such actors, with access, reach, and legitimacy, are crucial in the evolving peacebuilding consensus. This has allowed intervention upon a humanitarian basis to claim its own legitimacy, regardless of the norm of non-intervention, and furthermore has created an apparent normative requirement for such action in the event of conflicts and crisis on the part of the international community, as part of its commitment to the liberal peace. NGOs and other non-state actors, as well as international agencies, often go so far as to call for the use of force to clear the way, or provide security, for their own actions and interventions in conflict zones. In their conditional relationship with recipients, donors, international organisations and international financial institutions, non-state actors have developed the capacity for the most intimate forms of intervention in civil society in order to develop a civil peace and contribute the broader liberal peace project through the institutionalisation of bottom-up forms of governance, engendered in the liberal peace project. Indeed, it is through this conditionality that dominant actors of the international system pass on the norms and regimes associated with the liberal peace, and through which they receive any feedback at all from recipients and local actors. This process also has the inadvertent advantage of allowing states access to civil society, and providing non-state actors with the capacity to survive and become influential at the civil and global levels. The version of the liberal peace that emerges through this non-state actor level of the peacebuilding consensus tends to be more concerned with aspects of social justice, development, and identity, but also facilitates and legitimates intervention at this level through non-state actors which are influenced by their relationship with donors. Many such actors retain their agency by negotiating continuously with donors but even so the liberal peace regulates their behaviour.

This leads to one irreconcilable conclusion. The liberal peace has given rise to a situation where non-state actors may concur with its crusading aspect, perhaps even legitimating the use of force for the end of reproducing the liberal order. This crusading aspect can be legitimised by the establishment of a civil society, and a stable system of governance.[53] If the state cannot secure these aspects of the liberal peace, outside actors effectively take over.[54] Often human right violations or a lack of human security provides the basis for both state and non-state forms of intervention, whereby the governance of the state and existence of civil society comes to depend upon outside actors.[55] This provides external actors with both an ethical *obligation* to intervene far beyond the state and into civil society, if they are to live up human rights and humanitarian rhetoric, and also an *opportunity* to intervene at the level of both state and civil society. Clearly, the ideology of human security and the nature of the role of non-state actors in conflict zones in reproducing these types of dependencies mean that they are complicit in the reproduction of the liberal peace as the dominant form of conflict settlement. Because of this relationship of conditionality, this means that the civil peace general reflects the dominant concerns of states and donors (governance, capacity building, and ownership, are often mentioned in this context) and therefore is actually very close to the constitutional and institutional discourses of peace. Some actors happily accept this concurrence as inevitable in the context of the peacebuilding consensus, while others, perhaps more focused on issues of social justice, may resist it. In the context of capacity building via the peacebuilding consensus, the problem may well be that only a limited capacity is being built, but also that institutional and local capacity is being destroyed in target conflict environments.[56] These, and other issues, are the focus of the following chapters in this volume.

Notes

1 Henry F. Carey and Oliver P. Richmond, *Mitigating Conflict: The Role of NGOs*, Special Issue of *International Peacekeeping*, co-edited (London: Frank Cass, 2003).

2 A fourth component is the victor's peace, providing the liberal peace with a hegemonic character. For an elaboration of these different strands of the liberal peace see Oliver P. Richmond, *The Transformation of Peace* (London: Palgrave, 2005), forthcoming.

3 For more on this concept, see Mark Duffield, *Global Governance and the New Wars* (London: Zed Books, 2001), p. 11.

4 Oliver P. Richmond, 'The Globalisation of Approaches to Conflict', *Cooperation and Conflict*, 39/2 (2004).

5 Michael Mandelbaum, *The Ideas that Conquered the World* (New York: Public Affairs, 2002), p. 6.

6 United Nations Development Programme, *Human Development Report 2002* (Oxford University Press, 2003), p. 5.

7 Margaret E. Keck and Kathryn Sikkink, *Activists Beyond Borders: Advocacy Networks in Inernational Politics* (Cornell University Press, 1998), p. 11.

8 David Rieff, *A Bed for the Night* (London: Vintage, 2002), p. 79.

9 Peter van Tuijl, 'NGOs and Human Rights: Sources of Justice and Democracy', *Journal of International Affairs*, 52/2 (1999): 495.

10 Mark Duffield, *Global Governance and the New Wars* (London: Zed Books, 2002), p. 16.

11 David Chandler, *From Kosovo to Kabul* (London: Zed Books, 2002), p. 28.

12 John Keane, *Global Civil Society* (Cambridge: CUP, 2003), p. 2.

13 Rieff, p. 67.

14 Edward N. Luttwak, *Strategy: The Logic of War and Peace* (Cambridge, Massachusetts: Harvard, 1987), p. 66.

15 See in particular, Nicolas Leader, *The Politics of Principle: The Principles of Humanitarian Action in Practice*, Humanitarian Policy Group Report 2: Overseas Development Institute (March 2000), p. 49.

16 For more on this project see, <http://www.sphereproject.org/about/nl1.htm>.

17 Patrick James Flood, *The Effectiveness of UN Human Rights Institutions*, (Westport, CT: Praeger, 1998).

18 Felice D. Gaer, 'Implementing International Human Rights Norms: UN Human Rights Treaty Bodies and NGOs', in Henry F. Carey (guest ed.) *Journal of Human Rights* 2/3 (September 2002).

19 For the dynamics of this debate see John Keane, *Global Civil Society*.

20 Daphne Josselin and William Wallace (eds), *Non-State Actors in World Politics* (London: Palgrave, 2001), p. 253.

21 Mary B. Anderson, *Do No Harm* (Boulder: Lynne Rienner Publishers, February 1999). See also Johanna Macrae, 'The Death of Humanitarianism?', *Disasters*, 22/4 (1998): 312.

22 See, for example, Nicolas Stockton, 'In Defence of Humanitarianism', *Disasters*, 22/4 (1998): pp. 354-355.

23 See Chris Brown, 'The Idea of World Community', in Ken Booth and Steve Smith (eds), *International Relations Theory Today* (Cambridge; Polity Press, 1995), p. 106.

24 See Terry Nardin, *Law, Morality and the Relations of States* (Princeton, N.J.: Princeton University Press, 1983).

25 Brown, p. 106.

26 Ibid, p. 106.

27 Ibid.

28 Daphne Josselin and William Wallace, p. 1.

29 See, among others, UNDP *Development Report* 1994; Roland Paris, 'Human Security: Paradigm Shift or Hot Air?', *International Security*, 26/2 (2001): 87-102; *International Security*, 7/3 (July–Sept. 2001); Yuen Foong Khong, 'Human Security: A Shotgun Approach to Alleviating Human Misery?', *Global Governance*, 7/3 (July–Sept. 2001).

30 See in particular, John Keane, *Global Civil Society*.

31 Paris argues that the inclusion of development means that peacebuilding is effectively a new era in developed-developing world relations. Roland Paris, 'International Peacebuilding and the "Mission Civilisatrice"', *Review of International Studies*, 28/4 (2002): 638.

32 W. Reinicke, *Global Public Policy* (Washington DC: Brookings, 1998), p. 259.

33 Nicola Reindorp, 'Global Humanitarian Assistance', *Humanitarian Exchange*, 18 (March 2001), p. 31.

34 Mark Duffield, 'NGO Relief in War Zones', *Third World Quarterly*, 18/3 (1997): 527-542.

35 See Boutros Boutros Ghali, *An Agenda for Peace: Preventive Diplomacy, Peacemaking and Peace-Keeping*, A/47/277-S/24111, (17 June 1992); *An Agenda for Development: Report of the Secretary-General*, A/48/935, (6 May 1994); *An Agenda for Democratization*, A/50/332 AND A/51/512, (17 December 1996).

36 Kevin Watkins, *Oxfam Poverty Report* (Oxford: Oxfam Academic, 1995): International Commission on Intervention, *The Responsibility to Protect: The Report of the International Commission on Intervention and State Sovereignty* (Ottawa, Canada: International Development Research Centre, 2002).

37 With respect to the former point, one of the refrains of the humanitarian community is that '... intervention must take place without there being any intervention'. This has been repeated several times to me by several senior members of this community. Of course it raises the question of whether this is actually possible (which is very unlikely), and if it is how would such power be made accountable?

38 See 'Letters from the Secretary General to the President of the General Assembly and the President of the Security Council', Report of the Panel on UN Peace Operations, A/55/305-S/2000/809, (21 August 2000).

39 Kofi A. Annan, 'Democracy as an International Issue', *Global Governance*, Vol. 8, no.2 (April 2002), p. 135.

40 Ibid.

41 The UN has also established the Electoral Assistance Division to guide states making a transition to democracy.

42 Mark Duffield, 'Aid and Complicity', *Journal of Modern African Studies*, 40/1 (Spring 2002): 83.

43 Ibid, p. 90.

44 Ibid, pp. 11-13.

45 Michel Foucault, 'Governmentality', in Graham Burchell, Colin Gordon and Peter Miller (eds), *The Foucault Effect: Studies in Governmentality* (Hemel Hempstead: Harvester Wheatsheaf, 1991), pp. 87-104.

46 Michel Foucault, *The History of Sexuality*, 1 (London: Penguin, 1990 (1976)).

47 See *UN Security Council Resolution 1244* (10 June 1999), paragraphs 9-17.

48 Fiona Terry, *The Paradox of Humanitarian Action: Condemned to Repeat?* (Ithaca: Cornell, 2002), pp. 218-219.

49 Rieff, p. 64.

50 Mark Laffey, 'Chomsky and IR Theory After the Cold War', *Review of International Studies*, 29/4 (2003): 593.

51 Ibid.

52 Bruce Cronin, 'The Two Faces of the UN', *Global Governance*, 8 (2002): 68.

53 Richard J. Goldstone, 'Whither Kosovo? Whither Democracy?', *Global Governance*, Vol. 8, no.2 (April 2002), p. 144.

54 See Richard Falk, *Human Rights Horizons* (London: Routledge, 2000), p. 68.

55 Chandler, p. 194.

56 Francis Fukyama, *State Building: Governance and Order in the Twenty First Century* (London: Profile, 2004), p. 53.

Chapter 3

Up to No Good? Recent Critics and Critiques of NGOs

Kim D. Reimann

In the past two decades, the number and influence of NGOs has grown dramatically, leading many scholars and observers in recent years to argue that a paradigm shift has taken place in politics and international relations theory. While the tone of the much of the literature on NGOs has been positive and has presented them in a progressive and idealistic light, the rise of NGOs has not been without controversy or critics. As NGOs have grown in size and influence, their actions have come under much greater scrutiny. Their role as a promoter of good causes has been called into question on several accounts.

This chapter examines the various criticisms of NGOs and calls attention to both the validity of these criticisms as well as contradictions and inconsistencies. Critics of NGOs can be found across the political spectrum, ranging from rightists who object to NGOs in principle to leftists who criticize NGOs for their failures to advance a progressive agenda or for deferring to government preferences. Despite their ideological differences and ultimate objectives, however, critics are remarkably similar in terms of many of their main complaints about NGOs. During the course of the 1990s and early 2000s, a clearly defined set of critiques of NGOs have appeared focusing on: (1) their performance and actual effectiveness, (2) accountability issues, (3) issues of autonomy, (4) commercialisation, and (5) ideological and/or political interpretations of their rising influence. Now appearing with increasing regularity and frequency in the academic literature, the policy world, and the popular press, these critiques have been directed towards not only NGOs working in the area of conflict resolution (the main subject of this book), but to *all* NGOs: advocacy NGOs, service NGOs, and NGOs working in various issues areas. In order to provide both a comprehensive and a refined examination of the debate, this chapter will present the major criticisms of NGOs in general, while distinguishing critiques as they apply to various types of NGOs.

I. The Rise of NGOs as the Magic Bullet: 1980s–1990s

For NGOs working in the areas of international development, humanitarian crises and democracy promotion, the 1980s and 1990s were watershed years in terms of material resources available from external funders in the international donor community. From comparatively low levels in the 1960s and 1970s, official funding for NGOs tripled in the 1980s then doubled again in the 1990s.[1] By the mid to late 1990s, an estimated $6 to $7 billion dollars of official aid and foundation funding was being channeled through NGOs.[2] These increases in funding for NGOs marked a policy shift in the international donor community away from supporting state institutions towards a neoliberal, privatized approach to development and relief. NGOs were now heralded as the antidote to corrupt and failing states in developing and democratising countries since they would promote bottom-up, 'people-participatory' development and a thriving 'civil society' that would encourage the spread of democratic norms and practices.[3] Similarly, in the area of humanitarian crises, a shift towards aid privatisation took place in then 1980s and 1990s, with NGOs becoming the major funding recipients and service providers of relief in war-torn countries.[4]

The 1980s and 1990s also saw a rise in the amount of international funding and political support available for advocacy NGOs working in various issue areas, such as the environment, human rights, security issues and women's issues. Although US official aid, with the exception of democracy aid, was generally not available to advocacy NGOs, Canadian and European aid agencies were not shy about funding advocacy groups and provided funds for both international and developing country advocacy NGOs, especially those promoting environmental and human rights causes. However, it was private foundations, and in particular large American private foundations, that provided a major new surge of funding for advocacy NGOs. Starting in the 1980s, international programs of private foundations expanded rapidly, and by the late 1990s, $1.6 billion was annually spent on international programs by American foundations alone.[5] In this period, advocacy NGOs were also now normatively portrayed by foundations, the UN, and other international elite institutions as a necessary 'citizen' or 'civil society' component of global politics that would hold states and international organisations accountable, provide 'voice' to the underrepresented, promote new norms and universal values, and provide the UN a way to address its 'democratic deficit'.

In sum, the 1980s and 1990s were not only a time of rapid NGO growth, these decades were a period in which NGOs came to be enthusiastically promoted by powerful states, international organisations and private foundations. The rhetoric and propaganda used by these international actors portrayed NGOs as the new citizen saviors that would help solve world problems ranging from 'equitable and sustainable' development to world peace to the spread of democracy and human rights. In addition to their idealistic image as altruistic and selfless promoters of good causes, NGOs were now presented as *functionally* important and contributors to human progress.

II. Backlash: NGOs under Attack

Considering the excessively high expectations and the enormous amount of resources and political access given to NGOs in the 1980s and 1990s, it should not be surprising that numerous critics of NGOs have appeared. Appearing first in the literature on development aid and humanitarian crises in the mid 1990s and then spreading to other parts of academic literature and popular press in the late 1990s and 2000s, several general criticisms of NGOs emerged as the core complaints and concerns. While closely interrelated, these core criticisms can be divided into the five main categories of: (1) NGO performance and effectiveness in obtaining their goals; (2) issues concerning accountability, representation and transparency; (3) the question of dependence on external funding and NGO autonomy; (4) commercialisation and the emergence of a highly competitive charity and activist 'market', and (5) ideological and politically motivated critiques of the rising influence of Western NGOs.

Questioning Performance: Are NGOs a Force for Progress or Doing More Harm than Good?

Of all the criticisms directed towards NGOs, among the most serious are those focusing on NGO performance and effectiveness that claim NGOs have had a poor track record and have done more harm than good. These criticisms have been mainly directed at service NGOs working in the fields of international development and relief, but variations of these criticisms have also targeted advocacy NGOs.

International Development

In the area of international development, the question of NGO performance and effectiveness became a very central one given the fact that aid agencies and NGOs themselves were aggressively promoting NGOs as a cost effective and better way to reach the poor. Exceedingly high expectations for NGO-led development were bound to lead to disappointments and as early as the mid-1980s studies started to show that NGOs often performed poorly when it came to clear, measurable results and that NGOs did not seem to be living up to their image as vehicles for 'participatory' development.[6] By the mid 1990s, after billions of dollars had been poured into NGO development projects worldwide, Edwards and Hulme and other development scholars came to similar conclusions. While there were many cases of both NGO success and failure, the main body of evidence indicated that NGOs were not performing as effectively as the development paradigm had promised in terms of poverty reach, cost-effectiveness, sustainability, popular participation and flexibility and innovation.[7] Numerous government studies and evaluations on NGO performance and effectiveness have been undertaken since the 1990s, and most of them have found that while many individual NGO projects have often been judged 'successful', work done by NGOs still often falls short when it comes to sustainability, participation and significant improvements in socio-economic conditions or political empowerment.[8]

Humanitarian Crises

Compared with NGOs working in humanitarian crises and conflict situations, however, the performance failures of NGOs in the area of international development seem minor. Since the mid 1990s, humanitarian relief NGOs have faced intense criticism for not only failing to succeed in their goals but for also often making a bad situation even worse. These 'doing more harm than good' criticisms are among the most damaging for NGOs and they have had a wider impact on the public image of NGOs in general since they have been the frequent focus of negative press exposes.[9]

Although critiques of humanitarian relief NGOs existed in the 1970s and 1980s,[10] the more recent outpouring of criticism dates to the early to mid 1990s and flawed relief efforts in Somalia and Rwanda. The first critiques of NGOs performance in conflict zones came from NGOs themselves, with the report of the advocacy group African Rights in 1994 detailing the many problems and blunders caused by NGOs in Rwanda.[11] Since then, numerous studies, books and reports have come to similar conclusions and together comprise a general theory of how NGOs can, despite their best intentions, contribute to the prolongation and escalation of internal conflict.[12] Based on these various studies, relief NGOs are seen as potentially aiding conflict in five ways: (1) by providing resources to warring sides; (2) by contributing to market distortions; (3) by reinforcing societal divisions and conflict; (4) by freeing up internal resources for use in conflict; and (5) by legitimising warring sides.

Nearly all of the criticisms of the effectiveness and poor performance of humanitarian relief and other NGOs working in conflict situations fall into one of these five categories. One of the most common criticisms, for example, has focused on how relief aid and NGO presence in a conflict situation invariably brings in new resources from the outside that are used and manipulated by warring sides in ways that fuel and/or prolong conflict. Large-scale theft and misappropriation of relief aid has often led to substantial amounts of aid being channeled into war-related activities and NGOs often directly support warring factions when they hire local armed guards for protection, and when they pay fees and other sorts of payments to warlords in order to be allowed to operate in some conflict zones.[13] NGOs have come under harsh criticism for prolonging conflict and reinforcing divisions within society by appearing to take sides when they provide relief to a targeted victim group. As was the case in Rwandan and Cambodian refugee camps, relief can end up in the hands of the 'wrong' side and support new waves of violence and conflict.[14] Refugee camps themselves can be a strategic resource for one side in a conflict, providing an internationally protected base for regrouping and for recruiting soldiers.

Another huge source of criticism has emphasized the market and economic distortions that NGOs and relief aid either cause or reinforce and how NGOs contribute to the creation of dysfunctional wartime economies. Food aid has been repeatedly criticized for its negative economic effects such as creating food import dependency in formerly self-sufficient states, enriching corrupt elite and rebels who use food aid for power and personal enrichment, and putting small scale farmers and local distributors out of business by flooding the market with cheap imported food.[15] In addition to their role in providing food aid, NGOs also are criticized for their contribution to a dual war economy when they appear in the hundreds and pay exorbitantly high prices for housing, supplies, salaries for local staff and other local expenses.[16] In general, the aid industry has tended to reinforce pre-existing income disparities by disproportionately benefiting local educated elite (who own property and can speak English) and corrupt, powerful actors who are best positioned to exploit outsiders.[17] In cases where the aid industry becomes a major source of employment and business for the local population, it can unintentionally create a stake in the continuation of the conflict since peace would mean a potential withdrawal of aid and loss of jobs and economic livelihood.[18] By not adequately planning and preparing the local population for their eventual departure, NGOs have been criticized for creating dependency on aid and contributing to the general decline in local self-sufficiency and self-help that makes the transition back to a peacetime economy even more difficult.[19]

Advocacy NGOs

Although most of the criticisms of NGOs regarding effectiveness and performance have been directed towards service-providing NGOs, advocacy NGOs have not been immune to similar criticisms.

In area of democracy promotion, for example, advocacy NGOs have been criticized for failing to live up to the high expectations of international donors and although civil society aid has been successful in stimulating a surge in the number of advocacy NGOs in transition countries, this increase in the number of groups promoting democracy has not necessarily led to the vibrant, flourishing and independent Tocquevillian civil society as envisioned by Western donors. So far, assessments of effectiveness of advocacy NGOs have been mixed and largely negative with only scattered evidence that they are adequately performing the various functions of 'civil society' in supporting the growth of democratic practices and values. Most studies have found that these newly created NGOs function poorly, lack popular support and participation and, when they do perform well, tend to do so as elite lobbyists and trustee organisations located in a country's capital.[20]

Beyond the small world of democracy promotion, advocacy NGOs promoting a variety of causes internationally and transnationally in areas such as the environment, human rights, and trade have been criticized for misrepresenting facts and doing harm to those they intend to protect. Scientists, for example, have sharply criticized Greenpeace and other environmental NGOs for their strong stance against all genetically modified organisms (GMOs) which, they claim, has resulted in declining funding for GMOs in developing countries and has ended up hurting farmers there seeking to lower pesticide usage.[21] Similarly, advocacy NGOs protesting against child labor in developing countries have also been accused of doing more harm than good by depriving child workers and their families of needed income when multinational corporations like Nike shut down their overseas factories in response to boycotts and negative press.[22] In the past few years, scholars and practitioners have become more critical and discriminating in their study of transnational advocacy NGO effectiveness and have found that a wide variety of cases exist ranging from high profile success stories in which local populations were empowered and benefited from their ties to transnational actors to cases of miserable failures in which Western NGOs actually *disempowered* local groups. As Lisa Jordan and Peter van Tuijl have argued, not all international NGOs are 'politically responsible' about maintaining sufficient levels of communication and information exchange with the local populations they claim to represent. In such cases, Western NGOs have often ended up running campaigns that directly competed with campaigns and goals of local groups and ultimately led to 'solutions' contrary to the real interests of the local population.[23]

Watching the Watchdogs: Issues of Accountability, Representation and Transparency

Strongly interrelated to the question of NGO performance and effectiveness is the question of accountability. If NGOs are not performing well, how can they be held accountable for their mistakes and other questionable practices? Nearly all critics of NGOs, friendly and unfriendly, bring up the problematic issue of ensuring accountability due to the lack in many countries of a sufficient and useful set of regulations and standards for NGO performance, governance and transparency. In addition to performance accountability problems discussed in the previous section, accountability issues include questions of finance, representation and transparency.

In terms of financial accountability and corruption, a recurring problem mentioned frequently in the literature is the phenomenon of 'fake' NGOs set up in developing countries by local entrepreneurs, gangsters, for-profit businesses and government officials in order to tap into the many funding opportunities now available for NGOs.[24] Such NGO pretenders have become so prevalent in countries where international funding for NGOs is available that a whole new set of names and acronyms have been created to describe them: briefcase NGOs (BRINGO), come and go NGO (ComeN'Go), commercial NGO (CONGO), criminal NGO (CRINGO), government-owned NGO (GONGO), government-run and initiated NGO (GRINGO), mafia NGO (MANGO), party NGO (PANGO) and my own NGO (MONGO).[25] With the rise of these sort of NGOs, the difficulty of sorting out legitimate and 'good' NGOs from the corrupt, profit-seeing and 'fake' ones has led to general cynicism and skepticism towards NGOs, especially among local populations in the developing world.

Issues and criticisms relating to financial accountability are not, however, restricted to these most obvious cases of fake NGOs in developing countries. Legitimate NGOs with extensive operations and projects, particularly large Western-based service NGOs that operate worldwide, have been taken to task and criticized for spending too much money on overhead and administrative costs and too little on the on their actual projects. Pressure to keep overhead costs to a minimum have led many NGOs to 'fudge' some of their accounting, leading to criticisms and minor scandals when it is occasionally discovered that a portion of program costs was in fact spent by NGO headquarters for administrative expenses.[26] Some of the sensationalist criticisms of the 1990s aimed at NGOs involved accusations that a substantial percentage of private donations were not being used to help the poor but to fund large salaries, jet-setting costs of plane tickets and hotels, and other administrative costs.[27]

In addition to the financial bottom line, many critics have focused on issues of accountability related to representation, such as the so-called problems of a 'democracy deficit' and 'voice accountability'. Although supporters of NGOs and NGOs themselves have an idealized image of NGOs as representatives of 'the people' and 'civil society', critics have emerged who question the ability and the right of NGOs to make such grand claims.

No Longer Nongovernmental? Funding Dependence and Issues of Autonomy

Since governments and multilateral institutions began channeling billions of dollars of aid through NGOs in the 1980s and 1990s, an increasing number of NGOs have become dependent on official sources of funding for their activities. Various studies in the 1990s, for example, concluded that Western-based INGOs working in development and relief were 30-90 per cent dependent on official funding and a large number of Southern NGOs were 80-100 per cent dependent on foreign sources of aid.[28] As ties between many NGOs and the state have deepened, critics have accused NGOs of being coopted by the state and of effectively losing their autonomous 'nongovernmental' status as they become the subcontractors and policy instruments of states and IGOs. These criticisms have mainly applied to service NGOs working in international development and humanitarian relief which receive the bulk of official funds, but they have also extended to advocacy NGOs in developing countries working in the area of democracy, democratisation and 'civil society' representation which have also relied heavily on outside funding from bilateral aid agencies, multilateral donors and private foundations.

According to the critics, aid contracts and official funding rob NGOs of autonomy and legitimacy as an independent actor in several ways. First, as NGOs rely more on official funds, their projects and activities have often become more concerned with donor interests than with the needs of the local constituencies they claim to serve. To get funding, NGOs have become 'donor-driven' and have shifted their activities to match the goals of donors, starting projects not because there is bottom-up demand but rather because there is top-down supply of resources.[29] In addition, once on the government payroll, onerous reporting requirements and the need to respond to demands of donors can comprise NGOs by diverting their energy away from their grassroots constituencies and forcing them to sacrifice both institutional and programmatic integrity.

A second and related criticism is that as NGOs have become more dependent on official sources they have been less likely to be involved in advocacy or any activity that might be construed as overly political or critical of their donors.[30] Due to their eagerness for funding and their fear of losing funding once they get it, NGOs have been politically muzzled and have shied away from any meaningful 'empowerment' activities that could lead to real change for the poor they seek to serve.[31] According to critics in this area, this loss of political autonomy has meant that many NGOs have essentially become policy instruments of the state and IGOs.

Third, and finally, the issue of funding dependence on official sources raises problematic questions about legitimacy for Southern NGOs in developing countries where official funding is often foreign funding from a bilateral agency, an multilateral institution, or a Western foundation grant. Southern NGOs that depend on foreign funding have been attacked by their governments as 'agents' of Western cultural imperialism and their ties to Western governments and INGOs make Southern NGOs vulnerable to such accusations.[32] This has been particularly true for advocacy NGOs working in the democracy aid industry that promote human rights or in some way challenge states.[33] Almost inevitably, local NGOs that are heavily dependent on foreign funding will tend to be viewed by both governments and local populations as less legitimate and less authentic than those that receive no outside support.

Competing in the Do-Gooder Market: Commercialisation, Professionalisation and the Loss of the 'Voluntary' Spirit

In addition to concerns about NGOs losing the 'n' in 'nongovernmental organisation' abbreviation, some critics have also worried that NGOs are losing the 'n' in their status as non-profit organisations. As NGOs have grown both in number and in size in the past two decades, critics have also focused on how the growth in official funding and the emergence of a competitive charity market have transformed NGOs into large, highly professional organisations that behave less like voluntary, non-profit 'citizen' organisations and more like governments or for-profit organisations. In the process of becoming more professional, these critics argue, NGOs have also become increasingly bureaucratic and income-driven and have lost many of the original comparative advantages and features that made them special in the first place – i.e. their idealism, their spirit of voluntarism, their small scale and innovative flexibility, and their ability to engage with people at the grassroots level.

The surge of funding for NGOs since the 1980s has contributed to these trends in several ways. First, in the industrialized world, a substantial amount of official funding for development and relief has often gone to a small group of Western-based INGOs that have become multi-million dollar mega-NGOs with enormous staffs and operations worldwide. Donini and Smillie have noted how an oligopoly of eight families or confederations of INGOs controlled up to half of the total funds available for development and relief activities in the 1990s, with many of them having budgets of $500 million or more.[34] Similarly in the developing world, one can find numerous examples of Southern service-providing NGOs that expanded enormously as they became the favorites of donors as channels for 'people participatory' aid. In both cases, as these NGOs grew into mega-NGOs they quickly became more hierarchical, more bureaucratic and more like the governments that they were meant to be a pragmatic alternative to.[35] Although originally prized by aid agencies for their small-scale and innovative responses to local conditions, NGOs ironically started losing these traits and comparative advantages once they started applying for and getting large amounts of aid for 'scaling-up'.[36]

Secondly, critics point out that being part of the official aid industry itself has had a commercialising effect on NGOs and has remolded them into more corporate-like organisations. Because of the need to be accountable to official aid agencies for increasingly large sums of funding, NGOs have had to adopt a more market approach to their programs, measuring 'inputs' and 'outputs', costs and benefits and overall efficiency.[37] The result, these critics claim, is that NGOs have moved towards a corporate model and have lost touch with the original community-based, voluntaristic principles which made them special and separate from the market. As they have become more market-oriented, NGOs view communities as 'clients' and move away from principles of reciprocity, obligation and community solidarity.[38]

But official funding is just one part of the picture. The emergence of a lucrative 'charity market' of private donations in the 1980s and 1990s also brought about increasing levels of competition among NGOs, especially in the mid to late 1990s as funding levels stabilized. These market pressures and the desire of NGOs to increase or at least maintain their share of the market has encouraged a more corporate approach that emphasizes efficiency, market principles and professionalism.[39] Dichter, for example, has noted how large NGOs working in the area of international development have adopted management and corporate financial strategies such as transfer pricing and transfer fundraising. In organisational workshops and retreats, NGO executives and staff now refer to both beneficiaries and donors as 'customers' and discuss what specialty or niche their organisation should focus on.[40] Compared with the past, many people now working for NGOs see it as just another professional career – one that requires advanced degrees and may lead to work for the government or private sector – and appear to lack the personal and long-term commitment to the NGO 'cause' that previous generations showed.[41] Large, successful NGOs appear to be very similar to for-profit interest groups: they have nice offices, their executive staff get paid well, their staff jet-set around the world, and when they live abroad they inhabit an expatriate 'bubble' of privilege and relative luxury.[42]

Finally, market competition and the pressure to continually raise large sums from the general public have also caused NGOs to adopt questionable marketing and fundraising practices that have raised ethical questions about their integrity and real intentions. In the 1980s and 1990s, the use of images of starving children and refugees by development and relief NGOs in their ads and fundraising appeals led to a series of false advertising scandals and public outcry that NGOs be more accountable and less exploitative of the poor in their marketing.[43] These and other questionable practices also led some critics to view NGOs as profit-driven, self-serving 'business' organisations that care more about perpetuating their own organisational existence than helping victims of poverty and conflict.[44]

Although these various critiques were largely directed at large service-delivery NGOs working in the areas of development and humanitarian crises, advocacy NGOs have not been immune to these critiques of commercialisation and market-related opportunism. Large and well-funded advocacy NGOs also have become more professional and 'businesslike' in their appearance and practices in the 1980s and 1990s, with well educated, middle to upper middle class professional staff who work in pleasant offices next door to for-profit tenants.[45] Advocacy NGOs have adopted similar market-oriented, corporate models such as niche specialisation and logo merchandise; and their highly professional lobbying skills make them (at least in outward appearance) practically indistinguishable from high paid industry lobbyists.

As they have grown more influential, moreover, large advocacy INGOs in the West have also become powerful overseers of a global market of worthy and just causes spreading patterns of NGO 'marketisation' to the developing world. With their funding-raising skills, their ability to generate media coverage and their considerable political influence, large Western advocacy INGOs are now the gatekeepers of global activism, picking and choosing which of the many international causes are the most deserving of international attention.[46] To local movements and activists from developing countries, international activism is a 'Darwinian marketplace' where only the most savvy and well-packaged causes that meet the organisational needs of Western INGOs see the light of day. Movements with charismatic leaders that speak English, that espouse non-violence, and that can frame their cause in simplistic, universal terms that appeal to Western audiences are the ones most likely to get INGO support and attract global attention.[47] Once they get international support, local movements are usually given training in the West on how to market their cause to the media, get funding from foundations and other donors, and become a more 'professional' operation. This international marketisation and commercialisation of local movements in developing countries is not seen by critics as a positive development – to the contrary, they see these market forces as corrupting ones that divert local leadership from their original goals and potentially cause divisions within the movement as the international campaign becomes more and more removed from grassroots and local control.[48]

Ideological and Political Backlash

As they have become more influential and visible in world politics, NGOs have also faced ideological backlash from both the political left and right and have been depicted as a dangerous political force that threatens justice, freedom and the true will of the people. These critics have been equally harsh in their condemnation of NGOs and what they see as NGOs' 'real' political agenda, but their very different interpretations of this agenda have produced polar opposite conspiracy theories. While leftists accuse NGOs of being the agents for Western neoliberalism, capitalism and neocolonialism, right-wing critics bash NGOs for being the enemies of Western capitalism and democracy and the tools of left-wing radicals.

Ideological criticism of NGOs from the left and the developing world can be roughly divided into the two overlapping general conspiracy theories of hegemonic Western neoliberalism and neocolonialism. Both theories portray NGOs as part of a larger Western-led project of dividing the world into the haves (the West) and the have-nots (the rest).[49] Of the two, neoliberal conspiracy theories have been more common among Western scholars and observers and began appearing in the 1990s as official funding for NGOs working in developing countries skyrocketed.

Edwards and Hulme were the first to note the neoliberal market models underlying the new approach to aid and support of NGOs in the 1990s and warned that NGOs were at risk of becoming tools of an anti-state, pro-market 'New Policy Agenda'.[50] Others have similarly described how NGOs are part of a new Western approach to bilateral and multilateral aid that systematically weakens and 'decapitates' states by channeling funds to the private sector and by robbing states of policy autonomy through structural adjustment programs (SAPs).[51] NGOs have been important components of this neoliberal model, as the new privatized social welfare provider that both replaces state services and provides a social safety net and 'bottom-up' pressure valve, thereby allowing market forces to work their magic without causing excessive social disruption or resistance.[52]

The neocolonial conspiracy theories of NGOs build on and take these criticisms of the spread of neoliberal models even further and argue that NGOs are the 'advanced guard' of a new era of Western economic and political imperialism.[53] According to James Petras' leftist version of this argument, NGOs are the grassroots poster children for imperialist neoliberal (=global capitalist) forces that have appropriated the progressive rhetoric of 'civil society', 'sustainable development', 'empowerment', and 'bottom-up leadership'. Despite such noble-sounding phrases and goals, in practice NGOs usually disempower the poor and prevent them from effectively organising a united front against global capitalism. The proliferation of NGOs in developing countries in response to international funding opportunities, for example, has led to numerous, sometimes competing, small local projects that fragment poor communities into sectoral groupings and undermine their ability to see the larger, more systemic causes of their poverty and underdevelopment.[54] Unlike social movements which aim to mobilize mass populations for political and social empowerment, most Western-funded NGOs are apolitical and if anything have helped bring about the depoliticisation and demobilisation of the poor by discouraging mass-organized and class-based confrontational activities, by coopting potential movement leaders with the material promise of funding opportunities and by promoting 'self-help' projects that place the burden and responsibility of development not on the state or wealthy classes but on the poor themselves.[55] NGOs, thus, have proved to be ideal partners for global capitalist forces – NGOs have effectively helped contain potential bottom-up popular resistance to the neoliberal program and have promoted a privatized 'self-help' approach to development in which the poor are asked to exploit themselves.

These alarmist left-of-center interpretations of NGOs stand in sharp contrast to the equally alarmist views of political conservative and right-of-center NGO critics in America and other advanced industrialized countries. Instead of viewing NGOs as agents *promoting* the global spread of capitalism and neoliberalism, conspiracy theories from the political right interpret NGOs as a hegemonic leftist movement that *undermines* capitalism, democracy and the sovereign rights of states. This right-of-center set of critics emerged as an organized and coherent public voice in 2003 with the convening of a conference on NGOs by conservative think tanks in Washington, D.C., and the establishment of a web page called NGO Watch devoted to monitoring and exposing the dangerous growing power of

NGOs.[56] With the strong support of conservative think tanks such as American Enterprise Institute and the Federalist Society for Law and Public Policy, this new set of NGO critics worries that NGOs, in cahoots with the UN, are 'hijacking' democracy and seeking to impose their progressive, anti-corporate values on the entire world.[57] According to these critics, NGOs and their rising influence in national and international politics threaten democracy, capitalism and sovereignty of the nation-state.

The rise of the Global New Left NGOs threatens not only democracy, it also threatens national sovereignty. Since many politically conservative critics of NGOs are also critics of the United Nation and international treaties that constrain sovereignty in general, they often view relations and links between the UN and NGOs as a conspiracy to promote liberal internationalism and a quasi-world government. According to this analysis, NGOs have been able to advance their Global New Left cause by cooperating with the United Nations and other intergovernmental organisations (IGOs) under the banner of 'global governance'.[58] By channeling their efforts through IGOs and working with IGOs on the numerous issues that fall under the catchall category of global governance, NGOs have been able to influence international relations and set up international standards that potentially erode the sovereign rights of nations and put international pressure on states to fall in line with leftist NGO agendas in the areas of human rights, the environment, development, population policy, arms and security policies, health policy and many other issue areas.[59] Critics from the right are particularly alarmed by these developments since they believe that NGOs are often wrong in their policy prescriptions and that NGOs tend to advocate anti-market, anti-scientific and anti-democratic solutions that leave countries worse off. Bate and Tren, for example, have argued that the unbalanced and unscientific approach of NGOs calling for international bans of pesticides and genetically modified food products has led to 'international standards' and policies that have exacerbated malaria and food shortages in Africa.[60]

Finally, right wing critics of NGOs also claim that the New Global Left NGOs are enemies of corporations and have an anti-market orientation that seeks to undermine capitalism and free markets. As the major promoters of the concept of corporate social responsibility, for example, advocacy NGOs are trying to set standards for business behavior that conservative critics find unreasonable and detrimental to the normal functioning of businesses and free markets.[61] In addition to the NGO-led social investment movement and attempts to influence corporate policy through shareholder resolutions, NGOs have waged various all-out campaigns to hold corporations responsible for the many social and economic injustices of the world ranging from environmental degradation to human rights abuses and health-related problems.[62] In addition to causing reputational damage to corporations, these NGO campaigns have hampered capitalism by creating unrealistic expectations for what corporations are responsible for and by misinforming the public of the various misdeeds committed by corporations. In the latter case, the 'anti-science' view of NGOs that sees only danger in scientific and technological advancements (e.g. biotechnology, nuclear power, toxic but useful chemicals, etc.) has slowed down economic development and prevented capitalism from spreading gains from science to the market.[63]

III. Conclusion: Assessing NGOs and their Critics

Given their much larger presence and role in international politics in recent years, it should not be surprising that NGOs have come under increasing levels of scrutiny and criticism. In a sense, criticisms are natural and to be expected as part of a coming of age process; if NGOs were still minor players with absolutely no influence in international politics, they would not be attracting attention or criticism in the first place. As is the case with other important international actors – e.g., states, IGOs, and multinational corporations – NGOs are not infallible and bring with them their own set of organisational dysfunctions and pathologies. Criticisms are both inevitable and good since they force NGOs to grapple with the multitude of problems and issues that face *any* organisation that commands resources and power.

While these criticisms are sometimes exaggerations, most of them have more than a grain of truth to them and involve problems that many NGOs are well aware of. Larger international NGOs in particular have struggled with many of the issues described in this chapter and since the mid-1990s have made numerous attempts to address criticisms related to performance, accountability and marketing practices. Humanitarian and development NGOs were the first to devise self-imposed 'codes of conduct' in 1995 in response to NGO failures in Rwanda in 1994 and there are currently several initiatives now underway for monitoring and implementing so-called 'best' and 'good' practices. These include People in Aid's Code of Good Practice, the Active Learning Network for Accountability and Performance in Humanitarian Action, Humanitarian Accountability Partnership International and the Sphere Project.[64] Advocacy NGOs have been slower to respond, although there is now an active debate taking place among certain NGOs, with new projects appearing in recent years such as the International Council on Human Rights Policy's project on NGO accountability.[65]

Despite these efforts, however, there are reasons to believe that many of the problems NGOs face in the five areas mentioned in this chapter will not be easily solved and will require more than just efforts and changes on the part of NGOs. Problems that NGOs face are often embedded in larger structural problems and realities that are beyond their control. Additionally, some of the criticisms place contradictory and conflicting pressures on NGOs that are hard to respond to simultaneously. For NGOs to address many of the critiques found in the literature and media, it will also be necessary for states, IGOs and other actors to examine their roles and contributions to the problems. To conclude, the debate on NGOs is a complex one that will continue for some time to come. Now considered mainstream players in many areas of international relations, NGOs are finding themselves targets of many of the same criticisms that they themselves made of other influential actors. This is a healthy and a necessary stage in the historical development of the NGO sector, but one that should also be tempered with a deeper discussion of the larger set of structural challenges facing NGOs. Although NGOs are not the 'magic bullet' that will solve all problems and NGOs have earned many of the criticisms mentioned in this chapter, they have also provided relief and 'voice' to millions of people in practically all corners of the globe. To move from de-constructive criticism to constructive criticism, the debate on NGOs needs to be both broadened to present the bigger, structural challenges they face as well as fine-tuned to delineate when and how they can contribute to positive change.

Notes

1 David Hulme and Michael Edwards, 'NGOs, States and Donors: An Overview', in David Hulme and Michael Edwards (eds), *NGOs, States and Donors: Too Close for Comfort?* (London: MacMillan and Save the Children, 1997), p. 6.

2 Kim Reimann, 'International Politics, Norms and the Worldwide Growth of NGOs', paper presented at the Annual Meeting of the American Political Science Association (APSA), Boston, 28 August–1 September 2002.

3 Michael Edwards and David Hulme, 'NGO Performance and Accountability: Introduction and Overview', in Michael Edwards and David Hulme (eds), *Non-Governmental Organizations – Performance and Accountability: Beyond the Magic Bullet* (London: Earthscan, 1995); Marina Ottaway and Thomas Carothers (eds), *Funding Virtue. Civil Society Aid and Democracy Promotion*, (Washington, DC: Carnegie Endowment for International Peace, 2000).

4 Mark Duffield, 'NGO Relief in War Zones: Towards an Analysis of the New Aid Paradigm', *Third World Quarterly*, 18 (September 1997).

5 The Foundation Center, *Foundation Yearbook* (New York: The Foundation Center, 2000).

6 Judith Tendler, *Turning Private Voluntary Organizations into Development Agencies: Questions for Evaluation*, Evaluation Discussion Paper, No. 10 (Washington, D.C.: US Agency for International Development, 1982); Graham Hancock, *The Lords of Poverty* (New York: Atlantic Monthly Press, 1989).

7 Edwards and Hulme, pp. 6-7; Alan Fowler and Kees Biekart, 'Do Private Agencies Really Make a Difference?', in David Sogge (ed.), *Compassion and Calculation: The Business of Private Foreign Aid* (London: Pluto Press, 1996), p. 132; S. Akbar Zaidi, 'NGO Failure and the Need to Bring Back in the State', *Journal of International Development*, 11 (March/April 1999).

8 Ian Smillie, 'NGOs and Development Assistance: A Change in Mind-Set?', *Third World Quarterly*, 18 (September 1997): 571-572; Terge Tvedt, *Agents of Mercy or Development Diplomats? NGOs and Foreign Aid* (Trenton and Oxford: Africa World Press and James Curry, Ltd., 1998), ch. 6.

9 Ian Fisher, 'Can International Relief Do More Good than Harm?', *New York Times Magazine*, 11 February 2001; Jon Christensen, 'Asking the Do-Gooders to Prove They Do Good', *The New York Times*, (3 January 2004).

10 Ondine Barrow and Michael Jennings, 'Introduction', in Ondine Barrow and Michael Jennings (eds), *The Charitable Impulse: NGOs and Development in east and North-East Africa* (Oxford and Bloomfield, CT: James Currey and Kumarian Press, 2001), p. 22.

11 African Rights, *Humanitarianism Unbound? Current Dilemmas Facing Multi-Mandate Relief Operations in Political Emergencies* (London: African Rights, 1994).

12 Mary Anderson, *Do No Harm: How Aid Can Support Peace – Or War* (Boulder and London: Lynne Rienner, 1999); *Patronage or Partnership: Local Capacity Building in Humanitarian Crises*, ed. Ian Smillie (Bloomfield: Kumarian Press, 2001); Alex de Waal, *Famine Crimes: Politics and the Disaster Relief Industry in Africa* (Oxford and Bloomington: James Currey and Indiana University Press, 1997); John Prendergast, *Crisis Response: Humanitarian Band-Aids in Sudan and Somalia* (London and Chicago: Pluto Press, 1997); Peter Uvin, *Aiding Violence: The Development Enterprise in Rwanda* (West Hartford: Kumarian, 1998); Wafula Okumu, 'Humanitarian International NGOs and African Conflicts', in Henry F. Carey and Oliver P. Richmond (eds), *Mitigating Conflict: the Role of NGOs* (London and Portland, OR: Frank Cass, 2003); Michael Maren, *The Road to Hell: The Ravaging Effects of Foreign Aid and International Charity* (New York: Free Press, 1997).

13 Anderson (Ibid.); Prendergast (Ibid.); Maren (Ibid.); Okumu (Ibid.), pp. 126-27; Francis Kofi Abiew, 'NGO-Military Relations in Peace Operations', in Henry F. Carey and Oliver P. Richmond (eds), *Mitigating Conflict: the Role of NGOs* (London and Portland, OR: Frank Cass, 2003), p. 27.

14 Peter Gourevitch, *We Wish to Inform You that Tomorrow We Will Be Killed with Our Families: Stories from Rwanda* (New York: Picador, 1999); Smillie, p. 187; Okumu, pp. 124-126.

15 Anderson, *Do No Harm: How Aid Can Support Peace – Or War*; Maren, *The Road to Hell: The Ravaging Effects of Foreign Aid and International Charity*; Prendergast, *Crisis Response: Humanitarian Band-Aids in Sudan and Somalia*.

16 Anderson (Ibid); Maren (Ibid).

17 Maren (Ibid.).

18 Anderson, pp. 43-44.

19 Smillie, p. 9; Uvin, *Aiding Violence: The Development Enterprise in Rwanda*.

20 See various chapters in Ottaway and Carothers, *Funding Virtue*; Sarah E. Mendelson and John K. Glenn (eds) (New York: Columbia University Press, 2002).

21 Michael Bond, 'The Backlash against NGOs', *Prospect Magazine* (April 2000).

22 Sam Vaknin, 'The Self-Appointed Altruists', *United Press International (UPI)*, 9 October 2002.

23 Lisa Jordan and Peter Van Tuijl, 'Political Responsibility in Transnational NGO Advocacy', *World Development*, 28 (December 2000).

24 Maren, *The Road to Hell: The Ravaging Effects of Foreign Aid and International Charity*; Vaknin, 'The Self-Appointed Altruists'; Thomas W. Dichter, 'Globalization and Its Effects on NGOs: Efflorescence or Blurring of Roles and Relevance?', *Nonprofit and Voluntary Sector Quarterly*, 28 (Supplement 1999): 55-56; Alan Fowler, *Striking a Balance* (London: Earthscan, 1997), pp. 31-32.

25 Fowler, p. 32.

26 Smillie, pp. 566-570.

27 Maren, *The Road to Hell: The Ravaging Effects of Foreign Aid and International Charity*.

28 In the West, dependency on state funding is particularly high among NGOs in 'progressive' countries such as Scandinavia, the Netherlands and Canada. For various estimates on and examples of NGO dependency on state funds, see Hulme and Edwards, p. 7; Michael Edwards and David Hulme, 'Too Close for Comfort? The Impact of Official Aid on Nongovernmental Organizations', *World Development*, 24 (June 1996): 961-962; Syed Hashemi, 'NGO Accountability in Bangladesh: Beneficiaries, Donors and the State', in Michael Edwards and David Hulme (eds), *Non-Governmental Organizations – Performance and Accountability: Beyond the Magic Bullet* (London: Earthscan, 1995), p. 108; Odd Inge Steen, 'Autonomy or Dependency? Relations

between Non-Governmental International Aid Organizations and Government', *Voluntus,* 7 (1996).

29 Edwards and Hulme (Ibid.); Zaidi, p. 264; Silliman, pp. 29-30; Hashemi, p. 109; Ian Smillie, *The Alms Bazaar, Altruism Under Fire – Non-Profit Organizations and International Development* (London: IT Publications, 1995), Ch. 9.

30 Smillie (Ibid.); Silliman, p. 30; Edwards and Hulme, p. 962.

31 Silliman (Ibid); Zaidi, p. 265.

32 Zia Gariyo, 'NGOs in East Africa: A View from Below', and Mahbubul Karim, 'NGOs in Bangladesh: Issues of Legitimacy and Accountability', both in Michael Edwards and David Hulme (eds), *Non-Governmental Organizations – Performance and Accountability: Beyond the Magic Bullet* (London: Earthscan, 1995).

33 Christopher Landsberg, 'Voicing the Voiceless: Foreign Political Aid to Civil Society in South Africa', in Marina Ottaway and Thomas Carothers (eds), *Funding Virtue. Civil Society Aid and Democracy Promotion* (Washington, DC: Carnegie Endowment for International Peace, 2000).

34 Antonio Donini, 'The Bureaucracy and the Free Spirits: Stagnation and Innovation in the Relationship Between the UN and NGOs', in Thomas G. Weiss and Leon Gordenker (eds), *NGOs, the UN and Global Governance* (Boulder and London: Lynne Rienner, 1996), p. 91; Smillie, *The Alms Bazaar, Altruism Under Fire – Non-Profit Organizations and International Development.*

35 Dichter, p. 47.

36 Silliman, p. 37.

37 Silliman, p. 30; David Sogge and Simon Zadek, '"Laws" of the Market?', in David Sogge (ed.), *Compassion and Calculation. The Business of Private Foreign Aid* (London and Chicago: Pluto Press and Transnational Institute, 1996).

38 Sogge and Zadek, p. 69; Dichter, p. 54; Shelley Feldman, 'NGOs and Civil Society: (Un)stated Contradictions', *Annals AAPSS,* 554 (1997): 50.

39 Sogge and Zadek.

40 Sogge and Zadek, p. 78; Dichter, p. 53.

41 Dichter, p. 54.

42 Silliman, p. 30; Maren, pp. 257-261; Sogge and Zadek, p. 86.

43 Maren, pp. 22-24; Smillie, *The Alms Bazaar, Altruism Under Fire – Non-Profit Organizations and International Development;* Okumu, p. 129; de Waal, pp. 80-81.

44 Maren (Ibid.); de Waal (Ibid.).

45 Silliman, p. 30.

46 Clifford Bob, 'Merchants of Morality', *Foreign Policy* (March/April 2002).

47 Ibid.

48 Ibid.

49 Slim, pp. 210-11.

50 Edwards and Hulme, *Non-Governmental Organizations – Performance and Accountability: Beyond the Magic Bullet.*

51 Joseph Hanlon, 'An "Ambitious and Extensive Political Agenda": The Role of NGOs and the AID Industry', in Kendall Stiles (ed.), *Global Institutions and Local Empowerment: Competing Theoretical Perspectives* (London: MacMillan Press, 2000).

52 Ibid.; Duffield, 'NGO Relief in War Zones: Towards an Analysis of the New Aid Paradigm'; James Petras, 'Imperialism and NGOs', *Monthly Review,* 49 (December 1997).

53 Petras (Ibid); Yash Tandon, 'An African Perspective', in David Sogge (ed.), *Compassion and Calculation: The Business of Private Foreign Aid* (London and Chicago: Pluto Press and Transnational Institute, 1996).

54 Petras, pp. 14-15.

55 Petras, pp. 12-16.
56 See <http://www.ngowatch.org>.
57 Marguerite A. Peeters, 'Hijacking Democracy: The Power Shift to the Unelected', manuscript dated 2001, <http://www.aei.org/docLib/20030103_hijackingdemocracy.pdf>.
58 Peeters (Ibid); Jeremy Rabkin, 'Why the Left Dominates NGO Advocacy Networks', paper presented at an international conference, *Nongovernmental Organizations: The Growing Power of an Unelected Few*, 11 June 2003, Washington D.C. <http://www.aei.org/docLib/20040203_Rabkin.pdf>.
59 Peeters (Ibid); Rabkin (Ibid.); Roger Bate and Richard Tren, 'Do NGOs Improve Wealth and Health in Africa?', paper presented at an international conference, *Nongovernmental Organizations: The Growing Power of an Unelected Few*, 11 June 2003, Washington D.C. <http://www.aei.org/docLib/20030624_bate.pdf>.
60 Bate and Tren, *Malaria and the DDT Story* (Institute of Economic Affairs, 2001).
61 Gary Johns, 'The NGO Challenge: Whose Democracy Is It Anyway?', paper presented at an international conference Nongovernmental Organizations: The Growing Power of an Unelected Few, 11 June 2003, Washington D.C. <http://www.aei.org/docLib/20030630_johns.pdf>; Jon Entine, 'Capitalism's Trojan Horse: How the "Social Investment" Movement Undermines Stakeholder Relations and Emboldens the Anti-Free Market Activities of NGOs', paper presented at an international conference, *Nongovernmental Organizations: The Growing Power of an Unelected Few*, 11 June 2003, Washington D.C. <http://www.aei.org/docLib/20030624_entine.pdf>; Jarol B. Manheim, 'Biz-War: Origins, Structure and Strategy of Foundation-NGO Network Warfare on Corporations in the United States', paper presented at an international conference, *Nongovernmental Organizations: The Growing Power of an Unelected Few*, 11 June 2003, Washington D.C. <http://www.aei.org/docLib/20030612_manheimpub.pdf>.
62 Entine (Ibid); Manheim (Ibid); Johns, 'The NGO Challenge: Whose Democracy Is It Anyway?' Bate and Tren, *Malaria and the DDT Story*.
63 Johns (Ibid); Bate and Tren (Ibid).
64 See the following webpages for details on these NGO initiatives: <www.peopleinaid.org>, <www.apnap.org>, <www.hapgeneva.org> and <www.sphereproject.org>.
65 See <http://www.ichrp.org/index.html?project=119>.

Chapter 4

Politics Beyond the State: Globalisation, Migration and the Challenge of Non-State Actors

Fiona Adamson

What are the impacts of globalisation, broadly defined, on state security interests? In this chapter I address this question by focusing on one particular set of activities that is facilitated by globalisation: processes of transnational mobilisation, which are undertaken by non-state political entrepreneurs who operate across national boundaries. Just as forces of economic globalisation produce global shifts in patterns of economic activity, so too do they produce shifts in the resources, infrastructures and capacities available to non-state political entrepreneurs to engage in political mobilisation both transnationally and globally.

Globalisation and Changing Incentives for Transnational Political Mobilisation

Globalisation processes are accompanied by the increased mobility of people, capital and goods, and ideas and information across national borders. This increased mobility creates a number of pull factors for political entrepreneurs by facilitating the creation of new transnational networks and resource bases that emerge independently, but can then be harnessed by political entrepreneurs during the process of political mobilisation. Just as globalisation creates incentives for economic actors, such as firms and corporations, to move their production facilities overseas, and to operate transnationally and globally, so too does globalisation affect the calculations of would-be non-state political entrepreneurs by providing incentives for political entrepreneurs to move beyond the state and to engage in processes of political mobilisation that stretch across national boundaries. The globalisation of political mobilisation and contention, like the globalisation of economic production, transforms the interests of, and the international environment inhabited by, states. [1] Political resources become partially de-territorialized, accessible to non-state actors beyond the state, and open to mobilisation by organisational structures that stretch across national boundaries. As I outline below, the increased mobility of people, capital and goods, and ideas and information all combine to produce new resource bases and constituencies that can be tapped into by non-state political entrepreneurs in the process of political mobilisation.

Mobility of People – Migration and Migration-Based Networks

The world has become increasingly mobile. According to the United Nations, there are now 180 million people living outside their country of birth, which is up from 80 million three decades ago. The percentage of the world's population that can be classified as 'migrants' has been steadily increasing over the last 30 years, and now one out of every 35 persons in the world is a migrant.[2] Migration to both Europe and the United States has continued to increase over the past two decades and, as Held et al. note, 'There is now almost no state or part of the world that is not importing or exporting labor'.[3]

The impetus for migration can be economic or political or, often, a combination of both. Economic migrants leave their countries in search of economic opportunities and employment. Refugees and asylum seekers leave their countries to avoid the trauma of war or political persecution. As opportunities for economic migration have been restricted in Europe, the number of those attempting to enter European states via the asylum process has increased. In reality, it is often difficult to disentangle the political and economic factors that contribute to the production of migration flows.[4]

Mobility of Ideas, Information, and Identities – The Emergence of New Political Categories

The increased mobility of people and capital in the global economy is accompanied by the mobility of ideas, information and identities. It has become commonplace to associate globalisation with cultural changes ranging from the emergence of increasingly cosmopolitan global cities, to changes in consumption habits around the world, to the rise of mass popular culture and the homogenisation or Americanisation of global culture. Information and communication technologies allow for the instantaneous dissemination of ideas and information around the world.

Scholars of nationalism have pointed to the role that print capitalism, the development of vernacular languages, and nationally-bounded communication infrastructures have had on the rise of nationalism and the development of homogenous national identities.[5] Yet with new forms of global communication technologies, the 'fit' between national cultures and territorial spaces becomes more tenuous. Satellite dishes and the internet allow individuals access to the media and information source of their choice. Viewers around the globe during the war in Iraq could choose to receive their information from a variety of different news providers, whether CNN, the BBC or al-Jazeera. The availability of satellite television and other media outlets means that immigrants, travellers or tourists can remain linked to a virtual identity community that transcends any particular geographic locale. Thus, for example, Turkish migrants in Germany are able to stay linked to developments in Turkey by watching Turkish television, buying Turkish newspapers and logging into Turkish web sites. Despite being physically removed from Turkish territory, they experience the simultaneity of information that Anderson argues creates 'imagined communities'.

The global marketplace of ideas and identities also provides resources for non-state political entrepreneurs. It is relatively easy, for example, to set up a web site as a virtual gathering place for a transnationally-defined community, and to use it to 'market' a new identity category to a virtual community. The internet has become used by a number of different Islaamist groups to bypass imams and other traditional authority figures, allowing new independent actors to disseminate their own interpretations of Islam to transnational constituencies around the globe.[6] Similarly, independent groups can found television stations and broadcast across borders, thus challenging a state's monopoly on the provision of information and the articulation of a national identity. Al-Jazeera and al-Arabiya are currently doing this in the Arab World. In the 1990s independently run Kurdish television stations had a similar effect in Turkey, when they broadcast banned Kurdish language programming, including Kurdish language lessons, into Turkey from Europe.[7]

Transnational Political Mobilisation and Networks of Violence

New resources that arise due to processes of globalisation are part of a number of 'pull factors' that provide incentives to non-state political entrepreneurs to operate transnationally. Such pull factors are accompanied by 'push factors', such as the lack of political opportunities and resources within a state to pursue a given political project. Keck and Sikkink have coined the term 'boomerang pattern' to describe the process by which activists can bypass the blocked institutions of a state, and directly connect with transnational networks located in other states as a means of pursuing their political goals.[8] By doing so, political entrepreneurs can engage in political activities, such as making connections with international NGOs and intergovernmental organisations (IGOs), that are designed, in turn to effect political change in the target state. In the process of doing so, local political entrepreneurs attempt to market their political cause abroad, engaging in framing activities that will link their local political concerns with existing discourses that can bring them both political and material support.[9]

Yet, while liberal constructivists have elucidated this pattern as it relates to liberal groups that do not use violence, there has been less attention paid to how similar patterns define the activities of non-state actors who include violence in their repertoire of strategies of contention. In actuality, non-violent and violent tactics are often intermingled as part of a larger grand strategy that seeks to effect political change by drawing on resources and opportunities at the level of the international system. Non-state actors often engage transnationally in conflicts or civil wars by making identity claims and raise funds by drawing on transnational networks.[10]

Political entrepreneurs operating transnationally build up cross-border organisational structures that command political loyalties and mobilize resources. Groups such as the PKK, Hamas, or even al-Qaeda, in some respects, fall somewhere on the continuum of transnational social movements and networks of violence, terror and crime. They are not just involved in violence, but also promote a political agenda, as well as providing goods and services, such as welfare, policing, education, employment, membership, identity and existential meanings – to constituencies that are marginalized within the given political order.

The Intertwining of Transnational Political Mobilisation and Violence Prior to 9/11

Examples of how these various factors come together in transnationally-organized violent political movements, which are also arguably types of NGOs, can be seen in a number of examples taken from the 1990s. The Kosovar nationalist movement, for example, provides an example of how political entrepreneurs bypassed the state and drew on transnational migration networks and grey economy networks in order to construct a Kosovar nationalist movement. During the 1990s, almost a third of the Kosovar Albanian population spent time working or living abroad, with approximately 400,000 Kosovar Albanians migrating to Western Europe.[11] This meant that dense transnational social networks connected Kosovo with diaspora networks in Western Europe.

These diaspora networks were drawn upon by Ibrahim Rugova's League for a Democratic Kosovo (LDK) as a means of mobilising counter-hegemonic identities and as a source of revenue to fund the establishment of parallel political structures in Yugoslavia. The LDK had its headquarters first in Ljublijana and then in Bonn, Germany. Ninety per cent of the funds it raised abroad were spent on promoting a parallel education system and cultural activities. These transnational networks also contributed to funding an independent gray economy sector in Kosovo.

In the early 1990s, it was estimated that remittances and gray economy networks accounted for 70 per cent of all economic activity in Kosovo. In 1996, an organisation calling itself the Kosovo Liberation Army (KLA) was formed in Switzerland, and began to broadcast Albanian language programming from Switzerland that was beamed into Kosovo and tuned in to by the local population. Simultaneously, activists in the Western European Kosovar diaspora launched a political lobbying campaign in European capitals – targeting states, NGOs and IGOs, such as the Organisation for Security and Cooperation in Europe (OSCE), the European Union (EU) and the North Atlantic Treaty Organisation (NATO).

The KLA raised money from a transnational diaspora through its international 'Homeland Calling' fund, as well as from revenues from the sale of narcotics funneled to the KLA through transnational networks of organized crime. Even the KLA 'army' in Kosovo consisted largely of hastily trained recruits from the diaspora in Western Europe who spoke 'better German than Albanian', and who were able to take advantage of the collapse of the partial collapse of the Albanian state in 1997 to obtain weapons and establish training camps.[12] The decision to use violence as part of their overall strategy was also, some have claimed, directly linked to international 'pull' factors that existed beyond the Yugoslav state. Kuperman, for example, argues that the KLA deliberately used violence to incite a Serbian retaliation as a means of gaining the attention and sympathies of the international community, in the hope of provoking an international intervention that would benefit Kosovar nationalists.[13]

Another example from the 1990s is the Kurdish nationalist movement in Turkey. During the 1980s and 1990s, while expressions of Kurdish language, identity and politics were banned in Turkey, a number of Kurdish political entrepreneurs went emigrated from Turkey and began to directly mobilize 'Turkish' immigrant communities in Europe. They promoted a Kurdish identity and language, established cultural organisations, and numerous Kurdish newspapers in Europe.[14] Many, but not all, of the political entrepreneurs were somehow linked to the Kurdistan Workers' Party (PKK), which was headed up by Abdullah Ocalan, who had established headquarters in Damascus, Syria, after leaving Turkey following the 1980 military coup. From Syria, the PKK simultaneously undertook an armed conflict, using tactics of both insurgency and terrorism, in southeastern Turkey and engaged in political mobilisation activities throughout Europe.

Exiles in Germany and other countries in Europe set out to build a pan-European counterpart to the PKK's political wing beginning in 1985, and successfully created a transnational structure that was organized as a network of local cells that, in the words of van Bruinessen, became 'an almost invisible network spread around the globe'.[15] A European Central Committee headed up the PKK organisational structure within Western Europe, with headquarters in Cologne, Germany and Brussels, Belgium, and national organisations in Germany, Belgium, France, Holland, England, Switzerland, Italy and the Scandinavian countries.[16] Throughout the mid-1980s to early 1990s the political wing of the PKK operated legally in most of Europe, with its above-ground, cultural, social and political organisations existing side-by-side with a parallel covert and tightly organized underground structure.[17]

The organisational structure included student groups, women's organisations and youth clubs.[18] The PKK organized cultural festivals and political demonstrations, Kurdish language courses, immigrant support groups, youth camps and parents' clubs. Political demonstrations and cultural festivals organized by the PKK in Germany regularly attracted crowds of between 50,000 and 70,000, and were filmed and converted into videotapes that are circulated throughout the diaspora.[19] The PKK published a daily Turkish language newspaper, *Özgür Politika*, which reported on events in Turkey and in the Kurdish diaspora in Europe. This all occurred simultaneously with the pursuit of a violent armed strategy within Turkey, as well as with occasional terrorist threats directed at European tourists in Turkey, as well as threats to undertake terrorist actions, including suicide bombing campaigns, within Europe.

The PKK was particularly active in raising money within immigrant communities in Germany, where it harnessed material resources from the community by collecting voluntary donations and 'taxes' of up to 20 per cent of individual salaries and business profits. It also relied on extortion and protection money, business investments, criminal activity and the drug trade as other sources of revenue.[20] Money raised by the PKK in Europe from donations and criminal activities was used to purchase arms for the conflict in the southeast of Turkey, and the PKK, like the KLA, also recruited in the diaspora. Recruits would take up positions as guerrilla fighters following a period of training in Lebanon, and others work as 'organizers, diplomats, technicians of various sorts'.[21]

These two examples of the transnational structure of both the Kosovar and Kurdish movements could be supplemented with many other examples from the

1990s and earlier. For example, Tamil nationalists have been able to construct a transnational movement that functions both as a political movement and as an organisation that supports terrorism. Operating in Canada, the United Kingdom and other European states, Tamil nationalists groups, often associated with the Tamil Tigers (LTTE), had some of the most effective transnational fundraising organisations of non-state groups during the 1990s. A combination of direct donations by Tamil migrant communities, money skimmed off from the budgets of Tamil NGOs around the globe, human smuggling operations, and Tamil-run businesses provided the funds for their $50 million annual budget. Tamil diaspora communities in the United Kingdom, Canada and Australia are estimated to have provided $1.5 million a month via donations and informal taxes.[22] Until recently, Hamas operated openly in Europe as a transnational political organisation, and openly engaged in fundraising activities there. Similarly, Kashmiri groups have engaged in both fundraising and political lobbying of their local MPs in the United Kingdom, while simultaneously pursuing an armed strategy in Kashmir.[23]

In short, the combination of political entrepreneurs operating transnationally, activating diasporas as a source of revenue and political support and drawing on transnational gray economy networks to fund armed struggles in their 'home countries' was a common feature of the international political landscape during the 1990s. A number of scholars expressed alarm at the growth of this new form of 'long-distance nationalism' in which 'positioned in the First World, [the political entrepreneur] can send money and guns, circulate propaganda, and build intercontinental computer information circuits, all of which can have incalculable consequences in the zones of their ultimate destinations'.[24] By 2000, it was beginning to be recognized that this transnational political activity might actually be having a measurable effect on the course of violent conflicts around the world. A World Bank report noted a correlation between the existence of a significant diaspora population abroad and the probability of recurrent violence in a state that has already experienced violent conflict. Whereas countries with no or insignificant diasporas experience a 6 per cent chance of the recurrence of violent conflict, the probability of renewed violence goes up to 36 per cent in countries that have unusually large diasporas abroad.[25]

Most of the examples above are of political entrepreneurs who used the ideology of nationalism, and drew on national categories as a means of mobilising transnational networks and engaging in processes of transnational political mobilisation. Yet the phenomenon was not limited to political entrepreneurs pursuing nationalist political projects – in many places political entrepreneurs armed with religiously defined political categories and ideologies were directly competing with nationalists for constituents. This was the case, for example, in immigrant communities in Western Europe. In Germany, Turkish Islamists mobilized second generation Turks; in France, the GIA and other violent Islamist extremist organisation engaged in recruiting activities. By the late 1990s, there was increasing concern about the mobilisation activities of Islamists in Europe. During the 1990s, as well, Osama bin Laden's organisation al-Qaeda began to carry out violent attacks around the world, and it became increasingly clear that in many conflicts around the world there were links between militant Islamist fighters that stretched back to their common experience of training in Pakistan and Afghanistan, first in camps organized by the CIA and then in camps organized by Osama bin Laden's network.[26]

Indeed, al-Qaeda's transnational organisational structure, mobilisation activities, fundraising activities and recruiting and training techniques are not unique or anomalous – they follow the basic pattern of many other groups from the 1990s, including the fact that they are embedded in a larger political movement. The transnational fundraising techniques of al-Qaeda, which include the use of informal networks, legitimate businesses, such as the honey trade, criminal enterprises, such as the drug trade, and global fundraising via donations and skimming money off of NGOs and charity organisations, follow a common pattern of transnational resource mobilisation that has been used frequently by non-state actors mounting a violent challenge to the political status quo. The difference with al-Qaeda is largely their target and in the scale of violence they have been willing to use to achieve their political aims.[27]

Hypotheses on Globalisation, Political Mobilisation and National Security

I have argued so far that globalisation provides new incentives and opportunities for political entrepreneurs to operate transnationally, and I have argued that the use of terrorism and other forms of violence is best understood as a violent component of broader political movements. In this section, I conclude the discussion by returning to the question of national security and briefly lay out four hypotheses regarding the impact that globalisation has on national security. The hypotheses are derived from the preceding analysis, which treats the transnational activities of non-state political entrepreneurs as intervening variables between the independent variable of 'globalisation' and the dependent variable of 'national security'.

In the wake of 9/11 in the United States, it became clear that the functional differentiation between agencies responsible for internal and external intelligence gathering and surveillance had become increasingly dysfunctional, leading to calls for closer cooperation between the Federal Bureau of Investigation (FBI) and the Central Intelligence Agency (CIA). The creation of a Department of Homeland Security is symptomatic of the pressures for institutional restructuring which accompany globalisation and the emergence of transnationally-organized non-state actors willing to use violence.

Under Conditions of Globalisation, Weakly Institutionalized States Emerge as Security Threats

Whereas in traditional state-centric balance-of-power security paradigms, security threats are thought to emanate primarily from strong states, globalisation produces conditions in which weakly institutionalized states also become the sources of security threats. This is because weakly institutionalized states lack the political channels for non-state political entrepreneurs to channel political demands and grievances domestically, thus contributing to the 'push factors' that create incentives for political entrepreneurs to turn to transnational political mobilisation. Additionally, states that are weakly institutionalized have many of the characteristics of anarchy, thus creating pressures for political actors to engage in self-help strategies that emphasize the use of violence and force to achieve political objectives, rather than strategies that emphasize institutional channelling, bargaining and accommodation.[28]

Krasner notes that 'the character of transnational actors will reflect the institutional environment within which they must function'.[29] Transnational political movements that emanate from anarchic or weakly institutionalized environments develop organisational structures and strategies that are rooted in the political logic of anarchy. At the same time, in order to operate transnationally, they must partially adapt to the political logic of hierarchy – hence the emergence of hybrid political movements that partially resemble the social movements that are found in highly institutionalized political settings, and partially resemble mafia-style networks of terror, organized violence and crime.[30] Because weakly institutionalized settings provide institutional incentives both for transnational political mobilisation and for the use of violence as a political tool by non-state actors, the weakness of states (including the lack of participatory institutions) comes to be seen as not simply a domestic problem for those states, but as a security threat. State weakness emerges as an international security issue.[31]

Globalisation Leads to the 'Domesticisation' of the Global Security Environment

Transnational political mobilisation, the blurring of distinctions between internal and external security threats, and the increasing convergence of internal and external security strategies all combine to lead to what might be referred to as the 'domesticisation' of the global security environment. It has become common in the literature on transnational social movements to point to how politics at the level of the international system increasingly resemble aspects of domestic politics. The transnational activities of non-state actors are commonly thought to contribute to the development of a 'global civil society' and the interaction between non-state transnational networks and international institutions leads to the emergence of new patterns of authority in international politics and embryonic forms of 'global governance'.[32]

In a similar fashion, the effect of globalisation on international security is one in which threats to international security and stability increasingly resemble the types of domestic security challenges that are found within weakly institutionalized domestic settings. Indeed, a number of analysts have described the conflict between the US and al-Qaeda as resembling an insurgency or civil war occurring on a global scale.[33] Networks that use violence or political violence to achieve their goals are common to states that lack either institutional development or legitimacy. As Huntington observed in 1968, increased political mobilisation in settings that lack adequate institutionalisation create conditions of instability and political violence.[34] One could make the case that the current international system resembles a developing world polity that is as yet weakly and unevenly institutionalized, lacking an institutional infrastructure that can produce the required levels of legitimacy and authority for stability.

Conclusions

Globalisation, defined as the rise of stateless forces, brings with it both dangers and opportunities. This is well-illustrated by examining the phenomenon of transnational political mobilisation by non-state actors and the emergence of global political movements. The increased mobility of people, capital and goods, and ideas and information, combine to create incentives for political entrepreneurs to engage in transnational political mobilisation and to build social and political movements that stretch across state boundaries. Such activities can, on the one hand, contribute to the emergence of a global civil society defined by cross-cutting cleavages and interests and thus, as liberals have argued, increases levels of stability in the international system. On the other hand, an increase in transnational political mobilisation by non-state actors who use political violence and terrorism to pursue their goals is obviously a destabilising factor, not just for individual states, but for the international system as a whole.

I have argued in this chapter that it is more useful to view non-violent and violent forms of transnational social movements as existing on a continuum, rather than being wholly different categories of political action. Acts of political violence, including acts of terrorism and the use of insurgency techniques, are extreme tactics, but nevertheless still tactics that belong to broader repertoires of contention which political actors use to achieve political ends. As such, al-Qaeda differs from other transnational oppositional groups that were active in the 1990s in terms of the scale of violence used and chosen targets, but not necessarily in terms of its fundamental organisational logic or structure.

Like other types of global political movements – whether global human rights movements, environmental movements or the anti-globalisation movement – the activities of non-state actors who employ violence produce broader patterns of change in the international system. Both non-violent and violent transnational political movements contribute to increased levels of dynamic density and interaction in the international system as a whole, and to the emergence of a global civil (and uncivil) society.

Notes

1   On the internationalisation of production and its consequences for states see, for example, Richard Rosecrance, *The Rise of the Virtual State: Wealth and Power in the Coming Century* (New York: Basic Books, 2000); Robert Reich, *The Work of Nations: Preparing Ourselves for 21st Century Capitalism* (New York: Vintage Books, 1992).

2 *Migration Policy Issues: Facts and Figures on International Migration*, No. 2 (International Organisation for Migration, March 2003).

3 David Held, Anthony McGrew, David Goldblatt and Jonathan Perraton, *Global Transformations: Politics, Economics and Culture* (Oxford: Blackwell, 1999), p. 297.

4 Aristide Zolberg, Astri Suhrke, and Sergio Aguayo, *Escape From Violence: Conflict and the Refugee Crisis in the Developing World* (New York: Oxford University Press, 1989), pp. 30-33.

5 Benedict Anderson, *Imagined Communities* (London: Verso, 1983).

6 Peter Mandaville, *Transnational Muslim Politics: Reimagining the Umma* (London: Routledge, 2001).

7 Amir Hassanpour, 'Satellite Footprints as National Borders: MED-TV and the Extraterritoriality of State Sovereignty', *Journal of Muslim Minority Affairs*, 18/1 (1988): 53-72.

8 Keck and Sikkink, *Activists Beyond Borders: Advocacy Networks in International Politics* (Cornell University Press, 1998), p. 13.

9 Clifford Bob, 'Marketing Rebellion: Insurgent Groups, International Media and NGO Support', *International Politics*, 38/3 (September 2001): 311-33; Alison Brysk, *From Tribal Village to Global Village: Indian Rights and International Relations in Latin America* (Stanford: Stanford University Press, 2000).

10 Mary Kaldor, *New and Old Wars: Organized Violence in a Global Era* (Stanford: Stanford University Press, 1999).

11 The Independent International Commission on Kosovo, *The Kosovo Report: Conflict, International Response, Lessons Learned* (Oxford: Oxford University Press, 2000), pp. 42-64.

12 Chris Hedges, 'Ethnic Albanians Leave Northern Europe to Fight in Anti-Serb Rebellion in Kosovo', *New York Times*, 6 June 1988; Chris Hedges, 'Kosovo's Next Masters', *Foreign Affairs*, 78/3 (May/June 1999): 24-42.

13 Alan J. Kuperman, 'Transnational Causes of Genocide, or How the West Inadvertently Exacerbates Ethnic Conflict in the Post-Cold War Era', in Raju G.C. Thomas (ed.), *Yugoslavia Unraveled: Sovereignty, Self-Determination, Intervention* (Lanham, MD: Lexington Books, 2003).

14 There are also at least 25 Kurdish publishing houses based in Sweden, Switzerland, Germany and elsewhere. See Nicole F. Watts, 'Institutionalizing Virtual Kurdistan West: Pro-Kurdish Politics in Western Europe', in Joel Migdal (ed.), *States and Societies and the Struggle to Shape Identities and Local Practice* (forthcoming).

15 Bundesamt fuer Verfassungsschutz, *Die Arbeiterpartei Kurdistans (PKK) – Strukturen, Ziele, Aktivitaeten* (Cologne: Bundesamt fuer Verfassungsschutz, 1996), p. 7. Martin van Bruinessen, 'Shifting National and Ethnic Identities: The Kurds in Turkey and Europe', paper prepared for presentation at the International Symposium, 'Redefining the Nation, State and Citizen', Marmara University, Istanbul, 28–29 March 1996, p. 14.

16 Gottfried Stein, *Endkampf um Kurdistan? Die PKK, die Turkei und Deutschland* (Munchen: Bonn Aktuell, 1994), p. 91; Henri J. Barkey and Graham E. Fuller, *Turkey's Kurdish Question* (Lanham, MD: Rowman and Littlefield, 1998), p. 38.

17 Stein, p. 86.

18 Ibid., pp. 96-98.

19 Paul J. White, *Primitive Rebels or Revolutionary Modernizers? The Kurdish National Movement in Turkey* (London: Zed Books. 2001), p. 175.

20 *Süddeutsche Zeitung*, 8 August 1997, p. 6.

21 Martin van Bruinessen, 'Shifting National and Ethnic Identities: The Kurds in Turkey and the European Diaspora', *Journal of Muslim Minority Affairs*, 18/1 (1998): 45.

22 Byman (et al.), *Trends in Outside Support for Insurgent Movements* (RAND, 2001).

23 Patricia Ellis and Zafar Khan, 'The Kashmiri Diaspora: Influences in Kashmir', in al-Ali and Koser (eds), *New Approaches to Migration: Transnational Communities and the Transformation of Home* (Routledge, 2002).

24 Benedict Anderson, 'Long-Distance Nationalism', in *The Spectre of Comparisons: Nationalism, Southeast Asia and the World* (London: Verso, 1998), p. 74.

25 Paul Collier, 'Economic Causes of Civil Conflict and Their Implications for Policy', World Bank Working Paper, 15 June 2000, p. 6.

26 John K. Cooley, *Unholy Wars: Afghanistan, America and International Terrorism* (London: Pluto Press, 1999).

27 Although, it must be remembered, for example, that the GIA had planned to fly a hijacked Air France plane into the Eiffel Tour in the 1990s. They also engaged in subway bombing campaigns in Paris. The PKK threatened suicide bombing campaigns in Germany, as well as Turkey, as part of their struggle.

28 Jack Snyder and Robert Jervis, 'Civil War and the Security Dilemma', in Barbara F. Walter and Jack Snyder (eds), *Civil Wars, Insecurity and Intervention* (New York: Columbia University Press, 1999).

29 Stephen D. Krasner, 'Power Politics, Institutions, and Transnational Relations', in Thomas Risse-Kappen (ed.), *Bringing Transnational Relations Back In: Non-State Actors, Domestic Structures and International Institutions* (Cambridge: Cambridge University Press, 1995).

30 The reverse logic also holds. For example, western NGOs that operate in weakly institutionalized settings sometimes resort to logics of anarchy, such as bribery and coercion in order to implement their political programs. See Fiona B. Adamson, 'International Democracy Assistance in Uzbekistan and Kyrgyzstan: Building Democracy From the Outside?', in Sarah E. Mendelson and John K. Glenn (eds), *The Power and Limits of NGOs: A Critical Look at Building Democracy in Eastern Europe and Eurasia* (New York: Columbia University Press, 2002).

31 Robert I. Rotberg, 'Failed States in a World of Terror', *Foreign Affairs*, July/August 2002.

32 See Daniel Deudney, 'Global Environmental Rescue and the Emergence of World Domestic Politics', in Ronnie Lipshutz and Ken Conca (eds), *The State and Social Power in Global Environmental Politics* (New York: Columbia University Press, 1993); Mary Kaldor, *Global Civil Society: An Answer to War?* (Cambridge: Polity Press, 2003); Alejandro Colas, *International Civil Society* (Cambridge: Polity Press, 2002); John Keane, *Global Civil Society?* (Cambridge: Cambridge University Press, 2003); Rodney Bruce Hall and Thomas J. Biersteker (eds), *The Emergence of Private Authority in Global Governance* (Cambridge: Cambridge University Press, 2002).

33 Anonymous, 2003; Martha Crenshaw, 'Why America? The Globalization of Civil War', *Current History* (December 2001): 425-32; Stein Tonnesson, 'A Global Civil War?', *Security Dialogue*, 33/3 (September 2002).

34 Samuel P. Huntington, *Political Order in Changing Societies* (New Haven: Yale University Press, 1968).

Part Two:
NGOs in Peacemaking

Chapter 5

Building Peace Norwegian Style: Studies in Track I½ Diplomacy[1]

Ann Kelleher and James Larry Taulbee

Peacemaking, once the province of the powerful and prominent, has attracted many new participants in the post Cold War era. Both the numbers and types of actors involved have expanded exponentially. Not only did NGOs begin to play a more salient role, but states once considered peripheral players became engaged in major peacebuilding efforts. Among these new players is Norway, interesting because of its small population and location in the remote north. 'Norway is well-known for having played a leading role in the brokering of the Oslo Accord in the Israel/Palestine conflict, and more discreetly in peace processes such as those in Guatemala (1996), Haiti, Sudan, Cyprus, Kosovo (1999), and Colombia (2000).'[2] Given its presence amid so many negotiations in the post Cold War era, and the constructive, quiet, behind-the-scenes diplomacy it has sustained for the long years it often takes to achieve an agreement, the Norwegian involvement in peacemaking merits attention and analysis.

Though many would deny that Norway has a definitive model for peacemaking, Norwegian initiatives do seem to draw on a definite set of common operational principles. This chapter will analyze the characteristics of the Norwegian approach as they relate to the Guatemalan and Oslo Channel examples. It then will examine briefly Norwegian involvement in the ongoing peace efforts in the Sudan and Sri Lanka to determine if the process categories derived from the earlier experience fit the later projects in any meaningful fashion.

Styles of Engagement

The multitude of players and arenas has spawned ongoing debates over the particular roles and efficacy of non-traditional actors in peacemaking.[3] While a number of different analysts have proposed classification schemes in an effort to clarify the landscape, the traditional division between Track I and Track II diplomacy offers one way to approach the Norwegian initiatives analyzed here. As usually defined, Track I diplomacy involves the actions and direct participation of official representatives of governments, while Track II diplomacy involves non-official personnel, grass-roots activity and perhaps back channel discussions.[4] Analysts often refer to tensions between the two tracks, but in Norwegian practice boundary issues have little importance. In fact, some commentators have characterised the Norwegian involvement in the negotiations that led to the Oslo Accord as Track I, while others have placed it in Track II, raising questions about the essence of the process that produced the final settlement.[5]

The thesis of this article does not entail examination of the relative efficacy of either track, but rather focuses upon the imaginative blending of the advantages offered by both tracks to effect favorable outcomes. Because of the nature of the interaction in these cases – the permutations and combinations of actors, methods and means of access – we have chosen Track I½ as the appropriate designation. From the perspective of those involved in the missions discussed, the two traditional tracks exist in a symbiotic relationship. The Track I½ designation seems to reflect that perspective. In electing this characterisation, we are well aware that Track I½ is often used to describe the activities associated with the semi-official high profile missions of individuals like former President Jimmy Carter or former United States Senator George Mitchell.[6] We believe that the Norwegian approach in the four cases analyzed in this chapter draw upon the same set of advantages attributed to high profile Track I½ initiatives with the exception that the Norwegian approach eschews publicity, preferring instead the shroud of secrecy. Norwegian initiatives deal with both leaders in government and those of insurgency groups rather than the usual interlocutors of Track II mediators. Because those most directly involved find Norwegian initiatives useful, they grant access.[7]

Why Norway?

As a peacemaker, Norway sprang suddenly from amid the confusion associated with the reshuffling of international roles after the Cold War. A relatively small, homogeneous population that enjoys a high standard of living has produced a highly educated, closely connected governing circle whose members move easily between public, private and semi-official roles. The Norwegian domestic political process emphasizes consensus creation rather than confrontation. Norwegians are accustomed to the time consuming process of sorting out strongly held convictions and dealing with shifting coalitions of interests. They consider their consensus building political style as aptly suited to the ambiguities and uncertainties of peacemaking.

Five mutually supporting factors help explain why Norway has emerged as a broker in talks aimed at ending deeply rooted, long-lived sectarian violence. First, it has developed a domestic consensus that pragmatically synthesizes Social Democratic and Lutheran global concerns for the oppressed and less fortunate.[8] The country's leaders, supported by a strong public opinion, believe that Norway should actively do what it can to promote international peace. Second, Norway has an honest broker image at least partly resulting from its decades of advocacy for, and involvement in, the problems of developing countries. During the anti-colonial revolution, Norway consistently supported programs such as the New International Economic Order promoted by the newly independent states.[9] Because it lacks any history of modern colonialism or interventionism, Norway has been able to present itself as a credible neutral third party in peacemaking enterprises. Third, during the 1970s and 1980s, even prior to obtaining its oil wealth, Norwegian governments sought to chart an independent path. Although a member of NATO, Norway did not permit bases or troops other than its own within its territory, pursuing a posture based upon 'reassurance' with respect to the Soviet Union.[10] This has given credence to claims of disinterested independence.[11] Fourth, while distinct from each other, the peace processes have benefited from a flexible, carefully considered, mutually respectful government-NGO partnership. Fifth, oil wealth means that Norway can afford to pursue its selectively focused yet long-term peace initiatives.

In developing legitimacy, Foreign Ministry officials generally agree that close relationships with NGOs have played essential roles in building trust for in their peacemaking efforts.[12] The network of Norwegian NGOs benefits from the country's general honest broker image. Moreover, Foreign Ministry officials rely upon NGOs because, 'NGO people have the needed local knowledge', and because they also contribute by building public opinion support in Norway for particular initiatives.[13] The close personal relationships between NGO principals and government officials, often at the highest levels, means that Norwegian NGOs have access and influence not enjoyed by others.[14] The symbiotic relationship actively integrates the organisations into the process in important ways. In both Guatemala and the Oslo Channel negotiations, Norwegian NGOs played a significant role in getting the parties to the table.

Second, Norway prefers to operate behind the scenes. Building trust takes time, patience, persistence and discretion. Needless to say these factors relate very closely to the ability to establish trust in the prospective brokers. Warring parties have many reasons not to talk. Publicity often inhibits real negotiation even if the parties have come to the table.[15] Moving from conflict to constructive communication may entail years and a willingness to accept many short-term setbacks. Hence the patience of sponsors in bearing both the monetary and psychic costs over time forms an important component of the process. Isolated from critics and media demands, those in the process can concentrate on exploring common ground for solutions rather than playing to their respective constituencies.

Active facilitation relies upon the previous four elements. Norwegians emphasize their role as facilitation not mediation. Jan Egeland, a former deputy foreign minister noted: 'The United States has big sticks and carrots it can use to mediate, but we are activist facilitators'.[16] A recent deputy foreign minister reinforces the point:

> As facilitator, Norway's role is to assist the parties in their efforts to reach a political solution ... A significant part of our effort focuses on promoting understanding between the parties: we spend much of our time acting as a channel of communication and helping them find common ground between their respective positions.[17]

Norwegian intermediaries will do everything they can to get the parties together and keep them together. They will make suggestions, provide a place to meet away from the public spotlight, and allow time to work through deeply felt differences. Their normal role might be characterised as 'aggressive good offices', rather than mediation or shuttle diplomacy as usually conceived. Norwegian facilitators will take a more active part only if the principal participants approve.

The distinction between facilitation and mediation has become a staple of the negotiation and conflict resolution literature. Many analysts now perceive that the mediation efforts of the 1990s often failed to produce lasting peace.[18] Walker makes a critical distinction: facilitation occurs when 'an impartial "third" party provides procedural guidance to group participants to promote constructive communication, information exchange, learning and collaborative negotiations'[19] Van der Merwe notes:

> But perhaps the most important distinction is that between the role of facilitator and the role of mediator. I have come to the conclusion that at times when one or more of the parties were not ready for formal mediation or peacemaking the quiet process of facilitation of communication helped unobtrusively to pave the way for an eventual negotiated settlement. It is thus important to acknowledge and encourage the role of the facilitator in apparent intractable conflicts which seem to leave no room for the mediator.[20]

Finally, Norway seldom undertakes a mission where it serves as the sole facilitator. Its efforts normally support and complement other initiatives such as those of the United Nations in Guatemala and the United States in the Oslo Channel negotiations. On the one hand, the fact that Norway lacks 'big sticks' serves as a plus in terms of image and developing trust. On the other hand, the fact that it lacks both 'big sticks' and 'big carrots' may limit the nature of eventual settlements without the ability to draw on, or provide access to, the resources and activities of other states and organisations.

Guatemala and the Oslo Accord

Background

Guatemala's civil war had raged for 30 years when, in 1990, representatives of the government and the guerrillas signed an agreement in Oslo that formally inaugurated the country's peace process. The violence included levels of barbarity noteworthy even by the standards set by other Central American domestic wars. Negotiations as well as periods of intense violence continued until December 1996 when several agreements ended the fighting. One of them, the cease-fire, was signed in Oslo.

By 1993 Israel and the Palestinians, as well as several Arab states, had maintained a persistent hostility punctuated by all forms of violence for even longer than the Guatemalan civil war. Successive cycles of Jewish settler-Palestinian bloodshed had occurred even before Israel became a state in 1947. By the beginning of the 1990s, Israel and surrounding Arab States had fought five conventional wars (1948, 1956, 1967, 1973, 1982). Yet Palestinians did not become directly engaged in a peace process until the 1991 Madrid Conference and its successors. When it first began as one of the spinoffs of the first Persian Gulf War, the Madrid process involved the major front-line Arab states and Israel, with Israel insisting that individual Palestinians could participate only as part of the Jordanian delegation. To Israelis, because they characterised the PLO as a terrorist organisation, even a tacit recognition of it as speaking for the Palestinian people would undermine years of government policy and fly in the face of strongly held Israeli public opinion. Therefore the decision by a high-ranking Labour Party official to permit Israeli academics to meet secretly with high-ranking PLO officials under Norwegian facilitation in January of 1993 carried very high political risk for both sides. The back channel dialogue occurred because the Madrid process had become stalemated. The secret Norwegian back channel produced the breakthrough agreement between Israel and the PLO formally signed in Washington, D.C. in September, 1993.

NGOs and Personal Relationships

In Guatemala, three Norwegians played highly significant roles: Petter Skauen of Norwegian Church Aid, Gunnar Staalsett of Lutheran World Federation and Jan Egeland of the Foreign Ministry in Oslo.[21] Petter Skauen had gone to Guatemala following the devastating earthquake of 1976 that claimed at least 28,000 lives. It took many years to overcome the innate distrust of the Indian population. A brief biography of Skauen notes: 'After all, in many respects Guatemala was an apartheid state where the repression of the Indians was commonplace'.[22] Skauen not only helped bring the plight of the Maya to international attention, he developed a number of personal relationships with Guatemalan government officials as well. The personal contact proved essential in that 'Given an opportunity, some of them proved to be open to information that challenged their longstanding attitudes'.[23]

In the case of the Oslo Channel, Terje Rod Larsen served as the critical middle man. He arrived in the Middle East when his wife, Mona Juul, a Norwegian diplomat, received a posting in Egypt in 1988. As a Fafo Institute[24] researcher, Larsen began a project documenting standards of living of Palestinians in the territories. While his research project yielded close contacts with the Palestinians, it also furnished him with connections to the political department of the Trade Union Confederation in Israel. The fact that the Labour parties in Israel and Norway had a long history of close ties, made even more mutually supporting because Norway had strongly supported Israel for decades, helped Larsen forge the necessary links. A recent PRIO report notes that:

> The history of Norway's involvement with the Middle East conflict throughout the post-war period is surprisingly lacking from nearly every account of the Oslo Back Channel. Recent research has shown that a very special relationship did indeed exist between Norway and Israel, long before the exciting days of the secret Norwegian Back Channel.[25]

In 1992 an individual at the Trade Union Confederation organized the first meeting between Larsen and Yossi Beilin in Tel Aviv.[26] At the time, Beilin, a member of Israel's Labour Party, headed the Economic Cooperation Foundation and was researching the potential for developing closer economic links between Israel and the occupied territories.

During their initial conversation, Larsen noted that in January 1992 his wife had entertained a delegation of Palestinians from Tunis led by Abu Ala, Arafat's senior economic adviser. Larsen and Abu Ala had talked for hours. Larsen had become convinced that Fafo could facilitate an Israeli-Palestinian meeting. After the June 1992 elections in Israel, the Labour Party organized the governing coalition with Beilin assuming the position of Deputy Foreign Minister in the new government.

Secrecy

As a factor in the Guatemala process, secrecy as an important element has not received much attention from analysts. The very minimal commentary may be due to the years of multiple track meetings among myriad official and unofficial actors. In addition, the process included many publicly noted meetings as well as secret ones. Important clandestine conversations did take place during the lengthy Guatemalan process. Jonas notes that: 'Toward the end of this first period, before the negotiations came formally under UN moderation, there was at least one other channel, an informal negotiating "track" sponsored by Norway, which had been playing a similar role in the Middle East; even some of the same individuals were involved'.[27]

In contrast to Guatemala, the meetings and substance remained totally secret throughout the Oslo Channel's twelve multiple day sessions held between January and August 1993. The participants feared discovery, believing that public knowledge of the meetings would effectively end the negotiations. As an important side effect, removal from public scrutiny can create an informal and intense atmosphere conducive to candor and trust building. The Palestinians and Israelis in the Oslo Channel developed the ability to share a joke, to use humor to break an impasse or to deflect personal animosity over disagreements.[28]

Time and Patience

Building the essential relationships requires time and patience. While the two cases under discussion have different time frames, keeping the process moving required a great deal of persistence because talks stalled more than once during both. Jonas reminds us that: 'Finally, this quasi-comparative exercise is a reminder that despite the enormous investment by domestic actors and the international community in dozens of conflict situations, the successes are painfully slow and minimal in almost all cases'.[29]

In 1989, guerrilla leaders in Guatemala asked Bishop Staalsett, the head of the Lutheran World Federation, to set up contacts with Guatemalan governmental authorities. Staalsett rang up his old friend Knut Vollebaek, then serving as

Norway's State Secretary (deputy foreign minister) to ask for a safe place to hold meetings and for the money to underwrite the talks. Vollebaek told him he could have what he needed.[30] It took seven years and the dedication of many to bring the talks to fruition. Norway remained deeply committed to the diplomacy of the Guatemalan peace process despite the setbacks and crises that threatened to derail the entire enterprise.

The participants in the Oslo Channel considered themselves as rescuing the Madrid process that had begun in October 1991, some months after the Gulf War. In comparison with the Guatemalan talks, the Israeli-Palestinian talks moved rapidly, culminating in September 1993. Yet a true evaluation requires understanding that the Madrid-Washington series of conferences comprised the overall context. All of those working in the Oslo back channel considered themselves as working within the larger process.

Foreign Ministry Funding

With respect to Guatemala, Norway hosted several formal and back channel meetings. Norway hosted the talks in 1990 which produced an 'Oslo Accord' for Guatemala that opened up the possibility of further discussions between the rebels, various important societal groups, the army and the government. Norway then sponsored the ongoing informal Consultas Ecumincas during the early 1990s involving sectors of civil society when formal talks bogged down. When talks resumed under UN auspices, the process produced three more formal agreement signings in Oslo – the signing of two substantive agreements in 1994 and the final, definitive ceasefire in December 1996.[31] In the Israeli-Palestinian negotiations Norway underwrote the expenses of the twelve Oslo Channel sessions as well as the travel necessary to secure final agreement from the United States.

Activist Facilitation

Those who have written about the Guatemalan peace process and Oslo Channel have noted Norway's low-key approach and disinterested participation. In the case of the latter:

> Egeland and Larsen were determined their country would play the role of facilitator, not mediator. The Norwegians would bring the parties together, use their good offices to promote trust and explain the difficulties each side faced to the other party. If the meetings developed into negotiations they would not take a position on the substance of the talks, or suggest the routes that should be taken ... but they would be there at all times to help smooth the way.[32]

Jan Egeland has emphasized, 'We haven't made peace anywhere. The parties have'.[33] In any situation, peace does depend upon the political will of the internal actors, yet this does not minimize the significance of the role playerd by facilitators. In Guatemala, Norwegian initiatives combined with extensive UN involvement and participation by many other states widened the context and enabled the parties to move beyond the limited logic of old style Guatemalan politics.[34]

These observations do not mean that Norwegian participants stay completely outside the talks and never become dynamically involved. In evaluating this factor the emphasis should fall on the 'activist' part. Using the Oslo Channel as a precedent, their activism can include shuttle diplomacy as well as 'refereeing' actual negotiating sessions. During the Oslo Channel process, a succession of the highest level Norwegian Foreign Ministry officials intervened at crucial junctures. Even before the sessions began in January 1993, deputy foreign minister (State Secretary) Jan Egeland met with Yossi Beilin in September 1992 to confirm Norway's commitment to finance the meetings.[35]

At the fifth meeting in May 1993, the new Norwegian Foreign Minister, Johan Jorgan Holst, attended two sessions. Later in the summer, when the talks seemed stalled, Holst engaged in shuttle diplomacy, visiting Arafat in Tunis, then the Israelis in Jerusalem, returning to Tunis to meet again with Arafat. At one point Holst offered to shift from host to mediator if both sides agreed. He subsequently intervened again early in September 1993, only days before the final agreement was reached, to use his skills to defuse the potential deal breaking issue of mutual recognition.[36]

Back Channel Efforts in Support of Formal Negotiations

In most instances, Norwegian involvement supports the efforts of a lead facilitator.[37] In Guatemala, the United Nations had the formal lead role from January of 1994 until the final agreement. Norwegian efforts prior to that time were never aimed at assuming the lead role, but rather at paving the way for formal talks to resume. Similarly, the Norwegians always envisaged the Oslo Channel as only one part of the public Washington negotiations, a private confidence-building enterprise that could augment the more formal efforts by others. With the consent of both the Palestinians and Israelis, the Norwegian Foreign Minister, Thorvald Stoltenberg, informed US Secretary of State Warren Christopher about the existence of the initiative.[38]

The Guatemalan initiative illustrates the pivotal role of NGO contacts. The Lutheran World Federation worked with the Latin American Council of Churches, the World Council of Churches and the National Council of the Churches of Christ in the USA to convene four ecumenical 'consultations' between the negotiating parties and various representatives from Guatemala's civil society.[39] This deliberate effort to keep the parties talking in an international church context provided a way for civic representatives to have direct contact with the negotiating parties as well as focusing international attention on the issues. At many critical moments, these venues provided opportunities for exchange of opinions that would have been difficult, if not impossible, in other available venues within Guatemala.[40] In particular, during the 1995 electoral campaign when the official talks had come to a virtual halt, the fourth ecumenical conference kept the dialogue alive.[41]

Sri Lanka and Sudan

To what extent do the factors discussed above illustrate a general pattern of behavior beyond Guatemala and the Oslo Channel? To answer this question we will briefly examine two recent cases, Sri Lanka and the Sudan. In Sri Lanka, Norway has played an unexpected role as the sole outside facilitator. In the Sudan, it has joined the United Kingdom and the United States as one of three 'outside observers'. Analysis of these two current ongoing projects should provide evidence to evaluate how well the general operational guidelines derived from earlier cases fit later initiatives.

Background

When peace talks formally began in September 2002, Sri Lanka had suffered 19 years of war characterised by suicide bombings, presidential assassinations and scorched earth campaigns. By late 2003 six rounds of talks had been held between the government, dominated by the country's Sinhalese majority, and the Liberation Tigers of Tamil Eelam (LTTE), the guerrilla organisation made up of minority Tamils. LTTE had been fighting for an independent Tamil state, yet it and the Sri Lankan government had agreed to Norwegian facilitation in 1999. As of early 2004, talks had broken down although a cease-fire seemed generally to be holding despite violations on both sides.

By 2002 Sudan had suffered over 30 years of devastating war between the Muslim government and various Christian and animist groups in the country's south. Direct talks began in April 2002 between the Sudan government and the Sudan People's Liberation Movement (SPLM), an organisation that advocated independence for the south as its objective. The talks took place under the auspices of governments in the horn of Africa led by Kenya and organized as the Inter-Governmental Authority on Development (IGAD). Three outside 'observers', the United Kingdom, the United States and Norway, have supported the talks with financial and diplomatic assistance. In July 2002 the parties signed the Machakos Protocol perceived as a framework bargain that, in effect, traded self-determination in the south for government implementation of Islamic law in the north. This led to ongoing talks that by early 2004 had produced a partial cease-fire as well as agreements about military issues and the sharing of future oil wealth.

Initial Requirement

In one way, the Sri Lankan case might seem an exception to the observation that Norway will not engage until the relevant parties have agreed to hold face to face negotiations. Yet in another way Norway's actions illustrate the significance its foreign policy makers attribute to direct negotiations between the parties. Norway had tried for several years to arrange face-to-face meetings between the government and the LTTE (Liberation Tigers of Tamil Eelam). Government legislation designating the LTTE as outlaws formed an important barrier to formal face to face talks.[42] LTTE had also made some effort to ascertain the willingness of Norway to take on the task.[43]

In December 1999 President Chandrika Kumaratunga formally invited Norway to act as a facilitator between the government and LTTE. Foreign Minister Knut Vollebaek subsequently met with a representative of LTTE in London in February 2000 and with members of the Sri Lankan government in Colombo later the same month. Following up, a formal delegation headed by deputy foreign minister, Raymond Johanssen, again visited Colombo in May 2000 to meet with government officials. Subsequently a team consisting of Special Envoy Erik Solheim, the principal facilitator, new deputy foreign minister Vidar Helgesen, and the Norwegian ambassador in Colombo, Jon Westborg, engaged in shuttle diplomacy in an effort to arrange for the two sides to meet. The first formal negotiation session between the parties did not occur until September 2002.[44]

In the Sudan, direct talks began under the auspices of the Inter-Governmental Authority on Development (IGAD), chaired by Kenyan Ambassador General Lazaro Sumbeiywo in April 2002. These included at least one meeting between the leaders of the Sudan government and the Sudan People's Liberation Movement (SPLM).[45]

NGOs and Building Trust Through Personal Relationships

Norway's pattern of working with Norwegian NGOs that have contacts on both sides of a violent conflict holds for both Sri Lanka and Sudan. Arne Fjortoft, who first came to Sri Lanka in 1967 as a journalist, founded CEYNOR, a project that sought to revitalize and expand the fishing industry.[46] Fjortoft later initiated another NGO, Worldview International Foundation that focused on the development of communications facilities as a tool to help the poor and disadvantaged.[47] Save the Children Norway (Redd Barna) first came to Sri Lanka in 1974 to set up a health center in the North.[48] Erik Solheim, Norway's Special Envoy, had ties to the LTTE through his membership in the Socialist Left party. In addition the Norwegian government through NORAD (Norwegian Agency for Development Cooperation) has had a long official working relationship with the Sri Lankan government.

Two NGOs provided support in the Sudan. Norwegian Church Aid (NCA) and Norwegian People's Aid (NPA) had financed projects in northern Sudan. Jan Erickson, former Secretary General of NCA, actively engaged in discussions that led to peace talks.[49] A project director for NCA, Halvor Aschjem, was described as being 'involved in day-to-day issues' during the negotiation process.[50] Aschjem later became the Foreign Ministry's Counselor at the Norwegian embassy in Nairobi.[51] NPA has worked in Southern Sudan since 1986 in the areas of disaster preparedness, food security, health care, community development, vocational training, and education for minors.[52] NPA's Community Development Program focuses on facilitating long term economic recovery, promoting sustainable rural development, and strengthening local institutions. Complementing the NGO contacts, Norwegian International Development Minister Hilde Johnson has known John Garang, the leader of SPLM (Sudan People's Liberation Movement) as well as several Sudanese government officials for a number of years.[53]

As with the Oslo Channel, where informality and intensity helped to develop a distinctive atmosphere, some evidence points to the slow evolution of a relationship conducive to constructive interaction. 'The GOS (Government of Sudan) and SPLM have gradually and grudgingly allowed the concept of a partnership to take hold, and, as a result, we have seen a quantifiable increase in compromise and flexibility in recent talks.'[54] The back channel endeavor of Halvor Aschjem in hosting representatives of both sides on his farm in Norway may have moved the process along.[55] The two sides have recently signed a wealth-sharing agreement.[56] The parties had previously signed an agreement on military issues in September 2003.[57]

Time, Patience, Secrecy, Funding and Facilitation

Norway had supported the negotiations that led to the 1972 peace in Sudan that ended a 17 year civil war. Conflict broke out again in 1983. Initiatives to bring the parties together to begin negotiations date from 1988 when the Norwegian Ministry of Development Cooperation, in conjunction with the University of Bergen, one of the world's leading centers for Sudanese studies, decided to sponsor a conference. The meeting, the first to bring leading politicians and intellectuals from all major political factions in the Sudan together to discuss solutions to the ongoing conflict, was held at the University of Bergen in February 1989.[58] Despite considerable debate the Bergen proposals did not produce any major movement toward peace. Norway maintained its informal efforts until talks officially began in April 2002. In this endeavor, Norway returned to its support role, working with the United States and the United Kingdom.

While Norway has attempted to maintain the confidentiality of the negotiations themselves, its role in both the Sudan and Sri Lanka has been relatively high profile in comparison to that in earlier conflicts. As noted above, some evidence of back channel negotiations has surfaced with regard to the Sudan. Because of the ongoing process, principals are understandably quite reluctant to discuss the presence or absence of other such secret efforts.

In addition to humanitarian assistance directed both through NGOs and other intergovernmental organisations, Norway has contributed personnel and financial resources to the Joint Monitoring Commission (JMC) that monitors the ceasefire in Sudan's Nuba mountains, and to the Verification and Monitoring Team established to implement the ceasefire.[59] Norway has agreed to host a donor's conference to deal with reconstruction after the signing of a peace agreement. To support the continuing peace talks in Kenya on the Sudan and Somalia, the Norwegians pledged $500,000 USD in February 2003.[60] The Development Ministry pledged another $450,000 USD in February 2004 to be used for repatriation of refugees and mine clearing.[61]

The Sri Lankan case demonstrates the perils of publicity. The moves of the principals were under constant scrutiny from the beginning. Although Norwegian efforts produced six rounds of face to face meetings between the Sri Lankan government and LTTE from September 2002 to April 2003, the exact nature of the Norwegian role became a divisive topic in Sri Lankan party politics as well as an issue between the government and LTTE. Within the government, the bitter rivalry between President Chandrika Kumaratunga (People's Alliance) and Prime Minister

Ranil Wickremesinghe (United National Party) effectively stalled further progress after the February 2002 ceasefire.[62] Beyond the question of whether Norway should facilitate or mediate, government officials openly questioned the impartiality of the Special Envoy, Erik Solheim, because of his personal relationship with the LTTE leadership. Initiatives to help mend the split between the government's political parties and personalities to achieve a unified negotiating strategy generated angry charges of intervention from supporters of President Kumaratunga.[63] Because internal Sri Lankan party politics had become so contentious the Norwegian government officially suspended its efforts in November 2003, a little less than four years after the initial invitation.[64] While no exact figures exist on the total cost, the Norwegian government had completely funded activities associated with the negotiations.

Summary

These last two case studies confirm that successive Norwegian governments have shared a common approach to peacemaking over time. While Norway's role in the Sudan reflects all of the fundamental considerations discussed above, the decision to engage in Sri Lanka as a very public principal third party went against secrecy and 'team player' as important factors. Nonetheless, the process that led up to the public invitation to act as the lead 'facilitator' in Sri Lanka embodies all of the elements discussed above. The act of 'going public' clearly violated the general preference to conduct relevant activities under the 'radar screen' of public scrutiny. The consequent controversy over the Norwegian role highlights the potential hazards of publicity.

Conclusion

Of the six factors previously discussed, one stands out – the reliance upon Norwegian NGOs as a central component of peacemaking initiatives. Norwegian contributions to peacemaking in both Sudan and Sri Lanka have drawn upon the depth of contacts and trust developed by NGOs over a long period of time. When Norway uncharacteristically stepped up to take the lead role in Sri Lanka, it did so on the basis of a longstanding positive relationship that had evolved in large part through active support of NGO activity. Similarly, Norway's close ties with Sudan result from NGO activity, which has helped induce the Norwegian commitment to the peace process.

Recent work on NGOs has emphasized their changing role with respect to conflict management and resolution. Richmond has noted that Track II diplomacy can have a much more complex texture than many analysts have granted. In the right circumstances Track II offers a multi-track approach 'in which citizen and unofficial diplomacy incorporate many aspects of civil society'.[65] Track II offers a 'bottom up', building from the grass roots approach in contrast to the top down, mediated solutions often touted in the past. In this process, NGOs who have become deeply embedded in societies can act as facilitators and conduits, that is as agents who make productive exchange among players possible and who provide 'ground truth' to governments and other interested parties.[66] No matter how sophisticated or widespread, the difficulties of making such efforts an effective part of the peacemaking process in any conflict have usually stemmed from establishing and maintaining a firm connection between Track II organisations and activities and those engaged in Track I interactions. On the other hand, critics have noted the dilemmas such interaction can generate – the elements often cited as strengths of Track II processes can also produce significant problems because of personal relationships, limited experience, limited focus and divergent agendas.[67]

From a different perspective, that of traditional top down diplomacy, we would suggest that the role chosen by Norway in Track I, with the possible exception of Sri Lanka, actually fit into a Track I½ characterisation as well. The Norwegians fully understand that they are not a world power. They bring reputation, moral commitment and a willingness to apply what resources they can muster to the table, but acknowledge that successful outcomes in these ongoing conflicts will require the coordinated efforts, influence and resources of the major powers. Hence Norway regards itself as team player, filling in the gaps, rather than as a primary mover. This does not imply a passive or minor contribution. Because of its connections, its willingness to fill gaps and take on tasks major powers find difficult to assume, Norway has emerged as an important player in peacemaking.

Notes

1 We would like to acknowledge the research assistance of Kami Rynisch in tracking down some important materials for this article.

2 Alan Bullion, 'Norway and the Peace Process in Sri Lanka', *Civil Wars*, 4/3 (Autumn 2001): 76.

3 For example, see: Oliver P. Richmond, 'NGOs and an Emerging Form of Peacemaking: Post-Westphalian Approaches', International Studies Association 41st Annual Convention, Los Angeles, CA (13-18 March 2000), <http://www.ciaonet.org/isa/rio02/> (Accessed 4 March 2004); Pamela Aall, 'Nongovernmental Organizations and Peacemaking', in Chester Crocker, Fen Hampson and Pamela Aall (eds), *Managing Global Chaos* (Washington, D.C.: United States Institute of Peace Press, 1996), pp. 433-444.

4 For a discussion of the definitions see, 'The Conflict Management Toolkit: Approaches – Peacemaking, 'The Johns Hopkins School of Advanced International Studies', <http://cmtoolkit.sais-jhu.edu/index.php?name=pm-diplomacy> (Accessed March 2004).

5 Diana Chigas (<http://www.beyondintractability.org/m/track2_diplomacy.jsp>) cites the Oslo Accord as an example of 'intervention with decision makers' and therefore Track I. 'Who Are Track II Intermediaries and Diplomats?' <http://www.beyondintractability.org/ m/track2_diplomacy.jsp> (Accessed March 2004). The JHU-SAIS discussion of 'peacemaking' characterises the initiative as Track II. Cmtoolkit.sais-jhu.

6 Dayle E. Spencer and William J. Spencer, 'The International Negotiation Network: A New Method of Approaching Some Very Old Problems', Working Paper, The CarterCenter of Emory University (November 1992), p. 29; Columbia International Affairs Online (CIAO), <http://www.ciaonet.org/wpsfrm.html> (Accessed January 2004).

7   Jan Petersen quoted in Frank Bruni, 'A Nation That Exports Oil, Herring and Peace', *New York Times* (21 December 2002), p. A3.

8   See Vidar Helgesen, 'Peace, Mediation and Reconciliation: The Norwegian Experience', State Secretary of Foreign Affairs of Norway's presentation in Brussels on 21 May, 2003, <www.odin.dep.no> (Accessed 12 January 2004).

9   'When the Norwegians again took the initiative in inter-governmental fora, it was oriented to socio-economic rights and issues relevant to the Third World. The idea of a New International Economic Order in the 1960s and 1970s represented a new era for Norwegian activism.' Jan Egeland, *Impotent Superpower – Potent Small State* (London: Norwegian University Press, 1988), p. 40.

10 Johan J. Holst, 'Norway's Role in the Search for International peace and Security', *NUPI Notat*: 264/B (April 1983): 4.

11 Nils Morten Udgaard, a columnist for *Aftenposten*, a major Norwegian newspaper noted: 'We are not Americans and we are not Europeans.' Quoted in Bruni, 'A Nation That Exports Oil, Herring and Peace'.

12 Helgesen, p. 5.

13 Personal interview, Ambassador Knut Vollebaek, Norwegian Ambassador to the United States, 1 March 2004.

14 Ambassador Vollebaek repeatedly emphasized the importance of personal relationships in these efforts, Ibid.

15 Mary Boergers, 'Track 1 ½ Diplomacy in Northern Ireland', in David Smock (ed.), *Private Peacemaking – USIP-Assisted Peacemaking Projects of Nonprofit Organizations* (Washington D.C.: United States Institute of Peace, 1998), p. 26; Roberto Morozzo della Rocca, 'Community of St. Egidio in Kosovo', in Smock (ed.), p. 16; Jane Corbin, *Gaza First – The Secret Norway Channel to Peace Between Israel and the PLO* (London: Bloomsbury Publishing Limited, 1994), p. 211.

16 Peter Ford, 'Norway as Peacemaker', *Christian Science Monitor*, 31 May 2000, p. 10.

17 Helgesen, p. 3.

18 Richmond, 'NGOs and an Emerging Form of Peacemaking: Post-Westphalian Approaches'.

19 Gregg Walker, 'Third Parties and Managing Conflicts: Some Fundamentals of Conflict and Mediation', <http://oregonstate.edu/instruct/comm440-540/ConMedBasics.htm> (Accessed 15 May 2004).

20 Hendrick van der Merwe, 'Facilitation and Mediation in South Africa: Three Case Studies', <http://www.gmu.edu/academic/pcs/vander~1.htm> (Accessed 15 May 2004).

21 Susanne Jonas, *Of Centaurs and Doves – Guatemala's Peace Process* (Boulder, Colorado: Westview Press, 2000), p. 62.

22 Joar Hoel Larsen, 'Deacon and Diplomat – Apostle of Peace from Fredrikstad', *The Norseman* (January 2002), p. 27.

23 Joar Hoel Larsen, 'Norway, Latin America, and the Peace Process', *The Norseman* (January 2002), p. 22.

24 Founded by the Norwegian Confederation of Trade Unions in 1982, the Fafo Institute for Applied Social Science conducts research and studies in the fields of labor relations, welfare policy and living conditions, both nationally and internationally. <http://www.fafo.no/english>.

25 Hilde Henriksen Waage, 'Norwegians? Who Needs Norwegians? – Explaining the Oslo Back Channel: Norway's Political Past in the Middle East', a report prepared by PRIO International Peace Research Institute (Oslo, 2000), p. 2 (Summary) <www.odin.dep.no/ud/engelsk/publ> (Accessed 26 January 2004).

26 Yossi Beilin, *Touching Peace: From the Oslo Accord to a Final Agreement* (London: Weidenfeld and Nicholson, 1999), p. 57.

27 Jonas, p. 43.

28 Corbin, p. 87.

29 Jonas, p. 230.

30 Ford, p. 1.

31 'Key Actors through the Peace Process', in *Negotiating Rights: the Guatemalan Peace Process*, Conciliation Resources site, <www.c-r.org/accord> (Accessed 6 February 2004).

32 Corbin, p. 40.

33 Ford, p. 10.

34 Jonas, p. 58.

35 Beilin, p. 84.

36 Beilin, pp. 106-113.

37 Helgesen, p. 6.

38 Corbin, p. 66.

39 'Lutherans Welcome Guatemala Peace Accord', *ELCA News* (29 December 1996), p. 2; <www.wfn.org/1996> (Accessed 6 February 2004).

40 Jonas, p. 61.

41 'Chronology of the Peace Talks', in *Negotiating Rights*.

42 "'The removal of the proscription of the Liberation Tigers is an essential prerequisite for talks", Thamil Chelvam, the leader of the political wing of the LTTE, told Solheim, according to the radio.' 'Tigers in with Norway Envoy Insist Lifting of Ban is Key Issue', *Agence France Presse*, 18 May 2001 <lexisnexis@prod.lexisnexis.com> (Accessed 5 February 2004).

43 D.B.S. Jeyaraj, 'A Norwegian Initiative', *Frontline*, 17/5 (4-17 March 2000).

44 'Sri Lanka Peace Talks', Royal Norwegian Government Press Release, 19 September 2002, Official site of the Sri Lanka Government's Secretariat for Coordinating the Peace Process (SCOPP), <http://www.peaceinsrilanka.org> (Accessed 2 February 2004).

45 'Memorandum of Justification Regarding Determination under the Sudan Peace Act', The White House, 21 April 2003, p. 2, <http://www.state.gov/p/af/rls/19806.htm> (Assessed 16 February 2004).

46 'Arne Fjortoft Inspired Norway-Sri Lanka Friendship', *Sunday Observer*, 21 March 2004; <http://www.sundayobserver.lk/2004/03/21/bus20.html> (Accessed 8 April 2004). CEYNOR received considerable funding from the Norwegian government.

47 Arne Fjortoft, Founder, Worldview International Foundation <http://www.wtn.net/awards/awards2000/policy/arnefjortoft.html> (Accessed 5 April 2004).

48 In 1999, Redd Barna became a member of the International Save the Children Alliance resulting in the change in name and logo. <http://www.savethechildren.lk/history.htm> (Accessed 6 April 2004).

49 Personal interview, Ambassador Vollebaek, 1 March 2004.

50 'Dialogue or Destruction? Organising for Peace as the War in Sudan Escalates', *Africa Report*, No. 48, 27 June 2000, International Crisis Group, <http://www.crisisweb.org>. (Accessed 17 February 2003).

51 Rolleiv Solholm, 'Norway Hopeful about Peace for the Sudan', *The Norway Post*, 21 July 2002; <http://www.norwaypost.no> (Accessed 14 March 2004).

52 Norwegian People's Aid in Southern Sudan, Relief Web, <http://www.reliefweb.int/w/rwb.nsf/0/884eeb71cee8e5a0852566590059cfb4?OpenDocument>. (Accessed 8 April 2004).

53 Personal interview, Ambassador Vollebaek, 1 March 2004.

54 'Memorandum of Justification Regarding Determination Under the Sudan Peace Act', US Department of State site, 21 April 2003, <http://www.state.gov> (Accessed 15 February 2004).

55 Personal interview, Ambassador Vollebaek, 1 March 2004.

56 'Peace Negotiations on Sudan. Agreement Reached on Wealth-Sharing Issue', Norwegian Ministry of Foreign Affairs, 8 January 2004); <http://odin.dep.no/ud/engelsk/ aktuelt/pressem> (Accessed 4 April 2004).

57 Ibid.

58 Abdel Ghaffaar M. Ahmed and Gunnar M. Sorbo, *Management of the Crisis in the Sudan* (Bergen and Khartoum, 1989); <http://www.fou.uib.no/fd/1996/f/712001/preface.htm> (Accessed 7 April 2004).

59 'Peace negotiations on Sudan'.

60 'Norway to Donate 500,000 Dollars to Sudan/Somalia Peace Processes', *Agence France-Presse*, 17 February 2003; <http://www.reliefweb.int/w/rwb/nsf> (Accessed 6 April 2004).

61 'More Norwegian Economic Aid for the Sudan', *The Norway Post*, 17 February 2004; <http://www.sudan.net/news/posted/7784.htm> (Accessed 6 April 2004).

62 D.B.S. Jeyaraj, 'The Facilitator Fracas', *Frontline*, 18/3 (23 June–6 July 2001); <http://www.frontlineonnet.com/11813/18130440.htm> (Accessed 5 February 2004). 'Sri Lankan President Slams Norway Over Truce Deal', *Agence France Presse*, 1 March 2002, <http://www.lexis-nexis.com> (Accessed 5 February 2004).

63 K.T. Rajasingham, 'Political Commentary 14: Norway Interfering in the Internal Affairs of Sri Lanka', *Asian Tribune*, 12 December 2002; <http://www.asiantribune.com/ show_chapter.php?id=54> (Accessed 5 February 2004).

64 'Sri Lanka Peace Talks Impossible Until President, Premier Resolve Dispute: Norway', *The Associated Press*, 14 November 2003; <http://www. lexisnexis.com> (Accessed 5 February 2004).

65 Richmond, 'NGOs and an Emerging Form of Peacemaking: Post-Westphalian Approaches'.

66 For a commentary on 'ground truth', see Eva Bertram, 'Reinventing Governments: The Promise and Perils of United Nations Peace Building', *The Journal of Conflict Resolution*, 39/3 (Sep., 1995): 387-418.

67 See Andrew Natsios, in 'The Conflict Management Toolkit: Approaches – Peacemaking,' The Johns Hopkins School of Advanced International Studies, <http://cmtoolkit.sais-jhu.edu/index.php?name=pm-diplomacy> (Accessed March 2004).

Chapter 6

Voices from the Parallel Table:
The Role of Civil Sectors in the
Guatemalan Peace Process[1]

Susan Burgerman

The government of Guatemala and its guerrilla opposition fought a civil war off and on from the early 1960s through 1996, causing massive devastation in the rural areas. Popular, labor, and opposition organisations were virtually dismantled during the period of heaviest repression, from 1978–83. Throughout these three decades, Guatemala had the highest degree of socioeconomic inequality in Latin America.

The Guatemalan case is important because including NGOs at a parallel table created a precedent for democratising negotiated settlements. An analysis of the conditions that enabled this to happen, and of the obstacles, benefits, and costs, is timely and useful because of the likelihood that future negotiating agendas to end civil conflict will include some type of mechanism for civil sector input. Recent scholarly writing on NGOs in peace processes has focused on the much more visible role of international NGOs, especially in humanitarian services.[2] Work on multi-track diplomacy has focused on the intermediary roles of neutral third parties and on third channel diplomacy by major international actors such as Jimmy Carter or Oscar Arias.[3] The direct influence of *domestic* NGOs on the contents of peace accords is both rare and understudied.

The role of NGOs was promoted and consolidated at four junctures during the Guatemalan peace process. First, the convocation of a national dialogue in 1989 created an institutional mechanism for cooperation between civil sectors. Second, direct discussions between civil organisations and the guerrilla delegation on substantive topics were convened during the first phase of formal talks in 1990. This established the mechanisms for future direct contact between NGOs and the negotiating parties. Third, an attempted executive coup in May 1993 caused a mass, unified mobilisation of diverse civil organisations that gave strength, momentum, and moral force to the multisectoral coalition, increasing its presence in national debates over the format and inclusiveness of the peace process. Finally, an Assembly of Civil Society was created by accord in January 1994, which acted as a parallel negotiating table.

Following two meetings between the CNR and guerrilla delegates that produced no concrete results, Catholic Church leadership began the process that ultimately engaged the nongovernmental organisations in the peace process.[4] On 1 March 1989, Bishop Rudolfo Quezada Toruño convened a National Dialogue of 84 delegates from 47 trade, labor, political, popular, human rights, indigenous, educational and small business organisations. They represented all civil sectors with the exception of major producers, whose peak associations, the Coordinating Committee of Agricultural, Commercial, Industrial and Financial Associations (CACIF) and the National Agricultural Union (UNAGRO), abstained because they claimed that many of the popular organisations were guerrilla fronts. Their objections were not taken up by the other sectors. Representatives from the United Representation of the Guatemalan Opposition (RUOG) and the Guatemalan Human Rights Commission (CDHG), the two major Guatemalan groups in exile (both widely considered to be URNG front organisations), were present as observers but were not invited to participate.[5]

Fifteen commissions were formed to present working papers for discussion at plenary sessions on a variety of topics, with the ultimate goal of outlining an agenda for eventual direct negotiations between the URNG and the government.[6] The National Dialogue created an arena in which, for the first time in recent history, diverse members of Guatemalan society met as equals for the purpose of discussing contested issues and influencing the political agenda.

The first summit of URNG and government representatives took place in Oslo on 30 March 1990. At this point the official parties (the government, the military, and the URNG) had still not agreed to negotiate, and therefore the initiative in the process was held by nongovernmental actors – the CNR, the Church, and international NGOs – who had an interest in including domestic NGOs. The accord signed at Oslo called for the URNG and CNR to meet in the following weeks with representatives of the popular, religious, and business sectors, and political parties in order to develop solutions to Guatemala's problems. Bishop Quezada was to officiate at the meetings and a UN representative was to observe. Accordingly, the URNG met with representatives of the nine major political parties at El Escorial in Spain from 27 May–1 June 1990. The next meeting was held in Ottawa on 31 August–1 September with nine high level representatives of CACIF. Representatives of Catholic, Protestant, and Jewish religious communities met with the URNG in Quito on 24–26 September.[7] Finally, meetings were held with popular organisations on 23–25 October in Metepec, and with academic, professional, cooperative, and small business sectors on 27–28 October in Atlixco, both in Mexico. With the exception of the Ottawa meeting with CACIF, each round produced a joint declaration of principles that was disseminated to the interested public. By means of these five meetings, the URNG was able to incorporate key demands of civilian interest groups into its own negotiating strategy, and the NGOs had the opportunity to be the first to define the peace agenda.

The meeting with popular organisations in Metepec demonstrates the importance of cohesion and cooperation among NGOs, and the threat to cohesion that results from a perceived lack of autonomy from negotiating parties. Twenty labor and other popular and rights organisations met with the URNG at Metepec. Approximately 100 organisations made themselves available to participate; the

URNG selected five of these, including the Mutual Support Group (GAM), at the time the most prominent Guatemalan human rights organisation. The remaining 15 participants were internally elected. The URNG's selection created considerable dissension among the popular organisations. Some members of GAM's leadership were rumored to have extensive ties to the Guerrilla Army of the Poor (EGP), one of the component parts of the URNG. On that basis GAM's selection by the URNG was considered to indicate sympathy, if not outright affiliation.[8] The conflict was overcome for the purpose of the Metepec meeting, but this kind of tension within the civil society organisations would later emerge as public discord when they needed to cooperate in developing the terms of consensus proposals for the formal negotiations.

As with the National Dialogue, political opportunity for NGO participation during the Oslo round was provided by the terms of a signed accord, and by the accompaniment of strong institutional allies – in this case, the CNR, the Church, and the United Nations. Furthermore, direct contact with one of negotiating parties set a precedent for (albeit partial and indirect) access to the negotiating table. NGOs responded to the opportunity by, first, overcoming internal differences, and then by coalescing into two umbrella organisations that further increased their capacity for dialogue, despite the disunity that developed later.

Autogolpe

Facing threats of a general strike and uncontrollable student riots, on 25 May 1993 President Jorge Serrano (1991-May 1993) suspended the constitution and the other branches of government.[9] Within hours both Human Rights Ombudsman Ramiro de León Carpio and indigenous leader and Nobel Prize laureate Rigoberta Menchú appeared on television denouncing the coup and calling for popular mobilisation in protest.[10] A cross section of civil society immediately responded, including the board of directors of CACIF, who contacted trade unions, cooperatives, political party leaders, attorneys and judicial workers to form a Forum of Social Sectors (*Foro Multisectoral Social*). They were soon joined by religious leaders, popular organisations, academics, and journalists. On May 30, an Association for National Consensus (*Instancia Nacional de Consenso*) was created that included the full spectrum of NGOs. The original Forum continued throughout the days following the autogolpe to develop and circulate documents analysing the consequences of the crisis for all sectors of Guatemalan society. They specifically appealed to pragmatic members of the military high command with their analysis of what a coup would cost the country.[11] Demonstrations continued through the first week. Given the private sector's opposition to the autogolpe and the threat of international economic isolation, the majority of the high command joined the civil sectors in demanding Serrano's resignation. They agreed to comply with a June 4 Constitutional Court ruling that declared the presidency and vice presidency vacant and ordered Congress to designate a new executive. The *Instancia Nacional de Consenso* provided Congress with three approved candidates, and on June 5 Congress elected Ramiro de León Carpio to serve the remainder of Serrano's term.

During the final months of the year, the civil sectors were struggling to keep their issues from becoming sidelined. The *autogolpe* had given rise to an unprecedented degree of cohesion among the NGOs. Dissimilar groups had, if briefly, united to overcome a breach of the constitutional order. This event further consolidated the emergence of civil sectors in Guatemalan politics and gave impetus to their demands for direct participation in the peace process, even though the *Instancia Nacional de Consenso*'s cohesion failed to hold.

The Assembly of Civil Society

The United Nations Department of Political Affairs convoked a meeting of the parties in January 1994 in order to jumpstart the stalemated talks. The parties signed a new Framework Accord, the terms of which created a new institution, the Assembly of Civil Society (ASC), to consist of all legitimate, representative, and legal sectors of Guatemalan society. It was designed to produce recommendations for submission to the negotiating table on the topics yet to be addressed by the parties, and to evaluate the accords signed on those topics in order to facilitate in their implementation. The ASC was not given veto power over accords, nor was there a guarantee that the NGOs' consensus documents would be given equal weight to the negotiating parties' proposals. Nonetheless, the effect of their direct inclusion in the peace process was to hold the government and URNG accountable to their social bases.

Bishop Quezada was requested to act as President of the Assembly, and an Organising Committee was established comprising representatives of each of the sectors that had participated in the May-October 1990 Oslo round meetings, plus the indigenous organisations. CACIF was the only organisation that had participated in the Oslo round, and the only major NGO, to refuse membership. The absence of the major producers' peak association mainly weakened the ASC document on socioeconomic and agrarian issues, for which CACIF offered its own proposal.

The Assembly was formally established on 17 May 1994. Within the next few months, the delegates produced consensus documents on the resettlement of displaced populations, indigenous rights, the socioeconomic and agrarian situation, civil-military relations, and constitutional and electoral reforms. Despite the difficulties of achieving consensus on such controversial issues, the ASC had completed and submitted all of its proposals by the end of October 1994, before its December deadline and well in advance of the two negotiating parties' proposals.

The most significant line of confrontation was between maximalist indigenous organisations and the 'mainstreamed' human rights NGOs. Indigenous communities were at an overall disadvantage in this debate: they had a much lower level of literacy than the general population and their leadership on average was less educated than many of the human rights leaders; they had to contend with centuries-old language and cultural biases, and brought less in the way of organisational skills, training, and resources. The human rights NGOs by contrast were higher profile, commanded a great deal more international attention and publicity, and had comparatively elite educated leadership. Although the human rights and indigenous organisations had overlapping membership, tactics, and objectives, nevertheless real differences became apparent when they had to debate issues such as political autonomy and land restoration that mattered deeply to one sector but were considered diversionary or strategically misguided by the other.

In the end, Quezada's leadership and the growing cooperative norms among the Assembly delegates created sufficient cohesiveness to overcome the discord. A consensus document was produced on July 8, incorporating the majority of the Mayan sectors' proposals.

Negotiations on the final substantive accord, strengthening civilian authority and the role of the military in a democratic society, began the following month and an agreement was signed in September. Once again, the accord covered most of the key points in the ASC consensus document. The mandated reforms to the military, police, and intelligence apparatuses were particularly significant gains for the human rights organisations, as they restructured, downsized, or dismantled many of the institutions most directly responsible for egregious human rights violations.[12]

With this accord, negotiations on the topics for which the Assembly had submitted consensus documents were completed. Political opportunity during this final phase of negotiations was provided by the terms of the Framework Accord, which mandated NGO participation, and was institutionalized in the Assembly of Civil Society. Civil organisations were further able to take advantage of the political dynamics of the process by leveraging moments of weakness on the part of both the URNG and the government. Despite CACIF's abstention and the tensions surrounding the indigenous debate, the Assembly maintained its cohesion as long as needed to influence the accords. To a great extent this was due to Quezada's strong leadership and the members' increasing adoption of cooperative norms of engagement and dialogue. A final accord was signed on 29 December 1996, ending the period of civil war and opening a more complicated period of building the peace.

The process soon ran into severe obstacles, primarily of a political nature, but also stemming from a legacy of the negotiations: the agreements are unusually comprehensive, but also in many cases vague and lacking in specific benchmarks, indicators of compliance, means to achieve compliance, and assignment of specific parties to be held responsible for implementation. Some analysts consider this experiment to have been a failure, and cite it as evidence that NGO participation at a parallel table places inordinate demands on a peace process, by requiring warring parties to negotiate reforms that are too far-reaching, create unrealistic expectations, and diffuse the responsibility for implementation.[13] I argue that the benefits, especially the increased likelihood of addressing problems that led to the conflict in the first place, outweigh the detractions. Regardless of debates over the representativeness of the ASC or the implementation commissions, the process itself has created opportunities for popular ownership of the peace. And despite the spectacular descent into insecurity and violence that has taken place since 1998, and the collapse of the constitutional reforms necessary to implement the majority of security-related agreements, the Guatemalan peace process is not a complete failure. The government can be and is held accountable for the reforms it (as the Guatemalan state) negotiated, and reforms that do not depend on constitutional amendment have been implemented. Furthermore, the failures are not due to the participatory format of the negotiations and the implementation process, but rather to the strength and institutional support of peace spoilers who remain in power.

The role of NGOs in the Guatemalan peace process was unique. First, international human rights NGOs aligned with domestic activists to initiate the negotiations. Second, the process of dialogue in and of itself contributed to the development of tolerance and cooperative norms in one of the most divided and demoralized populations in Latin America. The necessity for political, economic, and military elites to cooperate with popular organisations in order to develop the agreements did lead to a much less polarized environment, despite the continuing anti-democratic behavior of atavistic leaders in government. Finally, NGOs directly participated in the design of an accords package that is remarkable in the breadth and substance of the issues addressed, although often vague and light on details, and certainly less than successful in guaranteeing the means for their implementation.

The Guatemalan experience highlights the need to coordinate the conflicting interests inherent in a participatory forum that encompasses diverse social and economic groups, including marginalized communities. At a critical moment in producing a consensus document on indigenous rights, contention between indigenous and other sectors nearly derailed the Assembly and temporarily cast a shadow on its credibility as a representative institution. One can easily imagine other such scenarios, for example disagreements between competing ethnic groups, or conflicting goals of women's and labor organisations.

Notes

1 Research for this chapter was assisted by an International Predissertation Fellowship from the Social Science Research Council and the American Council for Learned Societies, with funds provided by the Ford Foundation.
2 See 'Mitigating Conflict: The Role of NGOs', Henry F. Carey and Oliver P. Richmond (eds), *Journal Of International Peacekeeping*, 10/1 (Spring 2003).
3 See especially *Herding Cats: Multiparty Mediation in a Complex World*, Chester A. Crocker, Fen Osler Hampson and Pamela Aall (eds) (Washington, DC: United States Institute of Peace Press, 1999); also Crocker, Hampson, and Aall, 'A Crowded Stage: Liabilities and Benefits of Multiparty Mediation', *International Studies Perspectives*, 2/1 (February 2001); and Landon E. Hancock, 'To Act or Wait: A Two-Stage View of Ripeness', *International Studies Perspectives*, 2/2 (May 2001).
4 Tanya Palencia Prado, *Peace in the making: Civic groups in Guatemala*, trans. David Holiday and Matthew Creelman (London: Catholic Institute for International Relations, 1996), p. 11.
5 Robert H. Trudeau, *Guatemalan Politics: The Popular Struggle for Democracy* (Boulder: Lynne Rienner Publishers, 1993), p. 136.
6 Author's interview with Rolando Cabrera, director of FUNDAPAZD and secretary general of the Asamblea de la Sociedad Civil, 2 August 1995.

7 It should be noted that Mayan religious organisations were not invited to this meeting; they and various nontraditional evangelical groups protested their apparent exclusion.
8 Author's interview with Mario Polanco, GAM co-director, 6 March 1995.
9 For a comprehensive description of the May 1993 autogolpe, please see Rachel M. McCleary, *Dictating Democracy: Guatemala and the End of Violent Revolution* (Gainesville: University Press of Florida, 1999).
10 Rachel McCleary, 'The Constitutional Crisis in Guatemala: The Responses of the International Community and Guatemalan Society; A Report of an International Conference' (Washington, DC: United States Institute of Peace, 1994), p. 4.
11 McCleary, *Dictating Democracy*, pp. 109-114.
12 *Prensa Libre*, 'Gobierno y URNG firman ultimo acuerdo sustantivo de las negociaciones de paz', 20 September 1996.
13 See, for example, William Stanley and David Holiday, 'Everyone Participates, No One is Responsible: Peace Implementation in Guatemala', working paper contributed to the Stanford CISAC/International Peace Academy Project on Peace Plan Implementation, August 1999.

Chapter 7

Practicing Peace: The Role of NGOs in Assisting 'Zones of Peace' in Colombia

Catalina Rojas

Colombia's conflict is the oldest armed conflict in the Americas. Nearly four-decades of armed confrontations between several armed organisations, FARC (Colombian Revolutionary Armed Forces), ELN[1] (National Liberation Army), AUC[2] (Self Defense Units of Colombia) and the Colombian Army. Currently, all peace efforts from civil society organisations continue despite confrontations among the major-armed actors. Colombia's state is a fragile one, currently disputing political and territorial sovereignty with a number of violent actors including guerrillas, drugs traffickers, self-defense units, paramilitaries, and subject to common delinquency. Because of this complex association of violent actors, civilians are the most vulnerable.

Colombia's civil society, part of which is organized in NGOs, is quite complex and rich in its variety of actors including peasants, students, union workers, women, associations of relatives of kidnapped and disappeared people, and many others. Likewise, peace initiatives from various Colombian NGOs' and the citizens' peace movement in general, range from pressuring the national government to start a negotiation process; to organising thousands of women marching the streets of Bogotá and Putumayo in 2002 and 2003; to supporting local resistance processes of peace. One of the many local resistance processes conducted in Colombia in the last few years is the 'One Hundred Municipalities of Peace' conducted by REDEPAZ, the oldest peace network in Colombia. The peace umbrella organisation REDEPAZ is a network of more than 400 organisations with active presence in all the regions of the country. REDEPAZ mandate is to generate the conditions for a peaceful resolution of the conflict by pressuring all of the armed actors to stop the war. Such effort has been uninterrupted for the past ten years, amid exceptional security[3] and financial[4] constraints.

One example of how REDEPAZ has worked with local communities was the project 'One Hundred Municipalities of Peace', initiated in the year 2001. This project responded to the situation of the most vulnerable sector that is currently suffering the consequences of the armed confrontation in remote regions of Colombia, often under the control of armed actors and historically abandoned and unattended by the Colombian State. As some of the written material about the 'One Hundred Municipalities of Peace' states:

The project is thus based on the notion that *unarmed civilians are not only victims of armed confrontations but actors of peace*[5] within their own communities. Much has been said about the need to complement the formal negotiation process between the elites of the parties with democratising, bottom-up processes. Zones of Peace such as Mogotes, Samaniego and San Pablo are concrete examples of citizen, governmental and non-profit cooperation to protect the life, the land and the dignity of unarmed civilians.

The 'One Hundred Municipalities for Peace' project was inspired in a small community called 'Mogotes' whose citizens declared their town a peace territory in 1998. Hence, REDEPAZ used the case of 'Mogotes' as an example of local citizen peace initiative that could be reproduced in other locations such as municipalities, schools and neighborhoods. This is the origin of the project funded by the European Union.

By illustrating the process, development, obstacles and current challenges of establishing a zone of peace, I attempt to address the following themes:

1. Symbiosis *between NGOs and local communities* in creating and sustaining a ZOP.
2. *Violence resistance*: the process of developing the notion of 'active neutrality'.
3. The process of disarming the 'war machinery'[6] by reacquiring spaces for peace.

The event that triggered the decision of the inhabitants of Mogotes to declare their village a peace territory was after 150 armed men and women of ELN took control of the municipality the 11th of December, 1997, with the intention of judging the mayor charged with corruption. In that action, three policemen and one civilian were killed. As a response to the assassinations and subsequent crisis, the communal leaders called for a '*Municipal Constitutional Assembly*' in which two hundred people, some from Mogotes and some from the adjunct rural villages formed the assembly. Unanimously, the participants requested the guerrilla organisation free the mayor, Dorían Rodríguez, and for him to be democratically 'judged' by the citizens. After a popular vote, the town decided to discharge the major from his duties and called for new elections. José Angel Guadrón was subsequently elected the new mayor intending to implement the governance program suggested at the Municipal Assembly together with the process of municipal reform also suggested at the forum. The experience of Mogotes is one of citizen participation for social change and non-violent conflict resolution. Mogotes declared their municipality a ZOP in 1998. In 1999, Mogotes received national and worldwide recognition through the National Peace Prize. Diplomats, union leaders, non-profit leaders, Catholic Church priests, the media, all visited Mogotes. One year of receiving the award, an event was organized by the Municipal Assembly, REDEPAZ and the Catholic Offices in Santader to subscribe together a 'Commitment Letter' with the objective of strengthening Mogotes' engagement in peace.

As was mentioned before, Mogotes' experience was so powerful that it led REDEPAZ to replicate this process in one hundred municipalities all over the Colombian territory as has been described above. However, as in any process that is not based on force or coercion, the intent to isolate the community from the territorial, political, social and, economic influence of the violent actors with the use of non-violence, can prove hard. Hence, ELN executed the mayor originally charged of corruption in 1997. In retaliation, the major's relatives publicly accused one of the leaders of the Municipal Assembly and the process of political renovation and citizen power started to show 'signs of fracture'. After a while, the process regained force and the community began gaining cohesiveness after a Catholic father entered a 4-day hunger strike offering his life to the process. The community requested the violent actors to show respect for the process. The hunger strike was stopped when insurgents (armed actors) and REDEPAZ (NGOs) went to the town of Mogotes and reiterated a commitment to peace. The people of Mogotes are indeed remarkable. For example, they modified the title of mayor to one of *manager*, thus transforming the whole concept of public service, moving away from clientele-based politics to more efficiency and merits-based way of handling public affairs. Periodically he/she has to present a public report in the inhabitants in the public plaza. Long question and answers sessions are the ruling dynamics of social change, in a town characterized by unemployment and minimal presence of the state. Quoting the words of Diana Angel, a member of the REDEPAZ staff in Bogotá, who visited the village: 'Mogotes is the living example of a small Athens, in the middle of nowhere in Colombia'.

Today Mogotes is still under the threat of ELN forces. In addition, a much more deadly threat is attempting to enter the zone: the paramilitaries. Currently ELN and the paramilitaries are in dispute over control of the surrounding province of García Rovira. Despite the pressure from the paramilitaries, and the previous crisis, Mogotes still defines itself as an autonomous ZOP.

Samaniego has been another ZOP for the past three years. The town is under the direct influence of ELN, which monitors the process of elections.[7] The main problem however, is the situation of displaced people coming from Putumayo, as a result of the humanitarian crisis – a by-product of *Plan Colombia*. Therefore the Nariño Peace Table[8] sought organisations such as REDEPAZ (Bogotá Chapter), and the Catholic Church for advice and support. The people have already contacted the governor of Nariño to assure the continuity of the process and provide solutions to the incoming Internally Displaced People's (IDP) crisis. One of the big obstacles is the total absence of a humanitarian accord with the violent actors present in the region. Moreover, the people were losing faith in the past peace process which failed in 2002 between FARC and former President Andrés Pastrana, given that the continuation of violent actions kept targeting the civilians.

The process of establishing the town as a ZOP has been paralleled by the efforts of the Peace Table of Samaniego,[9] which gathers 25 representatives of private and public institutions, youth groups, children and all the members of the community that want Samaniego to be a peace territory. This process, as was stated above, is totally supported by the current mayor, which is convinced of the need of transforming the culture of confrontation and fear.

San Pablo represents the complexity of the war dynamics in southern Colombia. Partially an illegal crop cultivation area, San Pablo is currently disputed by all the violent actors seeking to benefit from the profits of coca and heroin. There have been hostilities between FARC and ELN and more recently the paramilitaries are starting to appear in the scene. In addition, the consequences of *Plan Colombia* are clearly seen in this municipality: displaced people coming from Putumayo (as in Samaniego) and a general escalation of the armed interventions, products of the *Plan Colombia*'s strategy in the southwestern part of the country. *Plan Colombia* started in 1999. It represents a US aid package to Colombia (*Plan Colombia*)[10] mostly focusing on military assistance. The recent history of San Pablo[11] (2000–2003) reveals six recent attacks from the insurgent fronts of FARC and ELN. The population decided to declare themselves a peace territory as a means of protecting the community from future attacks from any of the violent actors in the conflict. In November of 2000, the population publicly declared San Pablo a peace municipality. Unfortunately on March 9th 2001, FARC again attacked the town. San Pablo's citizens, together with the Nariño Peace Table and REDEPAZ expressed to FARC, the government, the paramilitaries and everyone else, that they were not going to stop the process of being a peace territory. The most urgent process is for the community and supporting institutions to make it clear to the violent actors that they should respect the voluntary and popular decision of letting San Pablo become a territory for peace. This process is far from easy and San Pablo's community is not very homogeneous for there are civilian sectors that follow some of the violent groups. There are conflicts between the civilians supporting FARC with those civilians supporting ELN. The intra-community divisions increase the complexity of the process. Francisco Angulo affirmed that San Pablo's political context is indeed very complex. The population is divided and has been influenced by different armed sectors, making it difficult to fully develop the notion of 'neutrality'. What has kept the process from been totally abandoned is the determination of the people to create conditions to protect themselves from violence. This is not an easy step, given the problems of division and intra-communal conflicts amongst the inhabitants. FARC sees the process of San Pablo as a real obstacle towards the power struggle for advancing economic, social and political power in the municipality. This is a real threat to the community, and, as was stated before, San Pablo has been attacked after the peace declaration, which means that FARC is really not respecting the popular will.

Regarding ZOP as a threatening entity to the advancement of war and war interests, Francisco Angulo argued that:

> ZOPs are posing a real obstacle to the violent actors. Because war is about controlling territories, and the Zones of Peace 'retake' those territories from the war confrontation. Hence, the violent actors 'frame' ZOPs as territories that they have 'lost'. This is why they [ZOPs] are a clear military target and this explains why FARC and ELN insist on hurting civilians.[12]

One of the few strategies of undermining this potential threat for all ZOPs in Colombia is to create enough pressure from different sectors inside and outside the country. Hence, any decision to undertake an attack or massacre on a ZOP will signify a high political cost for the violent groups, hence reducing the chances for attack. In this process, the international community and national and international NGOs play a relevant role.

One of the shortcomings identified in this project is that it encompasses a great number of different levels of both actions and actors, as indicated in the aforementioned strategies. Hence, there is a lack of an explicit description of which level and what types of activities ought to be implemented first. For instance, the project is not clear in delineating the level of importance between the pedagogical process and the establishment of the peace municipalities, or the creation of networks of different sectors of civilians working for peace. Therefore, more clarity is needed in the project as to which strategy should be considered the most relevant for the success of the project, or a systematic explanation of how these different strategies work.[13] The European Union was the main donor of the 18-month long initiative. However, the process of consolidating peace territories is much longer. The goal is to be able to foster the initial stages of the 100 peace municipalities in a year and a half. It is relevant to know that REDEPAZ supports communities that ask for advice, accompaniment, or any form of assistance under the parameters of peaceful coexistence. Hence, REDEPAZ does not arrive at the communities if the organisation has not been previously invited.

The process of building local resistance initiatives, such as the ZOP, exemplifies how communities can restore their social fabric by working on humanitarian goals in conditions of high levels of violence. One of the distinct features of local resistance processes is that citizens are able to organize themselves. Hence, the definition of ZOP used in this study is based on Colombian Human Rights expert, Alvarro Villaraga, who defines ZOP as:

> spaces in which armed actors are not allowed to enter, the only protection is symbolic, with signs and everything, but obviously this is symbolic, and reduces the risk of the community as well as distance them from the violent actors.[14]

The first point mentioned in the introduction was the symbiosis *between NGOs and local communities* in creating and sustaining a ZOP. Although there is not a single-actor in the assistance process of forming a ZOP, NGOs appear to be a relevant actor in most cases. In all the described municipalities, the assistance of an NGO, REDEAPZ, was present. Although a ZOP is a community-driven initiative, NGOs are usually effective in legitimising the process as well as providing training and in some cases even financial resources. However, in one of the cases above mentioned, REDEPAZ lack of funding to sustain some of the projects in Samaniego have affected negatively the development of that ZOP. Other, social actors include children, youth and women. They are gaining recognition as agents of social change, which can influence – in the long-term – the current culture of war and violence as the preferred strategy to deal with conflict.

The second element for discussion was *violence resistance*: the process of developing the notion of 'active neutrality'. The creation and sustainability of a ZOP included – among many other elements – unity amongst inhabitants with regards to dealing with physical and ideological differences with all violent actors. Intra-community division, as in San Pablo, clearly became an obstacle to the ZOP. As long as civilians continue their support without using force, a zone of peace can survive because it is their way of resisting their condition as victims of this conflict.

Lastly began the *process of disarming the 'war machinery'* by reacquiring spaces for peace. Incursions by most armed actors in all the cases described, proves that both the local community peace initiatives as the ZOP, and NGO projects such as the 'One Hundred Municipalities of Peace' poses threats to armed groups when they come to control of territory. The process of 'reacquiring' former war-controlled territories, affects the nature of the conflict in Colombia: control over its territory, people and resources.

The leading proposition of this essay was that timely collaboration and cooperation between NGOs and local communities can contribute to the creation of mechanisms for containing violence such as the Zones of Peace. ZOPs might contribute to the generation of identity-transformation changes with regards to the notion of being 'victims of the conflict'. In other words, ZOPs play a role in shifting from a victim-centered perspective towards one of resilience in which the local communities foster alternative mechanisms for reconciliation and transformation of conflicts in their own terms. After centuries of being attacked by the state authorities, by the insurgency and the paramilitaries; local rural communities started rejecting the power of weapons and are shifting towards the use non-violent mechanisms to produce social changes in their surroundings. *Perhaps they are not totally ready for peace, but they are certainly tired of war.* Many local communities and municipalities are aware that conflict is a natural part of everyday life, thus they are procuring dialogical practices as a preferred mechanism to resolve their differences. In some cases, local authorities are cooperating with communal initiatives. However, it has been due to the dedicated efforts to work with and learn from the communities that NGOs like REDEPAZ and many others became aware of the tremendous importance of this process. The role of NGOs in ZOP is difficult, especially given the precarious financial situation of the NGOs themselves. However, in the communities studied here, the presence, assistance and accompaniment of REDEPAZ proved to be very important in the invisible processes of people building peace in the midst of a civil war.

Notes

1 Left-wing guerillas.
2 Right-wing insurgencies.
3 Ana Teresa Bernal, REDEPAZ's director has been life-threatened in several occasions, local REDEPAZs have been forced to leave their communities and some of them have been killed.
4 On recent communication with the REDEPAZ director (April 2004), the NGO does not have enough funds to pay its staff and is in danger of being totally closed in a month's due.
5 Italics added by chapter's author.

6 By 'war machinery' I mean the geographical, psychological and cultural dynamics that fuel and perpetuate conflict and conflict behavior.

7 In the early 1990s the new constitution installed the 'decentralisation process', which, according to some analysts, is one of the big causes of why the guerrilla organisation gained so much territorial and political power in the regions.

8 REDEPAZ has regional chapters in different zones of the country. The Nariño peace table gathers the efforts of REDEPAZ in that specific region.

9 The Samaniego Peace Table is the local expression of REDEPAZ at the municipality.

10 For a detailed analysis look at: Catalina Rojas, 'What is the War on (T)ERRORISM? US Foreign Policy Towards Colombia in the Post-September 11 World: the End of the Peace Talks, the Beginning of the New-Old War', *Journal of the Political Studies Institute of UNAB University* (2002): 18.

11 Francisco Angulo, phone interview to the author, May 2001.

12 Francisco Angulo, phone interview to the author, May 2001.

13 The author of the article is not aware of any formal evaluations done either by REDEPAZ or by the donor.

14 Taken from a personal interview, *Women Waging Peace Report*, 17 October 2003.

Chapter 8

The NGOs' Dilemmas in the Post-War Iraq: From Stabilisation to Nation-Building

Mahmood Monshipouri

A difficult set of issues has complicated humanitarian NGO efforts to practice their routine and successful way of alleviating the suffering of the victims of post-conflict societies. NGOs in Iraq suffer from the lack of established infrastructure either in the country or in the neighbouring areas. There have been few NGOs operating in the country or in the region. This absence of on-the-ground experience among NGOs and most UN agencies hinders relief efforts.[1] In Afghanistan, Kosovo, and other recent emergencies, in contrast, the presence of extensive networks of NGOs in nearby countries have made it possible to mount an effective strategy of responding to humanitarian crises.[2] Because of sanction targeted against Iraq, US NGOs for a long time were forbidden to work in Iraq without a license from the Office of Foreign Asset Control (OFAC) of the US Treasury; they needed a license to travel to Iraq or import any item.[3] NGOs in post-war Iraq face several difficulties and dilemmas, of which the most crucial is to avoid politicising their responses.

Many NGOs have expressed serious concerns about the implications of the increased presence of military forces in the humanitarian arena. The International Committee of the Red Cross (ICRC) has insisted that humanitarian work must be disassociated from military operations. The connections with the military, ICRC members argue, risk compromising not only its identity but also the viability of its humanitarian operations. ICRC runs the risk of being seen as a fig leaf for the US military, non-neutral, and a 'justified' target of attack.[4] Some experts, however, raised serious concerns about the viability of many humanitarian operations where the security and safety of relief staff is not strengthened.[5] Further, the potential for confusion increases dramatically, as was the case in Afghanistan, when soldiers are seen to be distributing aid in civilian clothes, thus blurring the distinction between the military and NGOs. This practice not only interferes with the neutrality of humanitarian aid, it also can put NGO staff at risk of being mistakenly targeted by armed groups. This is in fact what happened in Afghanistan in December 2002, when one aid worker was killed and two others injured in a suicide bombing.[6]

Several humanitarian NGOs – such as Oxfam,[7] a UK famine relief agency operating to alleviate suffering caused by the war, and *Médecins sans Frontièrs*

(MSF), a French-based international NGO that provides medical care to people in need – have announced a policy of not taking funding from belligerent parties. Oxfam has refused to apply for an extra L3 million of funding put aside by the British government for emergency relief work in Iraq. Oxfam members have insisted it is crucial that for both the safety of their operations and the principle of impartiality they are not seen as an instrument of a belligerent party.[8]

The relief workers are clearly faced with an ethical dilemma: they wish to avoid acting as instruments of government foreign policy (Principle 4 of the 10-point Red Cross and Red Crescent Code of Conduct) while at the same time recognising that humanitarian imperatives come first (Principle 1).[9] Oxfam's statement reflects the way in which some NGOs deal with similar dilemmas: 'Oxfam will not accept funds from any source if doing so would increase poverty and suffering, undermine our humanitarian impartiality or public credibility to advocate'.[10] This means Oxfam will seek funds from the general public, European Union institutions and other institutions, including governments without military forces fighting in Iraq.

Many international NGOs, however, are dependent on government donors for their funding.[11] In post-war Iraq, peace enforcers and donors are essentially the same. NGOs such as International Rescue Committee (IRC), CARE, and Worldvision, which are financially dependent on USAID, are in fact large service providers that act as subcontracting agents of the occupying forces – that is, the United States and Great Britain.[12] The 1991 'Operation Provide Comfort' and Operation Northwatch' in northern Iraq made CARE a dependent organisation. Since 1991, Save the Children UK (SCF UK) has operated in northern Iraq's Kurdish sector on projects now costing about $1.5 million a year, with half of it met by the British government's Department for International Development.[13]

Some US NGOs have engaged in a 'hairsplitting' exercise, arguing that if the interlocutors are with State Department/USAID, then the funding is acceptable. They fail to realize that all branches of the US government are working toward the same overall objective. CARE USA has drafted a policy about determining what constitutes an unacceptable degree of 'military control', and what is meant by 'independence' and 'impartiality' in the current Iraq context. The real dilemma is that USAID is under the authority of Pentagon's Office of the Coalition Provisional Authority (OCPA).

Speaking on the 2003 InterAction Forum, USAID Director Andrew Natsios argued that NGOs under US contracts are indeed 'an arm of the US government', and that they should recognize the United States for providing funding. Natsios emphasized the point that international humanitarian leaders must promote their links to the US government and show results. Otherwise the Bush administration would find new partners for overseas assistance programs.[14] The leading US humanitarian organisations – IRC, CARE, Worldvision, and Save the Children – have major differences with the Pentagon's role in the rebuilding of Iraq. Three NGOs – CARE, Worldvision, and IRC – have not applied for the new funding, citing ongoing security problems that hinder their relief efforts, discomfort with oversight from occupying military officials, and the need to direct their staff and resources to more pressing humanitarian crises in other parts of the world.[15] The

IRC's President, George Rupp, noted that his organisation's projects in Iraq, which are under the direction of military officials, could compromise the organisation's independence.[16] Save the Children has amended an early draft of his agreement with US government to ensure that the organisation reported to civilian officials in USAID, rather than to military officials under the Pentagon's Office of the Coalition Provisional Authority (OCPA).[17]

Non-humanitarian NGOs run the risk of imposing practices and ways of thinking that are alien to the target countries. For example, in order to receive funds from USAID, Democracy Network in Bulgaria has focused on 'democracy building', 'civic participation', and 'community building', terms so foreign to the local society that even some NGOs have refrained from translating them.[18] Another risk, as noted above, is that the projects that NGOs are subcontracted to carry out could at times run counter to their own goals.[19] It is safe to conclude that those NGOs that are financially independent could avoid politicising humanitarian actions.

Doctors Without Borders (Médecins Sans Frontières – MSF)

As an influential actor in conflict regions and humanitarian crises, MSF has committed itself to two central objectives: 'providing medical aid whenever it is needed, regardless of race, religion, politics or sex and raising awareness of the plight of the people [they] help'.[20] The driving force behind this organisation's operation has been the commitment to offer professional services to alleviate suffering in humanitarian crises. As such, MSF refrains from engaging in the broader objective of nation building, reconstruction, or improving the political situation on the ground.[21]

MSF reported that before the war in Iraq started, most of the hospitals (34 hospitals in Baghdad) were well functioning, with full staff who treated patients fairly well. During the war, Al Kindi hospital treated 232 civilian casualties in two weeks, of whom 20 died either during treatment or in the emergency room. Following the fall of Baghdad and the subsequent looting and chaos, Al Kindi hospital, which had been working until the 8th of April and had 120 patients, had to close due to the lack of security. The failure to secure the hospitals subsequently cost an unacceptable amount of lives, sufferings, and disorder. Three weeks after the fall of Baghdad, most of the hospitals were in total disarray.[23]

Morten Rostrup, MSF International Council President, and Nicolas de Torrente, MSF-USA, have argued that addressing a health care system in disarray is as important as building a new administration in Iraq. They have raised serious concerns over the tendency to privatize health system in Iraq, fearing that the most vulnerable and the poorest part of the population may not get proper access to health care.[24]

Furthermore, MSF has consistently supported the cardinal principle of the International Humanitarian Law, namely, setting boundaries and limits to the means of warfare in Iraq. MSF has found the use of cluster bombs and cluster munitions unacceptable, in large part because of their indiscriminate nature. These bombs lead to unexploded ordnance capable of injuring civilians. In both Afghanistan and Kosovo, cluster bombs were used. These weapons, according to the International humanitarian law, must be banned.[25]

The most vexing problem facing MSF is their reliance on security provided by US occupying forces, without becoming submerged in the politico-military context in which they operate. The question persists: how to operate under the cover of the military while pursuing fundamentally non-military goals. Reflecting on this problem, Rafael Vila San Juan of MSF International argues: 'Our role is not to demonize the armed forces. We need to engage with them, since we work in the same sphere'.[26] He cautions, however, that 'civilian, humanitarian organisations cannot operate under the command of the military'.[27]

The International Committee of the Red Cross (ICRC)

With the rising guerrilla attacks in Iraq, the civilian and military cooperation on the humanitarian issues has become immensely complicated and perilous for NGOs. Following the deadly truck bombing of August 19, 2003, in which the UN headquarters in Baghdad was targeted, international aid groups, especially the International Monetary Fund and the World Bank, withdrew their staffs from Iraq, despite the fact that they vowed to remain active in Iraq. Instability and rising violence in Iraq have slowed down efforts to rebuild Iraqi oil production and to restore electricity. The resultant uncertainty has also scared off foreign investors and multinational corporations.[28] Concerned with the security situation in Iraq, the UN has pulled out some of its workers. The newly-appointed humanitarian coordinator, Ramiro Lopes da Silva, has insisted that the UN would stay the course to assist the Iraqi people.[29]

In the aftermath of another series of bombings in the late 2003, many NGOs either cut their personnel or left the country. Save the Children – UK, an international NGO, closed its offices in Baghdad and moved its workers to offices in the northern part of the country as well as to Jordan and Cyprus, at least temporarily. It kept offices open in the cities of Arbil and Sulaymaniyah in northern Iraq, where the security situation improved noticeably. Many other NGOs, including Oxfam and the International Organisation for Migration (IOM), left after these attacks. *Première Urgence*, a French NGO, took over the job of helping 8,000 internally-displaced people in Iraq since the IOM left. CARE International stayed while keeping a 'low profile'.[30]

The October 27, 2003 bombings of the ICRC offices in Baghdad left 12 people dead and proved beyond doubt that all Western organisations, including their international relief workers involved in the reconstruction of Iraq were targets. Humanitarian workers and coalition soldiers had become one in the minds of those who oppose the US-led occupation of the country. The Belgian branch of MSF cut back on its seven foreign staff in the country and the Greek branch of the organisation cut its overseas staffers from three to one. Mark Joolen of the Belgian MSF pointed out that 'the fact that a neutral organisation like the ICRC becomes a target represents a new development. It is increasingly difficult for independent organisations to disassociate themselves from the occupation forces.[31]

The guerilla attacks on the ICRC in fact marked the first time that a suicide bomber had struck the neutral ICRC in its 140-year history, and after two decades of humanitarian work in Iraq.[32] The ICRC has consistently stayed above the political fray in Iraq. Its sole mission has been to deliver lifesaving humanitarian aid.[33] Following these tragic assaults, Pierre Gassmann, head of the ICRC delegation in Iraq, noted that the agency would continue to refuse military protection: 'if we decide to ask for military protection, we will be exactly where the enemy is seen – at the side of the coalition troops'.[34] In the late 2003, ICRC decided to temporarily shut down its offices in Basra and Baghdad for the safety of its workers.[35]

Conclusion

In the case of Iraq, the military occupation has posed a major dilemma for HINGOs: should NGOs collaborate with the occupying forces? For NGOs, there is a real danger that such collaboration will cause them to lose their neutrality and/or independence. Without working with the military, however, NGOs will be unable to offer their relief services to the Iraqi people. Some NGOs have been operating as subcontracting agents of the military. The American and British troops have tried to stamp out resistance and retain Iraqi goodwill simultaneously.[36]

Concerns about military-humanitarian relations and the divisions among NGOs over their role have generated an intense debate about the extent to which NGOs' operations will be influenced by US government funding. The next logical question is how to maintain neutrality and operational independence given that financial autonomy is an important part of that operation. Many US NGOs remain largely dependent on heavy governmental funding. When the distinction between a soldier and an NGO worker is further blurred, both the cardinal principle of neutrality and the safety of NGO staff will be at risk. Given the dearth of NGOs' operational experience in Iraq, it is imperative to apply lessons learned from Afghanistan.

Although it is crucial for the military and NGOs to interact with one another, it is not clear how effectively they can work together amid the battle to stabilize and disarm the country. Some NGOs have been reluctant to work closely with the US military or the Pentagon's Office of Coalition Provisional Authority (OCPA). NGOs' conventional thinking, assets, and strategies have encountered a new challenge in post-war Iraq: how can they play an effective role in the creation of a legitimate state without addressing the issue of the 'victims' of violence and injustice? For now, however, insecurity has cast its specter over occupied Iraq, overshadowing such issues as good governance, development, civil society, and democratisation. Freedom without food, sanitation, minimal health care, and other basic services has become meaningless for the vast majority of the Iraqi people.

106 *Subcontracting Peace*

Notes

1 US Institute of Peace, 'Picturing Iraq at Peace', *Peace Watch*, 9/3 (April 2003): 1-2, and 9.
2 Gil Loescher, 'Be Prepared', *The World Today*, February 2003, pp. 7-9; see p. 8.
3 Ibid.
4 Andrew Harris and Peter Dombrowski, 'Military Collaboration with Humanitarian Organizations in Complex Emergencies', *Global Governance*, 8 (2002): 155-178; see 164.
5 Harris and Dombrowski, p. 173.
6 Erin Patrick, 'Reconstructing Afghanistan: Lessons for Post-War Iraq', *Migration Policy Institute*, 1 April 2003, available at <http://www.migrationinformation.org/Feature/display.cfm?ID=117> (Last visited on 16 June 2003).
7 The 12 member agencies of Oxfam international – Australia, Belgium, Canada, Germany, Hong Kong, Ireland, Netherlands, New Zealand, Quebec, Spain, Britain and the United States – have focused on fundraising from non-combatant nations, the European Union, the United Nations and individuals. See Nick Cater, *Alertnet*, 'Oxfam to Shun Iraq Funds From Belligerent States', March 4, 2003, available at <http://www.alertnet.org/thefacts/reliefresouces/602345?version=1> (Last visited on 9 June 2003).
8 Zahra Akkerhuys, Jean-Michel Piedagnel, Beverley Jones, and Nick Guttmann, 'Should NGOs Take Government Funding for Relief Work in Iraq?', *Third Sector*, 26 March 2003, p. 15.
9 Nicolas Pelham, op. cit.
10 Nick Cater, 'Oxfam to Shun Iraq Funds From Belligerent States', *Alertnet*, March 4, 2003, available <http://www.alertnet.org/thefacts/reliefresources/602345?version=1>. Last visited on June 9, 2003.
11 Ruth Gidley, 'NGOs Demand Access and Transparency in Humanitarian Aid', *Alertnet*, February 17, 2003, available at <http://www.globalpolicy.org/ngos/aid/2003/0217access.htm>. Last visited on June 9, 2003.
12 I thank Claude Bruderlein for sharing his thoughts with me on this issue.
13 Nick Cater, 'Oxfam to Shun Iraq Funds From Belligerent States', *Alertnet*, March 4, 2003, available <http://www.alertnet.org/thefacts/reliefresources/602345?version=1>. Last visited June 9, 2003.
14 Jack Epstein, 'Charities at Odds with Pentagon: Many Turn Down Work in Iraq Because of US Restrictions', *San Francisco Chronicle*, June 14, 2003, p. A11. See also, InterAction Forum 2003, 'The Challenge of Global Commitment: Advancing Relief and Development Goals Through Advocacy and Action', Synopses of Forum 2003 Panels, May 19–21, 2003, Washington Marriot, available at <http://www.interaction.org/content/forum2003/panels.html>. See section on 'Natsios: NGOs Must Show Results; Promote Ties to US or We Will "Find New Partners"'. Last visited on June 18, 2003.
15 David Bank, 'Humanitarian Groups Spurn Iraq', *The Wall Street Journal*, May 29, 2003, p. A6.
16 Ibid.
17 Ibid.
18 Katarina West, *Agents of Altruism: The Expansion of Humanitarian NGOs in Rwanda and Afghanistan*, Burlington, VT: Ashgate, 2001, p. 211.
19 Ibid., p. 222.
20 See http://www.msf.org.
21 I interviewed Dr. Nicholas de Torrente, the Director of Doctors Without Borders (Médecins Sans Frontières – MSF) on June 18, 2003. He emphasized that MSF's primary purpose is to help the victims of a failed state or any humanitarian crisis.
22 Joelle Tanguy and Fiona Terry, op. cit., p. 31.

23 See comments by Morten Rostrup and Nicolas de Torrence, 'Humanitarian Situation in Iraq', Transcript of Médecins Sans Frontières Conference, National Press Club, Washington D.C., May 2, 2003, available at <www.doctorswithoutborders.org/ publications/other/iraq_pressconference-5-2-2003.sh>. Last visited on June 6, 2003.

24 Ibid.

25 Ibid.

26 Quoted in Ruth Gidley, 'NGOs Demand Access and Transparency in Humanitarian Aid', Alernet, February 17, 2003, available at <http://www.globalpolicy.org/ngos/aid/2003/ 0217access.htm>. Last visited June 9, 2003.

27 Ibid.

28 Edmund L. Andrews, 'International Aid Groups Withdrawing Staffs From Iraq', *The New York Times* (August 21, 2003), p. A13.

29 Felicity Barringer, 'Questions Haunt a Saddened Annan', *The New York Times*, August 21, 2003, p. A13.

30 (Iraq: NGOs Scale down Presence, Office for the Coordination of Humanitarian Affairs (OCHA), Integrated Regional Information Network (IRIN), Sept. 29, 2003, available at <http://www.cidi.org/humanitarian/hsr/iraq/ix151.html>.

31 'Some Aid Workers Leaving Iraq After Red Cross Bombing', available at <http://uk.news.yahoo.com/031028/323/eceje.html>. Joolen continued: 'That merging of humanitarians and the military creates nervousness'.

32 See 'Foreigners behind Baghdad Bombs', BBC News – UK edn., available at <http://news.bbc.co.uk/1/hi/world/middle_east/3219993.stm>. Last visited on November 5, 2003.

33 See 'EU officials Express Outrage over Bombings in Baghdad', USA Today, available at <http://www. usatoday.com/news/world/Iraq2003-10-27-eu-reax_x.htm>. Last visited on November 5, 2003.

34 For more on the ICRC and police offices attacked see <http://www.dawn.com/ 2003/10/28/top18.htm>. Last visited on November 5, 2003.

35 Slobodan Lekic, 'We have Momentum Despite Rising Toll, Top aide Says', Chicago Sun-Times.Com. November 9, 2003. Available at <http://www.chicagosuntimes.com/ output/iraq/cst-nws-iside09.html>. Last visited on November 12, 2003.

36 Ann Scott Tyson, 'In Iraq, US Enters Tricky New Phase', *The Christian Science Monitor*, June 16, 2003, pp. 1 and 11.

Chapter 9

A Necessary Collaboration: NGOs, Peacekeepers and Credible Military Force – The Case of Sierra Leone and East Timor

Michael Gordon Jackson

In the 1990s, a bloody and savage civil war racked the failed-state of Sierra Leone. What turned the tide was the intervention of a robust and effective contingent of British troops in 2000 to help stabilize the situation and restore order. While their goals were limited and not open-ended, military intervention by the UK was vital in restoring order in Sierra Leone. In failed-state emergencies, the lack of security greatly hampers the ability of NGOs to complete their humanitarian missions. To succeed, NGOs in countries like Sierra Leone must have the backing of military forces such as the British or Australians in the East Timor intervention of 1999, which were perceived by all parties as reputable, professional and effective. Most UN peacekeeping forces lack these professional requisites. The quality of the military force is thereby crucial for NGO success.

During these two emergencies, many NGOs operated in these countries, both before and after intervention. The typology of Gordenker and Weiss, which characterizes NGOs by source of funding, is a useful method to outline the kinds of NGO missions taking place in Sierra Leone and East Timor.[1] For example, there were many private NGOs, with no connection to governmental funding, such as Amnesty International, Human Rights Watch, Oxfam GB, Catholic Relief Services, working side-by-side with quasi-NGOs (QUANGOs) such as the International Committee of the Red Cross (ICRC). Key donor-organized NGOs (DONGOs), such as United Nations Children's Fund (UNICEF) or United Nations Office of Coordination of Humanitarian Affairs (OCHA) also worked in these countries. How these NGOs perceived the security issue and the importance of the UK and Australian military interventions in establishing secure environments for humanitarian missions, will be emphasized in this analysis.

Sierra Leone and International Peacekeeping

During the war of the 1990s in Sierra Leone, NGOs were finding it nearly impossible to fulfill their missions in Sierra Leone because of the lack of security.[2] The UN Security Council on 22 October, 1999, with the purpose of solidifying the gains of the Lome Agreement, authorized the sending of 6000 international peacekeepers to Sierra Leone. Named the United Nations Mission in Sierra Leone (UNAMSIL), these peacekeepers received a mandate to collect weapons from rebels, disarm them, integrate them into the national armed forces, while protecting humanitarian aid workers and NGOs in Sierra Leone. Acting under Chapter VII of the UN Charter, the hope was that UNAMSIL would effectively enforce the peace mandate. However, on November 30, Amnesty International ominously reported that murders, rapes and acts of violence were accelerating since the Lome Agreement was signed.[3]

The UK announced on 10 October 2000 that a 100 man headquarters staff was to be deployed to Sierra Leone to 'command the overall UK effort and offer high-level operational advice to the Sierra Leone army'. 400 UK troops would remain in Sierra Leone. It was also announced that an UK brigade of 5,000 troops would be available for duty in Sierra Leone as a rapid reaction force if the security environment collapsed again. On 30 October, a six ship amphibious task force with 600 Royal Marines cruised off the coast of Sierra Leone to demonstrate British resolve to establish security. And, if the combat brigade were deployed, it would remain under strict British, not UNAMSIL control.[4] As Foreign Secretary Cook noted, the 5,000 force would underscore the UK's commitment; moreover as in the past, 'British forces were successful then in restoring stability. If necessary, this force will be able to do so again.'[5]

With this announcement, and the suppression of WSB, the security situation began to change significantly for the better. In mid November 2000, RUF and Kabbah signed an agreement for an immediate cease-fire, beginning a process of demobilisation and disarmament of all militia forces, and the full deployment of UNAMSIL forces in Sierra Leone. The political establishment and many Sierra Leonean citizens made it plain that they believed that the UK forces were the key factor in restoring some security in the country. On 23 November, 2000 pro-British demonstrators, organized by the influential Civil Society Movement in Sierra Leone, vociferously called for a continued UK presence.[6] President Kabbah again thanked the British for 'restoring discipline, loyalty and dignity' to the Sierra Leone army. 'With the support of the British ... things have changed dramatically and people have started coming in.'[7] By 18 January, the Sierra Leone government declared the 11-year-old civil war to be at an end.

The importance of the UK intervention should not be underestimated. A robust and professional military force from a 'lead nation' had restored order. 'The deployment of UK forces rescued the UN mission and certainly played a significant part in averting a full-scale humanitarian catastrophe in Sierra Leone.'[8]

When the crisis began to sharply worsen in the spring of 2000, many NGOs where outspoken in their support of British forces in Sierra Leone. Three private NGOs, the Catholic Agency for Overseas Development (CAFOD), Oxfam GB, and the Africa Office of Global Ministries, were especially vociferous in their support. CAFOD on 9 May strongly welcomed the intervention of British troops.[9] Oxfam GB released an even tougher statement in support of the British intervention. 'Oxfam GB welcomes the decision to deploy British troops to Sierra Leone ... it is difficult to imagine how UNAMSIL can succeed, with the required speed, without British troops being available to use force.'[10] The Africa Office of Global Ministries on 19 July 2000 criticized the weak performance of UNAMSIL and praised the ability of British troops to restore order.[11]

By every measure, the ability of NGOs to perform humanitarian and relief work, resettlement and repatriation of displaced persons, judicial reconciliation, and strengthening of civil authority in Sierra Leone began to significantly improve after the decision by the UK to intervene with combat forces. By 2002, the United Nations High Commissioner for Refugees (DONGO funding), announced that 15 international NGOs, 4 local NGOs and two UN agencies would work together and coordinate their efforts to reintegrate refugees into society; another DONGO, the United Nations Capital Development Fund (UNCDF) began critically needed microfinancing projects.[12] Medicins Sans Frontieres (MSF), a private NGO, began to effectively operate again.[13] And, with a secure environment, major private NGOs such as Amnesty International helped in the effort to revitalize the smashed Sierra Leone judicial system, along with the establishment of a Special Court for Sierra Leone to investigate and prosecute war crimes and the creation of a Truth and Reconciliation Commission to help create the conditions for national reconciliation.[14] Local and international NGOs also assisted with the successful efforts to hold national elections in Sierra Leone on 14 May 2002.[15]

Australian Intervention in East Timor

Similar to Sierra Leone after the UK military intervention, the security environment in East Timor after September 1999 improved greatly. After the United Nations Transitional Authority in East Timor (UNTAET) was established in October 1999, a range of private NGOs, QUANGOS and DONGOS found that it was possible again, in spite of hardships, to begin the process of reconstruction, relief and reconciliation to the East Timorese people.

Though human rights problems still persist in East Timor, the Australian-led INTERFET operation was crucial in creating a secure environment for NGOs. NGOs, like those in Sierra Leone in 2000, also were deeply aware that a true, professional military force had to be used to avert massacres and assist with relief operations in September 1999. On 3 September 1999, two dozen NGOs in the UK called upon Britain to press for the 'immediate dispatch of armed UN troops to East Timor to safeguard security'.[16] And once there, INTERFET generally had strong cooperative links with NGOs in the area. The UN command would consult NGOs regularly to get a sense of what was happening on the ground. Cooperation between INTERFET and NGOs became part of the normal processes. [17] INTERFET provided the secure environment, with credible and quality military professionals, while humanitarian agencies began the process of effectively giving relief to needy East Timorese.

As in Sierra Leone, NGOs heavily contributed to the strengthening of judicial mechanisms. For example, in May 2000, NGOs participated in the establishment of the Judicial System Monitoring Program, charged with reforming the court system in East Timor, monitoring the work of the Serious Crimes Panel in Dili, and disseminating legal information about the judiciary.[18] Other private human rights groups, along with the Catholic Church, helped the UNTAETs Human Rights Unit (DONGO) set up the Commission on Reception, Truth and Reconciliation (CRTR).[19] The United Nations Development Program (UNDP), a key DONGO, has also been very active in facilitating and coordinating relief operations with donors and NGOs.[20]

Conclusion

Throughout the 1990s, two debates about international peacekeeping operations and humanitarian aid converged. In the first, questions about the mandates, rules of engagement, force levels and the need for 'robust' UN international peacekeeping operations were raised. A parallel debate was also taking place within the NGO community about whether there was a clear link between effective military intervention and their own ability to successfully provide humanitarian assistance. By depending upon the use of military force by peacekeeping states and the implication of taking political sides in a conflict, could NGOs maintain their independence and neutrality among belligerents? Did the goal of achieving a 'secure environment' for NGO activities require a Faustian bargain with the military providers of that security? And if NGOs were being compelled by the nature of the conflicts they were operating in to cooperate much more closely with the military, what should be the 'quality' of military force required assisting them in their humanitarian missions?

A key question was asked in one NGO report, 'How can unarmed humanitarian actors operate in an environment dominated by the gun?' Thus, the challenge for aid organisations, 'How to conduct principled and effective humanitarian action in an environment where those principles are not accepted' by the parties to the conflict.[21] In the past, NGOs functioned with the consent of belligerents and promised to not take sides or interfere in the conflict. By necessity, humanitarian organisations were being forced to reconsider their traditional ambivalence about being too closely associated with peacekeeping forces.

Mary Anderson is quite right to note the relationship between humanitarian/relief aid and conflict. The difficulty of making theoretical sense of this interaction is complicated by the fact that, 'Each war is unique; each society has its own history, culture, personages, values, and tensions. Every aid project site is local and special.'[22] Making valid generalisations about the links between NGO activities, failed states, security, military intervention, and the quality of armed forces, is challenging.

The nature and scope of security threats faced by NGOs as profoundly changed how the aid and rights communities must do their business now and in the future. In order for many NGOs to perform their missions, collaboration with military forces in helping create a viable security environment is a given. Andrew Harris and Peter Dombroski rightly conclude, 'If humanitarian agencies are to perform their valuable functions of aiding those victimized by internal conflicts and regional warfare, they will need to cooperate more closely with military forces. In turn, military organisations will need to provide better support for the vital mission performed by UN humanitarian organisations and NGOs.'[23]

To them, the use of outside military interventions or 'tourniquet operations' may be indispensable to establishing proper security for NGOs. The military 'footprint', or the size, speed, and robustness of force that is applied, is vital for operational success. More rigorously drawn typologies are needed to help describe with analytical refinement the exact relationship between cases of complex emergencies, their contexts, the timing of international response, what calibration of force is needed for successful outcomes, the nature of that military force, and quality of those military forces that are committed by donor states or international bodies.

The question of how to define in more precise terms 'quality' armed forces in regards to CP and CM and their relationships with NGOs in conflict zones needs to be investigated more. Is quality only a list of tangible categories, such as numbers of peacekeepers, logistics, or weapons? As Hugo Slim noted in 1995, 'military humanitarianism' can be crucial in establishing preventive deployments, interposition, early warning, sanctions enforcement, protection and escort of NGO relief and agencies, demobilisation, disarmament, training of new security forces, and peace enforcement. Or, is quality also a matter of defining what intangible factors and skills are needed for positive CP/CM and relationships with the NGO community?

For example, Slim posits a productive line of approach with his description of British 'good peacekeeping practice'. He notes that the core of its peacekeeping doctrine rests on the principle of consent in the field. Consent is not a given but a variable in peacekeeping environments; it is 'dispersed' and 'uneven' in practice. 'Consent is something that the peacekeeper can expect to have bits of, from certain people, in certain places, for certain things, for certain periods of time.' British doctrine is focused on the 'management of consent – its generation, maintenance and retrieval'. It is an 'art' dedicated to convincing parties in the humanitarian emergency that its use of force is predicated on general consent.[24]

Do other states that field peacekeeping forces place a similar emphasis on managing consent? Can this measure of quality (or many others such as fair mindedness or discipline) be used to explain examples of when successful or unsuccessful peacekeeping take place? Comparative and systematic analysis of what constitutes quality, both tangible and intangible variables, between the armed forces of states like the UK, the US, or other donor countries when engaged in military humanitarianism, could result in useful generalisations about what is needed for successful peacekeeping and productive relationships with its NGO partners. Indeed, it is an analytical approach which might have some real utility in predicting successful outcomes in instances where NGOs and military forces operate in complex emergencies.

In conclusion, both the Sierra Leone and East Timor interventions highlight the need for a deeper analysis of UN peacekeeping reform efforts. Peace enforcement operations that have to contend with warlordism or chaotic failed state circumstances require quality forces, not just units of peacekeepers committed in piecemeal fashion. '... Local populations have most respect for peacekeepers who are also unmistakably professional soldiers, robust in their manner and well-equipped.'[25] Like it or not, these forces are only found in states such as UK, US, Australia, France and few others. Moreover, humanitarian NGOs, as noted by Thomas Weiss, have experienced a 'loss of innocence' regarding partnerships between robust peacekeepers and humanitarian agencies.[26] The necessity of collaboration has become all too clear.

Thus, successful peacekeeping operations of the future should consist of first class military forces, led by states with qualitatively superior armed forces, in partnership with NGOs on the ground. There is a distinct military dimension to the giving of humanitarian aid in complex emergencies. Success can best be achieved by a partnership between NGOs and the most qualified 'warriors' in the world. As NATO Secretary Lord Robertson stated, '... Civilians need a secure environment in which to do their work, and they depend on the militaries to provide that secure environment. For its part, the military depends on the civilians just as much.'[27]

Notes

1 L. Gordenker and T.G. Weiss, 'Pluralizing Global Governance: Analytical Approaches and Dimensions', in *NGOs, the United Nations, and Global Governance* (Boulder, CO: Lynne Rienner Publishers, 1996), pp. 19-21.
2 'Sierra Leone: The Forgotten Crisis – Report to the Minister of Foreign Affairs, the Honourable Lloyd Axworthy, P.C., M.P. from David Pratt, M.P., Nepean-Carleton, Special Envoy to Sierra Leone', 23 April 1999, <http://www.sierra-leone.org/pratt042399.html>.
3 'Sierra Leone: U.N. Peacekeepers Arrive; Other Development', *Facts on File*, 9 December 1999. Online.
4 'Sierra Leone: Deployment of Additional UN Forces', *Keesing's Record of World Events*, October 2000, p. 43781.
5 '5,000 British Troops Placed on Sierra Leone Alert', *PANA*, 11 October 2000. ReliefWeb.
6 'Sierra Leone: Civil Society Movt. Organizes Demonstration in Favor of UK Troops', *Agence France Presse*, 23 November 2000. ReliefWeb.
7 'British Defense Minister Supports Decision to Delay Sierra Leone Polls', *Agence France Presse*, 1 February 2001. Online.
8 P.R. Wilkinson, 'Peace Support Under Fire: Lessons from Sierra Leone', *ISIS Briefing on Humanitarian Intervention*, No. 2, June 2000. Online.
9 'People of Sierra Leone Need Peace Enforcers, Not Peace Keepers', *Catholic Agency for Overseas Development*, 9 May 2000. ReliefWeb.
10 'Sierra Leone: Oxfam GB Public Message', *Oxfam*, 10 May 2000. ReliefWeb.

11 'Statement on Sierra Leone', *Global Ministries – Africa*, 19 July 2000. <http://www.globalministries.org/africa/a072000.htm>.

12 'Sierra Leone – UNHCR 2002 Global Appeal', Online.

13 'Sierra Leone: Coping with a Permanent Medical Emergency', <http://www.msf.org/content>.

14 'Sierra Leone: International Community Must Stay Involved After Elections', *Amnesty International*, 1 May 2002. Online.

15 'Sierra Leone: Kabbah Reelected President', *Facts on File*, 23 May 2002. Online.

16 '27 British NGOs Call for Peacekeeping Troops in East Timor', 3 September 1999, <http://www.etan.org/et99b/september/1-4/3-27ngo.htm>.

17 M. Macan-Markar, 'Peacekeepers Put NGO High on List of Strategic Partners', *Asia Times*, 14 March 2002. Online.

18 'Justice in Practice: Human Rights in Court Administration, JSMP, Dili', *Crimes of War Project*, 10 December 2001, <http://www.crimesofwar.org/onnews/news-easttimor.html>.

19 S. Chesterman, 'Truth and Reconciliation in East Timor', May 2001, <http://www.globalpolicy.org/intljustice/general/2001/easttimor.htm>.

20 'UNDP Emergency Response Mission to East Timor', <http://www.undp.org/erd/east_timor/>.

21 'Humanitarian Policy Group Report: Terms of Engagement, Conditions and Conditionality in Humanitarian Action', *Overseas Development Institute*, July 2000, pp. 9-10.

22 Mary B. Anderson, *Do No Harm: How Aid Can Support Peace-Or-War* (Lynne Rienner, 1999), p. 1.

23 Karin Aggestam, 'Conflict Prevention: Old Wine in New Bottles?', *International Peacekeeping*, 10/1 (2003): 13-14.

24 Andrew Harris and Peter Dombrowski, 'Military Collaboration with Humanitarian Organizations in Complex Emegencies', *Global Governance*, 8/2 (Apr-Jun 2002). Retrieved from Academic Search Online.

25 Hugo Slim, 'Military Humanitarianism and the New Peacekeeping: An Agenda for Peace?', *The Journal of Humanitarian Assistance*, 3 June 2000. <http://www.jha.ac/articles/a003.htm>.

26 C. Bellamy, 'Combining Combat Readiness and Compassion', *NATO Review*, 49/2 (Summer 2001). Online.

27 M. Pugh, 'Military Intervention and Humanitarian Action: Trends and Issues', *Disasters*, 22/4 (1998): 340.

28 'Perspectives on Democratic Civil-Military Relations and Reform'.

Part Three:
NGOs in Peacebuilding

Chapter 10

When Civil Society Promotion Fails State-Building: The Inevitable Fault-Lines in Post-Conflict Reconstruction

Julie Mertus and Tazreena Sajjad

Over the past two decades, the clarion call for civil society to consolidate the nation-building process has grown louder. The space between the government and the people has been rapidly filled with institutions, organisations and movements with increasing legitimacy to voice the concerns of those outside power structures. Today, global trends of promoting democracy and the vehicle of democratisation in the process of state-building, either from the ashes of protracted violent conflict or from the ruins of authoritarian regimes, are incomplete without the component of civil society promoting the interests of the general public. In this framework, most often the focus is on the development of NGOs, at times to the extent that the term NGO is equated with 'civil society'. As a result, grassroots organisations and other alternative forms of social arrangements are squeezed out. In this climate the measure of a healthy democracy has, to a great extent, implied the NGO-centered infrastructure for elections and the establishment of a civil society network that challenges government and fills in the gaps in the provision of public services ... Civil society has hence emerged as a crucial component of democracies, and has been seen as one of the most essential elements for assisting a society into making the transition from conflict into the post-conflict stage and consolidating the peaceful politics.

In the heady democratisation climate, civil society tends to be invoked triumphantly, as a panacea to all that ails a state. States should be more wary, however, before they jump on the civil society bandwagon. A strong civil society and vibrant NGO sector has the potential to hinder, rather than enhance, civic nationalism and, thus, to create a weak state. This chapter explores the emerging tensions between civil society and nation-building in post-conflict situations. We argue that in several cases, civil society in fact fails the project of nation-building through undercutting the legitimacy and the potency of new states. Among other suggestions we urge patience in democratisation. Weak states, we believe, need time to consolidate its own institutions and gain legitimacy in the eyes of its constituents rather than following the continuing largely western dictated formula for functional and open societies.

Achilles' Heel: Questioning the 'Good' in Civil Society

Numerous actors at work on peace-building, ranging from the World Bank,[1] to the United States Agency for International Development (USAID),[2] to the Open Society Institute[3] have embraced the notion that state building and civil society go hand in hand. To take just one illustration, a recent USAID publication proclaims that civil society plays a critical role in democracies by 'informing citizens about their rights and responsibilities and ensuring that governments meet citizen needs'.[4] If all goes well, then the growth of civil society should support the development of a strong state, defined in terms of capacity (ability to devise policies and to see them through), autonomy (ability to independently of local and international actors) and legitimacy (defined in terms of acceptability of process and normative content).[5] Yet this is not always the case.

The experience of Bosnia and Herzegovina, Kosovo and more recently Afghanistan proves that civil society building may fail to support and, in some cases, even undercut state capacity, autonomy and legitimacy. The democracy template,[6] comprising of free and fair elections and state institutions and grounded on a diverse, active and independent civil society that articulates the interests of citizens and holds government accountable to its citizens seems rather incomplete, and devoid of an ingrained connection with local expectations and needs. Interestingly enough, looking through aid documents from the 1960s, one has a strong sense of déjà vu, reading about the importance of increasing participation, strengthening local governments, building community based advocacy groups, training women civic leaders, and the like.[7] Today, these visions have taken on more consolidated forms. More efficient, sophisticated NGOs and INGOs with strong bargaining positions can lobby for and help implement well-defined strategies and coherent timelines about how they could assist countries make permanent transitions from war, divisiveness and anarchy into functional, accepting, pluralistic nations of peace.

The problem lies is expecting civil society to take charge of, and transform overnight, the extent of this destruction and lead the way for social reconstruction. However, the sociopolitical nuances that need to be taken into consideration are for the most part denied to many of the forms of civil society, making its task largely unsustainable and impractical. Instead of challenging the particularly virulent forms of nationalism[8] prevalent at that time, many social organisations were either actively complicit in spreading nationalisms or were indirectly supportive, by failing to offer direct challenges and by organising themselves exclusively on ethnic lines.[9] It is for this reason that some commentators point to a 'stunted civil society' as a causal factor in both war and reconstruction reform.[10]

Civil Society as NGO Proliferation

Effective and functioning NGOs are said to contribute to a civic culture, and thus serve as precondition for and the result of effective and legitimate democratic institutions. NGOs are supposed to act as a counterweight to state power, protecting human rights, opening up channels of communication and participation, providing training grounds for activists and promoting pluralism. As a result of these developments, governments are prepared to provide increasing amounts of official aid to and through NGOs since they are seen to be effective vehicles for the promotion of economic and political objectives of aid packages. Consequently, today, nation-building processes working with the underpinning of democratic values and norms have led to the inevitable outcome – NGO proliferation. In developing countries as well as in post-conflict societies, international reformers conflate 'civil society' with NGOs and then use a head count as a crude index of the health of a civil society.[11] For the social and economic side of development, working with NGOs was thus often a means of avoiding governments rather than engaging them.[12]

If numbers of NGOs are indeed a lodestar of success, then civil society in post-conflict societies such as in Bosnia, Kosovo and Afghanistan are indeed thriving. Effective and functioning NGOs are said to contribute to a civic culture, and thus serve as precondition for and the result of effective and legitimate democratic institutions. On the whole, the local NGOs at work in post-conflict societies can be divided two broad categories: development or service NGOs and democracy NGOs. As the name suggests, development or service NGOs provide services that the state either cannot or will not provide, such as psychosocial counseling, prenatal heath care, or specific programs for the disabled, youth, women or the elderly. In the short term, however, service-oriented NGOs serve to energize the local population and encourage them to participate in their communities, thus readying them to be good citizens once their democratic state is up and running.[13] The problem, as one can predict, lies more in the long run, with civil society creating greater reliance on NGO services than on those provided by the state. This also means that to some extent, the state is disinclined to provide centralized public services to its constituencies. Consequently, when NGOs become cheap service providers and, in some cases even replace the local public sector, they undermine the country's long-term ability to develop an efficient state.[14]

Democracy NGOs, meanwhile, assume the functioning of a democratic government and seek to advance political agendas and influence policy formation and implementation.[15] By representing diverse interests and traditionally marginalized groups, they serve to undermine divisive nationalism and create a culture of tolerance necessary for participatory democracy to take root.[16] Given their close and immediate tie to democracy-promotion, democracy-NGOs are generally thought to be more important for state building than development or service provision NGOs.[17] The reality of power politics, continued ethnic tensions, poor economic performance and high levels of corruption indicate that the assumption that local NGOs will take on these tasks appears to be unfounded.

The increasing availability of official funding for both service and democracy NGOs and the popularity they enjoy can be viewed as 'both an opportunity and a danger'. Some NGOs may have the opportunity to scale-up their operations, and to demand more decision-making authority and autonomy from their donors. But for many others, more resources means even greater dependence and co-option into international agendas, erosion of local capacities and the weakening of state structures. Drawing from field research conducted in Bosnia in 2003, as well as from other field reports,[18] we now consider some of the reasons civil society projects have failed, on the whole, to make a significant contribution to the building of a strong state.

The focus of civil interventions under these circumstances should be on building a strong governmental infrastructure, legitimate in the eyes of, and accountable to its *local* constituency. Instead, the dynamics surrounding civil society seem to leapfrog beyond the intermediate stages of statehood into the realm of far more politically advanced countries where the public infrastructures are already established and where civil society has a long tradition of complimenting the process of participatory governance.

The formula of transplanting American-style advocacy NGOs to other countries is often unsuccessful, since advocacy NGOs are a product of the American experience and are alien to many socio-political cultures.[19] As Thomas Carothers has observed, American NGOs 'have grown out of particular aspects of America's social makeup and history – whether the immigrant character of society, the "frontier" mindset, the legacy of suspicion of central government authority, or the high degree of individualism'.[20] The political culture in many post-conflict societies on the other hand is decidedly different stemming from collective identity rather than the focus on individuality and individual's claims on the state.

Advocacy NGOs are not always an effective mechanism for voicing the general concerns of a population and for example, in many instances in the former Yugoslavia they are inappropriate. Advocacy NGOs are said to work when they promote civic participation and general human rights norms, as well as more specific expressions of public interest. However, advocacy-NGOs often promote the most 'popular' (that is, moneyed) causes, often at the expense of the real public interest. The problem is particularly acute in cases like Bosnia and Herzegovina where new NGOs emerged almost overnight, propped up by foreign dollars. While some of these NGOs perform admirable functions, the public see many of them as reflecting the values and interests of foreign governments and foreign NGOs, and not representative of the most pressing local concerns.[21] Indeed, many Bosnian NGOs lack ties to any grassroots base and instead reproduce concerns of elites.[22]

Observations from the field indicate that in a climate where Western models dominate, the imposition of inappropriate models may be difficult, if not impossible, to avoid. CARE has attempted to counter the Western development model with a 'non-directive' approach, which seeks to fund the activities of existing grassroots associations and self-help groups without requiring the sustainability of a particular structure. This allows CARE to be 'more concerned with the human resources and energies of the group and, in particular, its volunteers'.[23] Nonetheless, despite the efforts of CARE and some other donors to resist imposing Western models, the possibility of indirect promulgation exists. As Aida Bagic and Paul Stubbs write, 'The role of local staff, themselves trained in Western models of NGOs, and with their own preferences for particular kinds of groups, cannot be considered as neutral by definition, but needs to be looked at in practice'. In addition, international involvement in civil society development programs tends to be predominantly from Western European and North American traditions.[24] The priority given to NGOs may detract from other important voices such as official representatives and other community leaders who either have failed at attracting international support or who have chosen to not operate through an NGO.[25]

Dependency Syndrome/Imposition of Agendas

Drawing from the experience of developing countries, states making the transition to peace too are vulnerable to the political economy of aid dependence. Large amounts of aid delivered over long periods have the potential to undermine good governance and the quality of state institutions.[26] Furthermore, donor agencies and foreign experts often take over many of the critical functions of governance: substituting their own goals for an absent leadership vision, using foreign experts and project management units in place of weak or decaying public institutions. In these countries, aid has been part of the problem. And long-term dependence on aid creates disincentives for both donors and governments to change the rules of their engagement. [27] It maybe asserted that the international community's traditional strategy of trying to bring an end to the conflict by backing a proposed winner does not take into account precisely those people, who unlike warring factions have a stake in the rebuilding of institutions and the creation of a state responsive to their needs – a state with which they can interact as citizens.[28]

The cycle of dependency that emerges in post-conflict states as a consequence of foreign donors deciding and controlling agendas for local NGOs therefore, creates sharp division between the local populations and the well-intentioned bodies designed to serve them. Dependency on international actors draws the focus of accountability toward the international donor and away from the organisation's social base. In other words, donor-imposed systems of accountability do more than divert attention away from local constituents. In this new politics of accountability, the two dimensions of accountability – horizontal (concerned with the effective operation of the system of checks and balances and with due process in government decision-making) and the vertical (focused on the ways in which citizens control the government)[29] – are skewed. Ultimately, local communities may have a higher degree of accountability to an audience that is not on the receiving end of the services.[30] The consequences and implications for the state are clear: 'In this context, the advocacy role of civil society is better exercised by pressuring international civil servants rather than local political leaders'.[31]

In addition, the outcome-oriented nature of Western accountability models tends to restrict local creativity. As one influential study of NGOs concludes: 'Deriving from linear world views, with targets and sanctions to be imposed in the event of non-achievement, [Western accountability models] reinforce pressures for NGOs to transform themselves into routine service providers, reducing in the process their capacity to explore new ideas, or to tackle the more deep-seated or intractable problems of institutional development'.[32] Instead of long-term social change, emphasis is placed on immediately quantifiable results. What is expected is for local NGOs to speak the language of the donor community. While there is pressure to conform to existing donor template, there is also the reality of trying to compete with established international heavyweights for funding and all of this compounded by certain time-frames which organisations need to meet. Meanwhile, attempting to get assistance funds out of the door as rapidly as possible tempts aid providers to pay little attention to the actual local commitment to the projects and to put can do consultants and organisations in the nuances of local realities in charge of the work.[33] NGOs that depend on official funding often perform poorly in the crucial task of local institutional development, the gradual strengthening of capacities and capabilities among GROs to enable them to play a more effective and independent role in development[34]

The 'dependency trap' – to use Florian Beiber's terminology – effectively reduces the potential of local grass roots NGOs by creating 'numerous incentives based on assessments of Western donors and less on local needs'.[35] Local organisations are constrained by the necessity of designing projects around changing donor agendas rather than on the building of local constituencies. According to one local NGO leader, international assistance and bureaucratic efficiency takes a toll:

> Before [our intentions] were perfectly honest, and perfectly clear – to work for the good of our country. Now it has become[36] a job, one worth millions, in which continuing the job is the most important goal ... If the project looks good on paper then it is not at all important what happens.[37]

It is no wonder then that a study of youth groups funded by CARE in Bosnia found that 'those with significant international agency involvement in their founding, and/or with significant levels of funding, and/or with a salaried staff member, had much less chance of sustainability than those that were locally developed, organic, and realistic about the role and levels of funding required'.[38]

A survey of Bosnian NGOs conducted by the Bosnian office of the Open Society Institute (OSI) found that the majority of local NGOs are 'donor oriented', rather than 'program oriented' (those that focus on what they want to do and how, allowing for the possibility to learn how to do it). The OSI report further warned that:

> Authentic civil society requires primarily the 'program oriented' NGOs rather than those which plan and effect their actions in accordance with estimates and information on what the wishes of the donors are (in Bosnia and Herzegovina those are almost always foreign donors). The latter category of NGOs can hardly be the structure that long term development of an authentic third sector and thus an authentic civil society in Bosnia and Herzegovina can rest on.[39]

Interestingly, Bagic found that in the organisations initiated and sustained by internationals, 'the level of democratic development of some of the groups was extremely depressing ...'[40] and 'the real relationship of groups to ethnicized nationalism is masked by the expectation, on the part of some, that international agencies will require a clear statement of their "multi-national" membership'.[41] The imbalanced focus on how NGOs should be structured, what their agendas should be and who they should serve, based on the fancies of an international donor community, which may or may not have links to the actual needs and priorities of the Bosnian society, serve to curtail, rather than enhance, a robust process of nation-building.

Undermining of Local Efforts

State building efforts that advance their own models and agendas and fail to appreciate local efforts may be less effective and even harmful to the project of state building.[42] The reporting requirements and short time frame may be simply impractical and may break fledgling organisations; many small organisations cannot predict-for themselves, their staff or their beneficiaries-where funding will come from even in the near future.[43] Long-term organisational development is impaired where funding priorities shift constantly according to the 'discovery' of the day as dictated by internationals.[44] Moreover, the lack of stable, long-term funding leads to competition among NGOs and, as Sevima Sali-Terzic observes, 'this results in a low level of cooperation and coordination'.[45]

On the one hand, the functioning of grassroots NGOs suffers when the international actors overseeing the reconstruction project have the ability to hire the best and brightest local talent who might otherwise work for local groups.[46] But on the other hand, local capacities are also undercut when organisations use foreign experts and project management units in place of scouting local talent. In either case, an internationalized national civil society is created with little connection to the local community. The emerging 'project society' reflects not local concerns and local talents, but simply 'short term projects with a budget and a time schedule'.[47] Steven Sampson explains:

> Projects always end, ostensibly to be replaced by policy but normally to be replaced by another project. Project society entails a special kind of structure, beginning with the donor, the project identification mission, the appraisal, the selection of an implementing partner, the disbursement of funds, the monitoring, the evaluation, and, of course, the next project. Project society is about the allocation of resources in an organized, bureaucratic fashion.[48]

When internationals view building civil society as a technical task, as a matter of institution building and service delivery, they overlook the importance of addressing communal conflict and promoting cooperative power relationships. Unwittingly, trans-state forces solidify the power of nationalist and elite-based political institutions and create new power struggles within civil society. International involvement in civil society projects thus has the potential to alter existing relationships, contribute to greater social fragmentation and create new hierarchies, with those supported by the international community on top and those that are not on the bottom. In the long-run, a third wheel of socio-politics may be created that benefits a handful of the political elites and serves the interests of foreign donors and a few members of a foreign civil society leading ultimately to a lack of local ownership of aid projects. Assistance projects that are funded, designed, managed, and evaluated by foreigners are only occasionally backed by much real commitment or attachment from people in the recipient countries themselves.[49]

The ultimate problem then is the sustainability of NGOs as vital foundation stones of civil society. In places like Afghanistan, the NGO sector is widely seen as overpaid, and self-interested and dependent almost entirely on foreign funding. The salaries and services available in these NGOs are in sharp contrast to the reality of the dire socioeconomic realities of these countries.[50] The local talent, which could have been harnessed for local efforts in promoting sustainable programs, are instead lured away to work in blue-collar positions in international organisations where salaries are actually higher. In addition, the presence of foreign workers can displace growth in civil society.

Imposition of Norms

Finally, the legitimacy of the state depends, not only on the right process, but also on the right normative choices; in post-conflict societies such as Bosnia, Afghanistan and possibly in Iraq in the future, the normative choices of state and trans-state forces often do not resonate [and will not] with those of civil society. The western ideal for representative democracy involves free, multiparty elections and maintenance of civil liberties. Aristotle's prediction that a democracy can only flourish in a state with a large middle class[51] and the poverty facing many countries suggests a more complex reality: participatory democracy can be sustained only where a certain minimum social and economic standards are met, including minimum educational standards and freedom from severe material deprivation.[52] Washington's forceful recommendations of democratic governments, without taking into consideration social and economic rights on one hand and prioritising expediency over long-term sustainable strategies have led to catastrophic failures as witnessed in places like Congo, Guatemala, South Vietnam[53] and now in Haiti. Hence, the overt focus on and the implicit and explicit acceptance of norms of 'civic nationalism' and 'multiculturalism' coated within the accepted norms of democracy is continually paving the way for more tensions and irreconcilable differences between the state and the civil society.

Conclusion

The tensions between nation-building and civil society is pulling civil society in two directions. One direction is guided by the international community's vision for a post-conflict society and the other follows the aspirations of the constituents of the society. Thus the stage is set for possible fragmentation and cleavages within the new republic. One alternative is for the international community to become *better* state builders. They could guard against the creation of dependency relationships and stop imposing western models, foreign priorities and outsider norms.

Another alternative would be to temporarily *stop trying* to build a strong state. They could engage in the kind of projects that are needed to preserve the peace, such as building democratic institutions and quietly nurturing future leaders. This would entail standing by while a weak state (defined in terms of capacity, autonomy and legitimacy) wobbles and slowly finds its footing. This might be an uncomfortable one for liberals and nationalists alike, but in some cases it could be the only viable and sustainable option. Hence, in evaluating the impact of civil society on the ultimate state building process, rather than an evaluation of civil society's relationship with the state, a more relevant study can be found in examining whether civil society supports the kind of local political processes that may be a component of an eventual strong and just state.

Notes

1   <http://www.worldbank.org>; In particular, see World Bank, ECSSD, 'Bosnia and Herzegovina: Local Level Institutions and Social Capital Study, Volume 1', June 2002. Available from: <http://www.christophesolioz.ch/links/doc/wbbalocaljune2002.pdf>.

2   Http://www.usaid.gov; see, in particular USAID, 'Building Democracy in Bosnia and Herzegovina', available from <http://www.usaid.gov/democracy/ee/bosnia.html>.

3   <http://www.soros.org>; See, in particular, Open Society Fund Bosnia and Herzegovina, '2001 Report – Civil Society', Available from <http://www.soros.org.ba/en/programi/civilno_drustvo/izvjestaji.shtml>.

4   'Building Democracy in Bosnia and Hercegovina' (United States Agency for International Development, 2002). <http://www.usaid.gov/democracy/ee/bosnia.html>.

5   Marie-Joelle Zahar, book chapter draft on file with author.

6   Carothers, p. 86.

7   Carothers, p. 53.

8   Nationalism is used herein in the sense of 'ethnic nationalism', that is communities of sentiment, as opposed to civic nationalism, a concept more neatly tied to the need to create a state. Will Kymlicka, *Multicultural Citizenship* (Oxford Univ. Press, 1995), p. 24. 'Nationalism is a relational term whose identity derives from its inherence in a system of differences.'

9   It should be noted that great regional variations in the capacities of civil society organizations have always existed through Yugoslavia. Compare, e.g., Paul Stubbs, 'Nationalism, Globalization and Civil Society in Croatia and Slovenia', *Research in Social Movements, Conflict and Change*, 19 (1996): 1-26 and Jason Alpon and Victor Tanner, *Civil Society in Bosnia: Obstacles and Opportunities for Building Peace* (Washington, D.C.: Winston Foundation for World Peace, 2000).

10 United States Institute of Peace. 'Lawless Rule versus Rule of Law in the Balkans', *Special Report*, 97 (December 2002). Available from <http://www.usip.org/pubs/specialreports/sr97.pdf>.

11 Open Society Fund Bosnia and Herzegovina, '2001 Report – Civil Society', available from <http://www.soros.org.ba/en/programi/civilno_drustvo/izvjestaji.shtml>.

12 Open Society Fund, p. 214.

13 Carol Zabin and Andrea Brown, 'Bridging the NGO-Grassroots Gap', *Borderlines*, 4/3 (March 1996): 22.

14 Bellogini, 'Building Civil Society in Bosnia', pp. 4-9.

15 Roberto Belloni, 'Building Civil Society in Bosnia-Herzegovina', *Human Rights Working Papers*, No. 2, 12 January 2000. Available from <http://www.du.edu/humanrights/workingpapers/papers/02-belloni-01-00.pdf>.

16 For more on civil society development and its role in Yugoslavia, see David Chandler, 'Democratization in Bosnia: The Limits of Civil Society Building', *Democratization*, 5/4 (Winter 1998): 78-102.

17 Larry Diamond, 'What Civil Society Can do to Reform, Deepen, and Improve Democracy', Paper presented to the Workshop on Civil Society, Social Capital, and Civic Engagement in Japan and the United States, Sponsored by the Japan Foundation Center for Global Partnership, The Asia Foundation, and the Program for US–Japan Relations at Harvard University, 12–13 June 2001, Tokyo.

18 One of the most influential reports from the region is Zarko Papic (ed.), 'International Support Policies To See Countries-Lessons (Not) Learned In Bosnia-Herzegovina' (Open Society Institute, Bosnia and Herzegovina, 2001). <http://www.soros.org.ba/ en/dokumenti/ostali/book/index.shtml>. Particularly insightful field reports on specific civil society initiates include: Ulla Engberg and Paul Stubbs, *Social Capital and Integrate Development: a Civil Society Grants Programme in Travnik, Bosnia-Herzegovina*, Helsinki, GASPP, Occasional Papers (1999), No. 2; Ivar Evensmo, 'A case study on the Western Balkans: Evaluating Sida's support to the Olof Palme Centre (1988–1999)', *Assessment of Lessons Learned from SIDA Support to Conflict Management and Peace Building* (Stockholm: SIDA, 2000); and 'Dialogue Development, Bosnia Civil Society Development: Mapping, Characteristics and Strategies', EU Commission PHARE, consulting report (1997).

19 See generally Julie Mertus, 'The Liberal State and the Liberal Soul: Rule of Law Projects in Societies in Transition', *Social and Legal Studies*, 8/1 (1999); and Julie Mertus, 'Mapping Civil Society Transplants – A Preliminary Comparison of Eastern Europe and Latin America', *University of Miami Law Journal* and *University of Texas Hispanic Bar Journal* (1999).

20 Thomas Carothers, *The Learning Curve* (Washington DC: Carnegie Endowment for International Peace, 1999), p. 98.

21 Carothers, p. 212.

22 Paul Stubbs, 'Social Work and Civil Society in Bosnia and Herzegovina: Globalisation, Neo-feudalism and the State', *International Perspectives on Social Work* (1999): 55-64.

23 Aida Bagić and Paul Stubbs, 'Civil Society Development Programme An Independent Evaluation, CARE International Bosnia and Herzegovina and Croatia' (Zagreb, Croatia, 2000). <http://www.carecro.org/care/dok/CSD_report.doc>.

24 Ibid.

25 Mertus develops these thoughts in 'Improving International Peacebuilding Efforts: The Example of Human Rights Culture in Kosovo', *Global Governance* (forthcoming 2004).

26 D. Brautigam, *Aid Dependence and Governance* (Almquiest and Wiksell International, 2000).

27 Ibid.

28 Ana Cutter; 'Building Peace and Civil Society in Afghanistan: Challenges and Opportunities; Carnegie Council on Ethics and International Affairs', Symposium held in New York on 17 May and Washington D.C. on 18 May 2001.

29 Catalina Smulovitz and Enrique Peruzzotti, 'Societal Accountability in Latin America', *Journal of Democracy*, 11/4 (October 2000): 147.

30 Roberto Belloni, 'Building Civil Society in Bosnia Herzegovina', *Human Rights Working Papers*, No. 2, 12 January 2000; <http://www.du.edu/humanrights/ workingpapers/index.html>.

31 Ibid.

32 Vandana Desai and Mick Howes, 'Accountability and Participation: A Case from Bombay', in Michael Edwards and David Hulme (eds), *Nongovernmental Organisations – Performance and Accountability* (London: Earthscan Publications, 2002), p. 84.

33 Ibid, p. 261.

34 Ibid, p. 7.

35 Bieber, Florian, 'Aid Dependency in Bosnian Politics and Civil Society: Failures and Successs of Post-War Peacebuilding in Bosnia-Herzegovina', *Croatian International Relations Review* 8: 26/27 (Zagreb 2002). Available at: <www.policy.hu/bieber/Publications/BieberAidDependency2.pdf>.

36 *Peacebuilding: A Field Guide* (eds), Luc Reychler and Thania Paffenholz (Boulder, CO: Lynne Rienner, 2001).

37 Gordy, p. 5.

38 Bagić and Stubbs, 'Civil Society Development Programme An Independent Evaluation, CARE International Bosnia and Herzegovina and Croatia'.

39 'Open Society Fund 2001 Report – Civil Society', <http://www.soros.org.ba/en/programi/civilno_drustvo/izvjestaji.shtm391>.

40 Bagic and Stubbs, 'Civil Society Development Programme: An Independent Evaluation, CARE International Bosnia and Herzegovina and Croatia'.

41 Ibid.

42 See Report of the Panel on United Nations Peace Operations (Brahimi Report). Web: <http://www.un.org/peace/reports/peace_operations/>.

43 Ian Smillie, 'Non-Governmental Organizations in Bosnia and Herzegovina', CARE Canada (December 1996).

44 Bieber, 'Aid Dependency in Bosnian Politics and Civil Society: Failures and Successs of Post-War Peacebuilding in Bosnia-Herzegovina'.

45 Sali-Tezic, p. 140.

46 Ibid.

47 Steven Sampson, 'What Really Happens When We Export Democracy: Experiences from the Balkans', *Watson Institute Report*, Available at: <http://www.watsoninstitute.org/muabet/new_site/Helsink_helsinki.pdf>. See Steven Sampson, 'From Forms to Norms: Global Projects and Local Practices in the Balkan NGO Scene,' in Henry F. Carey (guest ed.), *Journal of Human Rights* 2/3 (September 2002).

48 Sampson, 'What Really Happens When We Export Democracy.'

49 Ibid, p. 260.

50 Ibid. p. 225.

51 Aristotle, *Politics*, Book VII, trans. H. Rackham (Cambridge MA: Harvard University Press, 1932).

52 Robert J. Barro, 'Don't Bank on Democracy in Afghanistan', *Businessweek*, 21 January 2002, p. 18-19. Available at: <http://proquest.ui.com/pqdweb?index=25&did=000000100510772&SrchMode=1>. (Viewed on 7 March 2004) Also see Robert J. Barro, 'Democracy in Afghanistan? Don't Hold Your Breath', *Hoover Digest* 2 (Spring 2002); Available at: <http://www-hoover.stanford.edu/publications/digest/022/barro.html> (Viewed on 8 March 2004).

53 Llewllyn D. Howell, Nation-building, *USA Today*, New York, January 2002, 130/2680, p. 30; Available at: <http://gateway.proquest.com/openurl?ctx_ver=z39.88-2003&res_id=xri:pqd&rft_val_fmy=ori:fmt:kev:mtx:journal&genre=article&rft_id=xri:pqd:dd=0000009> (Viewed on 7 March 2004).

Chapter 11

Private Military Companies in Peacebuilding

Marek Pavka

Even if sanctioned by the UN, NGOs utilising force have questionable legality as combatants under the Geneva Convention. Peacebuilding is probably the most ambitious form of peacekeeping, as it attempts to guarantee peace by establishing social, political and economical structures. Many authors argue that this task is too difficult for the UN. NGOs have undertaken various peacebuilding tasks, though the emergence of illegal mercenaries and 'legal' security services raises the question of what are the benefits and costs of NGOs using force?

What is a Private Military Company?

After the end of the Cold War developed states reduced their armed forces. In 1987 the number of armed forces personnel reached 28,320; in 1994 those numbers had dropped to approximately 23,500. Private military companies (PMC) have emerged in the disparity, left by the disinterest of economically developed countries concerning less developed areas of the world. PMCs offer a broad scale of services, including consultations, combat actions, and Third World governments.[1] These companies range from very small companies, as Deborah Avant comments, 'essentially a retired military guy sitting in a spare bedroom with a fax machine and Rolodex',[2] to big conglomerates such as the Hong Kong-based company, Securicor, which employs more than 100,000 people.

Among managers of private military companies are experts from armed forces and decision-making structures of states. For example, the CEO of Braddock, Dunn and McDonald Inc. (BDM), headquartered in McLean, Virginia, is former American Minister of Defense Frank Carlucci. Other notable managers and consultants at BDM include Philip Odeen, advisor to Henry Kissinger in the 1970s, and former Secretary of State James Baker. Likewise, two former Secretaries of Defense, William Perry and Melvin Laird, are board members at SAIC, as are two ex-CIA Directors, John Deutsch and Robert Gates.[3]

Similarly Military Professional Resources Inc. (MPRI), founded in 1987 and based in Alexandria, Virginia, has in its database six thousand former American soldiers, and among its employees are 17 retired generals. In addition, MPRI employs the former Commander of US troops in Europe, General Frederick

Kroensen, Chief of Staff of ground forces in 1987 to 1992; General Carl E. Vuono, Commander of American ground forces in Europe from 1988 to 1992; General Crosby E. Saint, former head of the Defense Intelligence Agency; General Harry Soyster and former Army Vice Chief of Staff General Ron Griffith. Tim Spicer, Director of the UK company, Sandline International, was Captain of the Scottish Guard in the Falkland war. Spicer also participated in the Gulf war in 1992 and in the UNPROFOR peacekeeping mission in Bosnia. Furthermore, the Chief of South African Executive Outcomes (EO), Eeben Barlow, was deputy commander of special battalion Buffalo. In the UK, Simon Mann managed EO in 1993. He was the former Deputy Commander of Unit 22 of SAS and by Tony Buckingham, another veteran of the SAS. Buckingham was also the manager of mining company Heritage Oil and Gas, in which former leader of the Liberal Party David Steel was also in management.

Such a connection to the establishment has predictable consequences. Barry Yeoman describes the relation of PMCs and government as existing 'based on years of camaraderie', although 'The companies do not rely on informal networking alone'. Seventeen leading US private military companies have pumped more than $12.4 million USD in congressional and presidential campaigns since 1999. Moreover, in 2001, according to federal disclosure forms, ten private military companies spent more than $32 million USD on lobbying.[4] Yeoman states that PMCs are:

> ... focusing much of their manpower on Capitol Hill. Many are staffed with retired military officers who are well connected at the Pentagon – putting them in a prime position to influence government policy and drive more business to their firms. In one instance, private contractors successfully pressured the government to lift a ban on American companies providing military assistance to Equatorial Guinea, a West African nation accused of brutal human-rights violations. Because they operate with little oversight, using contractors also enables the military to skirt troop limits imposed by Congress and to carry out clandestine operations without committing US troops or attracting public attention.[5]

Moreover DynCorp, a Virginia-based military and technology company that receives more than 96 per cent of its annual revenues from US federal government funding, retained two lobbying firms to block a bill that would have forced federal agencies to justify private contracts on cost-saving grounds. The lobbying was successful in 2001.[6] Furthermore, industry projections in 1997 suggested that revenues from the global international security market were about $55.6 billion USD in 1990 and were expected to rise to $202 billion USD in 2010.[7] With such a large international market, it would be foolish to believe other companies would not join the fray.

What are the Pros and Cons of Privatized Peacekeeping?

1) Absence of Political and Organisational Restrictions

Doug Brooks points out that PMCs lack both the cumbersome bureaucracy of the UN and the obsession of so called exit strategies by the USA.[8] Also, PMCs do not need to consider the body-bag effect and thus the impact on public opinion when pictures of killed soldiers are shown on television. Deborah Avant points out the contrast of the silence in the media concerning the fate of three US contractors working for California Microwave Systems, who have been captured by FARC guerillas in Colombia, and media coverage concerning the case of former POW Jessica Lynch in Iraq.[9] Barry Yeoman comments on PMC engagements in Colombia, 'If the government were shipping home soldiers' corpses from the coca fields, the public outcry would be tremendous. However, more than 20 private contractors have been killed in Colombia alone since 1998, and their deaths have been barely registered'.[10] PMCs' lower sensitivity to casualties is influenced by the fact that they have suffered only a few casualties. For example, EO records 18 killed employees in Angola and two in Sierra Leone.

As written by Johan Schulhofer-Wohl, 'No country wishes to embark on a peacekeeping mission and find its troop contribution being sent home in coffins. But the deaths of the soldiers of a private military company, to be blunt, would not cause the same political problem that the deaths of a country's nationals do'.[11] Furthermore PMCs are not exposed to transnational limits, which complicate operations undertaken by multinational forces. One example of such a limitation is communication and coordination problems that can occur among contingents from differing nations. Similarly PMCs do not suffer the degree of confusion concerning command of troops that multinational peace forces have.

Another advantage of private military companies in comparison with UN forces is a reduction in the time needed to deploy personnel. For example, UNOSOM was deployed three months after the Security Council gave its authorisation. EO claimed to be able to field personnel anywhere in the world within 72 hours.[12] Northbridge Services, a private military company founded by retired UK and US soldiers, asserts it could deploy 500 to 2,000 armed men in Liberia in three weeks to halt the fighting, which has raged around the capital of Monrovia.[13] Often the time needed for deployment is a decisive matter. Consider the genocide in Rwanda where at the peak of horror, 15,000 people were slaughtered each day. In 1992, when US Marines distributed relief supplies in Somalia, the military contracted Kellog, Brown and Root for logistical support. Don Trautner, who runs the US army logistics program, commented on the performance of the company, 'They had laborers and vehicles at the Port of Mogadishu within eleven hours after we had given them notice'.[14] Moreover, PMCs have their own intelligence components. The UN has resisted creating intelligence offices in their organisation.

2) Higher Efficiency

The efficiency of private military companies is shown by two actions in Africa. In March of 1993, Executive Outcomes, utilising only 50 employees, seized the important oil-producing district of Soyo. This success led to other contracts between EO and the Luanda government in 1994. After signing this contract, Executive Outcomes deployed 500 of its employees in Angola who, in a short time, reversed the outcome of the war and forced UNITA to sign a peace treaty in Lusaka in November of 1994.

Further proof of the efficiency of private military companies is the engagement of Executive Outcomes in the war in Sierra Leone. This engagement started in March of 1995 when the government of Valentine Strasser hired EO to defeat the forces of the Revolutionary United Front (RUF), in order to establish stability and to support democratic elections. The first combat action by EO took place in April of 1995. At that time, RUF units were only 36 kilometers from the capital, Freetown. In only nine days, Executive Outcomes was able to push the RUF forces away from the capital, to a distance of approximately 126 kilometers. After only ten months the civil war ended. The number of EO employees never reached higher than 250. As a result of EO activities in 1996, Sierra Leone held the first presidential elections in 27 years.

Deployment of EO in these two countries was very successful and in both cases forced rebel movements to sign peace treaties. However, the international community, which mediated peace negotiations, agreed to the terms of Jonas Savimbi (leader of UNITA) and Foday Sankoh (leader of RUF), who conditioned the signing of peace treaties with the withdrawal of EO from the country. Paradoxically, the peacemaker was blamed as the main obstruction of peace. It is no surprise that in February of 1997, only six months after withdrawal of Executive Outcomes from the country, a move enforced by the international community, another coup d'état occurred. Further instability plagued the country of Sierra Leone. Likewise, UNITA renewed the war in Angola after the withdrawal of EO from the country.

3) Financial Expediency

According to the evidence, it seems that engagement of private military companies could be much cheaper than using a UN peacekeeping force. Consider the following; the contract between EO and the government of Angola set a price of $40 million USD for one year of engagement. However, the cost for one year of a peace mission, UNAVEM III, in Angola cost the UN $135 million USD. In addition, the planned UN peacekeeping mission in Sierra Leone cost $47 million USD for eight months of commitment. Indeed, from 1995 to 1997 Executive Outcomes was paid $1.2 million USD a month for its Sierra Leone operation; it hammered the rebels so thoroughly that they ran to the negotiating table, clearing the way for an election. The firm was replaced in Sierra Leone by ECOMOG, and the rebels resumed their limb chopping. Then came a UN peace force, whose current performance is encouraging – but at a cost of $47 million USD a month.[15]

Executive Outcomes performed a business exploration of whether it would have had the capacity to intervene in Rwanda in 1994. Internal plans claim that the company could have had armed troops on the ground within 14 days of its hire and been fully deployed with over 1,500 of its own soldiers, along with air and fire support, within six weeks. The cost for a six-month operation to provide protected safe havens from the genocide was estimated at $150 million USD, or approximately $600,000 a day. This private option compares quite favourably with the eventual UN relief operation, which was deployed only after the killings. The UN operation costs averaged $3 million USD a day and did nothing to save hundreds of thousands of lives.[16]

However, as shown by Deborah Avant, there are many situations when the stipulations placed on military contracts preclude competition and flexibility. She cites the case of fuel delivery by Kellog, Brown and Root to the US army in Iraq that 'cost savings are neither automatic nor guaranteed'.[17] Also, many authors argue that use of PMCs in peacekeeping could be risky. They claim that these factors could undermine the efficiency of PMCs in peacekeeping:

4) The Bad Image of Mercenaries

David Shearer argues that perception of private military companies through the prism of engagement of mercenaries in Africa in the 1960s is the main obstruction to their legitimisation.[18] He argues, 'The term "mercenaries" is a label that incites rabid emotion at the expense of good analysis'.[19] This stereotype may have certain repercussions in public opinion, as exemplified by student demonstrations in Papua-New Guinea against making contracts with Sandline International or the rhetoric of Iraqi resistance movements. This problem stems from the aforementioned lack of difference in legal definition between classical mercenaries and private military companies. PMCs have put forth a strong effort to prove that they are not the classic depiction of mercenaries.

5) Lack of Accountability

Critics argue that private military companies are beyond public control and that they are under a strong influence from multinational corporations, in particular mining companies. As said Senator Patrick J. Leahy, Democrat from Vermont and the chairman of the Foreign Operations subcommittee, 'This is especially true when it involves "private" soldiers who are not as accountable as US military personnel. Accountability is a serious issue when it comes to carrying guns or flying helicopters in pursuit of US foreign policy goals'.[20] Representative Jan Schakowsky, Democrat from Illinois, has also argued that the United States' growing use of private military companies hides the financial, personal and political costs of military operations overseas, since the concerns face little public scrutiny. She denounced their use and said, 'I continue to oppose the use of military contractors who are not subject to the same kind of scrutiny and accountability as US soldiers'.[21]

Andrew Mackinlay, a member of the UK Commons Foreign Affairs Select Committee, said on the possibility of the use of PMCs, 'It would create the potential for wrongdoing by companies that could then dissolve themselves and lose themselves in remote parts of the world, unaccountable for their conduct or stewardship of war'.[22] Furthermore, Daniel Nelson, a former professor of civil-military relations at the Defense Department's Marshall European Center for Security Study, says that engagement of private military companies creates 'what we used to call "plausible deniability". It is disastrous for democracy'.[23]

Such arguments may be supported by the case of the Alabama-based firm, Aviation Development Corporation, which provided reconnaissance for the CIA in South America. In 2001 Aviation Development misidentified an errant plane as possibly belonging to cocaine traffickers. Based on the company's information, the Peruvian air force shot down the aircraft, killing a US missionary and her daughter. Afterward, when members of Congress tried to investigate, the State Department and the CIA refused to provide any information, citing privacy concerns. According to a source familiar with the incident, administration officials told Congress, 'We can't talk about it. It's a private entity. Call the company'.[24]

Private military companies reply by illustrating a willingness to submit to law, both national and international. At the national level there exists in some resident countries a certain degree of control of these companies by the state. Simon Sheppard states that PMCs are, in reality, tools of foreign policy for their resident countries in hot spots where the official engagement would be too risky. The deployments of MPRI in the former Yugoslavia or Vinnell in Vietnam are examples of companies under the control of national governments. Another example is the USA's requirement that PMCs obtain permission from the government, according to the Arms Export Control Act and the Export Administration Act.[25]

Besides these rules of the game declared by companies, some authors argue that international regulation is also necessary for legitimising PMCs, considering national norms could differ from country to country. Herbert Howe suggests a two-level mechanism of international control. First, an international institution, likely the UN, should be responsible for registering private military companies. The second level of control should be the approval of specific PMC projects given by an international institution. This resembles the South African legislation, which regulates both the existence of the companies and their operations. PMCs must be licensed to operate, and their maneuvers must also be licensed per each contract undertaken.[26]

6) Lack of Discipline

PMCs refute the criticism of a lack of discipline – a phenomenon typical of classical mercenaries – by emphasising their professionalism. Tim Spicer refers to the fact that PMCs are as professional, human and disciplined as armed forces of First World countries, especially considering these firms are often managed by former officers from such states. Moreover, there is evidence of recognition of such professionalism from some NGOs. For example, Executive Outcomes was praised by humanitarian organisations in Sierra Leone.

However, there are always two sides to a story. In Bosnia, employees of DynCorp were found to be operating a sex-slave ring of young women who were held for prostitution after their passports were confiscated. The two employees made similar accusations that while working in Bosnia, where DynCorp was providing military equipment maintenance services, DynCorp employees kept under-aged women as sex slaves, even videotaping a rape. Charges included DynCorp turning a blind eye while its employees trafficked in women – including buying one for $1,000. However, the DynCorp employees involved were not soldiers; therefore their actions were not subject to military discipline. Nor did the accused face local justice; they were simply fired and sent home.[27] Additionally, a couple of abuses produced by PMCs have been registered in Iraq. On December 1, 2003, Fijian mercenaries of Global Risk Strategies were involved in a massacre in the city of Samarra, where they indiscriminately fired on built-up areas after a currency changeover convoy came under attack. At least ten Iraqi civilians were killed and numerous others wounded.[28] Indeed, most recently it appears that two employees of the private security company CACI have been involved in the abuse of prisoners at Abu Ghraib in Iraq.[29]

P.W. Singer states that military firms should be brought under the control of the law, just like any other industry. 'This will require both the extension of the International Court of Justice to their activities and clear contract provisos that military firm personnel fall under the jurisdiction of international tribunals.'[30]

7) Erosion of the State

Another criticism of PMCs is the concern that engagement of such companies could undermine the host state. The concern is related to similar experiences with mercenaries, like Bob Denard in Africa. Some may argue that this imported instability is not typical of just the past. For example in the 1990s, Colombia accused former officers of the Israel Defence Forces of helping the drug cartels.

However, EO's commitments in Sierra Leone have not lead to the erosion of this state; instead, EO has contributed to strengthening it. In the short time of its engagement, this company gained extensive popularity, not just among people in the country, but among public officials as well. President Kabbah stated that, 'EO came at the right time, they provided a good service ... we appreciate that'. Leader of the military regime Maata Bio, who ousted another man on horseback, Valentine Strasser in January 1996, said of EO, 'We didn't consider them as mercenaries but as people bringing in some sanity'.[31] US Ambassador to Sierra Leone, John Leigh, stated, 'The government of Sierra Leone believes that Executive Outcomes can provide security in the country more efficiently than national armed forces'.[32]

One of the most eroded states in the world has been for a long time the Democratic Republic of the Congo. The reason for the erosion is war between Congolese armed factions and the forces of neighboring countries. Recently, a consortium of military firms, which range from aerial surveillance operators to a company of Gurkha veterans, interestingly entitled the 'International Peace Operations Association', has proposed that it be hired to work on behalf of the largely ineffectual MONUC peacekeeping operations in the Eastern Congo. This plan promises to keep peace in the Republic of the Congo and to stop its erosion. Moreover, already deployed is Saracen, a South African and Angolan security firm. Saracen was contracted by the World Wildlife Fund to train and protect the guards in a park where there are endangered white rhinos.

PMCs and Peacebuilding

We can divide the possible roles of PMCs in peacebuilding according to their services. The first category would be enforcement of peace, cease-fire or truce. Companies like Northbridge Services, Sandline International, Executive Outcomes, Hart Group or Blackwater, which have already been engaged in combat or which publicly offer such services, could perform these tasks.

An important element of every peacebuilding operation is monitoring and guarding of borders of the country. Border protection is important for many reasons, including too few personnel as a result of the disintegration of a country's armed forces, the possibility of smuggling arms or other contraband items, or to watch for movement of spoiler factions. Companies like AirScan Inc., which provides air, ground and maritime surveillance,[33] or Cubic Defense Applications, could perform these tasks. The US has already subcontracted DynCorp for aerial monitoring in the former Yugoslavia.

The second category involves the security transition of the host country. In particular, this consists of the demobilisation and/or integration of warring factions (which caused so many problems in Angola and Liberia) and the retrieval, destruction or storing of arms. Sandline International explicitly offers these types of services.[34] Space Mark International is also advertising its service of munitions handling and storage.[35] The firm USA Environmental has teams of weapons and explosive experts in Iraq and a $65 million USD contract to collect and destroy unexploded ordinances.[36] Wade-Boyd and Associates LLC offers explosives detection as one of its services. ArmorGroup provides de-mining, also considered a standard part of many peacebuilding operations.[37]

A third category involves the building of new armed forces in post-conflict countries. Companies like RAM Inc.,[38] Vinnell, MPRI, Cubic Defense Applications and Sandline International provide this service. In Iraq, DynCorp maintains a $50 million USD contract to train police officers. Vinnell, a subsidiary of Northman Grumman, has a $48 million USD contract to assist in the training of a new army.[39]

One of the core components of every peacebuilding operation is the international civilian police. Private actors already have a history in this field. Since the United States does not have an international civilian police force, nor do most states, in the 1990s it used private contractors to recruit and deploy international civilian police. The international civilian police the United States sent to Bosnia, Kosovo and East Timor were all DynCorp employees.[40] Some PMCs may perform some police functions. For instance, AMA Associated Limited, Hill and Associates Limited and ArmorGroup offer fraud investigation; Control Risks Group provides anti-money laundering, bomb threats and kidnapping investigations. Companies may also contribute to law enforcement. As an example, AECOM Government Services, Inc., offers implementation of law enforcement,[41] MPRI law enforcement expertise,[42] and Sandline International, more explicitly, combat, organized crime, provides protection of natural resources and key installations, anti-poaching operations, and anti-smuggling operations.[43]

However, security is not the only domain of PMCs' possible engagement in peacebuilding. Some firms also promote a democratisation process. MPRI offers 'democracy transition assistance programs',[44] while Sandline International can provide election securing and monitoring. Furthermore PMCs could also provide assistance to traditional NGO tasks; AECOM Government Services, Inc., offers convoy operations, airfield operations, port operations and environmental management;[45] MPRI offers humanitarian aid,[46] while Sandline International advertises its capabilities of humanitarian and disaster relief command and co-ordination, mine clearance, protection of aid agency personnel, medical support at all levels, air support, and water purification.[47]

Other PMCs may contribute to the reconstruction of infrastructure and economics in a post-conflict country. For example, Cubic Defense Applications offers training and modernisation of armed forces and radio communications for the civil market. Global Development Four, already active in Kosovo, offers a management of transport 'in any part of the world, no matter how difficult the terrain, how hostile the elements, or how unsympathetic the political climate'.[48] Often this is exactly the environment of many post-conflict countries. International Charter Incorporated of Oregon 'acts as a private military company in peacekeeping support and relief services. Past work includes Liberia, Haiti, Sierra Leone, Nigeria and Sudan'.[49] O´Gara-Hess and Eisenhardt provide similar services, 'no matter where in the world you live'.[50] Wade-Boyd and Associates LLC offers transportation in unstable environments. The often-discussed Halliburton presents reconstruction of oil and gas facilities, just as this firm is now reconstructing the Iraqi oil industry. ICP Group Limited is active in international banking and finance, energy and oil, media, the pharmaceutical industry and information technology.

P.W. Singer suggests they can protect NGOs, despite the fact that 'more Red Cross workers were killed in action in the 1990s than US Army personnel'. 'Thus, while the ability of humanitarian actors to create a consensual environment themselves is severely limited, military provider firms might be able to provide site and convoy protection to aid groups.' According to Singer, this is not all that unlikely, given that several UN agencies already use such firms to provide security for their own offices. Moreover, such suggestions are now raised at the level of state organisations, as was the discussion in the UK on the possibilities of the use of PMCs in peacekeeping. A Report of the Foreign Affairs Committee suggests these tasks for private military companies:

1. Assistance to weak but legitimate governments in establishing the security needed for development.
2. Provision of services of direct social and economic benefit, such as de-mining assistance to the UN in peacekeeping.
3. Protection of legitimate commercial and NGO activity in dangerous areas, raising the professional standards of local armed forces.

All such functions are standard processes of peacebuilding efforts. What is most striking, however, is the fact that some companies are already involved in UN peacebuilding, especially if we could consider monitoring as part of peacebuilding (as it usually is). In October of 1998, the US government subcontracted its involvement in the Kosovo monitoring force to DynCorp, and on its official web site, MPRI offers peacekeeping as one of its standard services.

The fate of the future use of private military or security companies in peacebuilding could be determined by their success in Iraq. Iraq has become the biggest test for PMCs, considering they are contributing as much as 20 per cent of the total US-led occupation force. At least 35 PMCs have contracts in Iraq, employing at least 5,000 heavily-armed foreign mercenaries and over 20,000 Iraqis to carry out military work in some of the most dangerous areas of the country. At least another 10,000 to 15,000 contractors from every corner of the globe are performing vital military logistical support roles such as driving, maintenance, training, communications and intelligence gathering. David Claridge, a director of a London security firm, has estimated that Iraq contracts have boosted the annual revenue of British-based PMCs alone from $320 million USD to over $1.7 billion USD.

Aside from the dubious legal status of Operation Iraqi Freedom, there are other impediments in Iraq, which could compromise the future of PMCs. One potential problem spot is the behavior of employees, which has been under harsh critique from opponents of the occupation of Iraq. However, it is not an accident that the Iraqi resistance movement systematically uses the term 'mercenaries' when referring to PMCs. It is not an accident that the World Socialist Website comments on PMC engagement by criticising that 'Mercenaries provide the Bush administration with a supply of hired killers to carry out the dirtiest aspects of colonial repression – from torture to provocations and assassination – which it would prefer the military was not directly involved in'.

Furthermore, disagreements and tensions between the US and the UN caused by the Iraqi campaign and the massive use of private actors in Iraq may galvanize the UN against PMCs more than ever. The UN may feel jealousy toward PMCs as they perform peacebuilding and peacekeeping functions in countries that are occupied against the will of the UN. As written by Deborah Avant:

> There are hints that private security could (…) easily provide a platform that competes with the UN as a tool for 'international' force. In the stabilisation portion of Operation Iraqi Freedom, for instance, estimates suggests that 20,000 PSC employees have been deployed to provide a wide variety of security-related functions – making private security the second largest portion of the 'coalition of the willing'. Given the general antipathy with which the 'international community' viewed the operation, one could view private security as an alternative mechanism to the UN for gaining additional personnel. (…) By offering a tool that works in an array of different forums, private security may reduce the need to work through the political processes that states have set up through multilateral institutions.[51]

Notes

1 See J. Selber and K. Jobarteh, 'From Enemy to Peacekeeper: The Role of Private Military Companies in Sub-Saharan Africa', <www.ippnw.org/MGS/V7N2Selber.pdf>.

2 Ibid.

3 <http://ad.doubleclick.net/jump/pg.news.com>.

4 D. Avant, 'The Privatization of Security and Change in the Control of Force', *International Studies Perspectives*, 5 (2004):155.

5 B. Yeoman, 'Need an Army? Just Pick Up the Phone', *NY Times*, 2 April 2004.

6 J. Schulhofer-Wohl, 'Should We Privatize the Peacekeeping?', *Washington Post*, 12 May 2000.

7 D. Shearer, *Private Armies and Military Intervention* (New York, 1998), p. 55.

8 S. Fidler and T. Catan, 'Private Military Companies Pursue the Peace Dividend', *Financial Times*, 24 July 2003.

9 Quoted in Yeoman, 'Need an Army? Just Pick Up the Phone'.

10 S. Mallaby, 'New Role for Mercenaries', *Los Angeles Times*, 8 March 2001.

11 P.W. Singer, 'Peacekeepers, Inc.', <www.policyreview.org/jun03/singer.html>.

12 Avant, p. 155.

13 D. Shearer, 'Outsourcing War', *Foreign Policy* (Fall 1998): 69.

14 D. Shearer, 'Privatising Protection', *World Today* (August/September 2001), <www.globalpolicy.org/peacekpg/reform/2001/private.htm>.

15 L. Wayne, 'America's For-Profit Secret Army', *NY Times*, 13 October 2002.

16 Quoted in J. Dao, 'Private US Guards Take Big Risks for Right Price', *NY Times*, 2 April 2004.

17 'Peacekeeping "Role" or Mercenaries', *BBC*, 13 Feb. 2002.

18 Quoted in B. Yeoman, 'Soldiers of Good Fortune', <www.motherjones.com/news/feature/2003/05/ma_365_01.html>.

19 Ibid.

20 However as noticed Esther Schrader, 'the firms say this prevents them from working with governments that the US disapproves of. When MPRI tried to get a license to train the Angolan army in 1994, for example, the State Department turned it down. But Congress is notified only of contracts worth more than $50 million. Sometimes there are conflicting views of what is in the US interest. And once a license is granted, there are no reporting requirements or oversight of work that typically lasts years and takes the firms' employees to remote, lawless areas'. E. Schrader, 'US Companies Hired to Train Foreign Armies', *Los Angeles Times*, 14 April 2002.

21 See K. O'Brien, 'Leash the Dogs of War', *Financial Times*, 20 Feb. 2002.

22 Wayne, 'America's For-Profit Secret Army'.

23 <www.wsws.org/articles/2004/may2004/pmcs-m03.shtml>.

24 *Washington Post*, 3 May 2004.

25 Singer, 'Peacekeepers, Inc.'.

26 Shearer, *Private Armies and Military Intervention*, p. 66.

27 Quoted in D. Isenberg, Soldiers of Fortune Ltd.: A Profile of Today's Private Sector Corporate Mercenary Groups', Center for Defense Information, Nov. 1997. <http//www.cdi.org/issues/mercenaries/>.

28 See <www.airscan.com>.

29 <www.sandline.com/site/index.html>.

30 <www.smiintl.com>.

31 <www.wsws.org/articles/2004/may2004/pmcs-m03.shtml>.

32 <www.armorgroup.com>.

33 See <www.ramincorp.com>.

34 <www.wsws.org/articles/2004/may2004/pmcs-m03.shtml>.

35 Avant, p. 154.

36 <www.AECOM-GSI.com>.

37 <www.mpri.com/site/capabilities.html>.

38 <www.sandline.com/site/index.html>.
39 <www.mpri.com/site/capabilities.html>.
40 <www.AECOM-GSI.com>.
41 <www.mpri.com/site/capabilities.html>.
42 <www.sandline.com/site/index.html>.
43 <www.gd4-kosova.com/>.
44 <www.icioregon.com/>.
45 <www.ogara-hess.com/Frameset.html>.
46 <www.mpri.com/site/capabilities.html>.
47 Singer.
48 Ninth Report of the Foreign Affairs Committee, 'Private Military Companies: Response of the Secretary of State for Foreign and Commonwealth Affairs', Session 2001–2002, Presented to the Parliament by the Secretary of State for Foreign and Commonwealth Affairs by Command of Her Majesty, October 2002.
49 O'Brien.
50 <www.wsws.org/articles/2004/may2004/pmcs-m03.shtml>.
51 Avant, pp. 156-157.

Chapter 12

Promoting NGOs as Agents of Social Stabilisation: Trauma Management and Crime Prevention Initiatives in the Southern African Region

Wole Olaleye and David Backer

Our chapter reports the findings from a survey of more than 100 NGOs active in the fields of trauma management and crime prevention across the Southern African Development Community (SADC).[1] The broad goal of the research, which was conducted by the Centre for the Study of Violence and Reconciliation (CSVR) during 2000–01, is to facilitate interventions aimed at alleviating violence in the region by addressing its causes, manifestations and consequences.[2,3] In particular, civil society initiatives exhibit visible contributions to peace-building and stabilisation efforts in Africa,[4] as well as many other areas of the world,[5] that appear to be worth advancing, whether independently or as part of multi-track strategies of conflict resolution.[6] Also, NGOs and other independent groups are widely viewed as playing a vital role in protecting human rights,[7] increasing pluralism,[8] providing an impetus towards democratisation,[9] and supplying services integral to processes of development.[10] One archetypal function is to mediate between state and society – and within society itself – on issues of justice and reconciliation.

The SADC Crime and Violence Prevention Project, in turn, sought to promote and consolidate the work of civil society around the region by encouraging further information sharing and networking among NGOs. An underlying logic is that interaction and collaboration both within and across countries fosters the diffusion of ideas and practices, stimulates learning and standard-setting, focuses energies on common causes and thereby economizes on scarce resources. The principal strategy in this capacity-building endeavor was to compile extensive details about the structure, personnel, assets and activities of relevant organisations. The resulting database affords valuable insight, from the unique perspective of civil society, into the priorities of social, political and human development in settings where turmoil and aggression have been routine. The profiles also reveal certain hurdles that NGOs face in approaching the task of trying to moderate such phenomena. Our chapter is then devoted to examining these two dimensions: in essence, what should be the aims of state and society in regards to violence, and to what extent can the existing organs of civil society complement – or substitute for, as may be warranted – official policies and programs.

During the 1980s and 1990s, over 40 of the 51 African countries were afflicted by either intrastate or interstate conflict.[11] Southern Africa was among the regions most deeply affected by violence and other sources of instability. War, civil and political strife and social and economic collapse in places like Angola, the Democratic Republic of Congo (DRC) and lately Zimbabwe constitute a serious threat to peace, stability and human security in these countries, not to mention the entire region. At the same time, many of the other SADC members states either experienced recent upheaval (Lesotho, Swaziland) or initiated processes of transformation only within the last 10-15 years, following transitions from protracted, brutal civil wars (Mozambique, Namibia), long-standing repressive regimes (Malawi, South Africa, Zambia) or periods of strict one-party rule (Seychelles, Tanzania). Several of these countries are now on more favourable trajectories: Malawi, Mozambique, Namibia, South Africa and Zambia have joined Botswana and Mauritius as relatively stable – albeit embryonic, to a greater or lesser degree – developing democracies. [12] Nevertheless, the necessity of addressing the residual effects of past eras, moderating ongoing discord, maintaining social order, tackling emergent problems such as humanitarian crises and the HIV/AIDS epidemic and achieving consistent economic growth has near-universal salience in the region.

Given this sort of context, NGOs assume a central role. Throughout Southern Africa, especially where the government's capacity to deliver on essential basic social and economic imperatives is weakest, NGOs have positioned themselves as essential service providers, in addition to supplying a critical link between the state and local communities. The same phenomenon has been observed in other notable (post-) conflict zones, including Cambodia, [13] East Timor, [14] Iraq, [15] and Sierra Leone.[16]

NGOs are especially suited to diffusing the co-ordinating role of the state by placing the benefits of reconstruction programmes into the hands of intended individual and community beneficiaries. Their presence also shifts the locus of power closer to the general population and helps to devolve responsibility for key aspects of decision-making and execution. This mitigates the risk of an expansive, unaccountable bureaucracy that assumes full responsibility for administering resources and transmitting policies from the upper echelons of power to the lower levels of implementation.[17] At the same time, given the pluralism that generally accompanies the profusion of NGOs and other organized interest groups, there is little risk of civil society imposing a homogenous agenda that crowds out the state or encroaches upon its ultimate authority. Instead, the relationship can and should be collaborative: the mediating influence of civil society ought to facilitate the incorporation of public input into both national and local policy-making processes.[18]

We should not be too sanguine, as the resort to NGO-based development schemes is not without its detractors.[19] Some of the concerns mirror those levied at the state: insufficient resources, a lack of reach – especially into rural and marginal communities – and low levels of internal democracy combined with high rates of mismanagement. Another common appraisal is the duplication and inadequate coordination of effort. Finally, many contend that the local NGOs active in developing settings are largely beholden to external interests (i.e. donors, foreign governments, international agencies), rather than focused on local realities. These critiques suggest factors that ought to be taken into account when assessing whether civil society is likely to have a consequential, positive impact on development processes.

We provide a non-random 'convenience' sample of just 118 organisations, representing 10 of the 14 SADC member countries, completed questionnaires and were included in the database. The fact that South African-based organisations constitute about two-thirds of the respondents raises two issues. One is a classical problem of selection bias: the South African organisations are more accessible, due to their proximity, superior telecommunication infrastructure and other factors. Arguably the bias is not too severe in this instance, as the imbalance generally corresponds to natural patterns such as the high number of trauma management and crime prevention NGOs – as well as the broader base of civil society – in South Africa relative to elsewhere in the region. Nevertheless, at least some caution should be exercised in drawing unqualified inferences from the aggregate data. A potentially more consequential problem arises if this imbalance unwittingly reproduces a (South African) viewpoint that prevails within the regional discourses around issues of reconstruction and development. To the extent that organisations from one country are disproportionately influential in setting agendas for regional collaboration, this tends to submerge the perspective of those in other distinctive settings and undermine the potential for strategic partnerships among NGOs from different countries in the region.

This pattern is partly attributable to the policies that prevailed under the authoritarian regimes and one-party states. Some used legal restrictions like registration requirements, but most resorted to political repression and/or violence to limit the extent of independent organisation. Furthermore, during this era mobilisation was often vectored into liberation movements. The wave of democratic transitions that swept the continent beginning in the late 1980s has opened the window for a wide variety of political activism. Given the short life of many of these organisations, it seems reasonable to expect, however, that civil society in Southern Africa is underdeveloped and fragile.

Scope

The next dimension is the geographic scope of activity. We find that over 60 per cent of the NGOs in the sample restrict their activities to local – mostly urban – communities. This pattern is consistent with their emergence as an important role player in providing critical services and intervention. Especially in South Africa, NGOs have carved a niche for themselves by selectively collaborating with certain government departments (e.g., safety and security, justice, social welfare and development, education, arts and culture, health). The state has accepted NGOs as collaborative partners because of their capacity to deliver services and interventions – drawing on funding from the government – to inaccessible areas where the state delivery have failed. In many instances, NGOs have shown greater responsiveness to the needs of specific communities and are able to work in flexible, informal and more efficient ways.

With the prevalence of local initiatives, however, there is the risk of insufficient coordination of activism, as well as a lack of standardisation of practices. The former concern has been raised previously about civil society in Sub-Saharan Africa.[20] The latter concern has been levied, among other areas, in the context of mental health services.[21] As we will describe in Section 5, networking among locally based organisations both within and across countries may help to counteract some of these tendencies. Ideally, such linkages should not be artificial constructs, but rather result from common views on shared causes and desires for collaboration.

Services

The next dimension is the services that the organisations provide in the two focal areas of trauma management and crime prevention. This dimension, in turn, has two principal components. One is the type, i.e. what sorts of issues do these NGOs address and what sorts of activity do they engage in as a result? The other is the target group, i.e. what constituenc(ies) feature in this work and who are services ultimately provided to as a result?

We found that our sample of NGOs provides a wide range of trauma management services, which we opted to group into five distinct categories. The most frequently cited category – counseling for victims of abuse – is notable for its lack of emphasis on addressing the effects of historical conflicts. Only 14 per cent of the organisations that offer such services conceive of them as being targeted to victims of war and/or conflict. By contrast, nearly 80 per cent offer general short-term counseling for women and children who are victims of abuse. Very few organisations cited an emphasis on research; even these cases likely view themselves as being involved primarily in community interventions as service providers. Nonetheless, this may also reflect a deficiency in skilled personnel with the capacity for reflecting on and evaluating the effectiveness of their services, thereby integrating a service delivery orientation with sophisticated research capacity. There is a need for organisations to do self-evaluations and engage in critical reflection on the theoretical and practical implications of the services offered and the social, political and cultural contexts in which they are applied. Moreover, they ought to interrogate the extent to which the interventions they offer are contributing towards promoting community reconciliation and empowering victims, rather than just offering a remedial assistance to victims. In so doing, organisations would be able to rethink their responses to the suffering brought about by war and reconsider their underlying assumptions from which these responses are derived.

Organisations in the region adopt a multi-faceted approach to crime prevention focusing on different types and victims of violence, highlighting problems in particular sectors, exploring the root causes, and engaging various parts of the government. Within these spheres of activity, organisations engage in training, research, conflict management or conciliation services, counseling to victims of violence, human rights advocacy, shelter provision and trauma interventions. Many of these activities are often not self-consciously referred to as crime prevention, yet all are critical in turning the tide of crime and building sustainable democratic governance in the region. Our results, therefore, illustrate the broad nature of the crime prevention agenda.

This information poses – but does not answer conclusively – some fascinating questions about the changing character of violence within the various countries of the region. For example, activities related to domestic violence constitute 72 per cent of the crime prevention activities engaged in by organisations, compared to 15 per cent that address political violence. Moreover, just 25 per cent of the organisations provide human rights training to police personnel; 14 per cent and 9 per cent, respectively, provide human rights training to magistrates and prosecutors. This contrast may imply an emerging trend away from a dominant emphasis upon political conflict, towards concerns about criminal and domestic violence. To the extent these dynamics penetrate the region more broadly, this has vital implications for targeted regional programs related to the prevention of violent crime. The survey responses indicate that the most vulnerable sectors of society and often the most direct victims of violent crime – i.e. women, children and youth – constitute the primary focus of the interventions and services provided by many of the agencies canvassed within the region. In excess of 80 per cent engage in interventions on behalf of women, and nearly 70 per cent do the same with respect to youths and sexually abused children. Meanwhile, only one in four are explicitly concerned with the plight of victims of torture, less than 20 per cent the members of various political organisations and a scant 10 per cent ex-combatants.

Capacity

Studies have shown that capacity is a key determinant of the range and types of organisational outputs.[22] In transitional settings, NGOs often have to contend with a brain drain, due to stiff competition from both the public and private sectors. Therefore, we focus initially on personnel, before turning our attention to other resources.

As might be expected, the NGOs in the sample are chronically under-staffed, in terms of both their full-time and skilled personnel. These findings suggest that skilled professionals are not attracted to the sector: despite the fields in which these organisations operate, less than half are staffed with social workers and counsellors, while full-time psychologists and psychiatrists are employed by only 15 per cent and 3 per cent, respectively. Many organisations instead make do with part-time assistance. Volunteers also play an important role.

Organisations were also asked about the kind of resources they have access to, as well as the areas in which they are deficient. One interesting finding is that 85 per cent indicate they have access to computers and more than 60 per cent indicated that they have access to Internet and email facilities. These figures are likely boosted by the high representation of South African NGOs in the sample. Recent studies indicate that the ratio of staff to computers in South African organisations is 1:1, compared to 4:1 or 5:1 in different parts of the region. It is estimated that there are currently a million account holders in Africa, 70 per cent of which are located in South Africa.[23]

Despite the prevalence of high technology among the organisations in the sample, one of the problems experienced in this research was accessing organisations via the Internet and email. Even where Internet and email facilities exits, it is often a single account shared by the entire staff within the organisation which often make communication difficult and/or impossible. These problems are compounded by insufficient bandwidth, which makes access to the resources of the Internet difficult, slow and inefficient. Interrelated with insufficient bandwidth is the lack of local penetration and poor quality of the underlying telecommunications network in most African countries acting, as a major obstacle to growth. Even where the access to the technology is available, lack of skills base necessary to maximize its use still presents problem. In some respects, these capabilities, rather than human capacity, experience differentials or even access to donor funding, play an important role in setting NGOs apart from one another within the region. This is also a factor that shapes the disparities within the region between South African NGOs and the reminder of the SADC countries. This problem is further compounded by the limited culture of sharing resources, especially information, within a historically divided region.

Consistent with the earlier discussion, 57 per cent of the organisations cited problems with staffing. Close to half indicated that they have difficulty accessing funds, which may signal a trend in donor funding strategy away from NGOs toward direct contribution to state-based developmental and reconstruction programmes. The challenges for many organisations is looking at innovative ways of shifting away from foreign donor dependency base to a more locally based foundation, such that government and businesses become major funding partner in exchange for rendering services. As observed earlier, this phenomenon is already evident in South Africa, where NGOs act as service providers and consultants at local and international levels. This raises issues about the ability of NGOs to maintain their critical, independent edge and perform a function that is generally considered vital to the maintenance of democracy.

Relationships among NGOs

Networking in the area of trauma management and crime prevention is increasingly recognised as an essential component of a more effective response to the challenge of violent crime in the region (especially in South Africa). Unfortunately, very little has been documented about the lessons learned in building and sustaining this kind of infrastructure. This oversight is regrettable, as such infrastructure can only be sustained and strengthen if networks reflect on their success, failures, capacities and weakness and share information with others. Therefore, we requested information from organisations with regards to national and regional (i.e. SADC) networking initiatives. The questionnaire addressed the structure of the network, the nature and forms of contact between organisations within the network and other related information. A surprising finding is that every single organisation in our sample participates in at least one network, primarily at the national level. The paucity of regional networking around issues of trauma management and crime prevention is perhaps not surprising, given unstable political climates, language differences, the limited transportation infrastructure, the lack of organisational capacity, etc. We also observed earlier that the NGOs in our sample have varying perspectives, especially across countries, which is not always conducive to formal, collaborative relationships among organisations. At the same time, it also means that they do not enjoy the full benefit of sharing information and skills – and thereby learning from – their compatriots in neighboring countries. Nevertheless, there is at least some effort to develop innovative ways for handling issues of common concern throughout the region.

Trauma management and crime prevention networks range from loose multi-purpose relationships for information sharing, capacity building, collaborative advocacy, and research to highly formalized structures with a central secretariat, paid staff, and explicit operating guidelines. In general, however, the networks to which the respondent NGOs belong are closer to the latter end of the spectrum. In theory, the prevalence of formal national networks provides a foundation – in terms of both precedent and infrastructure – for future collaborations among organisations at the regional level. On the other hand, it is interesting to note that the regional networks rely less on official structures. The reasons may have something to do with the difficulties of maintaining such relationships among organisations that are spread across countries and thus may not be able to interact frequently.

Most of the respondent organisations that participate in regional networks communicate with each other only once or twice a year. The pattern among organisations in national networks is just the opposite: interactions are typically quite frequent. The universal participation in national networks, combined with the frequency of contacts, suggests that these relationships are an important dimension of these organisations' activities. Technological advances clearly facilitate contact within networks, especially those existing at a regional level. Nevertheless, conventional means – personal interaction, conferences and ad hoc meetings – remain popular. A surprising finding is that members of regional networks rely upon the options at nearly the same rate as those in national networks. One would imagine that the close correspondence is a function of self-selection: engaging counterparts in the region presumes a certain scope of interest and level of capacity that only certain organisations enjoy.

While NGOs that belong to national networks communicate on a frequent basis, they collaborate somewhat less often. The members of regional networks, by contrast, apparently do not require such regular contacts in order to initiate and sustain collaborative projects. The latter finding, combined with our earlier observations about regional network members' heavy utilisation of information technology, suggest that recent advances have begun to blur geographical boundaries and allow for more ongoing relationships among NGOs.

Regional networks, by contrast, adopt a distinctive focus. A chief focus of collaborations is human rights training, cited by nearly all of the NGOs who participate in these networks. There is also a greater emphasis on trauma and conflict management, and tied to these agenda items more regular attention afforded to ex-combatants and victims of torture and landmines. The lack of interest in migrants, however, is somewhat of a surprise, given the large population movements throughout the region in response to political conflicts and economic pressures.

Conclusions

Our chapter presents findings concerning key characteristics of 118 NGOs engaged in the fields of trauma management and crime prevention across Southern Africa. Perhaps most significant, the survey captures their unique perspective on the issues and constituencies that should be priorities in development efforts for conflict-ridden, transitional and developing societies. The research reveals that NGOs play a critical role in the process of reconstruction through initiatives in areas such as community reconciliation and victim empowerment initiatives. While the increasing engagement of NGOs in the transformation of state institutions, with an eye towards cultivating a more democratic and service-oriented criminal justice system, is worth highlighting, it remains uncertain whether the nature of interventions offered by organisations sufficiently engages the deeply rooted conflicts of these societies.

The responses of the NGOs also afford insight into their self-perceived strengths and limitations as they endeavor to address these concerns and service these communities. In addition, they help to illuminate the strategies NGOs adopt in the interest of more effectively engaging government, their constituencies and each other, as well as non-state actors in the international community. Among the most prominent is the utilisation of networks to strengthen and actively engage in the process of reconstruction. This infrastructure allows organisations to address their common concerns in ways that promote effective reconciliation, co-operation, tolerance, security, respect for human rights, and social cohesion. It appears from the analysis that relationships at the regional level are weak and under-developed.

Despite these qualifications, we believe the sample affords a diverse and reasonably detailed picture of the status, priorities and needs of key NGOs that are active in fields of trauma management and crime prevention across Southern Africa. Our sincere hope is that increased awareness of and communication among these and other civil society organisations will assist efforts to ease conflict and combat its effects in the region.

Notes

1 SADC is comprised of 14 member states: Angola, Botswana, Democratic Republic of the Congo, Lesotho, Malawi, Mauritius, Mozambique, Namibia, Seychelles, South Africa, Swaziland, Tanzania, Zambia and Zimbabwe.

2 CSVR is an independently funded NGO with offices in Johannesburg and Cape Town, South Africa. Its spheres of engagement include criminal, domestic, political and gender violence, violence against children and violence associated with democratisation and developmental processes. CSVR adopts a multidisciplinary approach, employing social workers, psychologists, criminologists, lawyers, social scientists and education specialists.

3 The Directorate General for International Cooperation of the Belgium Government generously funded this project.

4 Perhaps the best-known book on these issues is Claude Welch, *Protecting Human Rights in Africa: Roles and Strategies of Non-Governmental Organizations* (Philadelphia: University of Pennsylvania Press, 1995). See also Ameen Jan, Chetan Kumar, Robert Orr, and Margaret Vogt, *IPA/OAU Consultation on Civil Society and Conflict Management in Africa* (New York: International Peace Academy, 1996); *Searching for Peace in Africa: An Overview of Conflict Prevention and Management Activities*, Paul Van Tongeren and Hans Van De Veen (eds) (Utrecht: International Books, 2000); Emily Frank, 'A Participatory Approach for Local Peace Initiatives: The Lodwar Border Harmonization Meeting', *Africa Today*, 49/4 (2002): 68-87; Augustine Toure, *The Role of Civil Society in National Reconciliation and Peacebuilding in Liberia* (New York: International Peace Academy, 2002); Angela Ndinga-Muvumba, *Civil Society Perspectives from the Mano River Union* (New York: International Peace Academy, 2003); and Michael O'Flaherty, 'Sierra Leone's Peace Process: The Role of the Human Rights Community', *Human Rights Quarterly*, 26/1 (2004): 29-62.

5 For analysis of specific settings, see Jonathan Goodhand and Nick Lewer, 'Sri Lanka: NGOs and Peace-building in Complex Political Emergencies', *Third World Quarterly*, 20/1 (1999): 69-87; Sean Byrne, 'Transformational Conflict Resolution and the Northern Ireland Conflict', *International Journal on World Peace*, 18/2 (2001): 3-22; Jon Barnett, Beth Eggleston and Michael Webber, 'Peace and Development in Post-War Iraq', *Middle East Policy*, 10/3 (2003): 22-32; Rebecca Engel, 'Reaching for Stability: Strengthening Civil Society-Donor Partnerships in East Timor', *Journal of International Affairs*, 57/1 (2003): 169-181. For general considerations, see Giovanni Rufini, 'The Potential of Non-Governmental Organizations in Peacekeeping Negotiation and Mediation', *Peacekeeping and International Relations*, 24/3 (1995): 5-7; Michael Edwards and Gita Sen, 'NGOs, Social Change and the Transformation of Human Relationships: A 21st Century Civic Agenda', *Third World Quarterly*, 21/4 (2000): 605-616; and Nicole Campos and Paul Farmer, 'Partners: Discernment and Humanitarian Efforts in Settings of Violence', *Journal of Law, Medicine and Ethics*, 31/4 (2003): 506-515; and David Hamburg, *No More Killing Fields: Preventing Deadly Conflict* (Lanham, MD: Rowman and Littlefield Publishers, 2003), especially chapter 4.

6 An oft-cited classic is Thomas Weiss and Leon Gordenker, *NGOs, the UN and Global Governance* (Boulder, CO: Lynne Reinner, 1996). See also Ben Rawlence, *Empowering Local Actors: The UN and Multi-Track Conflict Prevention* (New York: International Peace Academy, 2002).

7 There have been plentiful considerations of this topic over the years. In addition to Smith et al., see Ved Nanda, *Global Human Rights: Public Policies, Comparative Measures and NGO Strategies*, Paul Van Tongeren and Hans Van De Veen (eds) (Boulder, CO:

Westview Press, 1981); David Weissbrodt, 'The Contribution of International Nongovernmental Organizations to the Protection of Human Rights', in Theodor Meron (ed.), *Human Rights in International Law: Legal and Policy Issues* (Oxford: Clarendon Press, 1984); Henry Steiner, *Non-Governmental Organizations in the Human Rights Movement* (Cambridge, MA: Harvard Law School Human Rights Program, 1991); Kathryn Sikkink, 'Human Rights, Principled-Issue Networks and Sovereignty in Latin America', *International Organization*, 47/3 (1993): 411-441; Seamus Cleary, *The Role of NGOs under Authoritarian Political Systems* (New York: St. Martin's Press, 1997), and David Forsythe, *Human Rights in International Relations* (Cambridge: Cambridge University Press, 2000), especially chapter 7.

8 For a nuanced treatment of this subject in the African context, see Stephen Ndegwa, *The Two Faces of Civil Society: NGOs and Politics in Africa* (West Hartford, CT: Kumarian Press, 1996). See also Jesse Lubatingwa and Kenneth Gray, 'NGOs in Sub-Saharan Africa: Developing Critical Capacity for Policy Advocacy', *International Journal on World Peace*, 14/3 (1997): 35-70.

9 See, in particular, Margaret Keck and Kathryn Sikkink, *Activists Beyond Borders: Advocacy Networks in International Politics* (Ithaca, NY: Cornell University Press, 1998). The extensive literature also includes Julie Fisher, *Nongovernments: NGOs and the Political Development of the Third World* (West Hartford, CT: Kumarian Press, 1998); and Peter van Tuijl, 'NGOs and Human Rights: Sources of Justice and Democracy', *Journal of International Affairs*, 52/2 (1999): 493-512.

10 For a general perspective, see Ann Micou and Birgit Lindnaes, *The Role of Voluntary Organizations in Emerging Democracies* (Copenhagen: Danish Center for Human Rights and New York: Institute of International Education, 1993). See also David Backer and David Carroll, 'NGOs and Constructive Engagement: Promoting Civil Society, Good Governance and the Rule of Law in Liberia', *International Politics*, 38/1 (2001): 1-26; and Sue Downie and Damien Kingsbury, 'Political Development and the Re-emergence of Civil Society in Cambodia', *Contemporary Southeast Asia*, 23/1 (2001): 43-64.

11 Richard Joseph, 'The International Community and Armed Conflict in Africa – Post-Cold War Dilemmas', in Gunner M. Sørbø and Peter Vale (eds), *Out of Conflict: From War to Peace* (Uppsala: Africa Nordiska Institute, 1997). See also Chris Allen, 'Warfare, Endemic Violence and State Collapse in Africa', *Review of African Political Economy*, 81 (1999): 367-384.

12 South Africa has probably fared the best of the group. Malawi (in 2004) and Zambia (in 1996) both experienced serious controversies concerning election campaigns and results. President Sam Nujoma's increasing centralisation of authority and attempt to amend the Namibian Constitution to permit him to stand for a third term – though it ultimately failed – created a precarious political balance. Mozambique managed to have a more uneventful change in leadership, but the weak economy and inadequate infrastructure has hindered developmental progress.

13 Downie and Kingsbury examine the growth of civil society in the aftermath of Cambodia's 1993 multi-party elections.

14 Rebecca Engel, 'Reaching for Stability: Strengthening Civil Society-Donor Partnerships in East Timor', *Journal of International Affairs*, 57/1 (2003): 169-181.

15 Barnett et al. detail the tasks of reconstruction in Iraq and discuss the role of civil society in this process.

16 O'Flaherty argues that the human rights community made key contributions to conflict resolution in Sierra Leone.

17 In addition to Edwards and Sen, see Jonathan Goodhand and Nick Lewer, 'Sri Lanka: NGOs and Peace-building in Complex Political Emergencies', *Third World Quarterly*, 20/1 (1999): 69-87; June Rock, 'Relief and Rehabilitation in Eritrea: Lessons and Issues',

Third World Quarterly, 20/1 (1999): 129-142; and Jenny Pearce, 'Peace-building in the Periphery: Lessons from Central America', *Third World Quarterly*, 20/1 (1999): 51-68.

18 Keith Snavely and Uday Desai, 'Mapping Local Government – Nongovernmental Organization Interactions: A Conceptual Framework', *Journal of Public Administration Research and Theory*, 11/2 (2001): 245-263.

19 For a summary of these concerns, see Backer and Carroll.

20 Swedish NGO Foundation for Human Rights and the International Human Rights Internship Foundation, *The Status of Human Rights Organizations in Sub-Saharan Africa* (Stockholm: Swedish NGO Foundation for Human Rights and Washington, D.C.: International Human Rights Internship Foundation, 1994).

21 In addition to Baldwin-Ragaven et al., see Mike Mika, 'Group to Set Guidelines for Trauma Aid Training', *JAMA*, 284/1 (2000): 1230-1231.

22 The literature on this topic is vast; see, for example, Frederickson and London.

23 These figures are from Mike Jensen, *The African Internet – A Status Report* (<http://www3.sn.apc.org/africa/afstat.fhtm>, accessed on May 28, 2004) and Firoze Manji, Murtaza Jaffer and Emmanuel Njuguna, 'Using ICTs to enhance the capacity of human rights organizations in Southern Africa', *Voices from Africa*, 9 (2000): 19-31.

Chapter 13

A Rights-Based Approach to Natural Resources Management: Roles and Responsibilities of IGOs, States and NGOs

Clark Efaw and Avtar Kaul

A rights-based approach to programming recognises local populations as the primary stakeholders in their own development; they must live with the long-term outcome of development activities. In this approach, Agriculture and Natural Resources (ANR)-related interventions must focus on the ability of the rural poor to exercise their rights to participate in policy decisions and to have access to productive assets such as natural resources, credit and open markets. At the same time, expanding the capacity of people and local institutions to exercise their rights and responsibilities through training, education and advocacy. This approach forms the basis of all program activities and requires sustainability in project development at CARE (Cooperative for Assistance and Relief Everywhere):

> A rights-based approach emphasizes the right we all have as human beings to a secure, dignified existence and, at the same time, the responsibilities we all have to assist each other's realization of that right.[1]

A rights-based approach leads us to ask what we can do about the policies or the practices of policy makers that cause water poverty. Lack of access to water is not only a question of inadequate financial and technical resources, but is often the result of policies and practices above the individual or community level. A rights-based approach treats indigenous communities as responsible actors, and is more about helping people gain control than providing them with a specific product. CARE and other NGOs should expand assistance to local governments and communities in the planning and management of micro-watersheds, and promote institutional arrangements that take account of both the hydrogeological and political boundaries.

The role of indigenous communities as stewards of environmental resources obliges developed countries, as part users of those resources, to share the benefits with them. The role of major NGOs and of their partner organisations is to influence changes in policy and practice through training, advocacy and other means of increasing the communities' control over their resources. This role must cover both the developing country players as well as those in the developed countries who trade in the same.

As development NGOs, we define well-being in terms of income, child mortality, access to services (water, roads, electricity, health care), life expectancy, education and other easily measured improvements in lifestyle. But this tends to confine our thinking about well-being to only those easily-measured parameters. This neglects things like psychological and spiritual well-being, preservation of culture, the health of non-human species and ecosystems, and the likelihood that the current level of livelihood will be maintained or surpassed for the future. Their relative value can be argued in terms of priorities, but if we rank priorities in terms of measurable returns alone there will be a bias against the important contributors to quality of life which are supported by the conservation of natural resources.

In 2000, shifting from the 'needs-based' approach it has had since its inception at the end of WWII, CARE adopted a 'Rights-Based Approach' to development. With this change in its philosophy, CARE, which had been best known for direct delivery of needed supplies and services to poor and disaster-stricken communities, shifted its emphasis from mere delivering of packages of necessities and provision of relief to the facilitation of the empowerment of the poor. Also it meant working through local partners in the communities instead of reaching directly to individuals and families.

In September 2002, while attending the World Summit on Sustainable Development (WSSD) in Johannesburg, South Africa, CARE and the World Wildlife Fund (WWF) held a side meeting to discuss how they could join forces to address the issues of poverty and conservation of resources. The two organisations had been working side-by-side for many years, often in the same location or as infrequent partners on projects. This time they realized they had enough in common to form the basis of a partnership. CARE's interest had been in combating poverty for the poor and desperate people who often lived near environmentally-protected areas, and who depended directly on the natural resources around them. The WWF's role was to protect the wildlife in those reserves from the destructive influence of human activity. In years past, collaborations between conservation and development organisations had generated a dynamic tension originating from conflict between small income-generating activities of communities and maintaining the barriers between protected areas and the surrounding human habitat. Now the two sides came to the common viewpoint that it was going to be increasingly difficult to exclude people from protected areas. On the contrary, it was realized that people were potentially necessary to protect the environment.

The position papers which resulted from the meetings at Johannesburg between CARE and the WWF centered on two basic tenets: 1) that poor communities should have increased control over natural resources as well as the capacity to responsibly manage them; and that 2) they should be rewarded for their role as stewards of the environment. This declaration has taken the two organisations in a new direction. Simultaneously, it has raised a number of questions that both organisations will be explaining to their constituencies in the coming years. These include:

- What environmental services do the communities perform, and for whose benefit?
- How do we determine the value of the services, and how are the costs for the same to be shared?
- How will the process be governed, and how will we know if it is working?

By moving beyond their traditional roles as direct service providers, NGOs like CARE and the WWF are learning that they can play a vital part in shifting the balance toward a sustainable environment as well as economic development by promoting the political and economic empowerment of poor people living in environmentally-critical areas. Strategic partnership with local and national governments, businesses and other nonprofit partners could be decisive in reversing the factors that drive both environmental degradation and poverty. A concerted focus on a few areas would be effective.

NGOs can help promote sustainable trade favorable to poor countries. They can help small farmers and communities by advocating for the development of global markets for the exportation of goods and services, such as sale of carbon credits and alternative energy from geothermal sources and from biomass, including methane, ethanol and hydrogen.

In the absence of large corporate or governmental entities capable of negotiating with multinational agribusinesses, NGOs could play a significant role as honest brokers in organising and educating farmers, helping them to negotiate effectively on their own behalf, advocating for environmentally-safe and economically-just conditions of trade in agriculture inputs and products, and helping to build local capacity to enforce rules of governance that protect the economic and environmental rights of indigenous farmers.

NGOs can be instrumental in strengthening local markets. While gaining access to global markets will improve opportunity and the income-generating ability of developing country rural communities, dependence on that market exposes them to unacceptable levels of market risk and price volatility. At the same time, the local and national markets suffer from infrastructure deficiencies that cause local shortages and other symptoms of market inefficiency. A strong local market economy combined with global market access could achieve a suitable balance of agriculture and market diversification while protecting biodiversity and trade in traditional crop varieties.

Because of their strong relationships with both communities and governments, NGOs are in a position to push advocacy for land tenure. Neither tenant farmers nor the absentee landowners have sufficient incentive to invest time in the labor-intensive process of building soil structure and organic content to protect the topsoil. Terracing, composting, alley-cropping, planting nitrogen fixing varieties, organic farming and planting trees as live wind barriers or live fencing are among the techniques that will prevent topsoil erosion and improve soil productivity over the long term. But these often take years to take effect. In the absence of the assurance of future benefits to tillers, the land will continue to suffer depletion of its fertility. Land reform is important since it reduces the future risk to local farmers and protects the value of this vital resource.

NGOs can help link poor communities to carbon credit trade markets. The carbon-trading instruments of the Kyoto Treaty offer an innovative way to transfer payments from pollution producers to communities that facilitate removal of greenhouse gases (GHGs) by sequestration. GHG removal activities include building agricultural soil carbon, carbon-sink forest management, biomass-to-energy conversion, and solar energy utilisation. Participation in carbon trading markets seems complicated at first. NGOs are well positioned to play an important role in facilitating market participation by both buyers and sellers of carbon credits by serving as honest brokers in such trade.

NGOs can help communities increase their capacity to mitigate effects of climate change and environmental degradation. Some of the effects of climate change have already occurred, and they are changing the living conditions for the poorest people on the planet. The collective effects of climate change are projected to cause enough glacial melting to raise sea levels sufficiently to inundate much of the land mass of the Maldives and Bangladesh. Rivers in the dry zones of northern India, which were once fed through the dry season by the snowcaps of the Himalayas, only flow now during the rainy season. While populations of people living in the affected areas will need to adjust to climate changes, the major industrialized country polluters should share the costs of adjustment as well as halting global warming.

NGOs can help communities gain a larger share of profits by aiding value-added enterprises. Growing agricultural produce for sale to others in an unprocessed state is one of the least productive uses of land. NGOs can help improve productivity as well as add value to produce by arranging capital and technology for such enterprises. Also, they can provide environmentally-sustainable alternatives for economic development, including on and off-farm income generating activities and access to microfinance. Improvement in the productivity of land and the addition of value to farm products through techniques of selection, processing and packaging goods before shipment reduces the area of land required to produce sustainable flow of income. Formation of cooperatives to bargain from a position of power for agriculture inputs and sales of goods brings back more wealth directly to producers.

NGOs can assist communities in developing the capacity for environmental governance. For local communities to be effective partners in national and regional policy formation and enforcement, there must be a transparent process with oversight from community representatives. NGOs that already have an effective grassroots presence and support within communities could offer expertise in governance issues, conflict resolution, civil society strengthening and connection with regional partners in developing cooperative approaches to environmental issues.

Rights-based NGOs will need to engage parties in conflict resolution activities concerning such issues as rights to water and other natural resources, and in advocacy to prevent and mitigate pollution and other forms of often unintended encroachment on environmental rights.

The Next Steps

Helping local communities gain control over natural resources, to more effectively exercise their responsibility as stewards of those resources, and to realize their fair share of benefit for that role, means simultaneously identifying and addressing the underlying causes of poverty as well as environmental degradation. It also means addressing the power relationships that keep poor communities at a disadvantage when bargaining for their just and lawful rights. NGOs like CARE and WWF are taking on the task of changing the way natural resources are protected and exploited.

The model adopted by these NGOs involves risk taking on all sides. Conservation NGOs will be required to not only open protected areas but to entrust their care to people who have sometimes shown a propensity to either deplete scarce resources or trade the rights to those resources to parties who will exploit them even more exhaustingly. They will need to have effective monitoring and evaluation of such projects and will need to do a good job of selling the concept to their donors. Development NGOs will need to learn to see the environment as vital to the long-term future development of poor communities and invest resources on environmental programs. The poor communities and individuals themselves, who are probably the least able to bear risk, will need to make the greatest leap of faith of all. They will have to learn environmentally-sustainable ways of generating income, incorporating new technologies into their traditional lifestyles, and begin to interact effectively with a global economy that has always left them out in the past.

Education and advocacy will play a key role in this process of community empowerment. NGOs will need to remain open to new priorities and ideas from outside their own organisations. Donors, who have backed the traditional philosophies of their NGOs with financial commitment, will need to make decisions as to whether the new policies are in line with their own mission and values. International institutions, responsible for generating technology, both in the public as well as private sectors, will need to orient programs that are highly relevant and responsive to needs. Above all, local communities will have to become self-sufficient and knowledgeable about their needs and sources of inputs required to meet the same.

In order for communities to give themselves a comparative advantage, they will need to develop local markets and seek to participate in global markets for goods and services utilising their own natural resources – these may include but not be limited to such items as local varieties of crops and breeds of animals, carbon credit trading, renewable energy, non-timber forest products, sustainably managed timber, and tourism. Most developing world farmers and communities currently lack the negotiating skills necessary to successfully bargain with buyers. Moreover, locals lack the ability to provide goods and services in sufficient quantity and consistent quality to compete in global markets. As a result, the buying and distribution services are provided by intermediaries who are in business for themselves and who exploit the local people's lack of sophistication, market knowledge and negotiating skills for their own profit. Farmers and community leaders will have to become smart business people and gain access to computers and other sophisticated tools.

When developing countries seek to successfully participate in global markets, they will be entering a marketplace in which the rules have been set by the big players for their own advantage. NGOs like CARE and WWF have recently been showing an increasing propensity to play a more active role in advocating for trade rules more favorable to poor countries. CARE is very active in helping farmers form cooperative organisations to negotiate production contracts and more favorable prices for both agricultural inputs and outputs. They will need to help poor communities gain a voice and a seat at the table, and to participate in rewriting the rules.

Advocacy for environmental rights will involve acting in the interest of future generations, who, although they certainly have an interest in the disposition of natural resources, are not represented at the table – mainly because they do not exist. The future generations comprise the one group of people on whose behalf the environmental organisations, such as Green Peace, have done a better job of advocating than have the development NGOs and advocacy groups. Recognition of these generations' rights will require a more open and inclusive rights-based approach, which would in turn affect other sectors of development such as health, economic development, education, etc.

To improve governance and empowerment, there needs to be systematic collaboration between a range of organisations including government, international institutions, NGOs, and the private sector to:

- promote policies and approaches that respond effectively and efficiently to community demand for services including reorienting and building the capacity of local government;
- promote management by the user community, local government, and private sector, to ensure efficient and reliable services;
- support and facilitate decision-making processes for resource management with particular emphasis on the inclusion of women in decision-making.

Notes

1 Andrew Jones, *Promoting Rights and Responsibilities.* CARE, February 2002 (unpublished).

Chapter 14

The Challenges of an NGO in Post-Communist Europe: The Soros Health Education Program

Susan Shapiro

Although NGOs have re-emerged in Central and Eastern Europe, certain challenges still confront them. As Project Director of one such NGO, the Soros Foundation's Health Education Program (HEP), I dealt with these challenges on a daily basis. Utilising this program as a case study, this chapter will analyze this program's role in the transformation process in post-communist countries. I will examine the prescriptive ideas that have helped to change the health behaviour of teachers and students in post-communist countries so that other NGOs can recognize the key issues they might face in implementation of such a program. The following questions will be addressed: Why did this NGO implement a major health education program? What were the underlying factors that made it possible to integrate it into 23 countries? How was the framework of this NGO program adapted to different cultures? What were the key issues that most countries faced? Why were some countries more successful in the program's implementation than others? What can other NGOs learn from the challenges faced in this program?

The Structure of the Health Education Proram

In 1988, recognising that the Communist Party had placed little significance on health education, I applied to the Soros Foundation for a small grant to initiate a health education program in the Hungarian schools. By 1990, several schools within Hungary had developed and instituted a small-scale health education program. [1] This pilot project soon expanded into neighboring Romania. In September 1991, the Soros Foundation extended the program to include eight additional countries and by 1999, the Health Education Program was reaching millions of students in the following countries: Azerbaijan, Albania, Bulgaria, Belarus, Bosnia-Herzegovina, Croatia, Czech Republic, Estonia, Hungary, Kazakhstan, Kyrgyzstan, Lithuania, Latvia, Moldova, Macedonia, Mongolia, Poland, Romania, Russia, Slovenia, Slovakia, Ukraine and Yugoslavia. [2] The structure of the program had several components. Seven curricula were written that promoted attitudinal and behavioural changes and emphasized a proactive approach to learning, encouraging students to take responsibility for their own learning.[3] The courses were: *Nutrition and Your Health, Alcohol and Other Drugs, Smoking Prevention, An Introduction to Sexuality Education, and AIDS Education, Conflict and Communication: A Guide Through the Labyrinth of Conflict Management and Environment and Our Global Community.*[4]

The goal of the HEP was: to teach basic health education, to introduce elementary and secondary school teachers and health professionals to innovative ways to instruct their students in health education and to assist in the transformation of the fundamental process of educational methodology. But the underlying strength of the program went beyond factual information. It was to change the students' and teachers' way of thinking. A basic teacher training, given to health professionals and teachers in all 23 countries, served as the cornerstone of the program. It was a five day training that enhanced teachers' skills through new teaching methods and increased their knowledge of the subject matter of the curricula. Coordinators were hired in each of the countries to organize and establish the program within their country. They were chosen based on their participation in the basic training, their command of the English language, their interest in health education, and their ability to initiate a program. The Soros staff in the United States trained them in all areas of the program: administration, budget, organisation, and curriculum.

The Foundation hired an evaluation team, Metis Associates, to design a formal evaluation.[5] The evaluation analyzed the changes in participants' knowledge and awareness of teaching techniques, the quality of the locally run workshops and the extent and nature that the curricula were utilized. All aspects of the program received high ratings. In addition, a manual was developed by Metis that taught the trainers how to develop their own evaluation so that they could continually monitor their program and adapt it to meet their needs. As the HEP became integrated into the 23 countries, seven factors emerged that contributed to its achievements. Some of these factors were based on the guidelines of the health education program developed by the Soros Foundation; others were based on the philosophical changes that needed to occur in governments in transition.

1.   The Soros Foundation's Health Education Program seemed as though it was basic health education – factual information about health to students. It did not threaten either the old government or the government in transition. It was something that they could not help but approve. In Mr. Soros's words, 'We carefully balanced projects that would annoy the ideologues in the Party, with other projects that they couldn't help but approve, and we made sure that there was always a positive balance'.[6] The HEP went to the heart of the difference in communism versus an open society. It taught teachers and students how to communicate with one another and how to trust. It introduced teachers to the importance of creating an 'atmosphere' in the classroom. It focused on skills of problem-solving, decision making and behaviour modification.

2.   The HEP provided the transitional countries with critical, up-to-date health information that had been well researched in universities across the United States and through the Centers for Disease Control, the National Institute of Health and World Health Organisation. This information did not exist in the former communist era.[7] The Foundation worked directly with behavioural psychologists whose research targeted 'specific intervention topics selected for in-depth exploration – tobacco use ... nutrition, sexually transmitted diseases and teen pregnancy prevention'.[8] In addition, information from the communist era was sometimes inaccurate. For example, the Russian Ministry of Health claimed that alcoholism was not a problem throughout the country. Yet, the teachers said that many students came to school high on alcohol. In Mongolia, many teachers said that they believed that vegetables were only for animals, not human consumption. They were surprised to learn that they should include them in their daily diet.

3.   The HEP followed a train-the-trainer approach so that it could reach teachers and students across all regions. Fifty to sixty participants were trained in each country. A small number of these participants were selected to become part of the training network. They took an additional train-the-trainer course – a four-day workshop that taught them training skills. They became certified as trainers for the program. Each had a manual for all training sessions.

4.   The HEP hired coordinators in each country to administer the program within each nation. They were instrumental to the success of the program. The HEP staff observed all of the participants from the initial five-day training. They selected coordinators who seemed to have the potential to organize a program; who became confident in their ability to teach a new methodology; who were convinced of the positive effects of the information; and who attempted to improve their own health. The interview process was thorough and continued until the success of the person to serve as coordinator became evident.

5.   The HEP hired coordinators with professional backgrounds that would increase the probability of success; teachers, doctors, and school administrators. For example, in Romania a doctor, Dr. Dan Baciu, was hired as the country coordinator. He initiated a major health education program in schools across Romania and implemented a public health program that expanded throughout the country. He believed in the need for health education and fought resistance from former communist members. In Dr. Baciu's words, 'The Ministry of Education approved my program despite the opposition of several former communist officials who were still in power. I would not take no for an answer. I was so persistent.' He marketed the program so that professionals, ordinary citizens and students knew about it. The major bus company in Cluj-Napoca allowed him to put anti-smoking designs on the sides of city buses. He printed pamphlets and carried them to doctors' offices. He facilitated hundreds of workshops to teachers in dozens of cities:

If I didn't have enough money from the Soros Foundation to pay some of my expenses, I asked for contributions from people within the community. Owners of newly privatized restaurants supplied leftover food to feed the teachers during training. Businesses donated paper that I used to make hand-outs for teachers. Sanitoriums offered rooms at a discount for those teachers who lived too far away from the trainings and had to stay overnight. Friends made desserts for the participants of the workshop, and colleagues translated the curricula. I stretched the monies to render as many services as possible. And I presented the participants with materials that they could not get anywhere else.[9]

6.   The HEP gave intensive training to the coordinators so that they had skills to train others and to administer the program in their country. The coordinators had to learn how to budget; how to administer; how to communicate with others. They had trainings on the following topics: NGOs roles in society; strategic planning; program development and office management. They learned the process that one must go through in order to make change: decision-making skills, problem solving proficiency, motivational techniques and communication skills.

7.   The HEP implemented the program immediately after the fall of communism. The timing of the transition affected this program's impacts. Rather than waiting for a completely stabilized transitional country, the Soros Foundation introduced this program without a legally defined civil society. Clifford F. Zinnes and Sarah Bell argue for the early introduction of NGOs in transitional societies, explaining that '... NGOs should be encouraged to enter a country as soon as it is safe, rather than wait for a propitious legal environment'.[10]

Adaptation to Different Cultures

When communism collapsed, many of the countries suffered from a growth of racial hostility and intolerance toward minorities. Students therefore needed to gain knowledge about intercultural education. They had to learn new concepts, such as valuing differences, how to cope with changes, and how to respond to other cultures. In every country there were ethnic groups who had been suppressed in communism. In the former Yugoslavia, students had to learn about their own culture, evaluate theirs and others and to recognize that there is no justification for legal discrimination.

The HEP developed a network with other cultural diversity programs. For example, The Council of Europe had developed a European Youth Campaign against racism, xenophobia, anti-Semitism and intolerance. The Council developed an education pack for teachers on understanding difference and discrimination; a positive approach to differences; and methods and resources, to be used during diversity training.[11]

Finally, the HEP also assisted coordinators on intercultural education pilot projects. Their programs included human rights issues, developing policies in their schools to combat prejudice, and learning communication skills and mediation to emphasize cooperative behaviour.

Key Issues

In the 1990s, HEP was small and manageable. As the program expanded in the 1990s and became integrated into thousands of schools throughout the region, issues arose that were often unforeseen.

Dealing with Philosophical Differences

The HEP taught principles of democracy to counter the communist philosophy. Several lessons in the *Conflict and Communication* curriculum were based on basic rights, such as freedom of opinion and expression and freedom of life, liberty and the security of person.[12] Creative thinking and expression and taking responsibility were major objectives. Students were taught that freedom of speech is their right, and through classroom discussion, they learned how to express themselves. This was not as easy as it might seem on the teacher's or student's part since under communism, there was little tolerance for questioning a teacher or his/her authority.[13]

Lack of Independent Thinking

Under communist ideology people were led to believe that the government knew what was good for society, based on special knowledge of social and economic development. This special knowledge was rational state control. People were at risk when they defied the state. The program taught participants how to understand themselves, explore their own values and beliefs, and share them with others. The participants were asked to define physical, mental, emotional, social, personal and spiritual health according to their common, personal and cultural values. They were placed into groups, and each group had to decide upon its own definition of health. This was the first opportunity for many of them to realize that they could take responsibility for their own health and to express themselves openly to strangers in their group.

Teaching Civic Responsibility

The HEP felt that it was very important to address the concept that civic responsibility is part of one's responsibility in an open society. As George Soros states in *Underwriting Democracy*:

In a democracy people are allowed to decide questions of social organization for themselves. Solutions need not be final; they can be reversed by the same process by which they were reached. Everyone is at liberty to express his or her view, and, if the critical process is working effectively, the view that prevails may represent the common interests of all the participants.[14]

This statement was at the root of several lessons in the Alcohol and Other Drugs curriculum. In one such lesson, Drugs and The Law,[15] students were taught that in a democratic form of government, each person has a voice in creating (drug) laws by which the community must live. Students went through a process of writing laws so they could understand how a democratic society works and some responsibility for helping society. They learned that each citizen has the right to voice his/her opinion. Students wrote letters to government officials expressing their concerns about drug laws. They learned that civic responsibility includes communication with lawmakers and other government representatives.

Facing Job Insecurity

The HEP had to face the problem of teaching participants that an open society supports equal opportunity, not a guaranteed job or position. As Darko Jordanov, a teacher and conflict management consultant from the Republic of Macedonia, stated:

> Part of communist ideology was to pretend to have peace. Everybody must be equal and the same ... It is not realistic. I compare it to a race. My ideal is that everybody starts the race at the same time, but the one who runs the fastest is the winner. In communism, everybody was supposed to reach the end of the race at the same moment ... I see that it kills the race ... that is one of the reasons for the death of communism.[16]

The health education program was competitive in nature. Motivation and hard work were valued. Darko Jordonov said:

> Communism never found a way to motivate people to work hard. People used to say, 'Why should I work more when everybody earns the same amount of money?' It was enough for a decent life, but why not just go to work for eight hours, and do nothing, and then go home fresh? And if you wanted to work, people would not respect you for that.[17]

Resisting New Ideas because of Lingering Communist Ideology

It was a challenge for participants to be non-judgmental with one another when their views were contradictory. Some became angry with those who defended the old regime. Conversely, some were intolerant favoring an open society. In these transitional countries, the participants had little exposure to non-confrontational communication skills.

Evaluating the Cases

The most successful programs enjoyed high motivation and the capabilities of the country coordinators to conduct highly motivational training. The lack of success was often attributed to problems within the countries or internal problems within the Foundation.

Government Cooperation

The Foundation worked with coordinators and other NGOs to put pressure on the Ministry of Education to implement a health education program. The coordinators had information that they presented to their Ministries that explained the benefits of such a program. A government excited about HEP could induce its expansion. In Moldova, HEP was implemented. The teacher-trainers worked with the Ministry of Education to have HEP become mandatory in Moldovan schools. HEP was taught for two hours a week during biology classes. All biology teachers (over 1000 individuals) were trained to use the curricula.[18]

Instability in a Country

The stability, or lack of it, within a country affected AFP implementation. The Bosnian government in 1994 was not able to implement HEP, even though there was sufficient funding. Although the Soros Foundation did not meet direct resistance, the political situation was not stable enough. Because of the war, most children did not attend school. For a short time, the coordinator decided to put the health education program on the radio. The material in the health education curricula was not taught in Bosnia until the end of the war. A Pen Pals for Peace program was initiated. Students in Sarajevo exchanged letters with students in the United States. The Foundation then published a book, *Dear Unknown Friend, Children's Letters from Sarajevo*,[19] a collection of drawings and letters written by children living in Sarajevo during the siege of that city.

Internal Foundation Differences

The Soros staff within each country often influenced the outcome of HEP. Soros Foundations are autonomous institutions established in particular countries or regions to initiate and support open society activities.[20] They each have their own board. It was sometimes difficult for them to get assistance for HEP if the board within the local foundation did not fully support the program. In Lithuania the Soros Foundation board believed that there was a need for the health education program, and the government supported the initiative, so it became one of their priorities.

The situation in Russia was quite different; the board did not fully support HEP, and the government did not make it easy to implement the program. In 1987, Soros had difficulties organising a board with people who usually would not speak to one another. Management fell into the hands of a reformist clique of Communist Youth League officials. They formed a 'closed society for the promotion of open society'.[21] The Russian Foundation never got off to a good start, and problems persisted for several years. Between 1992 to 1998, the HEP developed in spite of these problems. Six hundred schools in St. Petersburg initiated the program.

In Samara, the program existed in nine pilot schools. More than 100 teachers and 20 psychologists were trained. In Novosibirsk, Siberia, the Ministry of Education approved the program. In regional centers around Siberia, in Tomsk, Omsk, Krasnayar and Irkutsk, the Foundation had requests for its implementation. In addition, the Pedagogical University used HEP teaching methods and received federal approval to incorporate the HEP philosophy into college-level programs.

In 1998, the Soros Foundation's Executive Director in New York took note that the Russian HEP, from 1992 until 1998,[22] made 336 workshops for 8000 participants. Fifty-two per cent were teachers; 48 per cent were from other professions, such as psychologists, pedagogic methodologists, and school principals. By the end of 1997, approximately 1,789 schools employed 2622 teachers and almost 70,000 students. Health education had become a priority. The program received support and additional funding from oblast budgets, retraining institutes, and local ministries of education. Their greatest challenges were a lack of materials and the need for curriculum adaptation to Russian culture.[23]

Needs of Coordinators in 23 Countries

The program grew so quickly that Participants introduced to it later did not have the same quality training as those who were involved early on. Coordinators selected from the first workshop had intensive training; with coordinators meetings at least twice a year, they had a support system, they had abundant supplies, the opportunity to spend two weeks in the US observing training, and access to Soros staff. Involved in the program immediately after the fall of communism, everything was new and exciting. As the program grew in size, Soros staff could not meet all the needs.

Lessons Learned

The HEP became integrated into 23 countries from 1989 through 1999. It aided in transforming post-Communist societies in several ways. It introduced critical information on health issues into schools. It emphasized interactive teaching to encourage behavioural change and individual and community responsibility – teaching students how to take responsibility for their own actions and their own health.

Those were the concrete, measurable successes of the program. But the program had its challenges. It could not easily change the old state mentality. It was a challenge for participants to learn how to express themselves, even though the program taught principles of freedom of speech and civic responsibility. This program could only offer teachers and students skills. Using these in everyday life takes much longer. Because of insufficient funds, participants often did not have enough training to become competent. The skills were taught typically in one five-day workshop and a few follow-up sessions.

There were missed opportunities by Soros staff. First, the World Health Organisation, Council of Europe, and the Commission of the European Communities developed a Health Promoting School Project in 1994 in four countries: the Czech Republic, Hungary, Slovak Republic and Poland. These four pilot countries paved the way for many other member states to join the European Network of Health-Promoting Schools.[24] A partnership with this pilot project would have benefited HEP. Second, the Soros Foundation should have hired someone to find matching funding. The Soros Foundation could not put endless dollars for the needs of thousands of teachers in 23 countries. Finally, a stronger US support network would have helped the coordinators, as well as establishing a board of health educators could have deepened HEP roots in the countries.

In spite of these problems, the HEP continues to exist in schools in all 23 countries. The curricula and school methodology have been instituted in many universities and pedagogical institutes, and teachers now teach with methods other than just lectures. Coordinators from several countries have created their own Foundations and NGOs that continue to fund and manage the HEP. In 2003, the Soros Foundation updated the curricula and placed them online for teachers and health professionals in all transitional countries.

Notes

1 *Refer* to Susan and Ronald Shapiro, *The Curtain Rises: Oral Histories of the Fall of Communism in Eastern Europe* (Jefferson, North Carolina: McFarland Publishers, 2004) <www.mcfarlandpub.com>. Chapter I, 'Behind the Curtain'. This chapter gives detailed information about the Egry József School in the XI district of Budapest and other Hungarian classrooms. See <www.mcfarlandpub.com>.

2 For more information on the individual country foundations, go to <www.soros.org> and refer to that particular region.

3 *See* the Health Education Curricula: Nutrition and Your Health, Smoking Prevention, Alcohol and Other Drugs, An Introduction to Human Sexuality and AIDS education. See <www.soros.org> for the curricula.

4 *See* the curriculum, *Conflict and Communication: A Guide Through the Labyrinth of Conflict Management*, developed and written by Daniel Shapiro, Ph.D., at <www.soros.org>. The curriculum is being adapted for schools in the United States by staff at the Harvard Law School Program on Negotiation (2004). Information can be obtained from Dr. Shapiro at the Harvard Law School Program on Negotiation, Pound Building, Massachusetts Avenue, Cambridge, Massachusetts 02138; Email: Dr. Shapiro at <dlshapir@law.harvard.edu>. *Environment and Our Global Community.* The authors

and their articles include: Albania, Irena Vangjeli, 'The Role of the Forest and Deforestation'; Bosnia, Refugees, Sanja Derviskadic-Jovaniovic and Sulejman Redzic, 'Their Lives and Their Environment: Environment and War'; Bulgaria, Virginia Valova, 'Discovering Nature: Declaration of Responsibility to Nature'; Croatia, Lidija Pavic and Bozica Jelusic, 'Bringing Earth Day to Your Community'; Czech Republic, Ivan Janik and Vera Janikova, 'Environment and The Law, Parts I, II and III'; Estonia, Sirje Aher, 'Reuse, Recycling and Waste Minimisation'; Hungary, Agnes Halacsy, Marta Szlka, and Dorottya Hollo, 'Air Pollution: Environmental Debate'; Latvia, Ruta Vocisa, 'Shoreline Ecosystems'; Lithuania, Laima Galkute, 'Water Pollution'; Macedonia, Tanevski Josif, 'Development of Ecological Organizations'; Moldova, Gacota Anatol and Kiseleva Oksana, 'Pesticides and the Food Chain'; Poland, Dorota Meerecz and Dr. Bohdan Dudek, 'Lead Poisoning'; Romania, Simona Botea, 'Cleaning The School and Neighborhood: Getting Involved'; Russia, Novosibirsk, Gryaznova Tatiana and Nizhny Novgorod, 'Protecting Endangered Species', Shwetz Irine, Shustov Sergej, and Dobrotina Nataly, 'Biodiversity, The Spice of Life', St. Petersburg, Moutchnick Boris Isaakovich, 'The Aquarium as a Model of an Ecosystem, The City as An Ecosystem, Future City'; Slovak Republic, Stefan Szabo and Silvia Szabova, 'Environmental Education: Steps Ahead'; Slovenia, Jorg Hodalic, M.S., 'Ground Water'; Ukraine, Natalia Pustovit, 'Radiation'; Yugoslavia, Aco Divac, 'Political Action: Writing Letters to Activate Interest in the Environment'. For further information contact Susan Shapiro at <rmdshapiro@aol.com> or the Soros Foundation at <www.soros.org>.

5   Developed by Metis Associates Inc., 80 Broad Street, Suite 1600, New York, New York 10004-2209 for the Soros Foundation, 'Health Education Program Report of the Phase I Quantitative Findings', January 1995, pp. 1-6. See <www.soros.org>.

6   George Soros with Byron Wien and Krisztina Koenen, *Soros on Soros, Staying Ahead of the Curve* (New York, NY: John Wiley and Sons, Inc., 1995), pp. 113-147.

7   The Health Education Program staff sent monthly updates of information that came from a variety of sources such as the CDC, NIH, and WHO. Newsletters were sent to coordinators from the various organisations.

8   John P. Elder, E. Scott Geller, Melbourne F. Hovell and Jonia A. Mayer, *Motivating Health Behavior* (Delmar Publishers, Inc., 1994).

9   Susan and Ronald Shapiro, *The Curtain Rises: Oral Histories of the Fall of Communism in Eastern Europe* (McFarland Publishers, 2004), p. 50.

10 See Zinnes and Bell, 'NGO Growth in Transition Economies', *Journal of Human Rights*, 2/3 (September, 2003): 389.

11 Council of Europe, 00-586 Warsaw, Poland, Flory Street 3. The Health Promoting School Network was a joint effort of the World Health Organisation, Europe; Council of Europe; and the Commission of the European Communities, 1994.

12 *See id.*

13 Daniel Shapiro, *Conflict and Communication: A Guide Through the Labyrinth of Conflict Management* (Central European University Press, 2004), p. 219.

14 George Soros, *Underwriting Democracy* (New York, New York: The Free Press, A Division of Macmillan, Inc., 1990), pp. 192, 193.

15 Alcohol and Other Drugs curriculum, pp. 83-89.

16 Susan and Ronald Shapiro, *The Curtain Rises: Oral Histories of the Fall of Communism in Eastern Europe* (Jefferson, North Carolina: McFarland Publishers, 2004), p. 210, <www.mcfarlandpub.com>.

17 See Susan and Ronald Shapiro, p. 204.

18 Report given to the Soros Foundation from Julia Moldovano, coordinator, the Soros Foundation Moldovan Foundation.

19 *Dear Unknown Friend, Children's Letters from Sarajevo*, First Edition (The Open Society Fund, 1994).

20 See <www.soros.org>.

21 Soros, Wien and Koenen, p. 128.

22 Soros Foundation Russian Evaluation Program, <www.soros.org>.

23 Susan Shapiro, Carol Flaherty-Zonis and Lisa Pilsitz, 'Russian Health Education Program Strategic Plan 1998–2000'. For further information contact Susan Shapiro at <rmdshapiro@aol.com> or Elizabeth Lorant at the Soros Foundation, New York.

24 Council of Europe 00-586 Warsaw, Poland, Flory Street 3. The Health Promoting School Network was a joint effort of the World Health Organisation, Europe; Council of Europe; and the Commission of the European Communities, 1994.

Chapter 15

Community Peacebuilding in Somalia – Comparative Advantages in NGO Peacebuilding – The Example of the Life and Peace Institute's Approach in Somalia (1990–2003)

Thania Paffenholz

The work of the Swedish 'Life and Peace Institute' (LPI) in Somalia is of particular interest for NGO-peacebuilding, firstly because it constitutes so many elements that are now acknowledged by most peacebuilding researchers and practitioners to be of strategic importance for supporting sustainable peacebuilding.[1] Secondly, it is significant because LPI has worked on all levels of NGO peacebuilding: with the UN mission UNOSOM on a track-one and a half level; later – when the UN left Somalia – it continued on at track-two level and also at a track-three level of empowering civil society. Thirdly, lessons learned from the study of LPI's experiences both confirm and challenge important paradigms of NGOs peacebuilding. We learn for example that the empowerment of civil society without an organized civil society in place is possible and that advocacy for people-based peace processes is as important as activities on the ground. Fourthly, LPI has developed its own 'community bottom-up peacebuilding' approach, which can be classified as a specific approach among the peacebuilding/conflict transformation approaches and thus adds a new dimension to these NGO approaches to peacebuilding.

In this article we analyze the development of the LPI approach to peacebuilding. The first section summarizes the conflict situation in Somalia, followed by a description of LPI's involvement in Somalia from 1990 to 2003. In the final parts, the LPI approach is analysed.

The Early LPI Phase 1983–1992: Research, Information, and Networking

LPI was founded in 1985 as an international ecumenical peace research institute. It represents a combination of peace research, action and education. The Institute aims at non-violent conflict transformation and support for local peacebuilding initiatives.

From 1987 onwards LPI started a Horn of Africa Programme. In the beginning the focus was based on research, networking and advocacy. In 1990, LPI held meetings with Somali Diaspora groups in North America and Sweden. LPI acted as facilitator, organizer and fundraiser.

Track-1 1/2 NGO-Peacebuilding: LPI and the UN 1992–1995

In 1992, it was already clear that a huge UN mission, United Nations Operation to Somalia (UNOSOM), was to go to Somalia. On the request of the Swedish mission to the UN, LPI started discussions with the UN on how to implement the UN mandate for reconciliation in Somalia. From then onwards, LPI cooperated with the UN on a track-1 ½-level of NGO peacebuilding.

At the same time as the new programme started, a conflict over responsibilities between the Horn of Africa Programme and LPI as an organisation started within the LPI office in Uppsala. The conflict went on for almost two years and overshadowed the entire work of LPI, as it divided the institution along the lines of the conflict. It had also some negative spillover effects on the programme in Somalia as this was the biggest programme of the LPI/HAP.[2] This tension finally involved the International Board of the LPI and was only ended with the LPI director and the director of the LPI/HAP both retiring.

LPI in Somalia: Handing Over to the Somalis 1999–2003

At the beginning of LPI's involvement there was a completely different situation on the ground with almost no independent, non-clan based civil society groups in place. As civil society was emerging, it was decided to incorporate local peace NGOs into the new three-year programme. A decision for a hand-over of the Somalia programme to the Somalis was made by the LPI Board in 1997 due to the long external involvement.

The hand over of the programme was seen as a process of some years. In November 2001, the official handing-over of the LPI/HAP Somalia programme took place, and a Somali civil society organisation was founded called 'Forum for Peace and Governance' (FOPAG) with offices all over Somalia. Its capacity was and is still made up mainly of former LPI/HAP Somali staff.

Lessons Learned

Requirements

A strength of the LPI approach was and is its long term involvement within the Somali context. Thus, not only could relationships and networks for empowerment be built, but also 'windows of opportunities' for peacebuilding could be used, when appropriate. LPI stayed along in Somalia when other external actors left the scene.

The Use of Many Different Implementation Strategies

A core strength of the approach is the comprehensiveness and richness of the strategies and instruments used to implement the approach

Unclear Relation to Track-1 Peacebuilding

The main shortcoming of the LPI approach is its unclear relation to track-1 (top-leadership) peacemaking. Other approaches to peacebuilding, such as the complementary approaches or Lederach's transformation approach, do not deny the existence of, and need for, track-1 peacemaking. While Lederach's peacebuilding approach advocates reaching the bottom and the top levels by empowering the middle-range multipliers of the conflict society, LPI focused more on the bottom plus the middle to reach out to the entire society. How the top level should be included in this picture is not clear.

For the further development of the LPI approach, it is necessary to clarify the relation to track-1 peacemaking. An unclear definition could limit the peacebuilding capacity of the approach, as the full range of networks, strategies and instruments might not be used.

Need for the Prioritisation of Strategies

While applying so many different strategies, LPI developed a menu of options for peacebuilding strategies. However, for further application of the approach by LPI or other organisations, these strategies need to be prioritized and put more into a comprehensive framework.

Sustainability Needs to be Introduced from the Very Beginning

LPI has come a long way from working with the UN to building a comprehensive LPI Somalia programme supporting to a new Somali-owned programme that was launched at the end of 2001. This has also been an important learning experience on sustainability. In the future, when LPI or other organisation want to practice the community bottom-up approach to peacebuilding, they should incorporate sustainability into programming at an early stage. Exit and handing-over strategies therefore need to be developed from the very beginning.

Thirteen Lessons Learned from LPI's experience

Lesson 1: The Need for Visions, Goals and Commitment

Prior to developing conflict transformation/intervention strategies, the underlying vision for the intervention should be examined. When intervening actors do not have a clear vision or goals for peacebuilding, there is a danger that interventions will be determined by 'the market' of suppliers, rather than by the real needs of the country or area in conflict. The strength of LPI's entire involvement in the Somali context was that their vision was the driving force behind all strategies.

Lesson 2: Towards a Clear Understanding of Roles

The LPI experience shows that it is essential for external peace actors to be clear as to their own role within a particular process. From the very beginning LPI defined its role as that of a facilitator. LPI facilitated many processes and also acted as an advocate for the interests of civil society. At a certain stage of the process, especially after UNOSOM left, LPI concentrated more on training aspects. Thus, it did not make full use of its capacity/role as a facilitator and advocate for the civil society.

Lesson 3: The Need to Design Concrete Strategies Combined with Good Analysis

Operating with a vision alone is not sufficient. Intervening actors need to turn their visions into operational intervention strategies. Goals can be best clarified through analysing an intervening actor's/institution's own capacities and limits, values, interests and adapting them to problems and needs for peacebuilding. Goals must be clear; however, strategies for reaching these goals can vary and be adapted or modified in the course of the process of peacebuilding.

Experience has shown the need for a combination of a given set of strategies with a flexible adaptation to the situation and a readiness to inculcate learning into the strategies.

As a precondition for designing strategies a good analysis of the conflict situation, as well as of the social-cultural background, is needed. LPI practiced this with the help of external studies and local analysis through its programme officers.

However, the limits and roles of an organisation should also be clarified prior to engaging in new strategies. A critical analysis of LPI's strategies used in Somalia shows that LPI was sometimes driven by external developments without sufficient reflection upon its own capacities. At other times, LPI was driven by implementing a specific strategy, like training, thereby sidelining other important strategies. Therefore it is necessary to be aware of the entire set of strategies an organisation needs and can cope with in order to implement its approach.

Lesson 4: Finding the Right Partners and Entry Points

Finding the right partners and entry points are two issues that are very closely linked. Often partners determine entry points and even strategies. There are 'natural' partners as well as selected partners or a combination of both. Governmental, track-1 actors and large donors have easier access to all sorts of actors, whereas non-governmental, track-2 and track-3 actors, usually have access only to their particular constituency or can be involved when they are invited.[3]

All potential partners bring strengths and weaknesses that need to be analyzed. While some lack resources, others lack capacity or strategies. Others differ in their perceived legitimacy in relation to the conflicting parties. These assets and liabilities must be considered in assessing possible partners.

Fundamental to successful interventions is the relationship between the external and the internal partners. Often local partners accept strategies of outside partners because they are in need of resources. It is of equal importance that both sides are clear about their interests and values.[4]

From LPI's experience we learn first of all that there are different sets of partners:

1.   *Organisations and Relevant Individuals*   The LPI experience shows the importance of people for processes. Whenever a set of like-minded people worked together the process was easiest. LPI was very effective in relating to people who shared the same values. However, when there were no such people around, LPI addressed relevant organisations and tried to inculcate the message in a sensitive manner and was able to develop a non-person based approach over the years.

2.   *Donors on Different Levels (Track 1, 2, 3)*   LPI has had mainly to deal with the European churches as donors, which provided basic funding for a lot of activities, whereas the Canadian Development Agency and later the European Union, were donors for the Somali programme. Good relations with the donor and a shared vision towards peacebuilding between the donor and LPI as implementing agency was key. Moreover, the more flexible the funds that were provided by donors, the more the programme could be implemented in an efficient way.

3.   *External Track-1 Actors from Outside the Conflict Area*   The main track-1 actor from outside the conflict area was UNOSOM and then later the UN, the EC and bilateral actors. The relation between UNOSOM and LPI in particular was not an easy one and showed clearly the difficult interface between track-1 and -2 actors in the field of peacebuilding. The precise definition of roles and tasks seems to be crucial for such a joint exercise. The advisory role LPI obtained has developed into a good example of a track-1/track-2 interface. However, as far as the implementation side is concerned, a set of partners for UNOSOM would have been a better choice than a single track-2 actor.

4.   *External Track 2 or 3 Actors from Outside the conflict Area*   In the beginning of LPI's involvement in Somalia, there was hardly any other NGO dealing with peacebuilding. Therefore there was no need for coordination. Later a few other NGOs started to implement peacebuilding projects. In the beginning this was a new situation for LPI which was accustomed to be on its own. It therefore took some time until LPI appreciated the new situation and began cooperating effectively with other peacebuilding organisations working in Somalia.

5.   *Internal Actors from Within the Conflict Area on Different Levels (Track 1, 2, 3)* There was a common understanding within LPI not to work with the 'warlords'. On the contrary, LPI always wanted to make clear that the 'warlords' needed to be excluded from any peacebuilding effort. According to LPI's approach it was civil society on track-3 and also track-2 which were the proper partners to empower and to work with.

        LPI empowered capable Somali experts by training them as trainers. The amount of resources and training put into the LPI Somali field staff has contributed tremendously to enhance their capacity for peacebuilding. The main reason for this was that there were no appropriate local NGOs to work with. This was a very good strategy, as there were no indigenous groups to relate to in the beginning of the 90s. In other countries, priority should be given to working with local groups to empower them. These groups should be chosen according to a clear set of criteria. For the civic education programme, participants are chosen in a participatory manner according to certain criteria that focus mainly on their ability to function as multipliers.

6.   *The role of the Diaspora* LPI had always worked a lot with expatriate diaspora groups. When LPI had become more established in the region, focus shifted to indigenous Somali groups. Nevertheless, the work, especially with expatriate Somali experts and researchers, showed that these groups and individuals can bring additional value to the process.

Lesson 5: Building Structures and Thinking in Processes

The conflict setting in Somalia as well as LPI's engagement shows that peacebuilding is a process. UNOSOM was a frustrating experience for the entire international community, but led to some positive developments. For example, the UN founded a Lessons Learned Unit in order to better understand positive and negative developments from their peacekeeping operations.

        For the entire Somali conflict, UNOSOM was just one phase of external involvement, mostly hindering the Somalis from taking up their own responsibilities for peacebuilding. LPI's immediate continuation after UNOSOM was possible only because peacebuilding was perceived as a process. The same is true for the Djibouti process. Many international actors saw Djibouti as the solution to the Somali problem. The same organisations, and sometimes even the same people who had always been against traditional reconciliation processes and have supported top-down negotiations with the 'warlords', became enthusiastic about bottom-up peacebuilding, ignoring obstacles to the process. LPI perceived the Djibouti process from the beginning as 'one brick in the wall of the house of peace'.

Lesson 6: Practice What You Preach

The LPI/HAP case in Somalia demonstrates that organisations which want to make a meaningful contribution towards long-term peacebuilding must practice their peacebuilding approach within their own organisations. Organisations that facilitate and implement peacebuilding programmes with a process-oriented participatory bottom up approach must have the same structures in place internally. If this is not the case, civil society representatives working with the organisation will not be able to take the organisation's approach seriously. In the case of LPI's Somali involvement this was more important, as LPI was directly working with the Somali civil society through and with the Somali field staff.

At the beginning of LPI's involvement, LPI used to be driven by people rather than by structures. This is a natural fact for a small organisation and might not have caused harm. However, it was beneficial that LPI moved away from a personality-driven to a structure-driven approach. In addition, the conflict in the LPI headquarters in Uppsala referred to earlier, also influenced the peacebuilding approach negatively, as it presented a bad image to the Somalis.

Lesson 7: Timing: The Need for Long-Term Engagement and 'Windows of Opportunities'

The concept of ripeness has provoked a debate in research, coming to the conclusion that the concept is helpful as it makes actors more sensitive to these indicators. However, the practical use of the concept is limited, as ripeness can usually only be analyzed ex post, or is empirically very difficult to distinguish from the success of outcomes. It becomes thereby tautological: If the conflict is not ripe, there is no chance of a successful peace intervention – if it succeeds, the conflict was ripe.[5] Moreover, in focusing on the concept of ripeness there is even a danger that external actors may remain inactive, as they may not see a ripe moment.[6]

Therefore, the term 'ripe moment(s)'[7] should be replaced by the term 'windows of opportunities'. While the term 'moment' implies a very short time frame and thereby limits chances for intervention, 'windows' can be opened and closed, thereby reflecting the reality that chances for intervention can come and go and therefore need to be monitored and analyzed. If peace interventions were left until a window is fully opened; this window might already be closed when the actor is ready to intervene. What are needed, therefore, are both long-term engagement and the ongoing analysis of potential 'windows of opportunity'. LPI was able to identify various 'windows of opportunity' and support them.

Lesson 8: Having the Right Donor

The LPI Somalia experience makes the importance of the relationship between the external track-2 or -3 actor and its funding agencies obvious. Looking at the two main donors of the LPI programme in Somalia it can be seen that donors supporting peace processes should be extremely flexible. Donors need to have a clear approach and adapt their instruments accordingly.

It was important for LPI that the European Commission funded the entire civic education programme. However, the programme had to be delayed and stopped several times, due to the complicated EU funding rules and regulations. Considering this, the EU is the best donor when it comes to funding for entire programmes that are not ad hoc or urgent, whereas bilateral donors, such as Sida/Sweden, are better donors for flexible, ad hoc and basic funding. The flexible support of local reconciliation conferences, the support for the transport and accommodation of Somalis to participate in important meetings, the flexible funding of conferences that could not be planned ahead (all core LPI strategies), could only be implemented with the understanding and trust of Sida in LPI in combination with adequate funding procedures.

Lesson 9: Co-operation and Co-ordination: Identifying Strategic Alliances for Peacebuilding

All actors on all levels of intervention believe in the usefulness of co-ordination. In practice, however, co-ordination hardly works. Co-ordination is useful only if certain preconditions are met: The objective of co-ordination must be clear and desirable for every actor involved. The LPI experiences demonstrate the difficulty of co-ordination and co-operation. In the beginning of the process, LPI and UNOSOM were engaged in a strategic partnership that contained all the difficult challenges of partners at different levels of intervention.[8] This strategic alliance had the advantage for LPI of being able to influence UN decision making in Somalia. This was an asset for the entire process. Nevertheless, it might have been even more efficient for peacebuilding in Somalia to have a strategic alliance with a set of actors on the ground.

Lesson 10: Being Flexible and Open to New Challenges

The challenge is to find the perfect mixture of clear strategies and instruments and a flexible way to implement them and adapt them to the process. LPI endeavoured to practice exactly this mixture. Over the years LPI found the right way to react to new challenges, although not always in a timely manner.

Lesson 11: Empowerment of Civil Society Works Without Organized Actors on the Ground

The concept of empowering civil society obviously needs an existing civil society in place as a precondition for engagement. This is often defined as existing organized civil society groups, like unions and associations or independent human rights or peace groups. If there are no such structures in place, external actors tend to see no avenue through which to practice this approach.

The LPI Somali experience teaches that civil society can be supported in the absence of such groups. Due to the disintegration of Somali society and the state structures, there were no operative and organized civil society groups in place in the early 90s. LPI therefore chose the following strategies to implement its approach:

- LPI trained their own trainers in order to implement the programme;
- LPI supported individual activists and larger groups belonging to the same category, like teachers, jurists, artists or women's groups. These groups were not organized but identified in a participatory process by the local LPI trainers;
- LPI also worked with entire communities.

This Had Several Effects: Non-clan and groups-based people could come together. This was a reconciliation exercise in itself. Moreover, sometimes the formation of groups could be facilitated through the workshops. The biggest success of this approach was probably the fact that so many different people could be involved. This can also be seen in the fact that more than 50 per cent of the Djibouti delegates had been trained by or involved with LPI in one way or another.[9] This success does not suggest, however, that existing civil society groups should not be supported. For some time now LPI has included the support of local NGOs in its programme.

Lesson 12: Build-in Learning Mechanisms

When working on peacebuilding, a great deal of knowledge is generated. However, lessons are mainly learned individually and not by organisations and institutions. When people leave an organisation, the lessons they learned disappear with them and have to be learned again by the next person to follow. Evaluation units of big organisations have also accumulated a great deal of knowledge, but usually lessons come only from individual cases. Not much emphasis is placed on the collective learning of organisations.

It is therefore essential to build in a learning process on all levels of intervention. The LPI example demonstrates the strength of several different built-in learning mechanisms from the reference groups, self-evaluation, permanent reflection and external evaluations, but most of all an ongoing culture of discussion. Also of importance is a feedback mechanism whereby learning is directly channeled back to the programme.

Lesson 13: Making the Process Sustainable

The goal of sustainability needs to be incorporated into intervention designs from the very beginning. Moreover, actors should develop an exit strategy prior to their engagement. It is necessary that external intervening actors be prepared to leave interventions to local actors or other external actors. The *process* must be sustainable, not the involvement of the external actor!

There are different possible strategies to make a process sustainable. It is important to develop a joint activity plan with a built-in follow-up component. Furthermore, there is a need to build in a monitoring system with a constant feed back mechanism for the constituency concerned. As a matter of trust and building of relationships a feed back mechanism is essential. That also ensures ongoing ownership of the process, which is the best guarantee for sustainability.[10]

Another approach to make a process more sustainable is to look for networking and collaboration partners to support the process. There is no need to co-operate for the sake of co-operation. On the contrary, coordination or collaboration should be established only if there is an added value for all partners involved. However, it is always necessary to elaborate the usefulness of strategic alliances.[11]

From LPI's involvement in Somalia we can learn that there was not enough focus on sustainability. LPI's main strategy for sustainability was to maintain the process of the broad-based empowerment of people in the society, but there was a lack of emphasis on the methodology to achieve this sustainability. Occasionally, LPI's long-term perspective was not helpful because it focused too much on the long-term trickle-down effect rather than also looking into medium-term strategies for sustainability. To empower people is the proper approach but, to continue processes, sustainable structures are also needed.

Notes

1 The findings of this article are based on the research study: Thania Paffenholz, *Community Bottom-Up Peacebuilding: The Life and Peace Institutes Experience in Somalia* (1990–2000), LPI Horn of Africa Series (Uppsala, 2003).
2 Discussions and Interviews with core LPI staff from Uppsala, Nairobi and Somalia.
3 Thania Paffenholz, 'Thirteen Characteristics of Successful Mediation in Mozambique', in Luc Reychler and Thania Paffenholz (eds), *Peacebuilding: A Field Guide* (Lynne Rienner Publishers 2000), pp. 121-127.
4 See Mott Foundation, *Reaching for Peace, Lessons Learned from the Mott Foundation* (November 1999), pp. 26-27.
5 Marieke Kleiboer, 'Ripeness of Conflict: A Fruitful Notion?', *Journal of Peace Research*, 31/1 (1994): 109-116.
6 Thania Paffenholz, *Konflikttransformation durch Vermittlung* (Mainz Grunewald, 1998), pp. 197-198 and 216.
7 *Elusive Peace: Negotiating an End to Civil Wars*, I. William Zartman (ed.) (Brookings Institution Press, 1995).
8 For an analysis of LPI and UNOSOM see Wolfgang Heinrich, *Building the Peace: Experiences of Collaborative Peacebuilding in Somalia 1993–1996* (The Life and Peace Institute Horn of Africa Series, 1997), pp. 152-167.
9 Questionnaires filled by Somali participants in Aarta in 2000.
10 See Thania Paffenholz, 'Designing Transformation and Intervention Processes', in *Berghof Handbook for Conflict Transformation*: <http://www.berghof-handbook.net/> (last viewed in Dec. 2004).
11 Thania Paffenholz, Ibid.

Chapter 16

The Role of NGOs in Institution-Building in Rwanda

Joanna Fisher

NGOs and the international community have failed Rwanda many times. Congratulating themselves on encouraging development indicators, few attempted to institute preventive mechanisms for the impending crisis of 1994.[1] In the immediate aftermath of the genocide, interventions of humanitarian organisations were again accused of having a severely pejorative effect. Local NGO representatives argued that the primary institution developed by international NGOs, which flooded into Rwanda after the genocide, was a culture of dependency in the population.[2] Recognising this negative impact, the Rwandan Government expelled many NGOs in 1995.[3]

In order to explore NGO involvement in institution building, this chapter will examine the role of NGOs in the introduction of two Rwandan institutions: *Ubudehe* and *Gacaca*. Both institutions are being developed from a combination of traditional and new practices. *Ubudehe* is a local government institution designed to encourage community co-operation and solidarity through participatory planning and implementation of activities for poverty reduction. *Gacaca* is a traditional conflict resolution mechanism, adapted to try those accused of genocide crimes. The institutions represent two distinct paths through which the Rwandan government is working towards reconciliation.

NGO interventions in Rwanda have failed repeatedly because they have left inequitable institutions untouched. Whilst 'institution-building' has quickly become a part of development rhetoric, only a minority of NGOs have given serious consideration to their role in developing institutions. There is evidence that the service provision approach has had very little long-term impact. A study commissioned by USAID found that in a sample of 212 projects, only 11 percent had a strong probability of continuing after aid was terminated.[4]

In the immediate aftermath of the genocide, NGOs mobilised enormous levels of resources to meet the basic needs of the displaced and disorientated population. As security was re-established in Rwanda, NGOs provided the means for the resettlement of refugees, both forced and voluntary. The material needs of the population overrode any qualms NGOs may have had over the nature of the resettlement programme. In the years since, the government has been content to encourage NGO involvement in service provision and improvement of living standards at a local level. The government has been reluctant to engage NGOs in the process of developing policy and institutions to ensure the long-term security and stability of Rwanda.

Most national civil society organisations describe themselves as weak and highly dependent on outsiders.[5] NGO strategy is affected by: a history of antagonistic relations between civil society and the government; the legacy of approximately 200 international humanitarian NGOs which flooded Rwanda in 1994; and cultural lack of appreciation of a civil society role in governance. This combination of self-reinforcing factors exacerbates problems limiting the intervention of NGOs.

Rwanda had high levels of associative action before the genocide.[6] However, associative life was closely controlled[7] and failed to impact the extremely hierarchical social structure through which the genocide was coordinated. These associations, or *abashyirahamwe*, more closely resemble small-scale enterprises than organisations that would provide a counterbalance to monolithic government authority structures.

Institution Building in Rwanda

Ubudehe and *Gacaca* were selected for study here because of their contrasting approaches and configurations as preventive mechanisms for future conflict. Their tangible and bounded nature, as opposed to diversely-conceptualised institutions such as good governance, enables an overview of interventions with a minimum of subjective generalisation.

Traditional '*Ubudehe*' in Rwanda was a custom by which the strong laboured for the weak at peak agricultural periods. The literal meaning of the word is 'working together to solve problems'. Active people from the community would spend a day working on the fields of those unable to cultivate alone, ending with a celebration. The government has developed a modern form of *Ubudehe*, combining the tradition of community co-operation to combat poverty with the emic analysis of poverty, a poverty reduction technique that has gained prominence in the last decade. The process aims to encourage community cohesion and reconciliation, fostering interdependency rather than dependency on external assistance. Modern *Ubudehe* employs Participatory Rural Appraisal (PRA) techniques, using familiar objects to symbolise aspects of poverty, as a basis for establishing local priorities for improvement of living conditions and for the design and implementation of interventions.[8]

The emic process is carried out within cellules (100-900 households). Each cellule has been allocated 1000 Euros by the government, funded by the European Commission. The community use leaves, twigs and other familiar objects to map their commune on the ground. The map shows the area's facilities and every household, marking the characteristics of poverty as elaborated by the community. Mapping is designed to be a non-threatening method of including the whole community in self-analysis. The community then discuss their understanding of poverty, its causes and consequences. They identify and analyse their problems, prioritising issues through 'preference scoring': a simple, participatory ranking process. Activities and resources needed to address the primary problem are identified and planned. Committees are elected for implementation and for monitoring.

The time is still too early to judge the success of *Ubudehe*. Clearly, in some cellules only the form and not the substance of the programme had been adopted, with previous decision-making hierarchies remaining intact. However, elsewhere the population reports a widespread involvement in decision-making, implementation of projects addressing issues of high priority to the whole community, and effective monitoring, with any member of the community able to verify whether implementation has followed the communally elaborated plan.

Inkiko Gacaca is a groundbreaking attempt to address an unprecedented problem, adapting an indigenous community mechanism to tackle a unique situation. *Gacaca* was a traditional process for conflict resolution, whereby the parties involved in a dispute voluntarily came together, in front of community elders (*nyangamugayo*), to explore the issues and agree upon a way forward. The outcome of *Gacaca* was negotiated and consensual. Gacaca literally refers to the grass on which the people sat to resolve the problems. *Inkiko* ('jurisdiction') *Gacaca* combines aspects of traditional Gacaca with a more formal, hierarchical system of justice imported through colonisation. The inhabitants of each cellule follow a seven-stage process.

The population is firstly called together to elect judges, respected and trusted members of the community, denominated *nyangamugayo*. The judges then establish time, location and ground-rules for subsequent meetings. The judges facilitate a process of reconstruction of the events of 1990-94. This commences with a community-compiled house-by-house census of those present at the time of the genocide. They then draw up lists of genocide-related victims and damage. The community is then required to testify against the perpetrators of the inventoried killing, rape and property damage. The accused are tried and subjected to a combination of punitive and reparative justice.[9]

Many tensions exist in transforming an informal, local, consensual and reparative system into a formal, hierarchical and primarily punitive system. *Inkiko Gacaca* fails to meet international legal standards ratified by the Government of Rwanda, including right to representation and the burden of guilt. However, it has been estimated that trying 'genocidaires' through the classic court system would take 100 to 200 years. Most actors have in principle accepted the system as an imperfect but necessary means for reconciliation. However, serious reservations remain.

Questioning the validity of the use of the traditional concept of *Gacaca* is pertinent here. The modern institution surrounding *Gacaca* is clearly centralised and arguably retains little more than the surface aspects of the original. Many of the institution's actors are concerned at the current balance between punitive and reconciliatory aspects of *Inkiko Gacaca*. In addition, the actors feel the development of the process has been dominated by lawyers and that, in its drive towards punitive justice, it risks failing to promote reconciliation. Not only was reconciliation the aim of traditional justice, but also stated as a primary aim of the Rwandan government.

The Role of NGOs in Establishing *Ubudehe* and *Gacaca*

Ubudehe has been developed through a policy action group composed of the Government of Rwanda, Action Aid, and two donors. Each actor had a distinct role reflecting the characteristics of their type of organisation, with Action Aid providing expertise in working at the community level. Action Aid worked closely with the government, making a considerable contribution of ideas and methodology to the programme. Action Aid built the capacity of Central and Local Government to take on their respective roles in the institutions. Action Aid also funded pre-pilots, which were used to explore the impact of the new institutional procedures on the community and on existing institutions. In addition, Action Aid has played a significant part in examining the process and feeding the findings back towards further development of the programme. *Ubudehe* would not have been formed without the intervention of Action Aid, and the programme faces potential sustainability problems, due to limited ownership. A danger exists that the work may not continue for long enough for the envisaged institution to mature.

Many different types of NGOs have been engaged in building the institution of *Inkiko Gacaca*. Those who were meaningfully involved included: international NGOs specialising in human rights, law and penal reform and Rwandan human rights NGOs, whose interest is primarily in the legal strength of the system. Also involved are Rwandan welfare NGOs, faith communities and international NGOs engaged in building civil society. Platform organisations bring together actors with varied positions and interests in the process. The organisations have distinctive roles according to their mandate, expertise and strategic positioning, aiming to provide a channel for feedback on the process at local or national levels. Some NGOs have had an, albeit limited, input in the design of technical aspects of the process and have provided logistical assistance and funding for effective management of the pilots. Local NGOs and faith communities worked to provide a helpful environment for the institution. Some international NGOs fostered the capacity of local NGOs to play a part in advocacy on behalf of the poor, in order to build and maintain local and sustainable, pluralistic input to the development of institutions.

Engagement with both institutions, particularly *Inkiko Gacaca*, has been problematic. *Gacaca* is highly political, and NGO input has generally been poorly received. The problem of attribution and the complexity of the interaction involved in institutions make it difficult to observe whether the overall impact from one or all NGOs has been positive or negative. Strategic decisions are difficult to justify, and outputs are intangible. Attribution of causality, externalities and the interaction between *Gacaca* and other institutions cannot be objectively verified.

The difficulties with both institutions are considerable, and NGOs engaged with *Gacaca* have had reason for ongoing serious evaluation of their interventions and their very involvement with the institution. It is pertinent to question the reasons why they have remained involved to this point, despite their acknowledgement that much of their work has had little impact. Evidently, mixed and differing agendas continue to exist. Unstated incentives, such as remuneration, politics, power and prestige of individuals and their organisation affect decision-making to varying degrees. However, for many, their continued presence results from comparing doubts about the impact of their interventions with the conviction that some kind of counterbalance to government control is essential. The NGOs believe that the people need to be represented and that they can take this role, trying to ensure that the institutions that develop are equitable rather than skewed by unequal power relations.

As relatively small and flexible organisations, often working in a variety of environments, NGOs can achieve a disproportionate impact through stimulating lesson learning. Klinmahorn and Ireland highlight the connection between the flexibility of NGOs and their potential influence as agents of change beyond the scale of resources applied. [10] NGOs are able to facilitate learning from the experiences of other countries, bring in expertise not otherwise available, provide alternative forms of linkages to grassroots communities and contribute to processes for feedback and adjustment of programmes. The NGOs involved in *Gacaca* and *Ubudehe* used a wide variety of mechanisms to contribute to the building of the institutions in this way.

The analysis and interventions of many international NGOs has been carried out in the light of experiences in other countries, such as the use of the PRA in *Ubudehe* and using the experience of informal and formal justice systems in Africa to inform policy decisions in *Gacaca*. Technical expertise, in law and other fields, has been provided by these international NGOs in order to compensate for Rwanda's extreme human resource deficits. NGOs have been able to encourage the use of pre-pilots, using their flexibility to provide funding for part or all of the experimentation and using their expertise in feeding lessons back into the policy process. Secondments have been used for the transfer of skills, values, methodologies and perspectives to national organisations. Action Aid has seconded an employee to the Ministry of Finance, enabling a two-way exchange of information and understanding. Within this framework, formal and informal linkages with government are able to overcome often adversarial relationships. Recommendations for improvement of *Ubudehe* have been informal and made in the context of trust and understanding.

NGOs engaged with *Gacaca* and *Ubudehe* have had to position themselves on the continuum between working in partnership with government and working at a distance from government. Action Aid opted to influence *Ubudehe* from within a close partnership with the government. This involvement provides an opportunity to instill their ideas, methodologies and values into the design and implementation of the institution. Rugwabiza stated, 'If NGOs want their views to be considered, they have to contribute. The more you participate, the easier it is to give ideas.'[11] If an NGO puts itself in a position in which it assumes part of the responsibility for an institution, the contribution of ideas or constructive criticism gains legitimacy in the eyes of the government. Such a position can overcome NGO 'tunnel vision', restricting their ability to make unrealistic demands. The partnership also creates formal and informal links, through which it is possible to pass constructive criticism more subtly and without confrontation.

Co-ordination Mechanisms

In a politically-sensitive arena, many organisations prefer ad hoc interest-based alliances to platforms, in order to maximise organisational strengths, without tying organisations to particular strategic options. This can be seen in some of the ways in which international NGOs engaged in *Gacaca* have worked together. They have no formal co-ordination structure, however, they have managed to avoid duplication and to maximise resources and information through informal collaboration. For example, confession forms, developed by ASF from a judicial perspective, were piloted by Penal Reform International, using the presence of their employees in prisons throughout the country. Another example can be found in a project, led by the National University's Centre for Conflict Prevention, which aims to compile a report focusing on the experiences of one cellule, with each chapter authored by a different NGO with a distinct focus. Such collaboration can make use of the strengths of distinctive strategic positions, access and specialities of different organisations.

A local platform organisation, PAPG, has been established for monitoring *Gacaca*. As has been found with other platform organisations in Rwanda, there is a growing consensus that such an organisation closes down political space and inevitably leads to conformance to the lowest common denominator. [12] An alternative role for a platform, as taken by the 'Coexistence Network', is to act as a conduit of information, providing a contact point through which information can be disseminated and through which NGOs can communicate regarding programmes and location, as a means of identifying opportunities for synergy.

Various donor/NGO round tables were established for *Gacaca*. Many saw the purpose of these as making use of the more powerful position of donors for advocating adaptations to the *Gacaca* process. However, PRI states that no consequent impact was observed from such meetings. [13] Some NGOs perceive that donors have failed them, due to the donors' own hidden agendas. However, donors are also constrained, and the Rwandan government is sensitive to conditional support and willing to reject it.

Institution building for *Inkiko Gacaca* allows us to observe the interaction of NGOs assuming close and distant relationships with the government. NGOs taking an extreme position of collaboration with the government cede control and independence. They effectively become subcontractors and sacrifice their civil society role. NGOs refusing to engage with the government become antagonistic and lose their power to influence. Few NGOs achieve and retain a position between these extremes. The Rwandan government, which considers all who are not with them to be against them, makes that balance harder to achieve. It requires constant stakeholder and institutional analysis, which is beyond the capacity of many NGOs. Effective, but informal, collaboration between NGOs can mimic equilibrium, the position of each complementing others.

NGOs in Rwanda are engaging at central and local government levels and with local communities. However, most international NGOs engaged with Rwandan institutions have rejected engagement with local NGOs due to their lack of capacity and independence. This is shortsighted and self-fulfilling. It fails to raise the capacity of a very weak civil society, to build an understanding of pluralism, or to open up space for local organisations to engage with institutions.

Notes

1 P. Uvin, *Aiding Violence: The Development Enterprise in Rwanda* (West Hartford, CT: Kumarian Press, 1998).
2 British Embassy, Kigali, *Report on Participation Training Workshop* (Kigali: unpublished, 2003).
3 Office of the Resident Coordinator Rwanda, *United Nations Situation Report* (Kigali: United Nations System's Operational Activities for Development in Rwanda, 1996), p. 7.
4 Cited in D. Rondinelli, 'The Dilemma of Development Administration: Coping with Complexity and Uncertainty', from *Development Projects as Policy Experiments* (London and New York: Routledge, 1993), p. 2.
5 Ibid., p. 3.
6 Trocaire, *Response to DFID Draft Concept* note (unpublished, 2003), p. 1.
7 DFID, p. 3.
8 For a description of PRA see Chambers, *Response to DFID Draft Concept* note.
9 For a more detailed exploration of Gacaca see Amnesty International, *Gacaca: A Question of Justice*, <web.amnesty.org/library/engafr47007202?open&eng-rwa, 2002>.
10 S. Klinmahorn and K. Ireland, 'NGO-government Collaboration in Bangkok', in M. Edwards and D. Hulme (eds), *Making a Difference: NGOs and Development in a Changing World* (London: Earthscan Publications Ltd, 1992), p. 68.
11 Rugwabiza, *Making a Difference: NGOs and Development in a Changing World* (London: Earthscan Publications Ltd, 1992).
12 For example, PAPG, *August Monitoring Report on Gacaca* (unpublished, 2003).
13 De Jong, p. 4.

Chapter 17

Orangi Pilot Project:
An NGO Helping to Build Community

Steven Barmazel

Amid the many efforts to spur development in Pakistan, one organisation stands out as a success. The Orangi Pilot Project (OPP) is based in the urban center of Orangi, the largest *katchi abadi* or squatter settlement in Karachi, the country's largest city.[1] Begun in 1980, OPP is an NGO.[2] It depends on its own resources for money, and has no authority – no sanctions – to enforce compliance with any of its directives.[3] Nonetheless, OPP has spurred great improvements throughout its target community. The Project first focused on creating a system of underground sewers. Using local materials and labor, it succeeded in laying hundreds of kilometers of pipe, along with auxiliary facilities.[4] Besides improving health, social interaction and property values in Orangi, OPP has midwifed a multitude of improvements. Within a decade of the organisation opening its doors, for example, residents had established schools, health clinics, women's work centers, cooperative stores and a credit organisation to finance enterprise projects. To assist with these various social improvements, OPP itself split into separate but linked institutions.

More than 1 million people crowd into Orangi's 3,200 hectares.[5] Though squatter settlements evoke images of destitute masses, most residents of Orangi are in fact working class.[6] 'They are day-laborers, skilled workers, artisans, small shopkeepers, peddlers and low-income white-collar workers.'[7] Orangi is as ethnically diverse as any neighborhood in Pakistan; it holds a mix of native Sindhis and Balochis, immigrants (and their descendents) from Punjab and the Northwest Frontier Province, as well as from India (Such immigrants are known as *Mohajirs*) and Bangladesh (known as *Biharis*).[8] Residents have dubbed the area a 'Mini Pakistan'.[9]

Short History of Orangi and its Pilot Project

Squatters began moving into Orangi in 1965.[10] Housing and commercial facilities developed without help from government agencies.[11] That meant that, even by Pakistani standards, authorities did not provide adequate water, power, health care, transport, education and – perhaps most significantly – sewerage.

In 1980 donors invited the late Dr. Akhtar Hameed Khan to start a development program to help the neighborhood. Khan was a veteran of the India

Civil Service before Partition and later an organizer of rural development projects in Comilla, East Pakistan (now Bangladesh). A relative newcomer to Karachi and inexperienced with urban projects, Khan began touring Orangi by jeep to explore the area and interview residents about their needs.[12]

Khan began work in Orangi less than a decade after Pakistan had endured the trauma of civil war and the secession of more than half its people. One result of Bangladesh's liberation war and subsequent independence was an influx of refugees. *Biharis* (immigrants from East Pakistan, named for an Indian state bordering Bengal) flocked into Pakistan's cities – even as Pakistan had yet to recover from the flood of millions of Mohajirs (immigrants from India, most of who arrived around the time of the 1947 Partition). Since 1972, the population of Orangi had surged.

Khan landed on the idea that focusing on sanitation and sewerage works would improve both the health and properties of residents. [13] Reviewing Orangi's subsequent progress, a United Nations agency looked back on the state of sanitation as Khan found it: 'In 1980, bucket latrines or soak-pits were the main means of disposal for human excreta and open sewers for the disposal of wastewater. The result was poor health with typhoid, malaria, diarrhea, dysentery and scabies being common. Poor drainage resulted in water logging and reduced property values.'[14]

Khan concluded that Orangi residents took no action to improve the situation for four reasons: Financial – they could not afford to have built conventional sanitary latrines and underground sewers. Psychological – they held that government agencies should build sewer lines without charge. Technical – local builders lacked the know-how to build underground sewer lines. Social – building underground lines required a high level of community organisation and cooperative action, which did not exist.[15]

OPP engaged technicians to survey routes and to prepare plans and cost estimates for each lane. Meanwhile, social organizers worked to help coordinate community efforts.[16] The communities engaged in these improvement efforts needed to be small enough to encourage beneficiaries to participate, yet large enough to undertake the sizable task of building a sewer system. 'The OPP chose the lane, consisting of 20-40 houses as the basic organisational unit, since it is small enough to ensure participation and large enough to ensure economies of scale.'[17]

Each lane needed a resident 'lane manager' to oversee the process, including collecting contributions, supervising work and resolving disputes. OPP itself steered clear of such work; it would provide technical advice and support social organisation, but only those living in a lane could be responsible for managing finances and contracting construction.[18] This spurred lane residents to new levels of cooperation, and created both financial and psychological 'buy-in' to the community effort and the resulting infrastructure.

Within a decade, OPP had transformed Orangi, concluded WaterAid, a UK-based NGO that supports integrated water, sanitation and hygiene education projects in developing countries.[19] 'Gone were the murky, stinking open sewers that crisscrossed the settlement and which posed considerable health and physical hazards to its residents … The OPP experience is … a most impressive demonstration of just how much urban poor communities can contribute to the development of quite complex large-scale infrastructure projects.'[20]

An Empirical Test

Empirical evidence of an NGO's effectiveness is rare. It is difficult to find an example of an identical (or even similar) community that develops without the benefit of an NGO's program during an identical period (in a scientific experiment called a *control group*). A seven-year collaboration with the United Nations Center for Human Settlements (UNCHS) to develop sanitation in Orangi indirectly provided control data about OPP. UNCHS offered in 1982 to provide technical advisors for OPP's sanitation and health public-health programs. The venture was funded by OPP's main benefactor, the Bank of Credit and Commerce International (BCCI). The Pilot Project's mode of operating was so at odds with the UN agency's, however, that within four months the venture broke down.[21] Pursuant to a request by UNCHS, sanitation improvement (essentially laying sewers and auxiliary improvements) in Orangi for the remainder of the venture's term was divided between OPP and a newly created agency under the auspices of UNCHS, called the Community Development Project (CDP). Dr. Khan wrote of the separation in OPP's 13th progress report:

> There will now be two projects in Orangi sponsored by BCCI: the three-year-old OPP which will follow its own approach, and a new project with UNHCS as the executive agency. The new project will receive two million dollars from BCCI in three years, while OPP will receive a small annual allocation in rupees ... [Besides OPP], the people of Orangi will also have the benefit of another project, characterized by UN munificence and guided by foreign experts.[22]

After the remaining six years were up, the CDP had spent some $625,000 and had developed sanitation in 36 lanes. OPP, meanwhile, had spent less than a third that amount and had laid sewers in more than 4,000 lanes. The CDP was wound up and its project area reverted to OPP.[23]

Attributes of OPP's Strategy

The challenges facing squatter settlements and other impoverished areas inadequately served by official agencies are too staggering to tackle without some government help.[24] Thus, Khan felt that the key function of NGOs and pilot projects that hoped to help residents of such areas was to develop strategies that could be integrated into official planning mechanisms.[25]

OPP officials feel that such strategies or models should meet three criteria. First, they should overcome 'constraints faced by government agencies in the rehabilitation [of the subject communities] without requiring major changes in their structure [or] any radical legislature'. Second, 'overheads, staff salaries and related costs should be [consistent with] government expenditure patterns and regulations, and the strategy should respect established state procedures'. Third, the processes of developing the model should be properly documented, and a demonstration area and effective training material created, 'without which replication is difficult, if not impossible'.[26]

Following these criteria, OPP does not view its efforts as development work. Instead, it 'promotes community organisations a co-operative action, and provides technical support to such initiatives'.[27] Nonetheless, it has helped manage and finance programs that improve the welfare of Orangi residents in many aspects of their lives. The programs include low-cost sanitation, housing, basic health and family planning, supervised credit for small-family enterprises, and education. In villages around Karachi, OPP also conducts a rural development program.[28]

Word of OPP's effectiveness spread. Organisations and activists from other *katchi abadis* in Karachi and elsewhere asked its help in replicating the Project in their home areas. By 1988, OPP felt overwhelmed by its expanded activities and created its five autonomous institutions.[29] The OPP Society oversees funding matters. The OPP Research and Training Institute manages sanitation, housing and social forestry programs; it also trains representatives of NGOs, government agencies, donor agencies and community organisations for all OPP programs. The Orangi Charitable Trust manages and promotes credit programs. And the Karachi Health and Social Development Association (KHASDA) manages the health program.[30]

In 1991 the World Bank commissioned OPP to consult on the Shelter for Low-Income Communities Project, a joint venture of the Bank and the Government of Pakistan.[31] The World Bank urged government involvement at all levels – motivating people, organising them and providing them technical advice.[32]

For a time, OPP tried lobbying and pressuring government agencies directly to get them to fulfill their obligations, such as paving roads, providing schools and other resources to communities.[33] 'However, the OPP "discovered that chasing government agencies is a full-time and unsuccessful job, and that this time can be better utilized."'[34] As a result, OPP changed its political strategy, and when it entered into a venture with the Karachi Municipal Corporation (KMC, the municipal government) that same year, it began arming community members with facts and figures regarding the project and the role the KMC was supposed to play. OPP also trained community members to monitor the work of KMC contractors. Thus the community itself shouldered the job of preventing substandard work.[35] After a turbulent beginning, OPP reported, good working relations developed between the community and KMC engineers and contractors.[36] OPP also reported, however, that the community was unable to get KMC to fulfill maintenance responsibilities.[37]

In joint ventures between, international agencies, local governments, OPP and communities, the Project had hoped that local government agencies would become effective partners. In general, OPP officials have been disappointed with the work of government agencies.[38]

There is one shining exception, however, and it is in OPP's own backyard. The Sindh Katchi Abadi Authority (SKAA) went so far as to adopt OPP techniques. The Authority was created to regularize land ownership in the province's katchi abadis and then to upgrade social and physical services. SKAA reduced red tape and applied low-cost technologies to its improvement projects. Instead of planning and executing development projects itself, the agency began to help communities to carry out *their* projects. There is seeming transparency in its account keeping and projects are regularly monitored and documented, as with the OPP.[39] As endorsement of SKAA's transformation and subsequent success, the Authority's director general, Tasneem Ahmed Siddiqui, received the 1999 Magsaysay Award.[40]

Violence

Even with OPP working in the neighborhood, violence has periodically rocked Orangi. In April 1985, a bus driving through Orangi hit and killed Bushra Zaidi, a teenaged girl. Zaidi was a Mohajir; the bus driver was a Pathan, a member of the dominant ethnic group of the NWFP and all of Afghanistan. Riots erupted, flaring to an intensity never before seen in the area. Orangi burned for days, and more than 100 people were killed in the violence.[41]

By the late 1980s, violence in the cities of Sindh province often had political overtones, influenced if not controlled outright from party organisations based outside Orangi.[42] Party thugs toting automatic weapons had firefights on the streets of Orangi as well as other poor and working-class districts of Karachi. Thousands died in this partisan war of terror and attrition. Orangi endured curfews for days on end.[43]

It is difficult to measure OPP's impact on dampening violence in Orangi. Pakistani communal conflicts and Pakistani politics both continue to veer into violence, and nowhere more so than in Karachi. Even if clashes begin elsewhere, they easily spill into Orangi, an ethnic and political cauldron. OPP has in fact been criticized for not intervening more directly against the eruptions that periodically rock Karachi, 'one of the most violent and divided cities of Asia'.[44] It does initiate repair and reconstruction of infrastructure, and also offers its offices as a meeting place for leaders of rival groups. OPP has argued that it is precisely its nonpartisan, noninterventionist stance that allows it to function and remain successful in Orangi.[45]

A 1990 incident illustrates how OPP's approach can be effective at repairing the community and even preventing bloodshed. An armed group of Mohajirs from outside Orangi entered the area and burned 68 houses in a neighborhood populated principally by Balochis. Some 1400 Balochis fled Orangi, most to homes of relatives. Some in the greater Baloch community tried to incite their Orangi-based brethren to make retaliatory raids on the katchi abadi's Mohajirs and Biharis. Swift and coordinated action by the government and the Orangi community prevented such a disaster. The government allocated money for rebuilding the destroyed homes. With technical help from OPP, the job was completed within two months. Local Biharis then went out and accompanied their Baloch neighbors home. There were no retaliatory raids by Baloch tribesmen, who are known to be heavily armed with automatic weapons, rocket launchers and grenades.[46]

OPP has helped alleviate the impact of specific violent events, and has even been able to prevent attacks that were almost sure to happen (as the 1990 incident illustrates). But these are merely sporadic incidents. To gauge OPP's more general effect on violence in the community, one would need to count how many incidents *fail* to occur, an impossibility. One can merely examine OPP's probable effect, by examining its impact on secondary factors that affect violence (health, wealth, education, uniting stakeholders). In these areas, the organisation's impact, by many accounts, has been significant.[47]

One statistic does indicate that Orangi is a community that has mobilized itself to community action. In 1984 Orangi boasted only 83 registered community organisations for purposes as diverse as education, athletics, religion, theater, cleanliness, and drug eradication. Within two years that number more than doubled, to 178.[48]

Still, the odds of effectively applying OPP's program elsewhere are considered steep. Successful communities tend not to follow OPP's model strictly, but to use it as a base from which to improvise and innovate to suit local circumstances.[49] OPP did not create its techniques, but it does claim to be the first to apply them in an urban setting.[50]

Notes

1 Aga Khan Rural Support Program (AKRSP) has also promoted substantial development in its target region, the remote mountains of Pakistan's Northern Areas, a federally administered territory set deep in the Hindu Kush Mountains. AKRSP programs have taken been inspired by the teachings and leadership of OPP's founder, the late Dr. Akhtar Hameed Khan. The International Bank for Reconstruction and Development/The World Bank, 'Annex 1: Description of the AKRSP Program', The Aga Khan Rural Support Program in Pakistan: A Second Interim Evaluation (Washington, D.C.: 1990), p. 87.
2 Arif Hasan, 'Introduction', Orangi Pilot Project: Reminiscences and Reflections (Oxford University Press: Karachi, 1996), p. 11.
3 Hasan, p. 11.
4 Television Trust for the Environment, Return of the Drain Gang – Pakistan, Hands On, Series 3. <http://www.tve.org/ho/doc.cfm?aid=854>.
5 Hasan, p. 19.
6 Dr. Akhtar Hameed Khan, 'What I Learnt in Comilla and Orangi', paper read at the South Asian Association for Regional Cooperation seminar (Islamabad, 1994).
7 Hasan, p. 19.
8 Hasan, p. 19; Dr. Akhtar Hameed Khan, 'What I Learnt in Comilla and Orangi'.
9 Dr. Akhtar Hameed Khan, 'Pacifying Violence in Orangi', Orangi Pilot Project: Reminiscences and Reflections (Oxford University Press: Karachi, 1996), p. 54.
10 Hasan, p. 19.
11 Hasan, p. 19
12 Dr. Akhtar Hameed Khan, 'What I learnt in Comilla and Orangi', p. 42.
13 United Nations Economic and Social Commission for Asia and the Pacific (UNESCAP), Good Practices Suite, Examples: Orangi Pilot Project. <http://www.unescap.org/drpad/vc/conference/bg_pk_5_opp.htm>.
14 Ibid.
15 Ibid.
16 Ibid.

17 Asian Development Bank, Beyond Boundaries: Extending Services to the Urban Poor, Chapter X, Resources, 'Orangi Pilot Project' (2002). <http://beyondboundaries.adb.org/chX/websites1o.htm>.

18 United Nations Economic and Social Commission for Asia and the Pacific (UNESCAP), Good Practices Suite, Examples: Orangi Pilot Project. <http://www.unescap.org/drpad/vc/conference/bg_pk_5_opp.htm>.

19 Akbar Zaidi, From the Lane to the City: The Impact of the Orangi Pilot Project's Low Cost Sanitation Model (A WaterAid Report) (WaterAid: London, 2001), p. 4.

20 Ibid.

21 Hasan, p. 24.

22 Hasan, p. 25.

23 Hasan, p. 26.

24 Hasan, p. 22.

25 Ibid.

26 Ibid.

27 Hasan, p. 21.

28 Hasan, p. 23.

29 Zaidi, p. 4.

30 Hasan, p. 26.

31 Hasan, p. 32.

32 Hasan, p. 33.

33 Hasan, pp. 36, 35.

34 Hasan, p. 35.

35 Ibid.

36 Ibid.

37 Ibid.

38 Hasan, p. 36.

39 Hasan, p. 36.

40 Shamim-ur-Rahman, 'The Home Maker: Tasneem Ahmed Siddiqui, Government Service', Asiaweek, 6 Aug 1999.

41 Laurent Gayer, A Divided City: 'Ethnic' and 'Religious' Conflicts in Karachi, Pakistan (Center for International Studies and Research: Paris, 2003), p. 7. <http://www.ceri-sciences-po.org/archive/mai03/artlg.pdf>.

42 Zaidi, p. 6.

43 Ibid.

44 Ibid.

45 Ibid.

46 Khan, 'Pacifying Violence in Orangi', p. 58.

47 See: Zaidi, p. 4; Asian Development Bank, Beyond Boundaries: Extending Services to the Urban Poor, Chapter X; Television Trust for the Environment, Return of the Drain Gang – Pakistan, Hands On, Series 3; UNESCAP, Good Practices Suite, Examples: Orangi Pilot Project.

48 Emma Duncan, Breaking the Curfew (Arrow Books: London, 1989), p. 182.

49 Zaidi, p. 14.

50 Hasan, p. 23.

Part Four:
NGOs and Norm Development and Monitoring

Chapter 18

Transnational Activism Against the Use of Child Soldiers

Heather Heckel

This chapter provides a case study of efforts to end the use of child soldiers, beginning with discussion of the issue. The chapter then highlights the central role of international NGOs (INGOs) in the emergence of the campaign. The case highlights common strategies of key INGOs as they sought to establish international human rights standards within the 1989 Convention on the Rights of the Child (CRC) and the 1999 Optional Protocol to the CRC. These strategies included information politics especially the collection of expert data, collaboration with the UN, and efforts to bypass limited political opportunity structures by utilising alternative venues for increased debate and awareness. Finally, the chapter emphasizes that INGOs are also increasingly using formal collaborative structures as a strategy for enhancing their legitimacy and influence.

In 2001, there were approximately 300,000 child soldiers actively fighting in over 30 conflicts.[1] The number of child soldiers rose rapidly in the late 20th century with expanding civilian involvement in wars and the proliferation of small arms.[2] Assessment of the exact numbers of child soldiers remains difficult due to disagreements over definitions and because many child soldiers live in underdeveloped nations and serve in non-state militaries. One could easily view the issue more broadly by including children in armed gangs, paramilitary groups, illegal networks of drug and diamond dealers, as well as those, especially girls, who act in combat support roles, such as cooking, running errands and as sexual servants.

Efforts by both NGOs and UNICEF to collect data on children in war were also evident in a series of mid 1980s workshops. In 1983, the first international symposium on children and war was held in March in Geneva, organized by three European based INGOs – the Geneva International Peace Research Institute (GIPRI), the International Peace Bureau (IPB) and the Peace Union of Finland.[3] In 1984, UNICEF hosted NGO workshops in Rome to discuss child victims of armed conflict. In 1985, Radda Barnen, the Swedish branch of Save the Children, hosted a workshop on psychotherapy of children impacted by Central America's violence.

INGO child soldier publications also increased in the late 1980s. In 1986, Human Rights Watch covered the role of children in Afghanistan in, *To Win the Children: Afghanistan's Other War*. Psychologist and Save the Children consultant, Neil Boothby raised awareness in the 1980s about child fighters in Cambodia,

Guatemala and Mozambique through publications on efforts to rehabilitate child soldiers and other child victims of war.[4] Meanwhile, the FWCC, under Woods' continued leadership, provided the UN Working Group with annually updated research on child soldiers. Woods' data received significant press coverage in August of 1988, in the *New York Times, Le Monde* and *La Nación*.

Some INGO research was drawn from rehabilitation programs operating in several war-torn states. Radda Barnen established the first rehabilitation program in Angola in 1985, but it failed when the Angolan military broke their agreement to demobilize.[5] Save the Children US conducted a more successful effort with the opening in 1988 of camps designed to promote the demobilisation and rehabilitation of child soldiers in Mozambique.[6]

Welcoming the UN Working Group's decision to consider child soldiers in 1986, INGO activists began calling for setting the age of recruitment and participation at 18.[7] Under Radda Barnen's project leadership, these INGOs argued that since early drafts of the CRC defined a child as a person under 18, child soldiers should also be defined using the age of 18. Additionally, Radda Barnen argued that since the ILO had defined 18 as the minimum age for working with hazardous materials in its 1973 Article 138, child soldiers clearly fell under those guidelines due to the handling of weapons.[8] As part of this campaign, the Swedish Red Cross Youth presented a petition on behalf of 654 organisations representing over 90 million young people from 118 states calling for an end to recruitment of all children under 18.[9]

The years after the CRC were characterized by INGO collaboration on the issue of children in war and the sub-topic of child soldiers along with NGO advocacy towards the UN and calls for collection of more accurate and comprehensive data on the issue. Collaboration was evident through the formation of two INGO alliances on children and armed conflict. Both emerged out of pre-existing networks oriented towards influencing UN negotiations. The first, the NGO Committee on UNICEF Sub-Working Group on Children and Armed Conflict (SWGCAC), grew out of the NGO Committee on UNICEF, which formed in 1952.[10] Established in 1989, the SWGCAC was designed as, 'a vehicle for sharing and disseminating information, improving coordination of programs raising public awareness and promoting policy change'.[11] The Women's Commission on Refugees based in Washington, DC chaired the group, whose members included Human Rights Watch, Amnesty International, Save the Children-US and the International Rescue Committee. The group met twice yearly and initially focused upon advocacy towards the UN for increasing research on the impact of armed conflict upon children.[12]

A second child soldier oriented alliance emerged in 1989 when the INAHG reorganized by establishing a permanent office to focus on monitoring the CRC and convening several sub-groups to address specific child rights issues.[13] One Sub-Group on Refugees and Children of War was designed to collect data on child soldiers and continue advocacy. Led by Human Rights Watch, this Sub-Group continued to lobby the UN, this time for the creation of a Special Representative on Children in Armed Conflict.

The Swedish Red Cross and Radda Barnen along with the Raoul Wallenberg Institute also collaborated by holding a Conference on Children of War in late May of 1991. At this conference, the attendees proposed prohibiting the recruitment and use of children under the age of 18 in armed conflicts and recommended a thorough study on the issue of children as soldiers.[14] After the conference, at the request of the participants, the Swedish and Icelandic Red Cross Societies took the recommendation for a study to the International Red Cross Council of Delegates.[15] In November 1991, the Council passed Resolution 14 requesting that the Henry Dunant Institute 'undertake a study ... on the recruitment and participation of children as soldiers in armed conflicts, and on measures to reduce and eventually eliminate such recruitment and participation'.[16] The research coordinators at the Institute established several goals for the study advocating for the 'non-recruitment and non-participation in hostilities of any child below the age of 18' and 'to signal the appropriateness of a Protocol to the CRC'.[17]

Rising attention to child soldiers contributed to expansion of child soldier programmatic efforts by several INGOs and within varied UN bodies. In 1995, Radda Barnen launched a new project intensifying its earlier efforts by creating a regular newsletter and the first on-line child soldier resource databases with relevant literature and agency contact information.[18]

The same year, the Secretary General appointed Graca Machel, a long-time advocate of children's rights, to conduct a 'Study on the Impact of Armed Conflict on Children', which had been authorized by the General Assembly in 1993. Machel requested that the NGO Sub-Group on Refugee Children and Armed Conflict conduct the child soldier research for the study. The Sub-Group established a 'Steering Group' to conduct the research including QUNO, ICCB, Radda Barnen, the Henry Dunant Institutue, the Lutheran World Federation, and World Vision International. QUNO and the ICCB coordinated the project, titled the Child Soldiers Information Project, under the direction of Rachel Brett and Margaret McCallin.[19] The study utilised a series of questionnaires developed by the Steering Group and distributed in 26 nations. The resulting documentation, published by both the UN and separately by Radda Barnen, greatly expanded recognition of the scope and breadth of child soldiering.

NGOs Utilize Collaboration to Increase Influence

To increase their influence and to avoid duplicating their efforts, six INGOs decided to form a collaborative alliance on child soldiers in 1998. Their decision was most likely motivated, in part, by the recent success of the International Coalition to Ban Landmines (ICBL) as their first director, Stuart Maslen, came from the ICBL.[20] On June 30, 1998, The International Coalition to Stop the Use of Child Soldiers (CSUCS) was launched. The Coalition was established by the members of its Steering Committee, Amnesty International, DCI, HRW, IFTDH, International Save the Children Alliance represented by Radda Barnen, the Jesuit Refugee Service and QUNO.[21] The CSUCS formed to:

advocate for the adoption of, and adherence to, national, regional and international legal standards (including an Optional Protocol to the CRC) prohibiting the military recruitment and use in hostilities of any person younger than 18 years of age; and the recognition and enforcement of this standard by all armed forces and armed groups, both governmental and non-governmental.[22]

The CSUCS immediately intensified the INGO's influence by pursuing several tactics resembling those of the ICBL. First, they sought to expand their own membership by creating national partner organisations and reaching out to any interested parties including development and human rights organisations. Second, they created a website for both dissemination of information to the public and networking among NGO partners. Third, they compiled existing research on child soldiers and collected new data to publish the first *Global Report on Child Soldiers* along with regular newsletters. Fourth, they conducted several high profile media events in which the organisation sought attention for the problem of child soldiers.

The CSCUS had an immediate regional impact on Europe, where on December 17, 1998, the European Parliament issued Resolution B4-1078, which stated, 'that an additional protocol to the international CRC should urgently be adopted which bans the recruitment of children under 18 and their participation in armed conflicts'.[23]

Concluding the Negotiations

By the Sixth Session of the Working Group, the key issues of recruitment and participation below the age of 18 remained unresolved. The majority support for the 'straight-18' position was now clearly apparent but the United States continued to oppose the use of 18 as a minimum standard for all recruitment.[24]

Meanwhile, the INGOs by unifying under the CSUCS umbrella and its national chapters, especially the Australian and US CSUCS, had increased their legitimacy, their outreach, and the data they were able to utilize to be influential. The multiple regional agreements along with direct lobbying of key states also enhanced their impact. By early 2000, the CSUCS had generated significant public pressure for the UN and states to address the problem of child soldiers.

The US and UK also argued against the participation standard of 18, primarily because if under-18s were allowed to join the military, then governments could not ensure that they did not participate.[25] Once again, the Working Group settled on a compromise based upon earlier standards – Article 83(2) of the CRC and Article 77(2) of Geneva Protocol I requiring only that states take all 'feasible measures' to ensure that children under 18 do not take a 'direct part in hostilities'.[26]

The third controversial decision was to continue to use the term 'direct' when referring to participation in hostilities. The ICRC and INGOs had long campaigned for the use of the term 'indirect' because so many children serve non-combatant roles within militaries including domestic work, preparation of weapons, message carriers, and sexual roles. The compromise text enabled the Group to reach consensus and to send the Optional Protocol on to the General Assembly, where it was adopted on May 25, 2000.[27]

Conclusions

The compromises in the Optional Protocol represented a clear defeat for supporters of the 'straight-18' ban. The use of 'feasible measures' and 'direct participation' in hostilities were terms that the INGOs and ICRC had been trying to change since 1984 and negotiations for the CRC.[28] However, the inability of INGOs to fully sway the US government position within the political opportunity structure of UN negotiations should not cloud the diverse accomplishments of these organisations and their transnational campaign.

From 1979, INGOs played the primary role in the emergence of the issue of child soldiers on the international agenda. Having convinced the UN to consider the issue in its negotiations for the CRC, these entrepreneurial INGOs broadened their impact by becoming the primary collectors of data and issue experts. Using information politics and contributing data and recommendations to the UN negotiations, the INGOs were able to convince participating states to include humanitarian law in the human rights CRC and to directly address preventing and protecting child soldiers.

Beyond the CRC negotiations, INGOs continued to advocate and collaborate ultimately creating a transnational coalition by 1994 – with multiple UN and INGOs engaged in programmatic and research efforts on the issue. The campaign conducted by this coalition raised global awareness of the problem, facilitated accurate and broad data collection, and maintained pressure on the UN to enhance the standards set in the CRC.

Throughout the campaign, INGOs utilized strategies of collaboration to overcome disunity, reduce overlap, and to enhance their data collection and perceived legitimacy. This strategy culminated in 1998 with the formation of the CSUCS and its efforts to build national and regional support to leverage a conclusion to negotiations on the Optional Protocol. Although the Protocol outcome was not ideal from the CSUCS perspective, multiple regional agreements were achieved, data was globally collected and disseminated, and arguably a global norm against allowing persons under 18 to participate in warfare was established.

The case of the campaign against the use of child soldiers illustrates the central role of INGOs in issue emergence, leadership of transnational advocacy and coalitions, and in contributing to enhanced international standards and norm consolidation. While UN offices, some states and others played important roles, key INGOs clearly led and continue to lead this child rights movement. Further research into this pattern and its applicability to other cases such as girls' education, sexual exploitation of children and transnational adoption regulations is needed to comparatively evaluate INGOs role within child rights activism.

Notes

1 Coalition to Stop the Use of Child Soldiers, *CSUCS Annual Report* (CSUCS, 2001).
2 N.G. Boothby and C.M. Knudsen. 'Children of the Gun', *Scientific American*, 282/6 (June 2000). The rise of child soldiers resembles increasing child and civilian victims of war. From 1985 to 1995, wars killed at least 2 million children, left more than 4 million disabled, made 12 million homeless and orphaned more than a million. UNICEF *State of the World's Children* (Oxford University Press, 1996).
3 Rosenblatt, 1983. The papers from this seminar were compiled into an edited volume, *Children of War*, published by Doubleday in 1983. One chapter, by the editor, Rosenblatt, focuses on the use of children in wartime and addresses perceived benefits of children fighting, as well as long-term challenges faced by those children.
4 Boothby consulted for Save the Children and coordinated several rehabilitation and reunification projects in Mozambique for child soldiers.
5 Boothby and Knudsen, 'Children of the Gun'. In 1987, Uganda sought to conduct its own rehabilitation without INGO assistance by simply announcing that children who had fought for President Museveni's National Resistance Army would be demobilized and returned to school. While praised for ending use of child soldiers, this approach to rehabilitation was not widely supported.
6 Boothby and Knudsen, 'Children of the Gun'.
7 G. Van Bueren. *The International Law on the Rights of the Child* (Martinus Nijhoff Publishers, 1995), p. 8.
8 Van Bueren, *The International Law on the Rights of the Child*.
9 Van Bueren, *The International Law on the Rights of the Child*.
10 The NGO Committee on UNICEF was designed to 'encourage consultation and cooperation among NGOs at all levels and with UNICEF to promote the well-being of children everywhere'. NGO Committee History; Maggie Black, *Children First: The Story of UNICEF* (Oxford: Oxford University Press, 1996), p. 141.
11 Women's Commission for Refugees and Children History available online at <www.womenscommission.org> (Last accessed February 2004).
12 The Sub-Group appears have to have become much more active after the publication of the Machel Study and the establishment of a UN Special Representative on Children in Armed Conflict in 1996.
13 NGO Group for the Convention Brochure Background and Structure. Available from DCI, at <www.defence-for-children.org> (Last accessed on 8 October 2003).
14 Children of War, *Report from the Conference on Children of War*, Stockholm, Sweden, 31 May–2 June, 1991. Raoul Wallenberg Institute, Report No. 10 (Cohn and Goodwin-Gill, 1994).
15 The Council of Delegates is the executive body of the ICRC. Cohn and Goodwin-Gill credit two individuals, with the initiative of the study, Kristina Hedlund Thulin, Head of the Swedish Red Cross International Department and Jakobina Thordardottir, Head of the International Department at the Icelandic Red Cross (Cohn and Goodwin-Gill, 1994), Preface 1.
16 Council of Delegates Resolution 14, as referenced in Cohn and Goodwin-Gill, pp. 58-59.
17 Cohn and Goodwin-Gill, p. 5.
18 Rachel Brett and Margaret McCallin, *Children: The Invisible Soldiers First Edition* (Radda Barnen, 1996). In 1998, this project was renamed the Radda Barnen Global Information Centre on Child Soldiers.
19 Brett and McCallin, *Children: The Invisible Soldiers First Edition*; Brett and McCallin, *Children: The Invisible Soldiers First Edition*.

20 See Don Hubert, 'Occasional Paper #42 The Landmine Ban: A Case Study in Humanitarian Advocacy' (The Thomas J. Watson Jr. Institute, Brown University, 2000).

21 'CSUCS Global Report 2001: About the Coalition'; Brett and McCallin, *Children: The Invisible Soldiers First Edition.*

22 'CSUCS Global Report 2001: About the Coalition', p. 1.

23 The European Parliament also called on the European Council to 'agree to a Joint Action in order to promote the adoption of the Optional Protocol and to make the fight against the use of child soldiers part of the Union's policy'.

24 Working Group on Involvement of Children in Armed Conflict, Report on its Sixth Session, UN Doc E/CN./1996/102.

25 Michael Dennis, 'Newly Adopted Protocols to the Convention on the Rights of the Child', *The American Journal of International Law*, 94/4 (Oct. 2000): 789-796; Brett and McCallin, *Children: The Invisible Soldiers First Edition.*

26 Feasible is understood as 'practicable or practically possible taking into account all circumstances ruling at the time, including humanitarian and military considerations'. Dennis, 'Newly Adopted Protocols to the Convention on the Rights of the Child'.

27 A/RES/54/263.

28 Report of the Working Group on a Draft Convention on the Rights of the Child, UN Doc. E/CN.4/1988/28 and UN Doc E/CN.4/1989/48. The ICRC had actually been trying to change them since the early 1970s and negotiations for the Geneva Protocols, where again the US had opposed them.

Chapter 19

NGOs and Depleted Uranium: Establishing a Credible and Legitimate Counter Narrative

Chenaz B. Seelarbokus

Introduction

The use of depleted uranium (DU) by the US and NATO in the Gulf War and in the Balkans has prompted numerous controversies regarding the potential health and environmental hazards associated with exposure to DU weaponry.[1] There have been debatable reports linking the use of DU weapons to the 'Gulf War Syndrome' and the 'Balkan Syndrome', typically characterized by chronic fatigue, muscle and joint pain, headache, memory loss, depression, sleep disturbance, rash, mental disorders, respiratory problems, infectious diseases, and gastrointestinal problems, *inter alia*.[2]

The prevalence of these 'unexplained symptoms' and 'ill-defined conditions'[3] of the veterans has prompted a host of studies on the veterans' illnesses. Unfortunately, despite all the scientific studies and investigations, the public debate on the DU issue remains highly contentious. There are three main contenders in the international discourse on DU: (i) the governments responsible for the use of DU weapons (mostly US and UK); (ii) the United Nations (UN); and (iii) NGOs (in cohort with independent scientists and activists).

While governmental bodies and various UN agencies (e.g. the World Health Organization (WHO) and the United Nations Environment Programme (UNEP)) maintain that there are no risks posed to the army or to the civilian population by the use of DU weapons,[4] major NGOs working on the DU issue are engaged in a discourse which is antithetic to that of governmental or UN agencies. NGOs are calling for a ban on the production and use of DU weapons and for state liability for the suffering of veterans and civilians. Will the NGOs succeed as narrators and framers of a new international discourse on the DU issue? It is this paper's argument that the success of NGOs in establishing their narrative on the international platform will depend on how well they manage to meet the following three main challenges: (i) the establishment of solid credibility through the dissemination of scientific evidence linking DU exposure to negative health and environmental impacts; (ii) the establishment of legitimacy through the grounding of a DU ban within current international law; and (iii) the securing of new rule of law through the effective diffusion and successful catalysis of norm development and rule creation.

Major NGOs active in the DU area

The number of NGOs focusing on the DU issue has increased over the past few years. There are both domestic and international NGOs concerned with the DU problem. Due to the nature of the issue area, the anti-DU campaigns of domestic NGOs often project the activities of the NGOs in the international arena, thereby meshing domestic with global concerns. Some of the main organisations involved in the anti-DU campaign include, *inter alia,* the following: Military Toxics Project (MTP), Maine, U;[5] Campaign Against Depleted Uranium (CADU), Manchester, UK,[6] and its Arabic counterpart, the Arabic Campaign Against Depleted Uranium;[7] International Action Center (IAC), New York, US;[8] the Laka Foundation, Documentation and Research Center on Nuclear Energy, Amsterdam, the Netherlands;[9] the National Gulf War Resource Center (NGWRC), Maryland, US;[10] Green Cross International (GCI), Geneva, Switzerland;[11] the International Depleted Uranium Study Team (IDUST), Colorado, US;[12] the International Coalition to Ban Uranium Weapons (ICBUW), Amsterdam, the Netherlands;[13] Medact, London, UK;[14] and the International Physicians for the Prevention of Nuclear War (IPPNW), Cambridge, Massachusetts.[15]

Most of the NGOs active on the DU issue have as objective the securing of an international ban on the production, testing and use of DU weapons (e.g. CADU, ICBUW, IDUST, and IPPNW). In attempting to successfully anchor their antithetic discourse on the international agenda, NGOs are faced with the three main challenges mentioned earlier – namely, gaining credibility, establishing the legitimacy of their stance, and successfully catalysing the process for new norms and rules regarding DU weapons. The next sections focus on the means and strategies being employed by NGOs in meeting those challenges to ultimately achieve their mission of instituting a ban on DU weapons.

Meeting the first challenge: Establishment of credibility

NGOs have been widely involved in compiling information on the problems associated with DU exposure, conducting independent research on their own, and collaborating with independent researchers, scientists and other NGOs to carry out investigations and provide a new interpretation of facts and events. This parallel research (as compared with government-commissioned studies or those of official bodies such as WHO or UNEP) elicits credibility due to the independent and comprehensive nature of the investigations; the professional credentials, methods and experience of the investigative teams; and the absence of economic, military and political interests which otherwise besiege governmental agencies or government-commissioned studies.

Typically, NGOs' narrative focuses on findings based on field surveys and case analyses of the target population, rather than simply relying on mere literature reviews of a selective number of peer-reviewed articles (as are the 1998 RAND study;[16] the 1999 Agency for Toxic Substances and Disease Registry (ATSDR) study on the 'Toxicological Profile for Uranium';[17] the 2000 studies conducted by the Institute of Medicine (IOM);[18] or the reports published by the UK Royal Society[19]). In one important aspect, therefore, NGOs' discourse tends to reflect reality better than governmental statements which mostly discard the real health problems being faced by veterans and civilians. For example, the MTP, in collaboration with Dr. Hari Sharma of the University of Waterloo, Canada, released in 1999 the results of their independent medical study of Gulf War veterans, which predicted an increase of 20,000-100,000 fatal cancers in Gulf War veterans and Iraqi citizens as a result of the use of DU weapons in the Gulf War.[20] The NGWRC, in collaboration with the MTP and the Swords to Plowshares, produced in March 1998 their investigative report *Depleted Uranium Exposures Case Narrative,* which documented that that as many as 400, 000 Persian Gulf War troops might have been exposed to hazardous particles of uranium from shells fired by American tanks and aircraft.[21] Other such investigative studies include the May 1999 Laka Foundation report (*Gulf War Veterans and DU*), based on the research conducted by Dr. Rosalie Bertell,[22] and the 1996 IAC *Depleted Uranium Education Project*, which produced the 1997 book '*Metal of Dishonor*'.[23] The Uranium Medical Research Center (UMRC) is also intricately involved in scientific research relating to DU exposure, utilising Mass Spectrometry equipment to distinguish between natural uranium and DU.[24]

NGOs are also intricately involved in questioning the accepted wisdom of official documents, refuting official evidence suggesting no DU exposure or no health effects of DU exposure, highlighting governmental cover-ups (e.g. about the exact number of veterans that had possibly been exposed to DU), and emphasising government failures in providing the appropriate warnings to troops or implementing precautionary measures such as instructing troops to wear protective gear. As stated by the NGWRC:

> Our investigations lead us to conclude the Department of Defense (DoD) has engaged in a deliberate attempt to avoid responsibility for consciously allowing the widespread exposure of hundreds of thousands of troops and civilians to more than 630,000 pounds of DU released by US tanks and aircraft during the Gulf War. The DoD's actions regarding DU exposures are characterized by a blatant disregard for existing laws and regulations, human rights, and common sense. The Pentagon's desire to ensure the expanded use of DU takes precedence over the need to protect troops and civilians from contamination. The DoD also fails their legal requirement to train soldiers about the hazards of DU and to provide medical care to veterans and civilians with health problems associated with DU.[25]

Similar misgivings about governmental negligence in informing combatants, support personnel and civilians (especially those of Kuwait, Saudi Arabia and Iraq) about DU hazards have been aired by other NGOs such as the Laka Foundation and CADU.[26] NGOs have also criticized the use of the ICRP (International

Commission on Radiological Protection) model for assessing internal exposure to DU particles, arguing that the model does not fit the case of internal exposures to high ionisation densities in local tissues as it is mostly applicable to external doses of radiation.[27] These criticisms prompted the UK government to set up a new committee (Committee Examining Radiation Risks from Internal Emitters (CERRIE)) in 2001 to determine the failures of the ICRP model as applied to internal radiation exposure.[28]

NGOs have also been instrumental in undermining the credibility of official governmental or UN reports by pointing out important methodological limitations and highlighting relevant studies which have been overlooked. For example, WHO's studies in the Balkans have been criticized due to the fact that WHO analyzed DU only 'as a heavy metal pollutant' rather than focusing also on its radiological hazards. UNEP's reliance on Geiger counters to conduct measurements in the Balkans have also been deemed inappropriate, for Geiger counters are deemed to be 'incapable of detecting the particular alpha radiation'[29] CADU has criticized the Royal Society reports, considering that their conclusions were based on incomplete data, thereby leaving them 'wide-open to misinterpretation' and amenable to exploitation by the government.[30]

Meeting the second challenge: Establishment of legitimacy

One of the major factors clouding the DU issue relates to the fact that DU weapons *per se* are not regulated by current international humanitarian law. The governmental narrative has self-servingly used this legal hiatus to emphasize the 'legality' of DU weapons and to shun any responsibilities under international law to clean up DU impacted sites. In December 2003, the UK Ministry of Defense stated:

> A nation which has fired DU in conflict is under no legal obligation per se to return to the region post-conflict to clear up any DU that remains. The civil administration for the area concerned assumes responsibility for clean-up. The legality of this issue has developed through custom: there are no special policies or conventions which address clearance of DU residue.[31]

UN agencies dealing with the DU issue have not pronounced on the legality or illegality of DU weapons, preferring to limit their statements to the potential health impacts or the precautionary measures to be adopted, *inter alia*.[32] However, there has been some ambivalence and controversies associated with the stance of the UN Sub-Commission on the Promotion and Protection of Human Rights (formerly the Sub-Commission on Prevention of Discrimination and Protection of Minorities). The Sub-Commission issued two resolutions in 1996 and 1997 (1996/16 and 1997/36), calling for limitations on the production and spread of DU weaponry (among several other weapons such as nuclear weapons, chemical weapons, fuel-air bombs, napalm, cluster bombs, and biological weaponry), considering that such weapons are 'incompatible with international human rights and/or humanitarian law' (Resolution 1997/36).[33] However, the activities of the

Sub-Commission have been particularly mired by controversial debates, polemics and delay tactics,[34] most specifically in regard to a working paper submitted by Justice Sik Yuen (Senior Puisne Judge of the Supreme Court of Mauritius, operating under Sub-Commission resolution 2001/36).[35] Much to the disapproval of the US and UK representatives, Justice Sik Yuen considered that, according to existing humanitarian and human rights law, DU weapons should be banned in view of their having indiscriminate effect and being of a nature to cause unnecessary suffering or superfluous injury.

If we now consider the NGO discourse, we find that NGOs squarely consider DU weapons to be illegal under current human rights and humanitarian law, thereby reflecting Justice Sik Yuen's standpoint on the matter. Whereas the governmental discourse tends to narrowly interpret current humanitarian and human rights law, NGOs, on the other hand, tend to adopt a more expansive interpretation thereof to claim that DU weapons are already outlawed by existing international law. NGOs substantiate and legitimize their claim about the illegality of DU weapons by quoting various provisions and principles of international humanitarian law.[36] NGOs commonly invoke various articles of the Protocol Additional to the Geneva Conventions of 12 August 1949 (Protocol 1) relating to: the protection of the civilian population and their safeguard from indiscriminate attacks (Articles 48 and 51.4); the prohibition of employing weapons which are of a nature to cause superfluous injury or unnecessary suffering (Article 35.2); and the prohibition of employing means of warfare which 'are intended, or may be expected, to cause widespread, long-term and severe damage to the natural environment' (Articles 35.3 and 55.1).

NGOs also often refer to the Martens Clause (embodied in the Preamble to the 1899 Hague Convention II),[37] which evokes the 'principles of international law, as they result from the usages established between civilized nations, from the laws of humanity and the requirements of the public conscience',[38] to safeguard the continual protection of civilians and belligerents.[39] Further, NGOs summon the Precautionary Principle[40] and the violation of human rights law (e.g. violation of the right to life[41] and the violation of women's rights due to the vulnerability of women's breast and uterine tissues to ionising radiation[42]) to attest for the inherent illegality of DU weaponry.

In more simplistic terms, NGOs legitimize their standpoint by using the following four criteria, based on current international humanitarian law,[43] to test for the legality of DU weapons: (i) the *territorial limitation*, whereby weapons must be limited in effect to the field of battle; (ii) the *temporal limitation*, which implies that weapons must be limited in effect to the time period of the armed conflict; (iii) the *environmental limitation*, which means that weapons must not unduly damage the environment; and (iv) the *humanity limitation*, which suggests that weapons must not be unduly inhumane.[44] Based on these four criteria, NGOs (e.g. CADU, IDUST and Traprock Peace Center) consider that DU weapons are 'inherently illegal'[45] as they fail 'all four tests'.[46]

According to the NGOs, DU weapons fail the territorial test since DU aerosol particles can travel long distances. CADU has documented that DU particles can travel at least 40 km, noting that Saudi Arabia, Greece and Bulgaria detected above normal radiation levels due to use of DU weapons in the Gulf War and in Kosovo.[47] DU weapons fail the temporal limitation since they have long-term impacts. DU particles can remain suspended in the air for years and soil particles can be resuspended by ground disturbance years after the impact time. Moreover, DU has been detected in the urine of US, UK and Canadian Gulf War veterans eight years after the end of war.[48] DU weapons fail the environmental limitation as DU can traverse through soils, water bodies, and the root systems of plants, as evidenced by DU weapons tests carried out by the US in the state of New Mexico from 1955-70,[49] and as per the recent May 2003 UNEP report which documented groundwater and air contamination by DU in Bosnia and Herzegovina more than seven years after the end of war.[50] Finally, DU weapons fail the humanity test since they can cause renal and neurological dysfunction, as well as genetic damage through the destruction of DNA and RNA in cells. Genetic malformations and health problems can continue for the whole life-span of the victims,[51] and chromosomal aberrations in the human genes can cause cancers and genetic illnesses to be passed to the next generation.[52]

Catalysing norm convergence and new rule of law

One of the crucial steps in engendering new norms in the international arena relates to effective information dissemination and public sensitisation to generate mass public support for the new norms and thereby facilitate norm convergence and rule creation. NGOs (e.g. IDUST, UMRC, NGWRC and CADU) have grown savvy in using the internet interface to publish their investigative reports, to provide an independent space and a forum for the posting of relevant scientific literature dealing with the environmental and health hazards of DU weapons, and to publicize papers, books and reports prepared by independent activists and researchers.

The creation of new rules and laws in the international arena often occurs within the purview of international seminars and conferences. NGOs have been successful in organising and participating in various international conferences and workshops, the main ones being the International Conference Against Depleted Uranium, Manchester, November 2000 and the International Weapons Conference, Hamburg, Germany, October 16-19 2003. NGOs have also been successful in mobilising the mass, as evidenced by the wide participation in the International Day of Action Against DU and the successful formation of international coalitions against DU weapons, such as the ICBUW and IDUST.

Conclusion

An evaluation of NGOs' narrative on the DU issue shows that NGOs are playing prominent and crucial leadership roles in promoting new rule of law regarding the use of DU weaponry. In the midst of controversies surrounding the DU issue, NGOs are acting as an independent 'antidote'[53] of information, and are providing a new framing of the issue area by being a credible 'deconstructor' and positive critic of the governmental (or UN) narrative. Without the NGOs acting as watchdogs and as value guardians, the governmental bodies will probably not have divulged information on either the locations where DU weapons were used, or on the risks to human health and the environment. NGOs therefore effectively act as a 'positive challenge to statism'[54] and as a main impetus of change, compelling governments to be accountable not only to domestic constituencies but also to those outside their territorial and jurisdictional borders.

The credibility of the NGO discourse is guaranteed by the quality of the investigations conducted and the co-optation of highly credentialed individuals to support the NGOs' cause. Using the electronic interface to establish inter-NGO networking, NGOs are demonstrating a 'unified front perspective' and a unity of discourse which is lacking on the governmental side, typically characterized by confusing reports and a focus on uncertainties. Moreover, NGOs typically do not suffer from the self-interested motivations which often assail governmental agencies. Concerns about mission drift, legitimacy, credibility and accountability ensure that NGOs generally exercise a high level of professionalism and care in the formulation of their standpoints. NGOs are also demonstrating potential for being a great advocate for the anti-DU campaign by focusing on the most important stakeholder: the victims of DU exposure. NGOs seem to be the main, if not the only, entity taking up the cases of the civilian populations potentially affected by DU weaponry, especially vulnerable groups such as old people, children and women.

The legitimacy of the NGOs' standpoint is validated by the latter's understanding and interpretation of international humanitarian and human rights law. NGOs focus on the protection of innocent civilians, condemning DU weapons for their capacity to cause unnecessary suffering and superfluous injury, and for their long-term impacts on the environment. The legitimacy of the NGO discourse is further strengthened by existing stipulations of international law dealing with the right to life and health (e.g. Articles 3 and 25 of the Universal Declaration of Human Rights (UDHR)). The emphasis placed on information and dissemination of case narratives by the NGOs also respects current international law dealing with the right to education (e.g. Article 26, UDHR) which, according to Gostin and Lazzarani,[55] includes 'information and counseling on health risk, disease prevention, and practical forms of self-protection'. Finally, the NGO narrative is in accord with current International Environmental Law which establishes basic principles such as liability in case of environmental contamination, the concept of inter-generational equity, the principle of sustainable development, and the Precautionary Principle, among others.

There have been many recent developments in the international arena or within the domestic legal context which can strengthen the cause of the NGOs. In February 2004, for example, a Pension Appeal Tribunal Service in Edinburgh awarded the first ever pension appeal to a Scots ex-soldier, Kenny Duncan, for being diagnosed with DU poisoning during the 1991 Gulf War while moving tanks destroyed by shells containing DU dust.[56] This may set a precedent for numerous other cases, both in the US and in UK. Moreover, in the US, the fate of two bills on

DU weapons (*DU Munitions Study Act of 2003 and DU Munitions Suspension and Study Act of 2001*) needs to be watched, in view of their possible future implications for the direction and pace of the evolution of domestic and international norms on DU weapons.[57]

In view of these developments and the success of NGOs in establishing a credible and legitimate narrative on the DU issue, it is not implausible for negotiations on the institutionalisation of a ban on DU weapons to proceed successfully in the near future. However, even if a ban on the use of DU weapons is achieved internationally, there are several issues that will remain problematic. If DU weapons are indeed deemed illegal, who will be responsible for the decontamination of impacted areas? Who will be responsible for health care costs of the victims and for allocating compensatory damages? Also, even if we pay the immediate victims of the recent bombardments, what about future generations who may be victims of altered DNA? What about future environmental contamination wrought about by the recent attacks? Though there have been precedents of compensation mechanisms such as the 1991 UN Compensation Commission set up to establish Iraq's liability for environmental damage and other loss caused by its illegal invasion and occupation of Kuwait, similar mechanisms may be a long way to come for the case of DU weapons. Major constraints will be due to the great economic, political and military strength of US or UK, the ambivalence regarding the 'legality' of the US invasion of Iraq or of the Balkan operations, and the complexities associated with the processing of cases brought by individual veterans and members of the civilian population.

Notes

1 For information on the quantity of DU munitions used in the Gulf or Balkan wars, see Fetter Steve and Frank von Hippel (1999. 'After the dust settles' *The Bulletin of the Atomic Scientists* 55, no 6, 42-5; Fahey, Dan. May 1999. 'Depleted Uranium Weapons. Lessons from the 1991 Gulf War'. In *DU: A Post-War Disaster for Environment and Health. Part 7.* Laka Foundation. <http://www.antenna.nl/wise/uranium/dhap992.html>; UNEP. 2003. *Desk Study on the Environment in Iraq.* Switzerland: UNEP. p. 68; CADU, 'Current Issues', <http://members.gn.apc.org/~cadu/current-issues.htm>; BBC News, 9 January 2001. *The Military Uses of DU.* <http://news.bbc.co.uk>.

2 *Gulf War and Health: Depleted Uranium, Pyridostigmine Bromide, Sarin, Vaccines,* Vol. 1, Carolyn E. Fulco, Catharyn T. Liverman and Harold C. Sox (eds) (Institute of Medicine, Washington, D.C.: National Academy Press, 2000), pp. 32, 42; General Accounting Office (GAO), 'Gulf War Illnesses: Procedural and Reporting Improvements Are Needed in DOD's Investigative Processes', GAO/NSIAD-99-59, February 1999, pp. 2, 12.

3 Fulco *et. al.* (2000), op. cit. pp. 39, 41.

4 For example, see Ministry of Defense. *Depleted Uranium: The Misconceptions* <http://www.mod.uk/issues/depleted_uranium/misconceptions.htm>; WHO. January 2001. Kosovo Mission report. op. cit. p. 25. <www.who.int/ionizing_radiation/env/du/en>.

5 The MTP runs an international campaign to ban DU weaponry since 1992. <http://www.miltoxproj.org>.

6 CADU was launched in 1999 pursuant to reports about birth defects and raised incidence of cancer in the population of southern Iraq and among the Gulf War veterans, and also

due to an increase in childhood leukemia near the British test site in the south west Scotland. <http://cadu.org.uk>.
7 The Arabic Campaign Against Depleted Uranium, <http://www.cadu.org.uk/news/14.htm>.
8 The International Action Center (IAC). <http://www.iacenter.org>.
9 The Laka Foundation, Documentation and Research Center on Nuclear Energy, <http://www.laka.org>.
10 The National Gulf War Resource Center (NGWRC), <http://www.ngwrc.org>.
11 Green Cross International, <http://www.greencrossinternational.net>.
12 IDUST is a group of international researchers, activists and scientists with a global strategy to stop the use of DU in military weapons by the year 2010. <http://www.nevadadesertexperience.org/poisonfireDU.html>.
13 The ICBUW was launched in October 2003 to achieve a ban on the military use of uranium and other radioactive materials in weaponry. <http://www.bandepleteduranium.org>.
14 Medact is a nonprofit organisation of doctors, nurses and other health professionals who are concerned about major threats to health such as violent conflict, poverty and environmental degradation. <www.medact.org>.
15 International Physicians for the Prevention of Nuclear War, <http://www.ippnw.org>.
16 Harley, Naomi H., Foulkes, Ernest C., Hudson, Arlene and Anthony C. Ross. 1998. *A Review of the Scientific Literature As It Pertains to Gulf War Illnesses. Depleted Uranium. Volume 7.* Washington, D.C.: RAND.
17 ATSDR. September 1999. *Toxicological Profile for Uranium.* <http://www.atsdr.cdc.gov/toxprofiles/phs150.html>.
18 Fulco *et al.* 2000. op. cit.
19 The Royal Society. 22 May, 2001. *The Health Hazards of Depleted Uranium Munitions. Part I.* Available through DOD's web page at <http://www.deploymentlink.osd.mil/du_library/health.shtml>.
20 Press Release. May 4, 1999. *Military Toxics Project Confirms NATO is Using DU Munitions in Yugoslavia and Releases Results of Medical Study Indicating Potential for Fatal Cancers.* <http://www.fas.org/man/dod-101/ops/docs99/990504-kosovo-du.htm>.
21 San Jose Mercury News, 1998; Also, NGWRC. 28 September 1998. *Depleted Uranium Case Narrative Released.* <http://www.ngwrc.org/news/default.asp>.
22 Bertell, Rosalie. May 1999. 'Gulf War Veterans and Depleted Uranium'. In Laka Foundation. *Depleted Uranium: A Post-War Disaster. Part 3.* <http://www.ratical.com/radiation/dhap/dhap993.html>.
23 Caldicott *et al.*, March 1997. *Metal of Dishonor: How the Pentagon Radiates Soldiers and Civilians with DU Weapons.* New York: IAC Depleted Uranium Education Project.
24 UMRC is registered as an NGO in US and Canada and is an international association of scientists and medical doctors. Since 1997, UMRC has been conducting independent scientific research on internal contamination of radioactive isotopes, including DU. <http://www.umrc.net>.
25 NGWRC Annual Report. 1999. Page 6. <http://www.ngwrc.org>.
26 Laka Foundation. May 1999. *Depleted Uranium: A Post-War Disaster for Environment and Health.Part 2.* <http://www.antenna.nl/wise/uranium>; CADU News Issue 6, <http://members.gn.apc.org/~cadu/news/news06/>.
27 Conference Resolutions. World Uranium Conference. *DU/Uranium Weapons: The Trojan Horses of Nuclear War.* Hamburg. October 16-19 2003. <www.uranwaffenkonferenz.de/media.htm>; <www.uraniumweaponsconference.de>.
28 Chris Busby, 'Health Risks following Exposure to Aerosols produced by the use of Depleted Uranium Weapons', Paper presented to the *Res Publica* conference on DU, Prague, Czech Republic, 24-25 November 2001, <http://www.llrc.org/du/duframes.htm>.

29 Carlo Pona, 'The Criminal Use of DU', Paper presented at the International Tribunal for US/NATO war crimes in Yugoslavia, International Action Center, 10 June 2000. <http://www.iacenter.org/warcrime/cpona.htm>.

30 CADU. *The Royal Society Debacle.* <http://www.cadu.org.uk/news/14.htm>.

31 UK Ministry of Defense. 5 December 2003. *Depleted Uranium. Middle East 2003.* <http://www.mod.uk/issues/depleted_uranium/middle_east_2003.htm>.

32 See, for example, WHO. January 2003. *Fact Sheet on Depleted Uranium.* N°257. <http://www.who.int/mediacentre/factsheets/fs257/en/>.

33 UN Sub-Commission on Prevention of Discrimination and Protection of Minorities Resolution 1996/16, August 29, 1996, E/CN.4/SUB.2/RES/1996/16; UN Sub-Commission on Prevention of Discrimination and Protection of Minorities Resolution 1997/36, August 28, 1997, E/CN.4/SUB.2/RES/1997/36; Also see Sub-Commission on Prevention of Discrimination and Protection of Minorities concludes forty-eighth session – Press release HR/CN/755, September 4, 1996. <http://www.unhchr.ch>.

34 See, for example, Lopez, Damacio A. *The Case for an Immediate Ban on the Military Use of Depleted Uranium.* Presented at a meeting of the European Parliament in Brussels, Belgium, on June 10, 2003. <www.idust.net>; The Geneva Report on Depleted Uranium, especially the Press Release and intervention by Sub-Commission member Justice Francoise Jane Hampson during the 55th Session of the Sub-Commission on The Promotion and Protection of Human Rights held in Geneva, Switzerland, on August 4, 2003. Available at <http://www.bandepleteduranium.org>; International Service for Human Rights. *Analytical Report of the 54th session, Geneva 29 July–16 August 2002. 'Other Matters Considered'*, and *Analytical Report of the 55th session, Geneva, 28 July–15 August 2003. 'Other Matters Considered'.* Reports available at <http://www.ishr.ch/>; Parker, Karen. *The Illegality of DU weaponry.* Paper prepared for the International Uranium Weapons Conference, Hamburg, Germany, 16-19 October 2003. Traprock Peace Center, http://www.traprockpeace.org/; Parker, Karen. February 2000. *Depleted Uranium at the United Nations: A Compilation of Documents and an Explanation and Strategy Analysis.* CADU and International Educational Development/Humanitarian Law Project (IED/HLP). <http://www.nucnews.net/2000/du/00du/0002duun.htm>.

35 Sub-Commission on the Promotion and Protection of Human Rights. 54th session. Geneva. 26 Jyly-16 August 2002 (E/CN.4/Sub.2/2002/38); 55th session. 28 July–15 August 2003 (E/CN.4/Sub.2/2003/35). 'Other Matters Considered'. <http://www.ishr.ch>; Yeung Sik Yuen, Y.K.J. *Human rights and weapons of mass destruction, or with indiscriminate effect, or of a nature to cause superfluous injury or unnecessary suffering.* Working paper submitted in accordance with Sub-Commission on the Promotion and Protection of Human Rights resolution 2001/36. Fifty-fourth session. Item 6 of the provisional agenda E/CN.4/Sub.2/2002/38.

36 Ramsey Clark, 'An International Appeal to Ban the Use of Depleted Uranium Weapons', International Action Center. <http://www.iacenter.org/depleted/appeal.htm>.

37 Full title: Convention With Respect to the Laws and Customs of War on Land. Hague. 29 July 1899.

38 1899 Hague Convention. Preamble.

39 Karen Parker. October 2003. op. cit. p. 6.

40 Dan Fahey, 'Policy Paper On The Use of Depleted Uranium in Ammunition', Military Toxics Project: Washington, D.C. December 15, 1999. <http://www.miltoxproj.org/DU/Policy.htm>; IPPNW. 19 February 2001. *Depleted Uranium Weapons and Acute Post-War Health Effects: An IPPNW Assessment.* <http://www.ippnw.org/DUStatement.html>.

41 Ramsey Clark. op. cit.

42 Catherine Euler and Karen Parker, 'Depleted Uranium Munitions: The Use of Radiological Weapons as a Violation of Human Rights', Joint intervention by the International Peace

Bureau, International Educational Development and Campaign Against Depleted Uranium, Sub-Commission on the Promotion and Protection of Human Rights, Fifty-first Session, August 1999, <http://www.webcom.com/hrin/parker/depleteduranium.html>.

43 Karen Parker. 2003. *The Illegality of DU Weaponry.* op. cit. p. 8.

44 IDUST. <http://www.idust.net/index.htm#HISTORY>.

45 Ibid.

46 Leuren Moret, 'US Nuclear Policy and Depleted Uranium Testimony', Public Hearing for the International Criminal Tribunal for War Crimes in Afghanistan, held at Chiba, Japan, ICTA/E-068, 28 June 2003; also Karen Parker, *The Illegality of DU Weaponry* (2003). Op. cit.

47 Euler and Parker. August 1999. op. cit.

48 Ibid.

49 Ibid.

50 UNEP. May 2003. *Depleted Uranium in Bosnia and Herzegovina: Post-Conflict Environmental Assessment.* Switzerland: UNEP. <http://postconflict.unep.ch> p. 10. UNEP Press Release. 25 March 2003. *Low-level DU contamination found in Bosnia and Herzegovina, UNEP calls for precaution.* <http://postconflict.unep.ch/pressbihdu25mar2003.htm>.

51 Euler and Parker. August 1999. op.cit.

52 Schröder, H., A. Heimers, R. Frentzel-Beyme, A. Schott and W. Hoffmann. 2003. 'Chromosome Aberration Analysis In Peripheral Lymphocytes Of Gulf War And Balkans War Veterans'. *Radiation Protection Dosimetry* 103(3). pp. 211-220. <http://www.antenna.nl/wise/uranium/diss.html#CHROMSCHOTT>.

53 Thomas, Jabine B. and Richard P. Claude (eds) 1992. *Human Rights and Statistics: Getting the Record Straight.* Philadelphia: University of Pennsylvania Press. p. 15.

54 Wapner, Paul. 1996. *Environmental Activism and World Civic Politics.* Albany, NY: SUNY Press. Page 120.

55 Gostin, Lawrence and Lazzarani, Zita. 1997. *Human Rights and Public Health in the AIDS Pandemic.* Oxford: Oxford University Press. p. 30.

56 Martin Williams. February 4, 2004. 'First Award for DU poisoning claim'. *The Herald. Web Issue* 1943. <http://www.theherald.co.uk/news/9272.html>.

57 For more information, see HR 1483, '*Depleted Uranium Munitions Study Act of 2003*', at the Traprock Peace center page <http://traprockpeace.org/DUBill24March03.html>; or at <http://thomas.loc.gov>. An earlier bill introduced in October 2001 by McKinney (Armed Services Bill IX H.R. 3155) '*DU Munitions Suspension and Study Act of 2001*', called for the suspension of the use, sale, development, production, testing and export of DU munitions pending the outcome of studies of the health effects of such munitions.

Chapter 20

Postconflict Election Observers

Henry F. Carey

By 2005, 140 of the world's 192 countries now hold at least nominally credible, multiparty-elections. If one assumes that democracy is only about a century old (unless one assumes that the franchise is limited by gender and wealth in England and the US, as well as by race in the US), then there is very limited historical experience to compare past experiences. Furthermore, only in the Third Wave was the franchise universal from the start. According to the 2002 UNDP *Human Development Report*, using rather lenient criteria for democracy, only 82 countries, or 57 per cent of the world's people, enjoy full democracy with free civil institutions and human rights. Eighty-one countries began democracy toward the end of the 20th century, 47 of which have become fully functioning democracies. Some such as Pakistan have returned to authoritarian rule, including 13 sub-Saharan states. Yet, even the UN, which in previous decades eschewed embraces of what was regarded as any ideology, has embraced democracy as the system that best frees individuals' and groups' need for free civil and economic rights and potential.[1]

Various NGOs actively supported their right to monitor any election. NGOs are often attracted to particular elections, such as in Ukraine 2004, but not in equally fraudulent Romania 2004,[2] by regime changing possibilities from monitoring, so that some elections of less importance to US interests still brought them in small, but greater numbers than ever before (e.g. the International Human Rights Law Group in Paraguay 1989, Korea 1988, and NDI and IRRI in both important and less important elections of interest to the US). What was truly important about the legally sanctioned monitoring of the right to elections was not the mere presence, but the resources provided, to assure not only election-day coverage, but increasingly election campaign monitoring, when the fairness of close elections could be checked and altered before it was too late.

Budgets for electoral administration and monitoring are expensive. To have printed ballots, computerized voter registration and balloting results cost about $2-5 million per million voters. Often, the cost is greater. In both 1990 and 1996 in Nicaragua, the US spent large sums, $9 million and $6 million respectively, for electorates of about 1.5 and 2 million voters respectively. An additional $8 million was requested in April 1996 to finance security expenditures in the north of Nicaragua, where fighting had already killed about 50 earlier in the year. For less than a few million voters more, the cost was more than $2 billion in 1993 to pay for a transitional government and resettling exiled refugees and attempting to demobilize armed insurgencies before elections in Cambodia. For the September 14, 1996 elections in Bosnia, foreign aid donors were planning to spend $155 million before the local elections were postponed two weeks before. In Western Sahara, for elections that never occurred, over $100 million was planned for elections of several hundred thousand voters.

Election observers can operate superficially with potentially devastating consequences. More than journalists who 'parachute' into a crisis without extensive knowledge, observers are effective participants in the elections. To exhort them to perform even better, I will expand upon the authors' lessons on observer effectiveness. In many cases, some observer missions have bias (eg-El Salvador 1982, Nicaragua 1984), insufficient resources (Pakistan 1988 and 1990, South Korea 1987, Paraguay 1989, Philippines 1987), or laziness (Dominican Republic 1990). Host governments may not permit access to the whole election process (Philippines 1986, Albania 1990).

Critics attack US-sponsored and observed elections, such as the constituent assembly vote in El Salvador in 1982. Observers overlooked that the 1982 constituent assembly election was a *de facto* exclusion of the left and constrained freedom of expression and assembly. They correctly note that the observers 'were in no position to see anything'. Yet, even more objective multilateral observations prior to the 1989 UN missions in Namibia and Nicaragua may miss crucial facts. Hundreds of on-site, UN campaign-process observers did not call public notice to the $36 million that SWAPO's opposition in Namibia received covertly from South Africa, or the approximate $750,000 given by the CIA to Contra leaders like Alfredo César to return to Nicaragua in order to campaign for the UNO in 1989.[3] The UN and OAS observers in Nicaragua also did not monitor the second round of regional counting, in the days after the Feb. 25, 1990 election. Some UNO leaders alleged that nullification of ballots cheated the UNO of four or five Deputies.[4] Thus, even under the best of circumstances, observers cannot see everything relevant. That may just be a fact of life, such as the dead Chicago voters that Richard Nixon may have had to live with in his narrow 1960 defeat.

The unseen or unseeable can become determinative if observers fail to monitor registration and tabulation of voters. Most of the observers at the first Sandinista-managed election in 1984, for example, did not question the absence of electoral control in the form of effective opposition parties or independent parallel vote count. The election was boycotted by probably the most important segment of the opposition. Few of the observers regarded it as significant at the time because it had the support of the US. Nor did most of the hundreds of foreign observers then question the validity of the registration and vote results, even though there was no independent electoral control. The vast majority praised the Sandinistas on the election. In fairness, the performance of the host government and the observers was not unlike many elections of that period. Some countries like Mexico, whom the Sandinistas emulated, still have not permitted serious observation. Until they do, the results of elections Mexican-style cannot be taken seriously, even if they may have some other liberalisation impacts.

Process observers today, if they even check for accurate registration, will have a difficult time persuading the local authorities to correct the problem. Quite often, observers need to decide when the election should be challenged for insufficient reliability in the registration rolls. The OAS in El Salvador in March 1991 estimated that 15 per cent of the citizens who applied for registration were not certified to vote for those legislative and local elections and another 10 per cent had registration cards, but were not found on the voters' lists.[5] After repeated meetings with the Central Electoral Council (CCE) Chairman Jaime Romero Ventura, and one public report, the OAS was unable to make much headway. 'Romero just did not understand what was the role of the OAS in the elections', complained OAS mission director Mario Gonzales Vargas, 'whereas his PDC colleague Ricardo Perdomo did try to make some changes, but he could not get his way'.[6] Just to determine the scope of the problem, observers need either a reliable, stratified sample as used by Nicaragua's UNO opposition in 1990 or else voter interviews like those commissioned by the Carter group in Guyana in 1991.

Romero maintains that only 60,000 Salvadorans (0.5 per cent) were denied the ability to vote for any reason, and 10,000 were able to vote on election day with merely their registration application in hand. Just 24 hours before the election day, the National Assembly legislated to allow any citizen who could produce his application to register would be allowed to vote. Romero attributed any disenfranchisement to the stringent requirements for verifying the voter's identity, precisely to avoid problems like the electoral fraud of 1972. Romero's colleague, Ricardo Perdomo, took a middle position, assigning responsibility for the disenfranchisement to both the rigorous requirements and problems within the electoral commission.

These disagreements over such an important manner, where as many as a quarter of Salvadorans may have been disenfranchised after a decade of preparing for elections, mean is that the multilateral observers were not able to resolve the issue in time and have refrained from providing an extensive public analysis of the problem. In this case, both the OAS and Romero are quite unhappy with each other's lack of understanding for each other's position. The OAS sometimes appears incompetent, but seems unwilling to take decisive action, perhaps for fear of alienating one of its member governments. Curiously, the OAS did not issue final reports for either its 1991 El Salvador or Haiti missions, suggesting either laxity or an unwillingness to criticize Member States.

NGO election observers should bargain with host rulers for an improved electoral environment. Most observer groups lack the stature of a Jimmy Carter, who negotiated with Nicaragua's Daniel Ortega, Haiti's Eartha Pascal Trouillot, and Zambia's Kenneth Kaunda, among other heads of state. It is not clear that others can and should attempt this role, which usually exceeds the explicit terms of their invitations. Reliable parallel vote counts, which they also advise, are very difficult to implement, and may report a biased result, even inadvertently. Short of a major change in state practices, most countries will not permit large UN teams to monitor their entire electoral processes.[7] Low-profile NGO missions, the more common observation vehicle, will have difficulty inducing sober fair play by those accustomed to the traditional excesses of partisan emotion and dishonesty.

Even the UN, which defers to the sovereignty of its Member States, insists only on 'verifying' prior agreements, despite its significant bargaining power.

Former Secretary-General Javier Pérez de Cuéllar brilliantly refused to let the UN participate in Haiti until and unless then-dictator Prosper Avril agreed to accept foreign military observers to work with the Haitian army. One of the reasons he fled Haiti in March 1990 was his unwillingness to agree publicly, despite earlier private comments of this commitment. His successor, Trouillot, was quite willing to let the security advisers in, who were essential to persuading the army to do its job in permitting the elections to occur.

Restricting Judgments

When judgments are necessary, observer groups should be more candid about their own doubts or disagreements. Observers are human beings that can be affected by cognitive or motivational misperception, as well as by the presence or absence of rallying during campaigns and protestors of fraud in the capital afterwards, factors that at best must be analyzed in context and are quite often not indicative of the most obvious interpretation. When judgments are necessary, observer groups should be more candid about internal disagreements. Where one individual decides on electoral fairness, as is apparently the case with the OAS Secretary General, decisions are too dictatorial. Delegations that operate on a consensus principle should attempt to avoid 'groupthink' pressures for conformity that would overlook uncertainty within delegations. Where significant, dissent or minority views should be acknowledged and published. Finally, delegations should participate in the writing or editing of final reports so that final judgments reflect the views of delegations and not the staff of an organisation.

Observers should limit their comments to what they saw themselves, or what *reliable* sources, of which there are always very few, have reported. As the second and third rounds of elections occur, the results will be closer and subtle fraud more adept. Observation will begin a new, less dramatic phase that will have great impact on the durability of democracy in countries without much experience at fair play. While observers may wish to offer an honest, balanced judgment on both the process and the results, international pressures for legitimacy will make difficult the choice of declaring a fair or unfair election.

Qualified judgments do not fill the need of those governments which directly or indirectly fund significant observer missions for a legitimated government with which to do business after the election. If observers find some major fault with an election, even unintentional or unavoidable, US and other official foreign donors, the IMF, the World Bank and defense departments will not be able to maintain overt relations unless current policy favoring democracies change. Yet, if observers are to be accurate, they must report what they see. It is often not a pleasant task.

The financing of observation teams is rarely consistent in terms of amount, type and direction of expenditures provided in different elections. Financing has less to do with the amount needed and more with the interests of the financing sources, which are usually governments with particular interests in the countries concerned. Sometimes, such as in Haiti, aid donors simply wanted to launch democracy, no matter what the quality of its elections. So, it was not surprising that most official reports omitted the facts that about 20 per cent of the ballots were lost randomly and that the votes for president were never counted, but estimated from a UN-OAS quick-count of less than 2 per cent of the precincts. Where there has been protracted war such as in Cambodia, there may be reluctance to notice unfairness so that the process succeeds. What is good for peace may conflict with electoral standards. Where US foreign policy concerns warrant, some who are normally neutral election observers have been sent to assist the opposition. Perhaps such assistance is justified if restricted to training poll watchers, such as in Nicaragua, but in Chile in 1988, US funds were provided for the opposition's media and polling expenses. In other first elections like in Zambia, Albania, Poland, Romania, and Pakistan, the US provided no aid to equally weak oppositions in countries where the dictator posed less of a threat to US interests.

Conclusion

Observers have helped to make free elections possible where they are invited and are permitted to promote competitive contests. There are aspects to foreign observation, unrelated to traditional concerns for national sovereignty, which makes their participation problematic. First, the standards are unclear on two levels of fairness: technical honesty and structural fairness, both of which are ambiguous in definition and not reflected in domestic law. The latter is the more debatable issue, with room for local standards. Concerns for the prerogatives resulting from the arrogance of power, *prepotencia* and *desgaste del poder*, as is oft stated in Latin America, are difficult to operationalize, but observer groups should systemize their criteria on key issues on registration, voting and counting, intimidation of opposition poll watchers, misuse of government resources and unequal access to media.

Secondly, observers have made incorrect judgments on the credibility of the results and the entire electoral process. False positives and false negatives are all too common in close elections and all constituency-based legislative and parliamentary elections. Observers have been insufficiently critical of 'traditional elections' with subtle intimidation and patronage typical of the semi-democracies in Asia than they have in Central America, where credible elections almost never have occurred.

Third, it is not clear how much range observers have or should have in a given electoral assignment. Beyond the issues of judgment, should they also reveal every irregularity observed, and if so under whose criteria? Or, should they seek to bolster young democracies' confidence by withholding criticism in the interests of discretion? Is the ambit of observer activity determined by custom, invitation, or by the observers themselves, some of whom attempt to bargain changes in the ground rules of an election? Should such matters be determined in advance under the terms of reference agreed upon between the host and the observers, with the latter refraining when not offered sufficient free reign? Even in cases where expansive activity is authorized in advance, such as when the United Nations manages a government, disarms guerrillas, and supervises every aspect of an election, as partly true in Namibia in 1988–89 and Cambodia 1992–93, the observers' self-restraint is sometimes the only significant check on the scope of their activities. There is a danger that observers undertake the scope of activities according to the priorities and interests of the funding government.

Caution in the use of election observers is needed. Observers operate under their own constraints such as limited budgetary resources, implied loyalty to those who fund their missions, and their own decision-making shortcomings. Their goals vary among observing, changing and judging the fairness of the overall electoral process and the accuracy of the results. Observer missions lack the resources to fully succeed, even massive, multilateral ones. Foreign observers, even honest ones, operate in a domestic and foreign political context that cannot be improved overnight, even with foreign security advisers working with a cooperative military.

Observers have improved immensely over the past decade, but even more formidable challenges lie ahead. Even if successful, they must also train local organisations so that they do not displace their functions. Cooperating with other foreign missions can enhance the possibility of effective process observation. Each electoral mission poses unique challenges, depending on the likely irregularities and the resources available to detect them. To the extent that observers can avoid the superficiality and partisanship that characterized perhaps a majority of observations before the 1990s, the conventional wisdom of NGO election observers in postconflict settings holds true. Great needs remain, not only more invitations for observation as the authors state, but also for a single UN agency for electoral assistance, as well as greater communication among observers and governments *after* elections to correct the problems identified.

Notes

1   UNDP, *Deepening Democracy in an Fragmented World* <www.undp.org/hdr2002/>.
2   See *Romania since 1989: Politics, Economics and Society*, Henry F. Carey (ed.) (Lanham, MD: Lexington Books/Rowman and Littlefield, 2004).
3   UNO Campaign Manager Antonio Lacayo denied receiving a cent from the CIA during the election. 'I never knew, nor spoke to, anyone from the CIA'. EFE, Managua, 16 October 1991.
4   If true, the allegations in Namibia and Nicaragua both prevented the victorious opposition from unilaterally amending the constitution.
5   The 15 per cent figure comes from interview with OAS Mission Director, Mario Gonzales Vargas, Washington, 15 October 1991. The 10 per cent figure comes from interview with OAS El Salvador Director (and former Brazilian Ambassador to El Salvador), Diaz Costa, San Salvador, 22 August 1991 with Tom Gibb of National Public Radio present. Both Gonzales and Diaz said that the there was no discrimination based on party and that the official results were basically accurate. Diaz suggested that there could be a bias the ARENA party was less likely to be discriminated against because its membership was more literate. Gibb and veteran election observer David Browning, who perhaps understands Salvadoran elections better than anyone, made similar estimates-confirm. An even larger problem, which went uncorrected in El Salvador until 1991, was that the ballots were numbered, preventing them from being truly secret. The numbers

were used for control, though duplicates with the same numbers could have been printed anyway. Now, the numbers are printed and then torn off prior to voting.

6 Interview, Washington, 15 October 1991.

8 When I asked about their reaction to having a comprehensive UN observation team, Mr. Justice Naimuddin, Chief Election Commissioner of Pakistan and Haydee Yorac, Acting COMELEC Chairperson in Pakistan, rejected the idea as inappropriate. Both the latter and her successor, Christian Monsod, welcomed the idea of UN technical assistance.

Chapter 21

NGOs and the Rule of Law in El Salvador and Guatemala

JoAnn Fagot Aviel

Peace Accords signed in El Salvador in 1992 and Guatemala in 1996 marked the official end of peace negotiations and the beginning of a still-ongoing process of building peace and democratisation. 'Without the rule of law, democracy cannot be fully realized.'[1] However the rule of law is often not defined. Guillermo O'Donnell states 'that its minimal (and historically original) meaning is that whatever law there is, this law is fairly applied by the relevant state institutions, including, but not exclusively, the judiciary'.[2] A Central American analyst has emphasized that NGOs in Central America are working to establish 'not any rule of law, but one that will be democratic'.[3] For the democratic rule of law, access to justice for the poor must also be included in any definition.[4]

The civil war in Guatemala lasted 36 years, from 1960 to 1996, while the civil war in El Salvador was shorter, from 1979 to 1992. Before the negotiation and signing of the Peace Accords, the principal function of human rights NGOs operating in the two countries was to gather, evaluate, and disseminate information on violations of human rights. Identified by Laurie Wiseberg, the other key function of human rights NGOs, that of creating political space for democratic forces, was much more difficult to operate.[5] Domestic human rights NGOs had difficulty even in surviving. Many of their members were killed and others had to flee into exile. Transnational networks of NGOs were especially important to their survival. Salvadoran and Guatemalan NGOs coordinated their activities with international NGOs like Human Rights Watch and Amnesty International. Some had foreign offices that helped them create solidarity networks.[6] Members of groups such as the Peace Brigades and the Christian Task Force on Central America acted as human shields for threatened Guatemalan and Salvadoran members, hoping that by accompanying them in their tasks they would be less liable to be assassinated or 'disappeared'. NGOs and solidarity organisations also worked to influence their governments' Central American policy.[7] The Central American Human Rights Commission (CODEHUCA), which was founded in Costa Rica in 1979 by various Central American leaders, obtained consultative status with the United Nations Economic and Social Council and helped gather denunciations from NGOs and presented them in appropriate UN meetings.[8]

In El Salvador, the Foundation of Studies for the Application of Law (FESPAD), founded by lawyers in 1988, utilized an 'unusual instrument which is generally considered in Latin America as an obstacle to social change: the law'.[9] FESPAD created the Center of Studies for the Application of Law (CESPAD) in 1988 to educate the public about legal issues and the need for reform. Students at the University of El Salvador working with an Argentine consultant, Alberto Binder, formed the Center of Penal Studies in El Salvador (CEPES) in 1993 under FESPAD's auspices and linked it to existing centers in Argentina and Guatemala.[10] The Center for Constitutional Studies and the Center for Juridical Information were established in 1998. FESPAD grew from only 5 persons in 1988 to 50 in 1998. Its external funding came principally from Europe: OXFAM, the Danish and Norwegian development agencies, and the European Union as well as the Ford Foundation. Fees paid for services such as workshops and legal information.[11] Another NGO, the Institute of Juridical Studies of El Salvador (IEJES) was also founded in 1988 by lawyers and law students from different Salvadoran universities in order 'to support the construction of democracy and the consolidation of the rule of law'.[12] The Institute of Women's Studies, 'Norma Virginia Guriola de Herrera' or CEMUJER, was founded in 1990 by Alba America Guriola after the assassination of her sister. CEMUJER aimed at achieving 'a gender democracy and a rule of law' by working with all sectors of society, including the army and government functionaries.[13]

In Guatemala, the new NGOs are not comparable in size and focus on the rule of law to those in El Salvador. The closest are the Guatemalan Association of Jurists (AGJ), founded in 1989 by a group of lawyers, and the Myrna Mack Foundation, founded by Helen Mack in 1993 after her sister was assassinated. The AGJ is dedicated to assisting communities needing legal aid and 'to contribute to the strengthening of the democratic process and the establishment of a rule of law'.[14] Although similar to FESPAD in its aims, the AGJ has a much smaller staff. As AGJ lawyer Huberto Estrada Soberanis stated, over 80 lawyers were killed during the civil war. Many lawyers did not want to get involved in politics. He himself had received threats for defending people.[15] The Mack Foundation is also dedicated to reforming the judicial process.[16] The Center for Legal Action in Human Rights (CALDH) is a Guatemalan NGO that began in Washington in 1990 and opened its offices in Guatemala in 1994. CALDH provides free legal advice and representation to victims of human rights abuses.[17] The Center for the Investigation, Study, and Promotion of Human Rights (CIEPRODH), was founded in Guatemala in 1987, to focus on promoting human rights. Additionally, numerous indigenous organisations have formed. Two have been especially concerned with strengthening the rule of law: the Menchú Foundation, founded by Rigoberta Menchú with money she received from winning the Nobel Peace Prize, and the *Defensoria Mayan*, founded in 1993 to promote the use of Mayan law.[18]

New legislation and administrative procedures have been necessary to democratize the judicial system in each country. Both the United Nations Observer Mission in El Salvador (ONUSAL) and the US Agency for International Development (AID) had parallel projects in judicial reform with insufficient coordination between them.[19] FESPAD and the Center for Judicial Studies proposed reforming the constitution's judicial provisions and reforming the governance of the judicial branch.[20] FESPAD drafted a proposed judicial reform law in 1991, and a year later its director served on the technical commission set up by the legislative assembly to draft the law.[21] FESPAD's director participated in a special committee in the Attorney General's office, that presented a diagnostic study and recommendations for judicial reform in September 2001.[22] FESPAD also helped to incorporate international human rights law in domestic legislation and policy. The International Committee of the Red Cross worked with NGOs, legislators, justice officials and the military in each country to implement international humanitarian law.[23] IEJES worked to modernize legislation and reform the administration of justice. Together with other NGOs, IEJES proposed methods to improve the administration of the National Academy of Public Security and to control delinquency as well as constitutional reform.[24] With the support of UNICEF, CEMUJER sponsored a forum on the Juridical Condition of Salvadoran Women in November 1990, attended by 29 government and nongovernmental organisations. As an outcome of this forum, CEMUJER organized a permanent-working group to study Salvadoran legislation with a gender focus and to present reforms. CEMUJER lobbied the legislature on proposals regarding the Family, Penal, and Labor Codes as well as domestic violence legislation.[25] The new Family Code and adoption of the new domestic violence law made it possible, for the first time, for women to obtain restraining orders against their abusers.[26]

In Guatemala, USAID suspended aid in 1991 until a new Criminal Procedure Code was passed and the Attorney General's office reorganized.[27] Although judicial reform thus began before the signing of the 1996 Peace Accords, the Accords called for the president to create a 'Justice Strengthening Commission' which included the president of an NGO working on justice issues and a legal advisor to Mayan organisations. The Commission held public meetings with representatives of governmental, Mayan, women's and human rights organisations, research and educational institutions, professional organisations, unions and other groups concerned with justice in Guatemala. The Commission's final report, issued in 1998, included a series of recommendations.[28] After the signing of the Peace Accords, NGOs such as the AGJ and the Mack Foundation also elaborated legislative proposals and studies.[29] Recommendations were included in the constitutional reforms that were defeated in a popular referendum in 1999. The World Bank funded a $33 million judicial reform project from 1999 to 2004 in partnership with MINAGUA, USAID, and various foreign governments in which members of the judiciary, indigenous groups, and NGOs participated.[30] In 2002 several human rights NGOs and the Institute of Comparative Studies in Penal Science (IECCPG) formed the Council of Monitoring and Support to Public Security to oversee the progress of reforms to the police.[31] In both El Salvador and Guatemala NGOs were involved in proposing new legislation, administrative procedures and lobbying, but international involvement and pressure were greater than that of civil society. Despite the reforms, the problem of impunity continued.

After the passage of the general amnesty law, FESPAD and other NGOs labeled it unconstitutional and contrary to international treaties that El Salvador ratified.[32] After failed attempts to modify the amnesty law, FESPAD chose to focus on more collaborative strategies to solve current problems and long-term efforts to change policy and attitudes regarding the rule of law. Other NGOs, such as the

Center for Promotion of Human Rights 'Madeleine Lagadec' and the Committee of Families of Victims of Human Rights Violations (CODEFAM), continued to document and publicize the horrors of war and protest against the amnesty law.[33] Although the Salvadoran government made no effort to distribute the Truth Commission's report, NGOs distributed it as well as popular comic book versions, but the report was not widely available or read.[34] To help preserve historical memory of the civil war, on December 10, 1998, 'Human Rights Day', San Salvador Mayor Hector Silva announced that a monument to the civilian victims of human rights violations during the war, for which a coalition of NGOs had campaigned, would be built in a city park.[35]

Since the passage of the National Reconciliation Law in 1996, NGOs have sought the prosecution of those who were exempted from the amnesty. Several NGO forensic teams helped provide evidence for prosecution of some of the worst human rights abuses.[36] In January 1999, in the first case brought against army soldiers for executions committed during the civil war, Rigoberta Menchú accused the military of 'buying judges, bribing judges and promising land to witnesses' to win a plea of justifiable homicide in the case.[37] In August 1999 the court sentenced twelve soldiers to five years in jail and the rest to the four years they had already served.[38] However this ruling was later overturned. The Menchú Foundation and other NGOs demanded a retrial.[39] In 1993 an army sergeant was convicted of the killing of Myra Mack, an anthropologist and human rights worker. Her sister Helen Mack and the Mack Foundation then worked to bring to trial those responsible for ordering the killing. In October 2002 they succeeded in obtaining the conviction of Col. Juan Valencia Osorio for her murder. This marked the first time that the Guatemalan military leadership had been held criminally accountable for crimes committed during the civil war.[40] After the Appeals Court overturned the conviction, the Mack Foundation brought a parallel case to the Inter-American Commission. In November 2003, the Inter-American Court ruled that the government was criminally responsible. This decision helped to influence the Guatemalan Supreme Court to reinstate the conviction in 2004.[41]

NGO Options when dealing with Governments

NGOs working to strengthen the rule of law in El Salvador and Guatemala are still establishing their identity and the nature of their relationship with government and society. The Peace Accords and outside assistance have made it possible for NGOs to add to the strategy, of documenting and disseminating information on human rights abuses, the strategies of education and training of government officials and citizens, legal assistance, proposal of legislation and lobbying for legislation. NGOs' choice of options ranges from confrontation to collaboration with governments. The type of government with which they are dealing, their own ideology and goals, the extent of international support and their assessment of the consequences will affect decision-making. Most NGOs chose confrontation with more repressive governments existing before the signing of the Peace Accords. Now the choice of confrontation and/or collaboration is debated both within and between NGOs. Collaboration involves weighing the benefits of increased resources and opportunities to influence policy against the dangers of losing people's confidence and antagonising current power structures. Confrontation involves weighing the benefits of mobilising support and pressure and refusing to compromise goals and missions with costs ranging from imprisonment and loss of life to lack of influence on policymaking. NGO choice of a confrontationist or cooperative strategy is affected by government response. For example, Salvadoran NGOs cooperated with the activist Dr. Victoria Velázquez, who held the post of Human Rights Prosecutor from March 1995 to July 1998. However, they confronted her successor, Eduardo Penate, whom they tried to prevent from being chosen because of his lack of support for human rights and the rule of law, and eventually succeeded in having him removed.[42] Although governments often view confrontationist strategies as partisan attacks especially when they support or are supported by oppositional political parties, Henry F. Carey points out that '... too much cooperation with governmental and political actors, in order to enhance local political coordination, also runs the risk of being co-opted into a partisan cause'.[43]

Collaborative strategies have been employed more in El Salvador than in Guatemala. In El Salvador the strength of the FMLN party in the National Assembly and some municipalities has meant support for some NGO policies. This was not the case in Guatemala, where the party supported by the former guerrillas had only a few seats in the National Assembly and the government was less willing to collaborate. Collaborative strategies have been adopted more by newer NGOs than those NGOs active during the civil war, which had been allied to the FMLN and have since found it more difficult to collaborate with rightist governments. The more equal balance of power between the government and the former guerrilla forces in El Salvador, and the existence of the Salvadoran general amnesty law also influenced the choice of more collaborative strategies by both the Salvadoran government and NGOs. However, the decision of the Salvadoran Supreme Court to grant exceptions to the implementation of the amnesty law after an NGO petition challenging the amnesty may prompt more confrontationist strategies. In contrast to El Salvador, NGOs in Guatemala more strongly opposed amnesty and insisted on prosecution of those exempted from the amnesty law. The recent appointments of NGO founders, LaRue and Menchú, to positions in the Berger administration indicate more collaborative strategies are now possible. While some NGOs in both countries have based their identity and legitimacy on focusing either on confrontation or collaboration, others have chosen to employ both strategies. Incomplete democratisation in both countries has led to a mixture of options with NGOs confronting governments on current abuses and impunity for past abuses while collaborating on reforms when given the opportunity.

Notes

1   Valerie Bunce, 'Comparative Democratization, Big and Bounded Generalizations', *Comparative Political Studies*, 33/67 (August/September 2000): 713.

2   Guillermo O'Donnell, 'Polyarchies and the (Un)Rule of Law in Latin America: A Partial Conclusion', in Juan E. Mendez, Guillermo O'Donnell and Paulo Sergio Pinheiro (eds), *The (Un) Rule of Law and the Underprivileged in Latin America* (Notre Dame, Indiana: University of Notre Dame Press, 1999), pp. 307-308.

3   Victor Hugo Mata Tobar, 'Nuevas perspectivas de trabajo de las organizaciones no gubernamentales (ONG) de los derechos humanos (dh) centroamericanas en la decada de los noventa, u.p.' (23 febrero 1993), p. 12.

4   See Alejandro M. Garro, 'Access to Justice for the Poor in Latin America', in Mendez, O'Donnell and Pinheiro (eds), *The (Un) Rule of Law and the Underprivileged in Latin America* (Notre Dame, Indiana: University of Notre Dame Press, 1999), pp. 278-302.

5   Wiseberg.

6   Mariette Uitdewilliger, *Las Organizaciones No Gubernamentales de Derechos Humanos de El Salvador, Guatemala, y Honduras: sus relaciones internacionales con enfasis en la Comision de Derechos Humanos de la ONU (1980–1990); Tesis presentadao optar al grado de Maestra en Relaciones Internacionales, Universidad para la Paz* (Costa Rica, 1996), pp. 110-115.

7   Susan D. Burgerman, 'Mobilizing Principles: The Role of Transnational Activists in Promoting Human Rights Principles', *Human Rights Quarterly*, 20/4 (1998): 905-923.

8   Uitdewilliger, p. 93.

9   *Fundacion de Estudios para la Applicacion del Derecho (FESPAD)* and *Centro de Estudios para la Aplicacion del Derecho* (CESPAD), *Cinco Anos Despues* (San Salvador: November 1993), p. 1.

10 Popkin, pp. 220-221.

11 FESPAD, *Cinco Anos Despues*, pp. 3-4; *10 anos*, pp. 18-19.

12 Instituto de Estudios Juridicos de El Salvador (IEJES), *Memoria de Labores, 1993–1994*, San Salvador, p. 1.

13 Instituto de Estudios de la Mujer, 'Norma Virginia Guirola de Herrer' (CEMUJER) *Memoria 1990–1998* (San Salvador, 1999), pp. 1-17 and interview with Alba America Guriola, San Salvador, 27 July 1999.

14 *Oficina de Consultoria y Asesoria Legal de la Asociacion Guatemalteca de Juristas, ACJ*, Guatemala, not dated.

15 Interview with Huberto Estrada Soberanis, Guatemala, 20 July 1999.

16 Interview with Iduvina Hernandez, Guatemala, 22 July 1999.

17 Amnesty   International, <www.amnestyusa.org/countries/guatemala/actions/peace_accords/caldh>.

18 *Defensoria Maya, Ruchomb'al, Rukub'ano, Rub'auil, Ruchak, Objetivos, Funciones, Estructura y Funcionamiento* (Guatemala, 20 November 1996), pp. 1-5.

19 Popkin, p. 221 and p. 244.

20 Popkin, p. 220.

21 FESPAD, *Haciendo Derecho*, pp. 110-120.

22 FESPAD, <http://fespad.org.sv/portal/html/HistoriaC.php>.

23 Interview with Tathiana Flores, Guatemala, 16 July 1999.

24 IEJES, pp. 11-23.

25 CEMUJER.

26 Popkin, p. 195.

27 Popkin, p. 262.

28 Popkin, pp. 258-259.

29 Interviews   with   Estrada   Soberanis   and   Hernandez;   <www.myrnamack.org.gt/fundacion_publ>.

30 World Bank, <www.worldbank.org/publicsector/guatemala2.htm>.

31 US Department of State, 'Country Reports on Human Rights Practices', 2002, <www.state.gov/g/drl/rls/hrrpt/2002/18333.htm>.
32 FESPAD, *Haciendo Derecho*, pp. 125-128.
33 *Centro para la Promocion de los Derechos Humanos 'Madeleine Lagadec', Memoria Historia* (1999), p. 9 and 'CODEFAM' <emendozaz@navegante.com.sv>, sent 1-21-2000.
34 Popkin, p. 122.
35 Popkin, p. 140.
36 Popkin, p. 142.
37 'Nobel laureate quits massacre trial in protest', *Associated Press*, 6 January 1999, <www.CNN.com>.
38 'Guatemalan Troops Guilty of Killing War Refugees', *San Francisco Chronicle*, 14 August 1999.
39 Allison Davenport, 'Rigoberta Menchú Challenges Berkeley', *Center for Latin American Studies, University of California, Berkeley Newsletter* (Fall 2000), p. 11.
40 *San Francisco Chronicle*, 4 October 2002.
41 'Guatemala: Victory for Human Rights, Rule of Law', <www.oneworld.net/article/view/77377/1>.
42 'CODEFAM' <emendozaz@navegante.com.sv>, e-mail sent 1-21-2000.
43 Henry F. Carey and Oliver P. Richmond, *Mitigating Conflict, The Role of NGOs* (London: Frank Cass, 2003), p. 175.

Chapter 22

Conclusion

Henry F. Carey

A UN Development Programme, 'Millennium Project Report: Investing in Development', issued on 24 January 2005, criticized the 'feeding frenzy' of foreign aid donations after wars on conflicts. This comes in the well-trod tradition of Bhoutros-Ghali's *Agenda for Peace* and the *Brahimi Report on Peacekeeping*, both of which emphasize the need for innovation, including utilising NGO resources. There are indeed many dilemmas for peacebuilders. When international organisations attempt to revive communities, too much money is wasted, even though money should certainly be spent, though more selectively to achieve goals completely, rather than just spending funds from reluctant donors. Of course, efficiency is not possible, but the pattern has been to disburse aid to actually avoid rebuilding values and systems that work as opposed to sustaining the values that caused the conflict in the first place. Of course, ensuring that funds are not wasted can be achieved best by giving the funds to local NGOs, which have a better idea about what is needed. If conflicts have existed for a long time, local NGOs know sensibly how not to refuel old conflicts by rebuilding what is needed at local levels, rather than financing ethnic and conflict entrepreneurs who have too much at stake. On the other hand, local NGOs may be part of the incentive structure for violence and ethnic conflict, as well as unaware or uninvolved in efforts at peacebuilding. Along with the dangers of dependency, foreign sponsorship of local NGOs, fundamental to most peacebuilding contexts, constitutes a dilemma for NGO action and policy.

The book illustrates the tension between the thematic, critical articles such as by Reimann, Richmond, and Mertus and Nasreen, versus the more appreciative articles in much of the rest of the book. None of their views are as critical as Arundhati Roy,. who defines NGOs as:

> semi-official groups, usually dependent on grants from governments or cautious and orthodox private foundations. The general relationship to mass protest and vigorous movements for social change is sedative, conservative and ultimately lethal ... there are NGOs doing valuable work. But it's important to consider the NGO phenomenon in broader political context ... Their real contribution is that they defuse political anger and dole out as aid or benevolence what people ought to have as right.[1]

As above, criticism of NGOs should recognise how much progress has been achieved and that various dilemmas limit effectiveness within some dimensions.

These dilemmas include: a) whether or not to take sides in a conflict; b) how to collaborate with the military when NGOs must rely on it for protection; c) short versus long-term actions and investments by NGOs. Paffenholz, Mertus and Nasreen, and others have emphasized that short-term goals are more reachable than long-term goals. Paffenholz notes that local alliances are key to short-term success, while engaging on the national scene is required over the long term. The latter course, however, can lead to politicisation and possible constraints by collaborating with governments. Paffenholz and Aviel note that political learning makes longer term success possible, but this requires 'trials and tribulations' along the way. For best results, she advises smaller-scale projects, which are least likely to have national scale impacts. There are d) risks and uncertainty in any situation. This could include working in a war zone, where casualties can not only harm the particular NGO's efforts, but the willingness of other NGOs to continue working there. Furthermore, should and how can NGOs operate in war zones with corrupt or ineffective peacekeeping forces. Finally, there is the law of diminishing returns and no panaceas, which is augmented by 'cookie-cutter solutions', as Paffenholz puts it.

This conclusion returns to questions posed by Chadwick Alger in his introduction and present answers to them asserted or implied by this study's contributors. (Questions four and five are combined here into a general analysis of Intergovernmental-NGO collaboration):

I. Are NGOs adequately prepared to undertake the functions listed in the field guide of Paffenholz and Reychler (viz., gather information, monitor, provide relief, train, impel free and responsible media, deal with the past, and enhance security)?

Generally, we find nuanced and varied results from the studies. Richmond concludes, 'NGOs often are the only ones working to promote peace without other objectives'. Jackson finds that only some NGOs are 'prepared to perform and find viable ways of providing aid by developing strategies to counterbalance the rising risks associated with humanitarian actions'. Efaw and Kaul conclude that NGOs are and need to be constantly learning. 'NGOs are somewhat prepared ... which made room for some error while creating new ideas. This means much trial-and-error in getting to their goals, which means that NGOs are nevertheless in a constant learning process themselves as they learn what it takes to achieve success.' Aviel also found NGOs improving after periods of political learning during and after the wars in Central America, tinkering with their strategy as time went on and making new alliances and taking advantage of new opportunities, resulting from long-term engagements on specialized issues. NGOs need to coordinate with the police and army so that each divides their labour appropriately, but also to assure that those with arms do not direct the NGOs, except as necessary to provide the NGOs shelter.

Many positive results are suggested by the case studies. Several authors note the benefits of the right kind of government collaboration. Barmazel showed how government and NGOs could run small projects, in the most violent region of Pakistan, Sindh province. He is far less sanguine about NGOs addressing violence and other larger-scale problems of Pakistan. Taulbee and Kelleher found that NGOs developed close ties with Norway to gain legitimacy and support. Each group is thus able to focus on their own expertise and goals. NGO success can be dependent on the right kind of government in power, as semi-democracies will constrain NGO efforts in postconflict peacebuilding. Shapiro found that the Health Education Program succeeded in teaching local populations a variety of health practices, rights and concerns. Success depended on the commitment of the Soros Foundation for initial support and then gaining national governments' finance to assure long-term viability. NGO efforts in information dissemination are beginning and need to be enhanced in the local communities they serve. With military protection, peacekeeping NGOs that succeed in maintaining their neutrality, according to Monshipouri, and can 'freely move back and forth and learn what the needs are from all sides'.

In norm advocacy, advocacy NGOs can affect norms and practices in peacebuilding, particularly at international conferences. NGOs have learned how prepare beforehand in writing draft legislation to be included in final UN conference documents. NGOs address many questions that the UN does not address, though sometimes the UN will address them after the NGOs have undertaken the needed research. NGOs brought successful pressure to close the US School of the Americas, now reopened and renamed. With small, adept units, particular types of NGOs can be more sophisticated and prepared in peacekeeping than even multilateral organisations like the UN. Pavka asserts that private military companies are more efficient, with more experience operating together and greater preparation, than larger multilateral forces put together at the last minute.

Among criticisms about NGO preparedness, Olaleye and Backer conclude NGOs are effective on short-term relief, but much less so on long-term efforts, such as 'combating world hunger'. Mertus and Nasreen agrees that NGOs are less effective than the state over the long term, even though NGOs can 'provide more aid and other services than the state over the short term. This should not be at the expense of the state in providing services, who (are supposed to) provide more long-term services. Monshipouri finds that the increasing military presence with NGOs has increasingly relegated NGOs to 'subservient status, merely overseeing rather than actually doing relief'. He also warns that if NGOs have to negotiate with the government to gain protection or access, they can become 'targets of the opposition'. Whether this would be military or merely political, it would encroach on the legal and political neutrality needed for them to operate effectively. Alger sees a 'hit or miss' process, where many efforts at mobilisation do not succeed. He advises approaching local actors to increase the chances of success. Reimann says that 'NGO success varies widely, which shows the mixed results of NGO preparedness ... NGOs are good at small-scale projects, but the large goals are often what eludes them'. Mertus and Nasreen find NGOs 'prepared at times, but only up to a point, for they do not serve as the cure-all to every problem'.

II. Do specific cases offer insights on how the mobilising and financing structures of NGOs have affected the performance of their specific peacebuilding activities?

Obviously, there is even greater dependence on governments, with some, like Norway, interfering as little as possible, and the US taking a more hands-on approach with how its money is spent. While NGOs are not profit-seeking, it is not fruitful to imagine that they are uninfluenced by monetary considerations. They do not have unlimited discretion.

In particular case studies, we see optimistic conclusions: Efaw and Kaul emphasize the necessity of CARE's programming to attain long-run financial self-sufficiency among local groups so that the poor can survive, instead of 'just throwing money around'. Outsider NGOs need to induce trust among local groups and promote 'greater interaction with communities in sustainable concepts'. Richmond finds NGOs providing local access through their networks and utilising their often neutral access to facilitate access for all groups to outside actors. He sees the most important mobilisation activity in enhancing human security at the local level. Shapiro reports that the Health Education Project succeeded in educating the local populations how to improve their health. The key to success was in persuading funding from both the Soros Foundation and from national governments. Heckel found that one woman was able to secure adequate funding from a foundation in order for NGOs to take action on reforming international laws on child soldiers, as well as strengthening norms, such as through the Cape Town Principles. Seelarbokus reports that NGOs can provide more reliable, independent reports than do reports commissioned and/or financed by governments or industries or with direct interests at stake in the research.

In terms of conflict situations, Rojas reports that REDEPAZ shows how NGOs can make a difference, in this case in rural communities in Colombia, 'through determination, non-violent demonstrations, and mobilising'. Focusing on Sierra Leone and East Timor, Jackson has a pluralistic view of aid dependency and concludes that NGO 'funding might be geared towards whom it is from, which explains the many different types of projects taking place'. Aviel found that after the peace agreements NGOs in El Salvador and Guatemala were able to secure funding, enabling them to monitor human rights without fear of violent retribution. Barmazel found that the Orangi Pilot Project provided innovative models for the Mazoor Colony and other projects to become self-financing, thereby sustaining the benefits of basic human needs to a community otherwise beset by political and ethnic violence.

More negative reports on NGO mobilisation and finance are also abundant in the book. NGO aid dependency leads to perceptions that NGOs are really only serving Western governments. Alger finds that donors and even the UN want 'instant results' and 'cost maximisation'. Paffenholz, while praising LPI's efforts at connecting with bottom and middle level actors, suggests that it should have linked with top leaders. Monshipouri notes the particularly intense pressure facing NGOs in Iraq to support US policy, thereby compromising their operational and legally mandated neutrality. Mertus and Nasreen says that NGO aid and advice dependence on Western models 'restrict NGO creativity, causing them to produce results immediately and disregard quality ... neglect local projects, further restricting innovativeness and anything resembling self-sufficiency'. Fisher finds that NGOs in Rwanda were deprived of respect because of their financial dependency, which also induces rigidity, as well as competitiveness for funds and less cooperation among NGOs.

In more balanced terms, reflecting positive and negative results, Olaleye and Backer found that access to funding produced large differences in access to technology and efficiency in African NGOs, where those NGOs in South Africa were greatly advantaged compared to their counterparts in the other African countries. NGOs that focus on values and norms are likely to be convincing because of their lack of material interests, though that does not seem to undermine the influence of materially influenced NGOs. When NGOs make a country 'feel guilty' about their practices, an obviously difficult proposition, NGOs can be more effective. Carey reports that obtaining sufficient funding to provide comprehensive monitoring throughout an election campaign is the only way to prevent fraud and induce fairness. This financing is actually more available in postconflict elections than for ordinary votes. When NGOs report electoral fraud against a dominant authoritarian or semi-democratic regime, they usually require outside support of foreign governments to prevail. The only other alternative is abandon neutrality and side internally with the weaker party, usually from the opposition. Shapiro found that even the well-endowed Soros Foundation, which 'single-handedly got the Health Education Program fully functioning', still 'had much difficulty getting things done' for reasons of inadequate finance, as well as in providing adequate supplies or solving communications problems. Still without the support of Soros, 'the Health Education Program could not exist or even operate'. Finally, Paffenholz finds that variation comes with the types of funding sources, which determine NGO direction. The LPI/Sida (Canada) cooperation succeeded because of its flexible funding, unlike the situation with the less flexible rules of the European Union.

III. How did decisions in IGOs affect NGO performance in specific cases?

As a general matter, Alger, who specializes in UN studies, argues for IGOs and NGOs to engage in dialogue to encourage greater flexibility in making decisions. However, Monshipouri warns that IGOs often lack the authority to become directly involved. He advises IGOs to protect local NGOs while ensuring that they maintain their neutrality, on which their rights to participation are legally protected. As with states, Reimann warns that NGOs can become subservient to IGOs, particularly when the latter contract for the services of the former. The dilemma, of course, is the greatly increasing NGO expenses and the correlative need to obtain funds to pay for those activities. Thus, IGO-NGO collaboration is needed to assure that NGO input into formulating the most effective action plans can be undertaken in practice. This allows IGOs both to lengthen their reach locally, while at the same time giving local NGOs more prestige at home and abroad.

In terms of specific cases concerning IGO effects on NGO performance, we have the pleasant task of reporting some successes. The UN helped foster NGO joint participation in the Guatemalan peace talks, as Burgerman depicts. This led to important concerns to be addressed, as well legitimating accords which otherwise did not address many issues of justice and accountability for the indigenous population, which arguably had suffered genocide by the state. This made the settlement 'more reasonable' for them. Burgerman found that the relatively weak position of the UN provided an incentive for the UN to seek the participation of local NGOs. She concludes that the local NGOs, not the UN, were the parties which really effected the peace agreement with the Guatemalan military. Similarly, Barmazel concluded that UNDP inefficiency in promoting sanitation in Sindh, Pakistan, allowed the Orangi Pilot Project to fill in the gap. Paffenholz praises the UN and LPI for cooperating in Somalia to obtain fair cooperation in peace negotiations. The UN provided face-saving for warlords there to make peace and permit space for the local NGOs to operate openly in return. Jackson concludes that the UN did its best to stop violence in Sierra Leone during the civil war's latter stages of the 1990s, including negotiating the peace accords of 1998. The UN then protected the NGOs that were already working there so that they would not feel it necessary to withdraw. UNAMSIL attempted to convert rebel soldiers into members of the national armed forces, which, among other duties, protect NGO workers. Heckel reports that UN permission for NGO permission, led to setting age limits on child soldiers, to restrict the practice. On the other hand, NGOs, like the US-based, National Rifle Association, helped obstruct the SALW initiative to monitor and reduce small arms trafficking worldwide. Burgerman cites the conditions placed on military aid to Guatemala after its democratic transition commenced, which allowed for more civilian control over the military, as well as requiring NGO participation in the peace process and permitting the monitoring of human rights thereafter. Of course, the situation remains far from ideal, but progress, compared to the exigencies of civil war, are notable. Fisher found the World Bank helpful in encouraging NGOs to focus on input from local populations in Rwanda. She adds that the support of local NGOs is necessary to assure that IGO goals are met.

Efaw and Kaul sees the UN as 'delivering goals', which give NGOs 'some direction, some sense of purpose in pursuing how they coordinate their operations'. In the particular issue of postconflict elections, Carey found that IGOs, like the UN and OAS set electoral norm standards for domestic electoral authorities and parties, as well as international and local NGO observing and judging elections. If monitored well, this becomes a form of norm implementation. If not, then it becomes the basis for local party manipulation against the interests of local civil society and its NGOs who are caught unaware or worse, collaborating in rigging the results. More comprehensive UN observation teams in the late 1980s began monitoring elections, after less comprehensive local and international NGOs had made the initial efforts in election monitoring. Previously, UN monitoring by the UNDP Country Director was largely a peripheral exercise. Any country that came to have a full UN mission, beginning in 1989 in Namibia and in Nicaragua in 1990, had the 'gold standard' in NGO monitoring of an entire electoral process. Of course, just as the gold standard is an anachronism, such comprehensive missions effectively replace local efforts by local parties and NGOs to undertake what they must eventually perform on their own during elections. To the extent that such efforts by the UN and/or International NGOs replace local NGOs and parties, they may not serve the political development of the country concerned in the long run, despite the short-term contributions to free elections.

Among the negative findings about IGO decisions affecting NGOs, Aviel found that UN inefficacy led to repression of human rights NGOs in El Salvador in Guatemala during their civil wars. The UN took no action in East Timor to send in observers or authorize action to counter the aggression in the Indonesia invasion, which ultimately resulted in genocide. Yet, NGOs went into that new colony and mobilized worldwide attention and eventually, 25 years later, UN peacekeepers to stop the post-election paramilitary slaughter. Seelarbokus reports that the UN downplayed the negative effects of Depleted Uranium in weapons. NGOs brought more facts about health risks to the table. Yet, the European Union has been marginalising NGOs who criticize authoritarianism in candidate countries for membership.

As usually is the case, IGO have mixed effects on NGO performance. The UN and international law has never sanctioned private military companies, and 'mercenaries' have been deemed illegal in various UN fora. International humanitarian law (IHL) only covers governments. Many argue that IHL covers only state militaries. Anyone else fighting without state authority are unlawful combatants. That the US contracts many private military companies is a particular irony in this regard. Yet, Pavka, while commenting positively about such NGOs, also worries about their lack of neutrality as NGOs operating in humanitarian contexts.

IV. Is there any evidence in specific case studies of IGO involvement in these NGOs?

Tensions can have positive, as well as negative consequences. NGO-IGO partnerships are essential for improving local conditions. On a general level, NGOs are entering international fora, such as stalling the Cancun World Trade Organisation talks and being admitted as observers to the EU Agricultural Council. NGOs help IGOs penetrate local settings, while the latter, through its military and peacekeeping forces provide absolutely needed protection for NGOs to operate. Human rights NGOs supply the UN and other IGOs with key monitoring reports, which are used in official settings, like the treaty-based human rights committees. The UN has come to rely on NGOs to disburse emergency aid to the state, to local NGOs and directly to individuals in refugee camps and elsewhere in conflict zones.

Certainly, NGOs brought human rights violations to the UN's attention, beginning in the early 1980s with the UN Human Rights Commission's first country specific condemnations, aside from South Africa and Israel, against Chile, Argentina and Iran. This quickly generalized the UN's human rights concerns, which have remained less particular, though hardly universal, in the past quarter-century. Aside from the UN, the European Union has been increasingly active in working with NGOs, such as the REDEPAZ peace community project in Colombia.

In particular cases, we find some instances of positive tension. Certainly, NGOs providing relief tend to help enhance the legitimacy of relief operations, where the alternative is to have outside combatants from the North distribute aid. Clearly, tensions arise when some NGOs are funded and/or created by UN financing, such as in large peacekeeping missions such as Cambodia in the early 1990s. This becomes particularly acute when the NGOs concerned are scams. As a rule, NGOs at the UN, particularly those with consultative status at ECOSOC, which determines their participatory rights in UN fora, are largely from the North. Southern based NGOs are clearly under-represented. Similarly, as Alger reminds us, NGOs able to ally themselves with the UN, are usually better able to become funded than those who are less visible.

NGOs in social movements and NGOs like OWINFS (Our World is not for Sale) which oppose the WTO are not welcome there, or in the World Bank or IMF. Paffenholz found that UNOSOM so feared the warlords in Somalia that the UN asked the LPI NGO to stop the District Council process. The UN was then blamed for not stopping the District Council and for caving into pressure. Paffenholz concludes that the LPI could not have operated in Somalia without the collaboration of the UNOSOM peacekeeping force, whose security allowed LPI to think in longer term goals and efforts. As a result, 'the UN Lessons Learned Unit displayed an open-door policy for new outside actors (like NGOs) who wanted to provide services in the Horn of Africa'. Heckel reports that International NGOs ensured that banning child soldiers would remain an important issue in future UN fora after they had raised initial attention to the issue. In particular, she cites NGO lobbying at the UN Working Group, where a new minimum age for soldiers was promulgated for adoption. Alger sees the same process of NGOs lobbying and educating IGO delegations at play, such as the Neptune Group about the laws of the sea and the lobby coalition that participated in planning the statute of the International Criminal Court in Rome in 1998. Seelarbokus shows how NGOs countered the UN's method of measuring the extent of Depleted Uranium contamination and possible health effects to peacekeeping troops and especially the civilians living in Iraq and Bosnia. UN agencies were more interested in avoiding anger from Western governments, especially the US, which relies on this type of monition. Carey finds UN participation of election monitoring to have raised the standards that NGOs were able to apply in the larger majority of elections when the UN is not involved.

Of course, tension can inhibit UN-NGO collaboration. In the case of UN peacekeeping efforts in the genocides in Rwanda and Bosnia, NGOs were unable to mobilize greater UN peacekeeping efforts to protect the innocent from mass murder or even to focus attention on the atrocities. Part of the problem resulted from the lack of NGO consensus on whether military intervention was desirable. Jackson reports that NGOs in Somalia found the UNAMSIL troops to be inadequate and called for additional support from the UK and US. In Iraq, tension has emerged, as Monshipouri explains, between NGOs opposed to US military intervention and those NGOs sponsored by the US to build on the 'liberation'. The former NGOs advocate refugees being placed under UNHCR protection and not under the US-funded NGOs and those under US military protection. Aside from views of US policy, there is a perception that the few remaining NGOs operating in the face of fierce danger from jihadists and insurgents violate the legal rule of operational neutrality. Mertus and Nasreen emphasize that large amounts of funding available in the larger missions tends to steer projects toward the US or the UN and away from local NGOs. In the Guatemalan peace negotiations, the UN attempted to persuade the military and the governments to accept NGO representatives in negotiations with civil society, but the former refused. So, the NGOs sought observer status instead, from which they were still able to exert considerable influence. The Sri Lankan negotiations failed, despite the earnest efforts of the Government of Norway to sponsor Track 1 and 1/2 Diplomacy. The resulted, according to Taulbee and Kelleher because of the tension in the relationship between the government of Sri Lanka and LTTE, which was close to the Norwegian government. This thereby compromised the latter's perceived neutrality. Rojas documents the tension that was aroused by NGOs like REDPAZ after the European Union decided to stop funding the Municipalities project in Colombia. Finally, Heckel reports that the UN has often deferred to the US and other states in opposing raising the age requirement for soldiers, even though the ICRC and other International NGOs have clearly advocated soldiers to be at least 18 years old.

Despite all the risks of NGO-UN collaboration, Pavka, who is sanguine about private military companies, has noted that the UN has opposed their use, since they are not objects or subjects of international humanitarian law. Yet, this type of NGO is respectful of legal norms, but some wayward NGOs have spoiled the reputation of the industry at the UN. In the Congo, which Pavka concludes has run out of options, private military companies have joined forces with Congolese government and the MONUC peacekeeping forces. This is potentially a dangerous combination. The UN 'does not seem immune to tempting offers from such private NGO groups, as one small case here shows'.

The more effective the peacekeeping forces, the more effective the NGOs are in war and post-war situations. NGOs are more restrained if they have to worry about the integrity or effectiveness of peacekeeping forces. In the worst cases, like Afghanistan or Iraq, they reduce or eliminate their numbers entirely. Certainly, NGOs disagree and the UN sometimes has to mediate. MSF and the ICRC disagree over the neutrality principle in humanitarian interventions, and whether the legal protection accruing from it is jeopardized by criticising governments.

V. In what way has NGO involvement in specific cases affected the degree to which outcomes are more or less democratic?

Certainly, there were positive aspects in all of the cases and the future is for NGOs is bright, albeit constrained by many realities and dilemmas. One can say that in peace zones and humanitarian aid, life and death opportunities and risks abound. In lobbying IGOs, such as the UN, the World Bank, IMF and regional organisations, NGOs have made great strides in norm development, particularly when linked with media coverage of tragic circumstances. Certainly, the UN and other NGOs have strengthened NGO roles in humanitarian missions, as well as in monitoring human rights. To be realistic, however, it must be conceded that states and IGOs still finance and control what NGOs can achieve. Thus, lobbying and educating IGOs, states and public opinion remains a constant, necessary effort. Otherwise, the latitude NGOs need to link local and international societies will not be achieved.

Reimann cites the bottom-up operations that are essential to sustaining democratisation. Efaw and Kaul praise how NGOs, more than governments or militaries, do not exploit local citizens. Taulbee and Kelleher note that the Guatemalan Catholic Church help lead the peace negotiations toward a successful conclusion. Paffenholz credits LPI with successfully providing 'the means for dialogue' between disputing groups in Somalia, including for women. Barmazel cites the Orangi Pilot Projects defusing of ethnic violence by rebuilding houses destroyed by ethnic rivals in just two months. No subsequent ethnic violence occurred there, despite constant tit-for-tat communal violence between ethnic Mohajirs and Sindhis in the province. Aviel cites the precedent established by NGO activism in Guatemala in obtaining the prosecution of former President Rios Montt. Of course, the vast majority of murderers were free with effective immunity. Pavka cites private military companies helping to effect peace settlements. Richmond cites NGO roles that military operations usually cannot provide, except on an emergency basis: building a democratic process, education, medical care, rights protection, and institutional reform.

Monshipouri underscores NGO emergency relief efforts, citing Doctors Without Borders for both helping the most needy, while maintaining a critical eye on injustice in aid allocation and access. Fisher cites ASF's work in Rwandan prisons, designing confession forms. Shapiro cites the promotion of ethnic tolerance through the Health Education Program, while Mertus and Nasreen urge that state-building occur in the context of multi-cultural tolerance rather than a unitary one. This can be achieved if NGOs work with several ethnic groups, rather than following the tendency of serving only one. In addition, Mertus and Nasreen focus on 'democracy NGOs' transmitting foreign aid to local initiatives, where many local NGOs often are unaware of the appropriate norms of democracy. These observations imply that there is tension between the desire to allow local NGOs to operate freely and still conform to the norms of free elections, rule of law, minority protection, and the like. Jackson cites the efforts of NGOs in East Timor in court reform, albeit incremental, as well as monitoring human rights.

Among negative consequences, Alger cautions that not all NGOs are structured or act like democratic institutions. However, they are varied and more representative of civil society's viewpoints at the table in IGO deliberations. Regional conferences, as Heckel reminds us, may be an important new direction for NGOs to influence regional norm development and public opinion. Certainly, southern NGOs, even more than ones from the North, need to be represented more fully in IGO bodies, particularly the UNSC, where peacekeeping policy is formed. Another important example was how NGOs encouraged victims of *apartheid* repression to come forward in South Africa's Truth and Reconciliation commission, so that the true extent of the regime's atrocities and repression could be documented. Reimann finds NGOs creating a dependency that contradicts democratic notions of independence and popular sovereignty in practice, by 'overemphasising aid to the point where local communities revolve around these NGOs'. She also warns that NGOs tend to serve the elites, not the masses and 'still need work on bring all the locals together'. Efaw and Kaul advocate an ambitious 'rights-based approach' to financing postconflict development and peacebuilding, where NGOs respect all human and environmental rights. Burgerman add to the list, NGO advocacy of land restoration and political autonomy of indigenous groups. Aviel's priority for the future is NGO cooperation to bring genocidal and war criminals to justice, particularly former heads of state and military chiefs of staff who set such policy in action. Finally, the contributors generally call for NGOs to practice what they preach so that hypocrisy does not interfere with their well-meant messages.

Fisher's experience in Rwanda leads her to conclude that NGOs can be self-serving, with life-and-death consequences. 'NGOs may be benefiting their own image rather than that of the populace that they serve; they plan strategically at times so as to worry more about proving their worth to get funding instead of worrying about if those helped can survive in the long-term, after NGOs leave.' Carey notes that NGO election observers have failed to identify rigged or unreasonably incompetent elections, such as in Romania in 1992, 1996, 2000 and 2004; in Haiti in 1990, 1995, and 2000; Russia in 1995 and 1996 and in many other cases. They are unconsciously influenced by which governments are financing their expenses and which parties and candidacies they want to win, even though they are officially and consciously neutral. They rarely or never acknowledge such mistakes, or they often deny or cover them up. Pavka notes that private military companies are less legally and politically accountable than the more regulated state militaries, and thus receive less attention and thus more effective, because their risks are lower.

VI. Do any of the actors in specific cases reveal a future vision for NGO involvement in peacebuilding?

As always, NGOs need to be vigilant in monitoring human rights violations and seeking prosecutions, in distributing aid, as well as strengthening international law norms and institutions. Deepening NGO networks globally will be essential to these tasks. We cannot be sure if one NGO dies, another will spring up to take its place. While we have not lost sight of the critical remarks in many of the chapters, there is overwhelming evidence of positive advances. One can speak of 'mitigating anarchy' in international and domestic politics in ways that do not appear to have systematically occurred in contemporary peacekeeping efforts, both formal and informal.

Richmond and Olaleye and Backer recommend upward and downward mapping, networking, information and operations-sharing, as well as even for pursuing financial support among local, regional and international NGOs and associated governments and IGOs. Many contributors underscore the threats and dilemmas of NGO neutrality in war zones, and they imply that 'muddling through' is the best recourse when it becomes necessary to take sides. How to decide when that is necessary, of course, is left to each NGO. However, as Jackson and Rojas emphasise, if relying on one side's armed forces is the only way to achieve it, then neutrality becomes the less viable value, since saving lives is the highest priorities. However, many NGOs have decided no longer to send their civilians into war-zones, like Chechnya and Iraq, where NGO lives are not respected.

Taulbee and Kelleher recommend more combinations of Track One and Track Two diplomacy, what they call 'Track One and a Half', to obtain productive results by governments collaborating with, and deferring to NGOs in negotiations. Similarly, Shapiro sees government support for NGO initiatives to be essential to finance important ideas, particularly in transitional situations where resources are scarce. The self-reliance of so many new NGOs nearly not yet realistic. Ideally, funding should not be dependent on a single source. Of course, if NGOs are to be professional, they will have to rely on whomever provides the resources. The stipulations attached to the aid can be considered on a case-by-case basis.

Pavka recommends that private military companies be used more often, particularly in postconflict police training, as well as even in rebuilding infrastructure and markets, where militarisation of these functions cannot be avoided. There remains disagreement among our contributors about the extent to which NGOs can focus on long-term issues, with Mertus and Nasreen and Paffenholz advocating expansion, while Reimann cautioning that NGOs should focus on their short-term comparative advantage alone.

Jackson sees that 'stability is a must for success in humanitarian missions, or where there is chaos and difficulty of reaching those in need'. This requires a careful attempt not to jeopardise NGOs neutral status, while building on a necessarily difficult arrangement with the military, which makes many operational decisions on the grounds of military necessity, even though NGOs do not wish to lose their strategic autonomy. The San Pablo, ZOP and REDEPAZ peace zone in Colombia, ASF in Rwanda, the Orangi Pilot Project in Pakistan, the Health Education Program in Eastern Europe, LPI/HAP in Somalia, are all specific success stories. The book has also detailed the efforts of international NGOs like Doctors Without Borders, CARE, and the Soros Foundation.

To conclude, there are no checks on the integrity of NGOs, other than the free flow of information and competition. Since most transitional and postconflict societies are still partly closed, NGOs will remain partial, with incomplete, biased, inaccurate and ideological information, particularly in polarized societies. Since NGOs are not a panacea, efforts have to be coordinated with states and other NGOs with opposed agenda to agree on action plans that do not conflict with each other and perhaps can compliment. Implementation of tasks will always remain incomplete. In some cases, such as decontaminating areas with depleted uranium weapons and munitions, implementation has not even begun.

In the realm of NGO activities in mitigating conflict and building peace, contemporary theory has moved from panacea to bounded expectations. There is no pretence of analysing NGOs as maximisers of utility or rationality, as scholars have generally been drawn to theorising about their normative roles in generating humane rules and shaming the tyrannical. In the ambit of this study, our contributors have modestly focused on the norm generating activities that remain, such as banning child soldiers and eliminating depleted-uranium weapons to pierce armor. The larger focus, however, has been the pragmatic concerns involving emergency relief and fostering post-conflict reconciliation and institution building. Paradoxically, the world continues to grow in its reliance on NGOs, despite these predicaments. Given the propensity for conflicts to recur and the uncertain prospects of NGO contributions to reduce the chances and severity of renewed hostility, the field remains under-theorized. What this volume has done, however, is to clarify what theories can be generated from the wealth of experiences presented.

NGOs have a vital role in supporting societies emerging from conflicts, half of whom are relapsed old conflicts where earlier efforts at peacebuilding and prevention has failed. Greater assessments of best practices and lessons learned about the vast growth of NGO activity, both acting independently and in partnership with the UN, is needed. Analysis of ways to improve these approaches needs to evaluate how to improve both the political will and level of resources applied to these tasks. Finally, more investigation of how to empower local NGOs, which still depend on external resources in most cases, needs to be undertaken.

NGOs, in theory, promote peace and democracy and protect civil, political, economic, social and cultural rights. Most scholarship has concentrated on NGO monitoring, legislating, information dissemination, propaganda, education and lobbying for causes like democratisation and human rights. A search on Amazon.com reveals over 350 titles on of NGOs. Equally large numbers of diplomatic conferences, NGO lawyers and lobbyists, and inter-disciplinary studies, both have indicated that NGOs have greatly increased the extent of their activities, even if their longstanding efforts to strengthen the rule of law is unclear.

While it is true that many commentators have identified conflicts between state funding and NGO participation, there is no systematic study of how NGOs actually affect the design and monitoring of postconflict state institutions. This is understandable: until the peace agreements in Guatemala and Burundi, NGOs were largely excluded from the actual peace negotiations. Furthermore, most local NGOs which have been commissioned in postconflict peacebuilding have essentially created by foreign donors while existing local NGOs have been ignored. However, the abject failure of peacebuilding in Haiti and the troubled situations in Cambodia, Bosnia, and Kosovo, with the verdict in Afghanistan and Iraq still open to interpretation, the need for local NGOs to be directly or at least indirectly involved in their countries is apparent. The IMF, World Bank and many foreign governments have now established binding rulings to make sure that foreign assistance facilitates 'local ownership' of post conflict, development assistance.

The new world order may not be post-Westphalian, but new techniques have been attempted with different results in a variety of contexts, including the post 11 September world, in which states have reasserted their sovereign prerogatives in the name of counter-terrorism. This will challenge states not to abandon the progress of the late Twentieth Century during which international civil society, usually through NGO activism, was able to increasingly hold states accountable for their misdeeds. Now, with some of the NGO community seeking to valourise security over human rights, there is a renewed challenge for the larger NGO community to democratise the effort to combat terrorism, while also attempting to rebuild post-conflict societies. NGOs also face the difficulty of engagement in conflict zones from Kosovo to Iraq in which the US and UK have used force to overthrow corrupt regimes without international consent. A similar challenge is to mitigate the negative effects of globalisation, from fragmentation to marketisation.

Note

1 'Arundhati Roy Explains NGOs to You'; See also Alexander Cockburn, *The Nation*, 27 September 2004, p. 28.

Index

abashyirahamwe, 184
A Bed for the Night:
    Humanitarianism in Crisis, 14
Abu Ghraib, 137
accountability, 42, 214
    horizontal, 123
    vertical, 123
Action Aid, 186-188
Active Learning Network for
    Accountability and Performance
    in Humanitarian Action, 49
active neutrality, 102
Activists Beyond Borders, 4
actors
    traditional, 19
    local, 19
Additional Protocol I, 213
Additional Protocol I to the Geneva
    Conventions, 214-215
advocacy movements, 25
AECOM Government Services, Inc,
    138-139
Afghanistan, 8, 101, 104, 105, 120,
    121, 126, 201, 245, 249
Africa, 48, 141, 143
Africa Office of Global Ministries,
    110
African Rights, 40
Agenda for Peace, Democratization,
    and Development, 27, 28, 237
aggressive good offices, 71
Agriculture and Natural Resources
    (ANR)-related interventions, 155
Aid industry, 41
AirScan Inc, 141
AIDS Education, 162
Ala, Abu, 73
Albania, 222, 225
Alcohol and Other Drugs, 162, 166

Alger, Chad, 238, 244, 246
AMA Associated Limited, 138
American Enterprise Institute, 48
Amnesty International, 27, 109, 110,
    111, 189, 202, 203, 229
anachronism, 243
Anderson, Mary, 112
Angel, Diana, 95
Angel, José, 94
Angola, 29, 133, 134, 137, 138, 144
Angulo, Francisco, 96
*An Introduction to Sexuality
    Education*, 162
Annan, Kofi, 3, 16, 29
anti-colonial revolution, 69-70
anti-DU Campaign 210, 214
anti-Semitism, 164
anti-science view, 49
apartheid repression, 246
Arabic Campaign Against Depleted
    Uranium, 210
Arab States, 71
Arafat, 73, 75
Arbil, 104
Argentina, 5, 243
Aristotle, 126
armed opposition, 4
ArmorGroup, 138, 139
Arms Export Control Act, 136
Arias, Oscar, 85
Article 3, 214
Article 25, 214
Article 26, 214
Article 35.2, 213
Articles 35(3) and 55, 214
Articles 48 and 51.4, 214
Article 77(2), 204
Article 83(2), 204
Article 138, 202

Aschjem, Halvor, 77
ASF (Assembly of Civil Society)
188, 219, 222-4
Asia, 225
Asian Development Bank, 22
Asian Tsunami, 21
Assembly of Civil Society, 85, 88
Association for National Consensus
(*Instancia Nacional de
Consenso*), 87, 88
ATSDR analysis, 211
AUC (Self Defense Units of
Colombia), 93
autogolpe, 87-88
autonomy, 43, 120, 122, 127
Avant, Deborah, 131, 133, 135, 140
Aviation Development Corporation,
136
Aviel, 238, 240, 243, 246, 247
Avril, Prosper, 224
Azerbaijan, 161

Backer, 239, 241, 248
Baciu, Dr. Dan, 163
Baghdad, 103-105
Bagic, Aida and Paul Stubbs, 123,
125
Baker, James, III, 131
Balkans, 209, 212, 214
Balochis, 191, 195
Bangladesh, 158
Barlow, Eeben, 132
Barmazel, 238, 240, 242, 246
Barnen, Radda, 201-203
Bate and Tren, 48-9
Beiber, Florian, 129
Beilin, Yossi, 72-73, 75
Belarus, 161
Bell, Sarah, 164
Berger administration, 233
Bertell, Dr. Rosalie, 211
Biafran crisis, 24
Biharis, 191-192, 195
bilateral aid agencies, 43
bilateral state agencies, 4
Binder, Alberto, 230

bio-power, 30
bio-technology, 49
Blackwater, 138
Bogotá, 93, 95
'boomerang' pattern, 57
Boothby, Neil, 201
Bosnia, 120-125, 126, 136, 132, 138,
143, 161, 167, 244, 249
Bosnia-Herzegovina, 161
Botswana, 144
Braddock, Dunn and McDonald Inc,
131
Brahimi Report on Peacekeeping,
237
Brett, Rachel, 203
Brooks, Doug, 132
Brown, 26
Buckingham, Tony, 132
Bulgaria, 103, 161
bureaucratic efficiency, 124
Burgerman, 242, 247

CACI, 137
CACIF (Coordinating Committee of
Agricultural, Commercial,
Industrial, and Financial
Associations), 86-89
California Microwave Systems, 133
Cambodia, 29, 145, 201, 225, 226,
244, 249
Cambodian refugee camps, 40
Campaign Against Depleted Uranium
(CADU), 210-211, 212-213
Canadian aid agency, 38
Cancun World Trade Organization
talks, 244
Capacity (of mercenary groups in
Rwanda), 134
Cape Town Principles, 240
Capitol Hill, 132
carbon credit trading, 153, 157-159
carbon trading markets, 158
CARE (Cooperative for Assistance
and Relief Everywhere), 102-104,
122-124, 155-157, 159-160, 240,
248

Carey, Henry F., 233, 241, 242, 245, 248
Carlucci, Frank, 131
Carothers, Thomas, 122
Carpio, Ramiro de León, 87
Carter, President Jimmy, 69, 85
Castro, Fidel, 21
Catholic Relief Service, 21, 109
Catholic Agency for Overseas Development (CAFOD), 110
Cellules, 184-185, 188
CEMUJER (The Institute of Women's Studies, 'Norma Virginia Guriola de Herrera'), 230-231
Center for Constitutional Studies and the Center for Juridical Information, 230
Center of Studies for the Application of Law (CESPAD), 230
Centers for Disease Control, 163
Center for Promotion of Human Rights, 230-232
Center for the Investigation, Study, and Promotion of Human Rights (CIEPRODH), 230
Central America, 201, 225, 229, 238
Central American domestic wars, 71
Central American Human Rights Commission (CODEHUCA), 229
Central Electoral Council (CCE), 223
Central Europe, 137
Centre for the Study of Violence and Reconciliation (CSVR), 144
César, Alfredo, 222
charity market, 45
Chechnya, 248
Childers, 15
child labor, 41
child soldiers, 201-205, 242, 249
Chile, 225, 244
Christian Task Force on Central America, 229
Christopher, Warren, 75
CIA, 131, 136

civic nationalism, 119, 126
civic responsibility, 165-166, 169
civil intervention, 122
civil peace, 20-23, 26, 38
civil society, 43, 47, 74-75, 78-79, 110, 122-127
civil society aid, 41
Civil Society Discourse of Peace, 23
Clark, Ann Marie, 7
Clark, Ramsey 213
Claridge, David, 140
Cluj-Napoca, 163
CNR, 85-86
Coalition for the International Criminal Court, 15
Coalition to Stop the Use of Child Soldiers, 15
codes of conduct, 49
Coexistence, 188
Cold War, 68-69
Cold War era, 68-69
Colombia, 68, 93-98, 133, 137, 240, 249
Colombian Army, 93
commercialization, 44, 46
Commission of the European Communities, 169
Commission on Reception, 112
Commitment Letter, 94
Committee Against Torture, 7
Committee Examining Radiation Risks from Internal Emitters (CERRIE), 212
Committee of Families of Victims of Human Rights Violations (CODEFAM), 232
Committee on the Elimination of Discrimination Against Women, 7
common delinquency, 93
Communism, 162, 164-168
communist ideology, 165-166
Communist Party, 162
Communist Youth League officials, 168
community reconciliation, 87
Conference on Children of War, 203

Conflict and Communication, 162, 165

Conflict and Communication: A Guide Through the Labyrinth of Conflict Management and Environment and Our Global Community, 162

Conflict environments, 33

conflict resolution, 71, 183, 185

conflict zones, 19, 24, 27, 32, 40

Congo, 126, 245

Constitutional Discourse of Peace, 23

Consultas Ecumincas, 74

Contemporary International Relations, 20

Contras, 222

Control Risks Group, 138

Convention on the Rights of the Child (CRC), 201-205
Optional Protocol to the CRC, 201, 203-205

Cook, 110

Coordinating Committee of Agricultural, Commercial, Industrial, and Financial Associations (CACIF), 86-89

coordination, 3

Council of Europe, 164, 169

Council of Monitoring and Support to Public Security, 231

credibility, 209-215

crime prevention, 143-150

crime prevention agenda, 147

Croatia, 161

Cubic Defense Applications, 138-139

Cuéllar, Javier Pérez de, 224

Cyprus, 68

Czech Republic, 161, 169

Darwinian marketization, 46

DCI, 203

Dealing with Moral Dilemmas, 13

Dealing with the Past and Imagining the Future, 12

Dear Unknown Friend, Children's Letters from Sarajevo, 167

de facto, 222

Defensoria Mayan, 230

demobilization, 47

democratic deficit, 38, 43

Democratic Republic of Congo (DRC), 137, 144

Denard, Bob, 137

Department for International Development, 102 Department of Defense (DOD), 209, 212

Department of Defense Investigations of Gulf War Chemical and Biological Incidents, 212

Department of Veterans Affairs (VA), 209

dependency syndrome, 123-124, 127

dependency trap, 124

depleted uranium (DU), 209-216, 243, 245, 249

Depleted Uranium (DU) Exposure 209-211, 214

Depleted Uranium Exposures Case Narrative, 211

Depoliticization, 174, 178

Deputy Foreign Minister, 70

Designing the Mediation Process, 11

Deutsch, John, 131

development strategies, 20

Dialogue and Listening, 13

diaspora, 174

Diaspora groups, 174, 178

Dichter, 45-6

District Councils, 202, 245

Djibouti, 178-179, 182

Djibouti process, 178

Dinka, 30

disarming, 94, 98

go-gooder market, 44

Dominican Republic, 222

Donini and Smillie, 44-5

Dombroski, Peter, 115

Drugs and The Law, 166

drug cartels, 137

drugs traffickers, 93

Duffield, 30

DU Munitions Study Act of 2003 and DU Munitions Suspension and Study Act of 2001, 215
Duncan, Kenny, 215
DynCorp, 132, 136-138, 140

Earth Action, 7
East Timor, 5, 29, 109, 111-112, 138, 144, 240, 243, 247
Eastern Congo, 137
Eastern Europe, 161
Economic and Social Council, 6
Economic Cooperation Foundation, 73
Edwards and Hulme, 39, 47
Efaw, 238, 240, 242, 246, 247
Egeland, Jan, 70, 72, 74-75
Egypt, 72
Eisenhardt, 139
electoral fraud, 223, 241
election observers, 221-226, foreign observers, 222, 226 observer groups, 223-225
elections, US financing, 221-225
ELN (National Liberation Army), 93-96
El Salvador, 29, 222-223, 229-233, 240, 243
emergency relief, 249
environmental limitation, 213
epistemic communities, 25
Equatorial Guinea, 132
Erickson, Jan, 77
Esquivel, Perez, 5
Estonia, 161
ethanol, 157
EU Humanitarian Aid Office, 28
European aid agency, 38
European Commission, 184
European Council, 215
European Network of Health-Promoting Schools, 169
European Parliament, 204, 215
European Union, 94, 98, 180, 230, 241, 243-245
European Youth Campaign, 164

Executive Outcomes (EO), 132-134, 136-138
Export Administration Act, 136

Fafo Institute, 72
Fahey, Dan, 212
FARC (Colombian Revolutionary Armed Forces), 93, 95-96
Faustian bargain, 112
Federalist Society for Law and Public Policy, 48
female circumcision, 3, 4
FESPAD (Foundation of Studies for the Application of Law), 229-231
field activities, 5, 8 humanitarian, 8
first international symposium, 201
Fisher, 242, 247
Fjortoft, Arne, 77
FMLN party, 233
foot binding, 3
Ford Foundation, 230
Foreign Affairs Committee, 139
Foreign Asset Control (OFAC), 101
Foreign Ministry, 70, 73
Foreign Operations subcommittee, 135
Forum for Peace and Governance (FOPAG), 174
Forum of Civil Society, 15
Forum of Social Sectors (*Foro Multisectoral Social*), 221
Foundation of Studies for the Application of Law (FESPAD), 229-231
Framework Accord, 88-89
free elections, 225
free market economies, 20
FWCC, 202

Gacaca, 183-188
Garang, John, 77
Garber, 131
Gassmann, Pierre, 105
genetically modified food products, 48

genetically modified organisms
    (GMOs), 41
general humanitarian, 9
General Assembly, 6
Geneva Convention, 131, 213
Geneva International Peace Research
    Institute (GIPRI), 201
Geneva Protocol I, 204
genocide, 183-185, 242, 243
genocidaires, 185
geothermal sources, 157
Ghali, Boutros Boutros, 8, 237
global capitalist, 47
global civil society, 20-1, 25, 27
Global Communication Center for
    Developmental Organizations, 15
global concerns, 69
    Social Democratic, 69
    Lutheran, 69
Global Development Four, 139
global economy, 159
global governance, 23
globalization, 21
Global Policy Forum, 7, 15
global politics, 4
Global Report on Child Soldiers,
    204
Global Risk Strategies, 137
global warming, 158
gold standard, 243
Gordenker and Weiss, 109
Gostin, 214-215
governance issues, 158
governmentality, 30
GOS (Government of Sudan), 78
Government of Rwanda, 185-186
grassroots approach, 68, 79
Green Cross International (GCI),
    210
greenhouse gases (GHGs), 158
Greenpeace, 27, 41, 160
Griffith, General Ron, 132
groupthink pressures, 224
Guadrón, José Angel, 94
Guatemala, 5, 70-76, 85-89, 202,
    229-233, 240, 242, 246

Guatemalan Association of Jurists
    (AGJ), 230
Guatemalan Catholic Church, 246
Guatemalan civil war, 71
Guatemalan Human Rights
    Commission (CDHG), 86
Guatemalan peace negotiations, 245
Guatemalan peace process, 85, 89-90
Guatemalan peace talks, 242
Guatemalan Supreme Court, 232
Guerrilla Army of the Poor (EGP),
    87
Guerrillas, 105
Gulf War, 22, 209-212, 215
Gulf War Syndrome 209-212, 215
Gurkha veterans, 137
Guyana, 223

Haiti, 68, 126, 139, 223-225, 248
Halliburton, 139
Hamburg, 212
Harris, Andrew, 113
Hart Group, 138
Health Education Program (HEP),
    161-168, 239-241, 247, 249
Health Promoting School Project,
    169
Heckel, 240, 242, 245, 247
hegemonic act, 23
hegemonic liberal peace discourse,
    24
hegemonic peace, 30
hegemonic Western liberalism, 47
hegemonic Western neocolonialism,
    47
Helgesen, Vidar, 77
Henry Dunant Institute, 203, 204
Heritage Oil and Gas, 132
Herzegovina, 120-122, 124
Hill and Associates Limited, 138
Himalayas, 158
HIV/AIDS epidemic, 144
Holst, 75
Horn of Africa, 76
Horn of Africa Program (HAP), 76-
    77, 174, 245

host government, 4
Howe, Herbert, 136
HRW, 203
Huberto Estrada Soberanis, 230
Hulme, 39, 47
Humanitarian Accountability
    Partnership International, 49
humanitarian assistance, 20
humanitarian crises, 39
humanitarian idealists, 23
humanitarian pragmatists, 23
humanitarianism, 21, 25, 32
humanity limitation, 213
Human Rights Committee, 7
Human Rights Day, 232
Human Rights Links, 15
Human Rights Ombudsman Ramiro
    de León Carpio, 87
Human Rights Watch, 109, 201, 202,
    229
human security, 20-21, 25-26, 28,
    30-32
Hungarian refugees, 21
Hungary, 161, 169
Hutu, 24
hydrogen., 157

IAC *Depleted Uranium Education
    Project*, 211
ICCB, 203
ICP Group Limited, 139
ICRC (International Committee of
    the Red Cross), 23-4, 101, 104-
    105
Identifying Key Actors in Mediation,
    11
ideological backlash, 46
IEJES (Institute of Juridical Studies
    of El Salvador), 230-231
IFIs, 20, 26, 30, 31
IFTDH, 203
IGO secretariats, 7
illegal mercenaries, 131
ILO, 202
IMF, 224
imperialist neo-liberal forces, 47

INAHG, 202
India, 158
Inkiko Gacaca, see Gacaca
Inspection Panel, 22
Institute of Comparative Studies in
    Penal Science (IECCPG), 231
Institute of Juridical Studies of El
    Salvador (IEJES), 230
Institute of Women's Studies,
    'Norma Virginia Guriola de
    Herrera' or CEMUJER, 230
institution building, 183-184, 188,
    249
Institutional Discourse of Peace, 23
institutional peace, 20
insurgents, 245
inter-action, 8
Inter-American Court, 232
INTERFET operation, 111-112
intergovernmental agenda, 32
intergovernmental actors, 4
Inter-Governmental Authority on
    Development (IGAD), 76-77
inter-governmentalism, 32
Internal actors, 178
International Action Center (IAC),
    210-211
International Action Network on
    Small Arms, 15
International bans of pesticides, 48
International Campaign to Ban
    Landmines, 15
International Charter Incorporated of
    Oregon, 139
International Coalition to Ban
    Landmines (ICBL), 203-204
International Coalition to Ban
    Uranium Weapons (ICBUW), 210
International Coalition to Stop the
    Use of Child Soldiers (CSUCS),
    203-205
ICRP (International Commission on
    Radiological Protection), 212
International Committee of the Red
    Cross (ICRC), 4, 21, 101, 104-105
International Community, 97

International Council on Human
    Rights Policy, 49
International Court of Justice, 137
International Criminal Court, 245
International Depleted Uranium
    Study Team (IDUST), 213
International development, 39
International Environmental Law,
    215
International Federation for Human
    Rights, 15
International financial institutions,
    19, 32
international fora, 243
International Fund for Agricultural
    Development, 8
international government
    organizations (IGOs), 5, 6, 20
international hegemonies, 26
International Human Rights Law
    Group, 221
International Humanitarian Law,
    103, 243, 245
International Network for a Second
    Assembly, 15
International Organization for
    Migration (IOM), 104
International Peace Bureau (IPB),
    201
International Peace Operations
    Association, 137
International Physicians for the
    Prevention of Nuclear War
    (IPPNW), 210
International Red Cross Council of
    Delegates. 203
international relations, 26
International Rescue Committee
    (IRC), 21, 102-103, 202
International Save the Children
    Alliance, 203
inter-state cooperation, 7
inter-state organizations, 4, 19
International Suffrage Movement, 3
Internally Displaced Peoples (IDP),
    95

Intolerance, 164
IOM report, 211
IOs, 30, 31
Iran, 244
Iraq, 101-105, 121, 123, 126, 133,
    135, 137-140, 144, 245, 246, 248
Irkutsk, 168
IRRI, 221
Israel, 68, 71-75, 244
Israel Defence Forces, 137
Israel/Palestine conflict, 68, 71-74

Jackson, 238, 240, 242, 245, 247,
    248, 249
Jesuit Refugee Service, 204
Jihadists, 245
Johannesburg, 156
Johanssen, Raymond, 77
Johnson, Hilde, 77
Joint Monitoring Commission
    (JMC), 78
Jonas, 73
Joolen, Mark, 104
Jordan, Lisa and Peter van Tuijl, 42
Jordanov, Darko, 166
Jordanian delegation, 72
Josselin, 25
Judicial System Monitoring
    Program, 112
Juridical Condition of Salvadoran
    Women, 231
Justice Strengthening Commission,
    231
Juul, Mona, 72

Karachi, 191-192, 194-195
Kaul, 238, 240, 242, 246, 247
katchi abadi, 191, 194-195
Kaunda, Kenneth, 223
Kazakhstan, 161
Keck and Sikkink, 3-4
Kelleher, 239, 245, 246, 248
Kellog, Brown, and Root, 133, 135
Kenya, 4, 76, 78
Khan, Dr. Akhtar Hameed, 191-193
Kikuyu, 4

Kindi, Al, 103
Kissinger, Henry, 131
Klinmahorn and Ireland, 187
Korea, 221
Kosovo, 29, 31, 68, 104, 121, 138-140
Kosovo Liberation Army (KLA), 58-60
Krasnayar, 168
Krasner, Stephen, D., 62
Kroensen, General Frederick, 132
Kumaratunga, President Chandrika, 77-80
Kurdistan Workers Party (PKK), 57-60
Kuwait, 214, 216
Kyoto Protocol (treaty), 158
Kyrgyzstan, 161

Labour Party, 72-73
Lagadec, Madeleine, 232
Laffey, 31-2
Laird, Melvin, 131
Laka Foundation, Documentation and Research Center on Nuclear Energy, 210
Laka Foundation report (*Gulf War Veterans and DU*), 211
La Nacion, 202
Larsen, Terje Rod, 72-74
Latin America, 85, 90
Latin American Council of Churches, 75
Latvia, 161
Law of the Sea, 7
Lawyers' Committee on Nuclear Policy, 7
Lazzarani, 215
League for a Democratic Kosovo (LDK), 58
Leahy, Senator Patrick J., 135
Lederach, 11
left of the center progressives, 37
legitimacy, 209-210, 213-215
Leigh, John, 137

Le Monde, 202
Lessons Learned Unit, 178, 245
Lesotho, 144
liberal actors, 20
liberal peace, 19, 21, 28, 32-3
liberal states, 20
liberal transnational framework, 32
Liberation Tigers of Tamil Eelam (LTTE), 60, 76-79, 245
Liberia, 133, 138-139
Life and Peace Institute (LPI), 173-183, 240-42, 244-7, 249
    International Board of the LPI, 174
    Somalia program, 174-175
Lithuania, 161, 167
logo merchandise, 46
Lome Agreement, 110-111
Lusaka, 134
Lutheran World Federation, 72, 203
Lynch, Jessica, 133

Maata Bio, 137
Macedonia, 161, 166
Machakos Protocol, 76
Machel, Graca, 203
Mack, Myra, 230
Mackinlay, Andrew, 135
Madrid process, 72, 74
magic bullet 37, 51
malaria, 48
Malawi, 144
Maldives, 158
Managing Stress, 13
Mann, Simon, 132
marketization, 46
Marshall European Center, 135
Martens Clause, 213
Maslen, Stuart, 203
Mass Spectrometry, 211
Mauritius, 144
Mazoor Colony, 240
McCallin, Margaret, 203
McCoy, 131
Media, 12

mediation, 11
Médicins Sans Frontières (MSF,
   Doctors without Borders), 23, 24,
   102-105, 111, 247, 249
Member States, 223
Menchú Foundation, 230-233
Menchú, Rigoberta, 87. 230, 232-
   233
Mercenaries, 131, 135-137, 140, 243
Mertus, 237-241, 245, 247
Metal of Dishonor, 211
Metepec, 86-87
methane, 157
Metis Associates, 162
Mexico, 222
Middle East, 72
migrants, 56-57
military humanitarianism, 113-114
Military Professional Resources, Inc.
   (MPRI), 131, 136, 138, 138-140
Military Toxics Project (MTP), 210-
   211
MINAGUA, 231
Minear and Weiss, 3
Ministry of Education, 163
Ministry of Finance, 187
Minnear, 3, 4
mission drift, 214
Mitchell, George, 69
Mojahirs, 191-192, 195
Mogotes, 94-95
Moldova, 161, 167
Mongolia, 161, 163
Monitoring, 11
Monrovia, 133
Monshipouri, 239, 241, 245, 247
Montt, President Rios, 246
MONUC, 137
Mozambique, 29, 144, 202
multiculturalism, 126
multilateral donors, 43
multilateral forces, 239
multinational agribusinesses, 157
Municipal Constitutional Assembly,
   94
Municipalities of Peace, 93-94, 97-98

Mutual Support Group (GAM), 87
Myrna Mack Foundation, 230-232

Nairobi, 77
Namibia, 144, 222, 226, 243
Nariño Peace Table, 95-96
Nasreen, 237-241, 245-248
National Academy of Public
   Security, 231
National Agricultural Union
   (UNAGRO), 86
National Assembly, 223
NATO, 70, 209
National Council of the Churches of
   Christ, 75
National Dialogue, 85-87
National Gulf War Resource Center
   (NGWRC), 210-211
National Institute of Health and
   World Health Organization, 163,
   169
NDI, 221
National Peace Prize, 94
National Reconciliation Law, 232
National Rifle Association, 242, 246
National University's Centre for
   Conflict Prevention, 188
needs-based approach, 156
negotiations, 3
Nelson, Daniel, 135
Neptune Group, 243
neoliberal conspiracy, 47
neoliberal model, 47
Neptune Group, 7
Networks
   global, 3-5, 14
   international, 26
   migration, 55-56, 58
   national 148-149
   NGO, 15
   regional, 149-150
   transnational, 4
   transnational advocacy, 4
New International Economic Order,
   69
New Policy Agenda, 47

New York Times, 202
Nicaragua, 221-223, 225, 243
niche specialization, 46
Nigeria, 139
Nike, 41
Nixon, Richard, 222
Nobel Peace Prize, 5, 87, 230
non-governmental organizations
    (NGOs), 3-16, 19-33, 37-50, 68-
    79, 85-90, 93-98, 101-105, 109-
    114, 119-127, 143-150, 155-160,
    161-164, 167, 169, 173-179, 183-
    188, 201-205, 209-215, 221-226,
    229-233, 237-49
    advocacy, 38, 41, 46, 122
    Bosnian, 122
    briefcase 42
    come and go (ComeN'Go) 42
    commercial 42
    criminal (CRINGO) 42
    democracy, 121-122
    development, 77, 177-178
    DONGOs (donor-organized),
        109, 111-112
    environmental, 41
    fake, 42-3
    for-profit, 42-3, 45-6
    government-owned (GONGO),
        42
    government-owned and initiated
        (GRINGO), 42
    human rights, 15
    international, 4
    local, 4
    mafia (MANGO), 42
    Mega, 45
    my own (MONGO), 42
    party (PANGO), 42
    quasi (QUANGOS), 109, 111
    rights-based, 158-159
    South African, 144-145, 148-149
NGO Links, 15
NGO proliferation, 120-121
NGO Watch, 48
non-timber forest products, 159
norm entrepreneurs, 25

norms development, 209
Northbridge Services, 133, 138
Northman Grumman, 138
NORAD (Norwegian Agency for
    Development Cooperation), 77
Norwegian approach, 68, 69
Norwegian Back Channel, 72
Norwegian Church Aid, 72, 77
Norwegian Foreign Ministry, 75
Norwegian Ministry of Development
    Cooperation, 78
Norwegian People's Aid (NPA), 77
Norway, 68-77, 239-240
NPAs Community Development
    Program, 77
nuclear power, 49
Nutrition and Your Health, 162
Nyangamugayo, 185

OAS, 222-225, 243
OAS Secretary General, 224
OCPA (Pentagon's Office of the
    Coalition Provisional Authority),
    102-103, 105
Odeen, Philip, 131
O'Donnell, Guillermo, 229
Office of Coordination of
    Humanitarian Affairs, 8
O´Gara-Hess, 139
Olaleye, 239, 241, 248
Omsk, 168
One Hundred Municipalities of
    Peace, 93-95
Open Society Institute (OSI), 120,
    124-125
Operation Iraqi Freedom, 140-141
Operation Northwatch, 102
Operation Provide Comfort, 102
operational neutrality, 245
Optional Protocol on to the General
    Assembly, 205
Orangi Pilot Project (OPP), 191-196,
    240, 242, 246, 249
Ortega, Daniel, 223
Oslo peace accords, 68-69, 71, 74-
    75, 86-88

Oslo Channel, 68-78
Osorio, Col. Juan Valencia, 232
OWINFS (Our World is not for
    Sale), 244, 246
Oxford Committee for Famine
    Relief (OXFAM), 21, 27, 101-
    102, 104, 109-111, 230

Paffenholz, 9, 238, 241, 242, 246,
    249
Pakistan, 191-192, 194-195, 221-
    222, 225, 239, 242, 249
Palestinians, 71-72, 75
PAPG, 188
Papua-New Guinea, 135
Paraguay, 221-222
paramilitaries, 93, 95-96, 98
Participatory Rural Appraisal (PRA),
    184
Pastor, 131
Pastrana, President Andrés, 95
Pavka, 239, 243, 245, 246, 249
Peace Accords, 229, 231-232
peace-as-governance, 20, 23
Peace Brigades, 229
peace-building, 3-16, 19-33, 173-
    174, 176-181, 237, 248
Peace-building: A Field Guide, 9
Peacemaking, 68-71, 79-80, 175
peace municipalities, 93-95, 97-98
Peace Table of Samaniego, 95
Peace Union of Finland, 201
Pedagogical University, 168
Penal Reform International, 188
Penate, Eduardo, 233
Pen Pals for Peace, 167
Pension Appeal Tribunal Service,
    215
Pentagon, 132
Pentagon's Office of the Coalition
    Provisional Authority (OCPA),
    102, 105
People in Aid's Code of Good
    Practice, 49
People's Millennium Forum, 15
Perdomo, Ricardo, 223

Perry, William, 131
pesticide usage, 41
Petras, James, 47-8
Philippines, 222
Plan Colombia, 96
plausible deniability, 135
Poland, 161, 169, 225
political backlash, 46
political democratization, 20
political empowerment, 39
Port of Mogadishu, 133
post-Communist societies, 168
post-conflict reconciliation, 249
Poverty Report, 29
PRA (Participatory Rural Appraisal),
    184, 187
practical association, 26
Preamble to the 1899 Hague
    Convention II, 213
Precautionary Principle, 213, 215
preference scoring, 184
Premiere Ugrence, 104
prenatal health care, 121
prepotencia and *desgaste del poder*,
    225
President Kabbah, 137
Presidential Oversight Board, 212
preventive, 9
PRI (Penal Reform International),
    188
Principle 4 of the 10-point Red
    Cross and Red Crescent Code of
    Conduct, 102
private foundations, 43
private meetings, 7, 14
private military companies (PMC),
    131-140, 239, 243
Privatized Peacekeeping, 132
professionalization, 44
protective, 9
project society, 125
Protocols Additional of 1977, 213
psychosocial counseling, 121
public meetings, 6-8
public participation, 5, 6, 8
'pull' factors, 55, 57-58

'push' factors, 57, 62
Putumayo, 93, 95-96

Quezada (Toruño), Bishop Rudolfo
    86-88
QUNO, 203

racism, 164
raison d'être, 5
RAM Inc, 138
RAND study, 211-212
Raoul Wallenberg Institute, 203
REDEPAZ, 93-99, 240, 244, 245,
    249
regional organizations, 19
Reimann, 237, 239, 242, 246, 247,
    249
relief, 9
*Relief Aid and Development
    Cooperation*, 12
renewable energy, 159
Report of the International
    Commission on Intervention, 29
Representation, 42
Republic of the Congo, 137
Republic of Macedonia, 166
Resolution B4-1078, 204
Resolution 14, 203
restorative, 9
Revolutionary United Front (RUF),
    134
Reychler, 9, 238
Richmond, 79, 238, 240, 246, 248
Rieff, 14
rights-based approach, 155-158
right-winged conservatives, 37
ripe moment(s), 179
Robertson, Lord, 114
Rodríguez, Dorían, 94
Rojas, 240, 245, 248
Romania, 161, 163, 221, 225, 248
Root (Kellogg, Brown, and Root),
    133, 135
ROs, 20, 30
Rostrup, Morten, 103
Rovira, García, 95

Roy, Arundhati, 237
Rugwabiza, 187
Rupp, George, 103
Russia, 168, 248
Russian Foundation, 168
Russian Ministry of Health, 163
Rwanda, 9, 40, 134, 183-188, 241,
    242, 245, 247, 249
Rwandan genocide, 24
Rwandan government, 183-189
Rwandan Patriotic Front, 24
Rwandan refugee camps, 40

SADC Crime and Violence
    Prevention Project, 148
Saint, General Crosby E., 132
Samaniego, 94-98
Samara, 137, 168
Sandinistas, 222
sanitation, 192-194
San Pablo, 96-98, 249
Santader, 94
Saracen, 137
Sali-Terzic, Sevima, 125
Sampson, Stephen, 125
Sandline International, 132, 135,
    138-139
Sankoh, Foday, 134
Sanitoriums, 164
Saudi Arabia, 214
Save the Children, 102-103, 201-203
Save the Children Norway, 77
Save the Children UK (SCF UK),
    104
Savimbi, Jonas, 134
Schakowski, Jan, 135
School of the Americas, 239
Schulhofer-Wohl, Johan, 133
Secretariats, 7
Security, 12
Security Council, 6, 110
Securicor, 131
Seelarbokus, 240, 243, 245
Selecting Approaches to Mediation,
    11
self-defense units, 93

Serrano President Jorge, 87-88
Serious Crimes Panel, 112
Seychelles, 144
Shapiro, 239-241, 247, 248
Sharma, Dr. Hari, 211
Shearer, David, 135
Sheppard, Simon, 137
Siberia, 168
SIDA (Canadian Development
    Assistance Institute), 180
Sierra Leone, 5, 109-111, 114, 133-
    134, 136-137, 139, 144, 240, 242
signs of fracture, 95
Sikkink, 3, 4
Silva, Ramiro Lopes da, 104
Singer, P.W., 137, 139
Sixth Session of the Working Group,
    204
Skauen, Petter, 72
Slim, Hugo, 113
Slovak Republic, 169
Slovakia, 161
Slovenia, 161
Smillie, 44
Smith, 3
Smoking Prevention, 162
Socialist Left party, 77
social reform, 20
socio-economic conditions, 39
Solheim, Erik, 77-79
Somalia, 40, 133, 173-180, 182, 242,
    245, 246, 249
Somali Diaspora groups, 174
Soros Foundation, 162-164, 167-
    169, 239-241, 249
Soros Foundation's Health
    Education Program (HEP), 161-
    169, 239-241, 249
Soros, George, 162, 165-166, 168
South Africa, 144-145, 148, 156,
    222, 244
Southern African Development
    Community (SADC), 143-145,
    148-149
South African legislation, 136
South America, 136

South Korea, 222
South Vietnam, 126
Soviet Union, 70
Soyo, 133
Soyster, General Harry, 132
Space Mark International, 138
Special Representative on Children
    in Armed Conflict, 202
SPHERE, 25
Sphere Project, 49
Spicer, Tim, 132, 136
Sri Lanka, 75-80, 155, 245
Sri Lankan negotiations, 245
Staalsett, Gunnar, 72-73
state sovereignty, 23
State Sovereignty on The
    Responsibility to Protect, 29
Steel, David, 132
Steering Group, 203
Stoltenberg, Thorvald, 75
Strasser, Valentine, 134, 137
strategic partnership, 157
structural adjustment programs
    (SAPS), 47
structural fairness, 225
Stubbs, Paul, 123
Study on the Impact of Armed
    Conflict on Children, 203
Sub-Commission on the Promotion
    and Protection of Human Rights
    (formerly the Sub-Commission
    on Prevention of Discrimination
    and Protection of Minorities),
    215-216
Sub-Group on Refugees and
    Children of War, 202
Sub-Group on Refugee Children and
    Armed Conflict, 203
sub-Saharan, 221
Sub-Saharan Africa, 146
Sub-Working Group on Children
    and Armed Conflict (SWGCAC),
    202
Sudan, 30, 68, 75-79, 139
Sudan People's Liberation
    Movement (SPLM), 76-78

Sulaymaniyah, 104
Sumbeiywo, General Lazaro, 77
Surviving in the Field, 13
sustainably managed timber, 159
SWAPO, 222
Swaziland, 144
Sweden, 174, 180
Swedish and Icelandic Red Cross
    Societies, 203
Swedish Red Cross Youth, 202
Symbiosis, 94

Tanzania, 144
Taulbee, 239, 245, 246, 248
technical honesty, 225
Tel Aviv, 72
temporal limitation, 213
territorial limitation, 213
The Role of Civil Society in the
    Prevention of Armed Conflict, 15
third party model of norm
    generation, 7
Third Wave, 221
Tocquevillian civil society, 41
Tomsk, 168
Torrente, Nicolas de, 103
Toruño, Bishop Rudolfo Quezada,
    86, 88-89
Tourism, 159
tourniquet operations, 113
*To Win the Children: Afghanistan's
    Other War*, 201
Track I diplomacy, 68, 80, 177-178,
    245, 248
Track I½ diplomacy, 69, 80, 245,
    249
Track II diplomacy, 68-69, 79-80,
    177-178, 245, 248
Trade Union Confederation, 72
Training Local Peace Builders, 12
transnational agenda, 32
transnational global movements, 4
transnational political mobilization,
    55-57, 60, 62-63
transnationalism, 32

transnational social movements
    (TSMOs), 4
transparency, 42
Traprock Peace Center, 213
trauma management, 143, 145-146,
    148-150, 85-7
Trautner, Don, 133
Tren, 48
Trouillot, Eartha Pascal, 223-224
Truth and Reconciliation
    Commission (CRTR), 112
Truth Commission's report, 232
Tunis, 73, 75
Tutsi, 24
Tuijl, Peter van, 42
typology, 8, 9, 11

Ubudehe, 183-187
Underwriting Democracy, 165
UK Commons Foreign Affairs select
    committee, 135
Ukraine, 161
UN, 20, 22, 48, 73-75, 86-88, 139-
    140, 201-205, 210, 213, 215-216,
    221-226, 241-43, 245, 246
UN Agenda, 27
UNAMSIL (United Nations Mission
    in Sierra Leone), 110-111
UNAVEM III, 134
United Nations Capital Development
    Fund (UNCDF), 111
UN Charter, 6, 22, 25
UN Compensation Commission, 215
United Nations Department of
    Political Affairs, 88
UNDP, 22, 31, 242
UNDP *Human Development Report*,
    221
UNEP, 211-212
United Nations Economic and Social
    Council, 229
UN General Assembly, 15
UNHCR, 22, 245
UN High Commission for Human
    Rights, 22

UN High Commissioner for
Refugees, 8, 111-112
UN Human Rights Commission,
242-243
UN Human Rights System, 21
UNICEF, 201-202, 231
UNITA, 134
UN Interim Administration
(UNMIK), 31
United Nations Mission in Sierra
Leone (UNAMSIL), 110-111,
242
United Nations Observer Mission in
El Salvador (ONUSAL), 230
UN Operation to Somalia
(UNOSOM), 133, 173-174, 176-
178, 180, 202, 245
UN Parliamentary Assembly, 15
UNPROFOR, 132
UN Secretariats, 6
UN Security Council, 22, 133
UN System, 4, 25
UN Sub-Commission, 215
UN Transitional Authority in East
Timor (UNTAET), 111-112
UN Working Group, 202
United Representation of the
Guatemalan Opposition (RUOG),
86
United States Agency for
International Development
(USAID), 102-103, 120-121, 231
USA Environmental, 138
Universal Declaration of Human
Rights, 214
universal normative structure, 26
University of Bergen, 78-79
University of El Salvador, 230
Universal Declaration of Human
Rights, 3, 21
University of Waterloo, 211
URNG, 86-89
Urquhart, 15

Van der Merwe, 71
Vargas, Mario Gonzales, 223

Velázquez, Dr. Victoria, 233
Ventura, Jaime Romero, 223
Verification and Monitoring Team,
78
victim empowerment initiatives, 150
victims of the conflict, 101
Vietnam, 136
Villaraga, Alvarro, 97
Vinnell, 136, 138-139
Violence resistance, 94, 98
Vollebaek, Knut, 73, 77
voluntary spirit, 44
voice accountability, 43
Vuono, General Carl E, 132

Wade-Boyd and Associates LLC,
138-139
Wallace and Josselin, 25
war machinery, 94, 98
warlords, 178, 242
Weiss, 3, 109, 114
West, Katrina, 3, 9-10, 14-15
Westborg, Jon, 77
western capitalism, 47
western cultural imperialism, 44
western neocolonialism, 47
western neoliberalism, 47
Western Sahara, 222
WHO, 163, 169, 211
Wickremesinghe, Ranil, 79
Wilsonian Triad, 20
'windows of opportunities', 175,
179-180
Wiseberg, Laurie, 229
Women's Commission on Refugees,
202
Working in the Field, 10
World Bank, 8, 22, 120, 224, 231,
242, 246
World Council of Churches, 7, 75
World Federalist Movement, 7
World Organization Against Torture
(OMTC), 15
World Socialist Website, 140
World Summit on Sustainable
Development (WSSD), 156

World Trade Organization (WTO), 8, 22, 244, 246
World Uranium Conference, 212
World Wildlife Fund (WWF), 137, 156-160
Worldvision International, 21, 102, 203
World War II, 156

xenophobia, 164

Yeoman, Barry, 132-133
Yuen, Sik, 212
Yugoslavia, 122, 136, 161, 164

Zambia, 144, 223
Zinnes, Clifford F. and Sarah Bell, 164
zones of peace (ZOPs), 94-98, 249